Data Analysis witl

Second Edition

A comprehensive guide to manipulating, analyzing, and visualizing data in R

Tony Fischetti

BIRMINGHAM - MUMBAI

Data Analysis with R
Second Edition

Author: Tony Fischetti
Commissioning Editor: Amey Varangaonkar
Acquisition Editor: Tushar Gupta
Content Development Editor: Tejas Limkar
Technical Editor: Danish Shaikh
Copy Editor: Safis Editing
Project Coordinator: Manthan Patel
Proofreader: Safis Editing
Indexer: Tejal Daruwale Soni
Graphics: Tania Dutta
Production Coordinator: Shantanu Zagade

First published: December 2015
Second edition: March 2018

Production reference: 1270318

Published by Packt Publishing Ltd.
Livery Place
35 Livery Street
Birmingham
B3 2PB, UK.

ISBN 978-1-78839-372-0

www.packtpub.com

`mapt.io`

Mapt is an online digital library that gives you full access to over 5,000 books and videos, as well as industry leading tools to help you plan your personal development and advance your career. For more information, please visit our website.

Why subscribe?

- Spend less time learning and more time coding with practical eBooks and Videos from over 4,000 industry professionals

- Improve your learning with Skill Plans built especially for you

- Get a free eBook or video every month

- Mapt is fully searchable

- Copy and paste, print, and bookmark content

PacktPub.com

Did you know that Packt offers eBook versions of every book published, with PDF and ePub files available? You can upgrade to the eBook version at `www.PacktPub.com` and as a print book customer, you are entitled to a discount on the eBook copy. Get in touch with us at `service@packtpub.com` for more details.

At `www.PacktPub.com`, you can also read a collection of free technical articles, sign up for a range of free newsletters, and receive exclusive discounts and offers on Packt books and eBooks.

Contributors

About the author

Tony Fischetti is a data scientist at the New York Public Library, where he uses R everyday. He graduated in cognitive and computer science from Rensselaer Polytechnic Institute. His thesis was strongly focused on using statistics to study visual short-term memory.

He enjoys writing and contributing to open source software, blogging at *On The Lambda* (`http://www.onthelambda.com/`), writing about himself in the third person, and sharing knowledge using simple, approachable language and engaging examples.

I'd like to thank the NYPL, the R community, my support network of millions, Toblerone, Ignatius, Lex, and Pierre, and Bethany Wickham. I'd like to give a huge thanks to Andrea Fischetti for her love and support, and for keeping me warm and human. Finally, I thank my father, to whom I owe my love of learning and my interest in science and statistics, and my mother for her love and unwavering support.

About the reviewers

Manoj Kumar is a seasoned consultant with more than 15 years of versatile experience and exposure to implementing process improvement and operation optimization in typical manufacturing environments and production industries using advanced predictive and prescriptive analytics such as machine learning, deep learning, symbolic dynamics, neural dynamics, circuit mechanisms, and Markov decision process.

His domain experience is in:

- Transportation and Supply Chain Management
- Process and manufacturing
- Mining and energy
- Retail, CPG, Healthcare, Marketing, and F&A

Davor Lozić is a senior software engineer interested in various subjects, especially computer security, algorithms, and data structures. He manages teams of 15+ engineers and is a part-time assistant professor who lectures about database systems, Java, and interoperability. You can visit his website at http://warriorkitty.com and contact him from there. He likes cats! If you want to talk about any aspect of technology or if you have funny pictures of cats, feel free to contact him.

Packt is searching for authors like you

If you're interested in becoming an author for Packt, please visit authors.packtpub.com and apply today. We have worked with thousands of developers and tech professionals, just like you, to help them share their insight with the global tech community. You can make a general application, apply for a specific hot topic that we are recruiting an author for, or submit your own idea.

Table of Contents

Preface

I'm going to shoot it to you straight. There are a lot of books about data analysis and the R programming language. I'll take it for granted that you already know why it's extremely helpful and fruitful to learn R and data analysis (if not, why are you reading this preface?!) but allow me to make a case for choosing this book to guide you in your journey.

For one, this subject didn't come naturally to me. There are those with an innate talent for grasping the intricacies of statistics the first time it is taught to them; I don't think I'm one of them. I kept at it because I love science and research, and I knew that data analysis was necessary, not because it immediately made sense to me. Today, I love the subject in and of itself rather than instrumentally, but this came only after months of heartache. Eventually, as I consumed resource after resource, the pieces of the puzzle started to come together. After this, I started tutoring interested friends in the subject—and have seen them trip over the same obstacles that I had to learn to climb. I think that coming from this background gives me a unique perspective of the plight of the statistics student and it allows me to reach them in a way that others may not be able to. By the way, don't let the fact that statistics used to baffle me scare you; I have it on fairly good authority that I know what I'm talking about today.

Secondly, this book was born of the frustration that most statistics texts tend to be written in the driest manner possible. In contrast, I adopt a light-hearted buoyant approach—but without becoming agonizingly flippant.

Third, this book includes a lot of material that I wished were covered in more of the resources I used when I was learning data analysis in R. For example, the entire last unit specifically covers topics that present enormous challenges to R analysts when they first go out to apply their knowledge to imperfect real-world data.

Lastly, I thought long and hard about how to lay out this book and which order of topics was optimal. And when I say "long and hard," I mean I wrote a library and designed algorithms to do this. The order in which I present the topics in this book was very carefully considered to (a) build on top of each other, (b) follow a reasonable level of difficulty progression allowing for periodic chapters of relatively simpler material (psychologists call this intermittent reinforcement), (c) group highly related topics together, and (d) minimize the number of topics that require knowledge of yet unlearned topics (this is, unfortunately, common in statistics). If you're interested, I've detailed this procedure in a blog post that you can read at `http://bit.ly/teach-stats`.

The point is that the book you're holding is a very special one—one that I poured my soul into. Nevertheless, data analysis can be a notoriously difficult subject, and there may be times where nothing seems to make sense. During these times, remember that many others (including myself) have felt stuck too. Persevere... the reward is great. And remember, if a blockhead like me can do it, you can too. Go you!

Who this book is for

Whether you are learning data analysis for the first time or you want to deepen the understanding you already have, this book will prove an invaluable resource. If you are looking for a book to bring you all the way through the fundamentals to the application of advanced and effective analytics methodologies—and if you have some prior programming experience and a mathematical background—then this is for you.

What this book covers

Chapter 1, *RefresheR,* reviews the aspects of R that subsequent chapters will assume knowledge of. Here, we learn the basics of R syntax, learn of R's major data structures, write functions, load data, and install packages.

Chapter 2, *The Shape of Data,* discusses univariate data. We learn about different data types, how to describe univariate data, and how to visualize the shape of this data.

Chapter 3, *Describing Relationships,* covers multivariate data. In particular, we learn about the three main classes of bivariate relationships and learn how to describe them.

Chapter 4, *Probability,* kicks off a new unit by laying its foundations. We learn about basic probability theory, Bayes' theorem, and probability distributions.

Chapter 5, *Using Data to Reason about the World,* discusses sampling and estimation theory. Through examples, we learn of the central limit theorem, point estimation, and confidence intervals.

Chapter 6, *Testing Hypotheses,* introduces the subject of Null Hypothesis Significance Testing (NHST). We learn of many popular hypothesis tests and their non-parametric alternatives. Perhaps most importantly, we gain a thorough understanding of the misconceptions and gotchas of NHST.

Chapter 7, *Bayesian Methods,* presents an alternative to NHST based on a more intuitive view of probability. We learn the advantages and drawbacks of this approach too.

Chapter 8, *The Bootstrap*, details another approach to NHST by using a technique called *resampling*. We learn of its advantages and shortcomings. In addition, this chapter serves as a great reinforcement of the material in chapters 5 and 6.

Chapter 9, *Predicting Continuous Variables*, kicks off our new unit on predictive analytics and thoroughly discusses linear regression. Before the chapter's conclusion, we learn all about the technique, when to use it, and what traps to look out for.

Chapter 10, *Predicting Categorical Variables*, introduces four of the most popular classification techniques. By using all four on the same examples, we gain an appreciation for what makes each technique shine.

Chapter 11, *Predicting Changes with Time*, closes our unit of predictive analytics by introducing the topics of time series analysis and forecasting. This ends with a firm foundation on one of the premier methods of time series forecasting.

Chapter 12, *Sources of Data*, begins the final unit detailing data analysis in the *real world*. This chapter is all about how to use different data sources in R. In particular, we learn how to interface with databases, and request and load JSON and XML via an engaging example.

Chapter 13, *Dealing with Missing Data*, details what missing data is, how to identify types of missing data, some not-so-great methods for dealing with them, and two principled methods for handling them.

Chapter 14, *Dealing with Messy Data*, introduces some of the snags of working with less-than-perfect data in practice. This includes checking for unexpected input, wielding regex, and verifying data veracity with *assertr*.

Chapter 15, *Dealing with Large Data*, discusses some of the techniques that can be used to cope with data sets larger than what can be handled swiftly without a little planning. The key components of this chapter are on parallelization and Rcpp.

Chapter 16, *Working with Popular R Packages*, acknowledges that we've already wielded a lot of popular packages in this unit, but this chapter fills in some of the gaps and introduces some of the most modern packages that make speed and ease of use a priority.

Chapter 17, *Reproducibility and Best Practices*, closes with the extremely important (but often ignored) topic of how to use R like a professional. This includes learning about tooling, organization, and reproducibility.

To get the most out of this book

All code in this book has been written against the latest version of R—3.4.3 at time of writing. As a matter of good practice, you should keep your R version up to date but most, if not all, code should work with any reasonably recent version of R. Some of the R packages we will be installing will require more recent versions though. For the other software that this book uses, instructions will be furnished *pro re nata*. If you want to get a head start, however, install RStudio, JAGS, and a C++ compiler (or Rtools if you use windows).

Download the example code files

You can download the example code files for this book from your account at www.packtpub.com. If you purchased this book elsewhere, you can visit www.packtpub.com/support and register to have the files emailed directly to you.

You can download the code files by following these steps:

1. Log in or register at www.packtpub.com.
2. Select the **SUPPORT** tab.
3. Click on **Code Downloads & Errata**.
4. Enter the name of the book in the **Search** box and follow the onscreen instructions.

Once the file is downloaded, please make sure that you unzip or extract the folder using the latest version of:

- WinRAR/7-Zip for Windows
- Zipeg/iZip/UnRarX for Mac
- 7-Zip/PeaZip for Linux

The code bundle for the book is also hosted on GitHub at https://github.com/PacktPublishing/Data-Analysis-with-R-Second-Edition. We also have other code bundles from our rich catalog of books and videos available at https://github.com/PacktPublishing/. Check them out!

Conventions used

There are a number of text conventions used throughout this book.

CodeInText: Indicates code words in text, database table names, folder names, filenames, file extensions, pathnames, dummy URLs, user input, and Twitter handles. Here is an example: "Mount the downloaded WebStorm-10*.dmg disk image file as another disk in your system."

A block of code is set as follows:

```
# don't worry about memorizing this
temp.density <- density(airquality$Temp)
pdf <- approxfun(temp.density$x, temp.density$y, rule=2)
integrate(pdf, 80, 90)
```

When we wish to draw your attention to a particular part of a code block or output, the relevant lines or items are set in bold:

```
table(mtcars$carb) / length(mtcars$carb)
      1       2       3       4       6       8
0.21875 0.31250 0.09375 0.31250 0.03125 0.03125
```

Bold: Indicates a new term, an important word, or words that you see onscreen. For example, words in menus or dialog boxes appear in the text like this. Here is an example: "Select **System info** from the **Administration** panel."

Warnings or important notes appear like this.

Tips and tricks appear like this.

Get in touch

Feedback from our readers is always welcome.

General feedback: Email `feedback@packtpub.com` and mention the book title in the subject of your message. If you have questions about any aspect of this book, please email us at `questions@packtpub.com`.

Errata: Although we have taken every care to ensure the accuracy of our content, mistakes do happen. If you have found a mistake in this book, we would be grateful if you would report this to us. Please visit `www.packtpub.com/submit-errata`, selecting your book, clicking on the Errata Submission Form link, and entering the details.

Piracy: If you come across any illegal copies of our works in any form on the Internet, we would be grateful if you would provide us with the location address or website name. Please contact us at `copyright@packtpub.com` with a link to the material.

If you are interested in becoming an author: If there is a topic that you have expertise in and you are interested in either writing or contributing to a book, please visit `authors.packtpub.com`.

Reviews

Please leave a review. Once you have read and used this book, why not leave a review on the site that you purchased it from? Potential readers can then see and use your unbiased opinion to make purchase decisions, we at Packt can understand what you think about our products, and our authors can see your feedback on their book. Thank you!

For more information about Packt, please visit `packtpub.com`.

1
RefresheR

Before we dive into the (other) fun stuff (sampling multi-dimensional probability distributions, using convex optimization to fit data models, and so on), it would be helpful if we review those aspects of R that all subsequent chapters will assume knowledge of.

If you fancy yourself an R guru, you should still, at least, skim through this chapter, because you'll almost certainly find the idioms, packages, and style introduced here to be beneficial for following the rest of the material.

If you don't care much about R (yet), and are just in this for the statistics, you can heave a heavy sigh of relief that, for the most part, you can run the code given in this book in the interactive R interpreter with very little modification and just follow along with the ideas. However, it is my belief (read: delusion) that by the end of this book, you'll cultivate a newfound appreciation for R alongside a robust understanding of methods in data analysis.

Fire up your R interpreter and let's get started!

Navigating the basics

In the interactive R interpreter, any line starting with a > character denotes R asking for input. (If you see a + prompt, it means that you didn't finish typing a statement at the prompt and R is asking you to provide the rest of the expression). Striking the return key will send your input to R to be evaluated. R's response is then spit back at you in the line immediately following your input, after which R asks for more input. This is called a **REPL (Read-Evaluate-Print-Loop)**. It is also possible for R to read a batch of commands saved in a file (unsurprisingly called **batch mode**), but we'll be using the interactive mode for most of the book.

As you might imagine, R supports all the familiar mathematical operators as with most other languages.

Arithmetic and assignment

Check out the following example:

```
> 2 + 2
[1] 4

> 9 / 3
[1] 3

> 5 %% 2      # modulus operator (remainder of 5 divided by 2)
[1] 1
```

Anything that occurs after the octothorpe or pound sign, #, (or hash-tag for you young'uns), is ignored by the R interpreter. This is useful to document the code in natural language. These are called **comments**.

In a multi-operation arithmetic expression, R will follow the standard order of operations from math. In order to override this natural order, you have to use parentheses flanking the sub-expression that you'd like to be performed first:

```
> 3 + 2 - 10 ^ 2        # ^ is the exponent operator
[1] -95
> 3 + (2 - 10) ^ 2
[1] 67
```

In practice, almost all compound expressions are split up with intermediate values assigned to variables that, when used in future expressions, are just like substituting the variable with the value that was assigned to it. The (primary) assignment operator is <-:

```
> # assignments follow the form VARIABLE <- VALUE
> var <- 10
> var
[1] 10
> var ^ 2
[1] 100
> VAR / 2              # variable names are case-sensitive
Error: object 'VAR' not found
```

Notice that the first and second lines in the preceding code snippet didn't have an output to be displayed, so R just immediately asked for more input. This is because assignments don't have a return value. Their only job is to give a value to a variable or change the existing value of a variable. Generally, operations and functions on variables in R don't change the value of the variable. Instead, they return the result of the operation. If you want to change a variable to the result of an operation using that variable, you have to reassign that variable as follows:

```
> var              # var is 10
[1] 10
> var ^ 2
[1] 100
> var              # var is still 10
[1] 10
> var <- var ^ 2   # no return value
> var              # var is now 100
[1] 100
```

Be aware that variable names may contain numbers, underscores, and periods; this is something that trips up a lot of people who are familiar with other programming languages that disallow using periods in variable names. The only further restrictions on variable names are that they must start with a letter (or a period and then a letter), and that it must not be one of the reserved words in R such as TRUE, Inf, and so on.

Although the arithmetic operators that we've seen thus far are functions in their own right, most functions in R take the form, function_name(value(s) supplied to the function). The values supplied to the function are called **arguments** of that function:

```
> cos(3.14159)     # cosine function
[1] -1
> cos(pi)          # pi is a constant that R provides
[1] -1
> acos(-1)         # arccosine function
[1] 3.141593
> acos(cos(pi)) + 10
[1] 13.14159
> # functions can be used as arguments to other functions
```

If you paid attention in math class, you'll know that the cosine of pi is -1 and that arccosine is the inverse function of cosine.

There are hundreds of such useful functions defined in base R, only a handful of which we will see in this book. Two sections from now, we will be building our very own functions.

Before we move on from arithmetic, it will serve us well to visit some of the odd values that may result from certain operations:

```
> 1 / 0
[1] Inf
> 0 / 0
[1] NaN
```

It is common during practical usage of R to accidentally divide by zero. As you can see, this undefined operation yields an infinite value in R. Dividing zero by zero yields the value NaN, which stands for **Not a Number**.

Logicals and characters

So far, we've only been dealing with numerics, but there are other atomic data types in R:

```
> foo <- TRUE          # foo is of the logical data type
> class(foo)           # class() tells us the type
[1] "logical"
> bar <- "hi!"         # bar is of the character data type
> class(bar)
[1] "character"
```

The logical data type (also called **Booleans**) can hold the values TRUE or FALSE or, equivalently, T or F. The familiar operators from Boolean algebra are defined for these types:

```
> foo
[1] TRUE
> foo && TRUE                # boolean and
[1] TRUE
> foo && FALSE
[1] FALSE
> foo || FALSE               # boolean or
[1] TRUE
> !foo                       # negation operator
[1] FALSE
```

In a Boolean expression with a logical value and a number, any number that is not 0 is interpreted as TRUE:

```
> foo && 1
[1] TRUE
> foo && 2
[1] TRUE
> foo && 0
[1] FALSE
```

Additionally, there are functions and operators that return logical values such as the following:

```
> 4 < 2          # less than operator
[1] FALSE
> 4 >= 4         # greater than or equal to
[1] TRUE
> 3 == 3         # equality operator
[1] TRUE
> 3 != 2         # inequality operator
[1] TRUE
```

Just as there are functions in R that are only defined for work on the numeric and logical data type, there are other functions that are designed to work only with the character data type, also known as **strings**:

```
> lang.domain <- "statistics"
> lang.domain <- toupper(lang.domain)
> print(lang.domain)
[1] "STATISTICS"
> # retrieves substring from first character to fourth character
> substr(lang.domain, 1, 4)
[1] "STAT"
> gsub("I", "1", lang.domain)  # substitutes every "I" for "1"
[1] "STAT1ST1CS"
> # combines character strings
> paste("R does", lang.domain, "!!!")
[1] "R does STATISTICS !!!"
```

Flow of control

The last topic in this section will be *flow of control* constructs.

The most basic flow of control construct is the `if` statement. The argument to an `if` statement (what goes between the parentheses) is an expression that returns a logical value. The block of code following the `if` statement gets executed only if the expression yields TRUE:

```
> if(2 + 2 == 4)
+    print("very good")
[1] "very good"
> if(2 + 2 == 5)
+    print("all hail to the thief")
```

It is possible to execute more than one statement if an `if` condition is triggered; you just have to use curly brackets ({ }) to contain the statements:

```
> if((4/2==2) && (2*2==4)){
+    print("four divided by two is two...")
+    print("and two times two is four")
+ }
[1] "four divided by two is two..."
[1] "and two times two is four"
```

It is also possible to specify a block of code that will get executed if the `if` conditional is FALSE:

```
> closing.time <- TRUE
> if(closing.time){
+    print("you don't have to go home")
+    print("but you can't stay here")
+ } else{
+    print("you can stay here!")
+ }
[1] "you don't have to go home"
[1] "but you can't stay here"
> if(!closing.time){
+    print("you don't have to go home")
+    print("but you can't stay here")
+ } else{
+    print("you can stay here!")
+ }
[1] "you can stay here!"
```

There are other flow of control constructs (like `while` and `for`), but we won't be directly using them much in this text.

Getting help in R

Before we go further, it would serve us well to have a brief section detailing how to get help in R. Most R tutorials leave this for one of the last sections--if it is even included at all! In my own personal experience, though, getting help is going to be one of the first things you will want to do as you add more bricks to your R knowledge castle. Learning R doesn't have to be difficult; just take it slowly, ask questions, and get help early. Go you!

It is easy to get help with R right at the console. Running the `help.start()` function at the prompt will start a manual browser. From here, you can do anything from going over the basics of R to reading the nitty-gritty details on how R works internally.

You can get help with a particular function in R if you know its name, by supplying that name as an argument to the `help` function. For example, let's say you want to know more about the `gsub()` function that I sprang on you before. Check out the following code:

```
> help("gsub")
> # or simply
> ?gsub
```

This will display a manual page documenting what the function is, how to use it, and examples of its usage.

This rapid accessibility to documentation means that I'm never hopelessly lost when I encounter a function that I haven't seen before. The downside to this extraordinarily convenient help mechanism is that I rarely bother to remember the order of arguments as looking them up is just seconds away.

Occasionally, you won't quite remember the exact name of the function that you're looking for, but you'll have an idea about what the name should be. For this, you can use the `help.search()` function:

```
> help.search("chisquare")
> # or simply
> ??chisquare
```

For tougher, more semantic queries, nothing beats a good old fashioned web search engine. If you don't get relevant results the first time, try adding the term **programming** or **statistics** in there for good measure.

Vectors

Vectors are the most basic data structures in R, and they are ubiquitous indeed. In fact, even the single values that we've been working with thus far were actually vectors of length 1. That's why the interactive R console has been printing [1] along with all of our output.

Vectors are essentially *an ordered collection of values of the same atomic data type*. Vectors can be arbitrarily large (with some limitations) or they can be just one single value.

The canonical way of building vectors manually is using the c() function (which stands for **combine**):

```
> our.vect <- c(8, 6, 7, 5, 3, 0, 9)
> our.vect
[1] 8 6 7 5 3 0 9
```

In the preceding example, we created a numeric vector of length 7 (namely, Jenny's telephone number).

Let's try to put character data types into this vector as follows:

```
> another.vect <- c("8", 6, 7, "-", 3, "0", 9)
> another.vect
[1] "8" "6" "7" "-" "3" "0" "9"
```

R would convert all the items in the vector (called **elements**) into character data types to satisfy the condition that all elements of a vector must be of the same type. A similar thing happens when you try to use logical values in a vector with numbers; the logical values would be converted into 1 and 0 (for TRUE and FALSE, respectively). These logicals will turn into TRUE and FALSE (note the quotation marks) when used in a vector that contains characters.

Subsetting

It is very common to want to extract one or more elements from a vector. For this, we use a technique called **indexing** or **subsetting**. After the vector, we put an integer in square brackets ([ ]) called the **subscript operator**. This instructs R to return the element at that index. The indices (plural for index, in case you were wondering!) for vectors in R start at 1 and stop at the length of the vector:

```
> our.vect[1]                    # to get the first value
[1] 8
> # the function length() returns the length of a vector
> length(our.vect)
[1] 7
> our.vect[length(our.vect)]     # get the last element of a vector
[1] 9
```

Note that in the preceding code, we used a function in the subscript operator. In cases like these, R evaluates the expression in the subscript operator and uses the number it returns as the index to extract.

If we get greedy and try to extract an element from an index that doesn't exist, R will respond with NA, meaning, **not available**. We see this special value cropping up from time to time throughout this text:

```
> our.vect[10]
[1] NA
```

One of the most powerful ideas in R is that you can use vectors to subset other vectors:

```
> # extract the first, third, fifth, and
> # seventh element from our vector
> our.vect[c(1, 3, 5, 7)]
[1] 8 7 3 9
```

The ability to use vectors to index other vectors may not seem like much now, but its usefulness will become clear soon.

Another way to create vectors is using sequences:

```
> other.vector <- 1:10
> other.vector
[1]  1  2  3  4  5  6  7  8  9 10
> another.vector <- seq(50, 30, by=-2)
> another.vector
[1] 50 48 46 44 42 40 38 36 34 32 30
```

Here, the `1:10` statement creates a vector from 1 to 10. `10:1` would have created the same 10-element vector, but in reverse. The `seq()` function is more general in that it allows sequences to be made using steps (among many other things).

Combining our knowledge of sequences and vectors subsetting vectors, we can get the first five digits of Jenny's number:

```
> our.vect[1:5]
[1] 8 6 7 5 3
```

Vectorized functions

Part of what makes R so powerful is that many of R's functions take vectors as arguments. These vectorized functions are usually extremely fast and efficient. We've already seen one such function, `length()`, but there are many, many others:

```
> # takes the mean of a vector
> mean(our.vect)
[1] 5.428571
> sd(our.vect)      # standard deviation
[1] 3.101459
> min(our.vect)
[1] 0
> max(1:10)
[1] 10
> sum(c(1, 2, 3))
[1] 6
```

In practical settings, such as when reading data from files, it is common to have NA values in vectors:

```
> messy.vector <- c(8, 6, NA, 7, 5, NA, 3, 0, 9)
> messy.vector
[1]  8  6 NA  7  5 NA  3  0  9
> length(messy.vector)
[1] 9
```

Some vectorized functions will not allow NA values by default. In these cases, an extra keyword argument must be supplied along with the first argument to the function:

```
> mean(messy.vector)
[1] NA
> mean(messy.vector, na.rm=TRUE)
[1] 5.428571
> sum(messy.vector, na.rm=FALSE)
```

```
[1] NA
> sum(messy.vector, na.rm=TRUE)
[1] 38
```

As mentioned previously, vectors can be constructed from logical values as well:

```
> log.vector <- c(TRUE, TRUE, FALSE)
> log.vector
[1]   TRUE TRUE FALSE
```

Since logical values can be coerced into behaving like numerics, as we saw earlier, if we try to sum a logical vector as follows:

```
> sum(log.vector)
[1] 2
```

We will, essentially, get a count of the number of TRUE values in that vector.

There are many functions in R that operate on vectors and return logical vectors. is.na() is one such function. It returns a logical vector, that is, the same length as the vector supplied as an argument, with a TRUE in the position of every NA value. Remember our messy vector (from just a minute ago)?

```
> messy.vector
[1]   8   6 NA   7   5 NA   3   0   9
> is.na(messy.vector)
[1] FALSE FALSE   TRUE FALSE FALSE   TRUE FALSE FALSE FALSE
> #   8   6     NA   7   5     NA   3     0   9
```

Putting together these pieces of information, we can get a count of the number of NA values in a vector as follows:

```
> sum(is.na(messy.vector))
[1] 2
```

When you use Boolean operators on vectors, they also return logical vectors of the same length as the vector being operated on:

```
> our.vect > 5
[1]   TRUE   TRUE   TRUE FALSE FALSE FALSE   TRUE
```

If we wanted to--and we do--count the number of digits in Jenny's phone number that are greater than five, we would do so in the following manner:

```
> sum(our.vect > 5)
[1] 4
```

Advanced subsetting

Did I mention that we can use vectors to subset other vectors! When we subset vectors using logical vectors of the same length, only the elements corresponding to the TRUE values are extracted. Hopefully, light bulbs are starting to go off in your head. If we wanted to extract only the legitimate non-NA digits from Jenny's number, we can do it as follows:

```
> messy.vector[!is.na(messy.vector)]
[1] 8 6 7 5 3 0 9
```

This is a very critical trait of R, so let's take our time understanding it; this idiom will come up again and again throughout this book.

The logical vector that yields TRUE when an NA value occurs in messy.vector (from is.na()) is then negated (the whole thing) by the negation operator, !. The resultant vector is TRUE whenever the corresponding value in messy.vector is not NA. When this logical vector is used to subset the original messy vector, it only extracts the non-NA values from it.

Similarly, we can show all the digits in Jenny's phone number that are greater than five as follows:

```
> our.vect[our.vect > 5]
[1] 8 6 7 9
```

Thus far, we've only been displaying elements that have been extracted from a vector. However, just as we've been assigning and reassigning variables, we can assign values to various indices of a vector and change the vector as a result. For example, if Jenny tells us that we have the first digit of her phone number wrong (it's really 9), we can reassign just that element without modifying the others:

```
> our.vect
[1] 8 6 7 5 3 0 9
> our.vect[1] <- 9
> our.vect
[1] 9 6 7 5 3 0 9
```

Sometimes, it may be required to replace all the NA values in a vector with the value 0. To do this with our messy vector, we can execute the following command:

```
> messy.vector[is.na(messy.vector)] <- 0
> messy.vector
[1] 8 6 0 7 5 0 3 0 9
```

Elegant though the preceding solution is, modifying a vector in place is usually discouraged in favor of creating a copy of the original vector and modifying the copy. One such technique to perform this is using the `ifelse()` function.

Not to be confused with the if/else control construct, `ifelse()` is a function that takes three arguments: a test that returns a logical/Boolean value, a value to use if the element passes the test, and one to return if the element fails the test.

The preceding in-place modification solution could be reimplemented with `ifelse` as follows:

```
> ifelse(is.na(messy.vector), 0, messy.vector)
[1] 8 6 0 7 5 0 3 0 9
```

Recycling

The last important property of vectors and vector operations in R is that they can be recycled. To understand what I mean, examine the following expression:

```
> our.vect + 3
[1] 12  9 10  8  6  3 12
```

This expression adds three to each digit in Jenny's phone number. Although it may look so, R is not performing this operation between a vector and a single value. Remember when I said that single values are actually vectors of the length 1? What is really happening here is that R is told to perform element-wise addition on a vector of length 7 and a vector of length 1. As element-wise addition is not defined for vectors of differing lengths, R recycles the smaller vector until it reaches the same length as that of the bigger vector. Once both the vectors are the same size, then R, element by element, performs the addition and returns the result:

```
> our.vect + 3
[1] 12  9 10  8  6  3 12
```

This is tantamount to the following:

```
> our.vect + c(3, 3, 3, 3, 3, 3, 3)
[1] 12  9 10  8  6  3 12
```

If we wanted to extract every other digit from Jenny's phone number, we can do so in the following manner:

```
> our.vect[c(TRUE, FALSE)]
[1] 9 7 3 9
```

This works because the vector `c(TRUE, FALSE)` is repeated until it is of the length 7, making it equivalent to the following:

```
> our.vect[c(TRUE, FALSE, TRUE, FALSE, TRUE, FALSE, TRUE)]
[1] 9 7 3 9
```

One common snag related to vector recycling that R users (*useRs*, if I may) encounter is that during some arithmetic operations involving vectors of discrepant length, R will warn you if the smaller vector cannot be repeated a whole number of times to reach the length of the bigger vector. This is not a problem when doing vector arithmetic with single values as 1 can be repeated any number of times to match the length of any vector (which must, of course, be an integer). It would pose a problem, though, if we were looking to add three to every other element in Jenny's phone number:

```
> our.vect + c(3, 0)
[1] 12  6 10  5  6  0 12
Warning message:
In our.vect + c(3, 0) :
   longer object length is not a multiple of shorter object length
```

You will likely learn to love these warnings as they have stopped many useRs from making grave errors.

Before we move on to the next section, an important thing to note is that in a lot of other programming languages, many of the things that we did would have been implemented using `for` loops and other control structures. Although there is certainly a place for loops and such in R, often a more sophisticated solution exists in using just vector/matrix operations. In addition to elegance and brevity, the solution that exploits vectorization and recycling is often much more efficient.

Functions

If we need to perform some computation that isn't already a function in R a multiple number of times, we usually do so by defining our own functions. A custom function in R is defined using the following syntax:

```
> function.name <- function(argument1, argument2, ...){
+    # some functionality
+ }
```

For example, if we wanted to write a function that determined if a number supplied as an argument was even, we can do so in the following manner:

```
> is.even <- function(a.number){
+    remainder <- a.number %% 2
+    if(remainder==0)
+       return(TRUE)
+    return(FALSE)
+ }
> # testing it
> is.even(10)
[1] TRUE
> is.even(9)
[1] FALSE
```

As an example of a function that takes more than one argument, let's generalize the preceding function by creating a function that determines whether the first argument is divisible by its second argument:

```
> is.divisible.by <- function(large.number, smaller.number){
+    if(large.number %% smaller.number != 0)
+       return(FALSE)
+    return(TRUE)
+ }
> # testing it
> is.divisible.by(10, 2)
[1] TRUE
> is.divisible.by(10, 3)
[1] FALSE
> is.divisible.by(9, 3)
[1] TRUE
```

Our function, `is.even()`, could now be rewritten simply as follows:

```
> is.even <- function(num){
+    is.divisible.by(num, 2)
+ }
```

It is very common in R to want to apply a particular function to every element of a vector. Instead of using a loop to iterate over the elements of a vector, as we would do in many other languages, we use a function called `sapply()` to perform this. `sapply()` takes a vector and a function as its arguments. It then applies the function to every element and returns a vector of results. We can use `sapply()` in this manner to find out which digits in Jenny's phone number are even:

```
> sapply(our.vect, is.even)
[1] FALSE   TRUE FALSE FALSE FALSE   TRUE FALSE
```

This worked great because `sapply` takes each element and uses it as the argument in `is.even()`, which takes only one argument. If you wanted to find the digits that are divisible by three, it would require a little bit more work.

One option is just to define a function, `is.divisible.by.three()`, that takes only one argument and use this in `sapply`. The more common solution, however, is to define an unnamed function that does just that in the body of the `sapply` function call:

```
> sapply(our.vect, function(num){is.divisible.by(num, 3)})
[1]   TRUE   TRUE FALSE FALSE   TRUE   TRUE   TRUE
```

Here, we essentially created a function that checks whether its argument is divisible by three, except we don't assign it to a variable and use it directly in the `sapply` body instead. These one-time-use unnamed functions are called **anonymous functions** or **lambda functions**. (The name comes from Alonzo Church's invention of the lambda calculus, if you were wondering.)

This is somewhat of an advanced usage of R, but it is very useful as it comes up very often in practice.

If we wanted to extract the digits in Jenny's phone number that are divisible by both, two and three, we can write it as follows:

```
> where.even <- sapply(our.vect, is.even)
> where.div.3 <- sapply(our.vect, function(num){
+    is.divisible.by(num, 3)})
> # "&" is like the "&&" and operator but for vectors
> our.vect[where.even & where.div.3]
[1] 6 0
```

Neat-O!

Note that if we wanted to be sticklers, we would have a clause in the function bodies to preclude a modulus computation, where the first number was smaller than the second. If we had, our function would not have erroneously indicated that 0 was divisible by two and three. I'm not a stickler, though, so the function will remain as is. Fixing this function is left as an exercise for the (stickler) reader.

Matrices

In addition to the vector data structure, R has the matrix, data frame, list, and array data structures. Though we will be using all of these types (except arrays) in this book, we only need to review the first two in this chapter.

A matrix in R, like in math, is a rectangular array of values (of one type) arranged in rows and columns and can be manipulated as a whole. Operations on matrices are fundamental to data analysis.

One way of creating a matrix is to just supply a vector to the matrix() function:

```
> a.matrix <- matrix(c(1, 2, 3, 4, 5, 6))
> a.matrix
      [,1]
[1,]    1
[2,]    2
[3,]    3
[4,]    4
[5,]    5
[6,]    6
```

This produces a matrix with all the supplied values in a single column. We can make a similar matrix with two columns by supplying `matrix()` with an optional argument, `ncol`, that specifies the number of columns:

```
> a.matrix <- matrix(c(1, 2, 3, 4, 5, 6), ncol=2)
> a.matrix
     [,1] [,2]
[1,]    1    4
[2,]    2    5
[3,]    3    6
```

We could have produced the same matrix by binding two vectors, `c(1, 2, 3)` and `c(4, 5, 6)`, by columns using the `cbind()` function as follows:

```
> a2.matrix <- cbind(c(1, 2, 3), c(4, 5, 6))
```

We could create the transposition of this matrix (where rows and columns are switched) by binding these vectors by row instead:

```
> a3.matrix <- rbind(c(1, 2, 3), c(4, 5, 6))
> a3.matrix
     [,1] [,2] [,3]
[1,]    1    2    3
[2,]    4    5    6
```

We can do this by just using the matrix transposition function in R, `t()`:

```
> t(a2.matrix)
```

Some other functions that operate on whole vectors are `rowSums()`/`colSums()` and `rowMeans()`/`colMeans()`:

```
> a2.matrix
     [,1] [,2]
[1,]    1    4
[2,]    2    5
[3,]    3    6
> colSums(a2.matrix)
[1]  6 15
> rowMeans(a2.matrix)
[1] 2.5 3.5 4.5
```

If vectors have `sapply()`, then matrices have `apply()`. The preceding two functions could have been written, more verbosely, as follows:

```
> apply(a2.matrix, 2, sum)
[1]  6 15
> apply(a2.matrix, 1, mean)
[1] 2.5 3.5 4.5
```

Here, 1 instructs R to perform the supplied function over its rows, and 2, over its columns.

The matrix multiplication operator in R is `%*%`:

```
> a2.matrix %*% a2.matrix
Error in a2.matrix %*% a2.matrix : non-conformable arguments
```

Remember, matrix multiplication is only defined for matrices where the number of columns in the first matrix is equal to the number of rows in the second:

```
> a2.matrix
     [,1] [,2]
[1,]    1    4
[2,]    2    5
[3,]    3    6
> a3.matrix
     [,1] [,2] [,3]
[1,]    1    2    3
[2,]    4    5    6
> a2.matrix %*% a3.matrix
     [,1] [,2] [,3]
[1,]   17   22   27
[2,]   22   29   36
[3,]   27   36   45
> # dim() tells us how many rows and columns
> # (respectively) there are in the given matrix
> dim(a2.matrix)
[1] 3 2
```

To index the element of a matrix at the second row and first column, you need to supply both of these numbers into the subscripting operator:

```
> a2.matrix[2,1]
[1] 2
```

Many useRs get confused and forget the order in which the indices must appear; remember, it's row first, then columns!

If you leave one of the spaces empty, R will assume that you want that whole dimension:

```
> # returns the whole second column
a2.matrix[,2]
[1] 4 5 6
> # returns the first row
> a2.matrix[1,]
[1] 1 4
```

As always, we can use vectors in our subscript operator:

```
> # give me element in column 2 at the first and third row
> a2.matrix[c(1, 3), 2]
[1] 4 6
```

Loading data into R

Thus far, we've only been entering data directly into the interactive R console. For any dataset of non-trivial size, this is, obviously, an intractable solution. Fortunately for us, R has a robust suite of functions to read data directly from external files.

Go ahead and create a file on your hard disk called `favorites.txt` that looks like this:

```
flavor,number
pistachio,6
mint chocolate chip,7
vanilla,5
chocolate,10
strawberry,2
neopolitan,4
```

This data represents the number of students in a class that prefer a particular flavor of soy ice cream. We can read the file into a variable called `favs` as follows:

```
> favs <- read.table("favorites.txt", sep=",", header=TRUE)
```

If you get an error that there is no such file or directory, give R the full path name to your dataset or, alternatively, run the following command:

```
> favs <- read.table(file.choose(), sep=",", header=TRUE)
```

The preceding command brings up an open file dialog to let you navigate to the file that you've just created.

The `sep=","` argument tells R that each data element in a row is separated by a comma. Other common data formats have values separated by tabs and pipes (`"|"`). The value of `sep` should then be `"\t"` and `"|"`, respectively.

The `header=TRUE` argument tells R that the first row of the file should be interpreted as the names of the columns. Remember, you can enter `?read.table` at the console to learn more about these options.

Reading from files in this comma-separated values format (usually with the `.csv` file extension) is so common that R has a more specific function just for it. The preceding data import expression can be best written simply as follows:

```
> favs <- read.csv("favorites.txt")
```

Now, we have all the data in the file held in a variable of the `data.frame` class. A data frame can be thought of as a rectangular array of data that you might see in a spreadsheet application. In this way, a data frame can also be thought of as a matrix; indeed, we can use matrix-style indexing to extract elements from it. A data frame differs from a matrix, though, in that a data frame may have columns of differing types. For example, whereas a matrix would only allow one of these types, the dataset that we just loaded contains character data in its first column and numeric data in its second column.

Let's check out what we have using the `head()` command, which will show us the first few lines of a data frame:

```
> head(favs)
                 flavor number
1              pistachio      6
2 mint chocolate chip      7
3                vanilla      5
4              chocolate     10
5             strawberry      2
6             neopolitan      4

> class(favs)
[1] "data.frame"
> class(favs$flavor)
[1] "factor"
> class(favs$number)
[1] "numeric"
```

I lied, okay! So what?! Technically, `flavor` is a `factor` data type, not a character type.

We haven't seen factors yet, but the idea behind them is really simple. Essentially, factors are codings for categorical variables, which are variables that take on one of a finite number of categories--think `{"high", "medium", and "low"}` or `{"control", "experimental"}`.

Though factors are extremely useful in statistical modeling in R, the fact that R, by default, automatically interprets a column from the data read from disk as a type factor if it contains characters is something that trips up novices and seasoned useRs alike. Due to this, we will primarily prevent this behavior manually by adding the `stringsAsFactors` optional keyword argument to the `read.*` commands:

```
> favs <- read.csv("favorites.txt", stringsAsFactors=FALSE)
> class(favs$flavor)
[1] "character"
```

Much better, for now! If you'd like to make this behavior the new default, read the `?options` manual page. We can always convert to factors later on if we need to!

If you haven't noticed already, I've snuck a new operator on you--`$`, the extract operator. This is the most popular way to extract attributes (or columns) from a data frame. You can also use double square brackets (`[[` and `]]`) to do this.

These are both in addition to the canonical matrix indexing option. The following three statements are thus, in this context, functionally identical:

```
> favs$flavor
[1] "pistachio"       "mint chocolate chip" "vanilla"
[4] "chocolate"       "strawberry"          "neopolitan"
> favs[["flavor"]]
[1] "pistachio"       "mint chocolate chip" "vanilla"
[4] "chocolate"       "strawberry"          "neopolitan"
> favs[,1]
[1] "pistachio"       "mint chocolate chip" "vanilla"
[4] "chocolate"       "strawberry"          "neopolitan"
```

Notice how R has now printed another number in square brackets--besides `[1]`--along with our output. This is to show us that `chocolate` is the fourth element of the vector that was returned from the extraction.

You can use the `names()` function to get a list of the columns available in a data frame. You can even reassign names using the same:

```
> names(favs)
[1] "flavor" "number"
> names(favs)[1] <- "flav"
> names(favs)
[1] "flav"    "number"
```

Lastly, we can get a compact display of the structure of a data frame using the `str()` function on it:

```
> str(favs)
'data.frame': 6 obs. of  2 variables:
 $ flav  : chr  "pistachio" "mint chocolate chip" "vanilla"
 "chocolate" ...
 $ number: num  6 7 5 10 2 4
```

Actually, you can use this function on any R structure--the property of functions that change their behavior based on the type of input is called **polymorphism**.

Working with packages

Robust, performant, and numerous though base R functions are, we are by no means limited to them! Additional functionality is available in the form of packages. In fact, what makes R such a formidable statistics platform is the astonishing wealth of packages available (over 10,000 at the time of writing). R's ecosystem is second to none!

Most of these myriad packages exist on the **Comprehensive R Archive Network** (**CRAN**). CRAN is the primary repository for user-created packages.

One package that we are going to start using right away is the `ggplot2` package. `ggplot2` is a plotting system for R. `Base R` has sophisticated and advanced mechanisms to plot data, but many find `ggplot2` more consistent and easier to use. Further, the plots are often more aesthetically pleasing by default.

Let's install it:

```
> # downloads and installs from CRAN
> install.packages("ggplot2")
```

Now that we have the package downloaded, let's load it into the R session and test it out by plotting our data from the last section:

```
> library(ggplot2)
> ggplot(favs, aes(x=flav, y=number)) +
+     geom_bar(stat="identity") +
+     ggtitle("Soy ice cream flavor preferences")
```

The graph generated by the preceding code will be as follows:

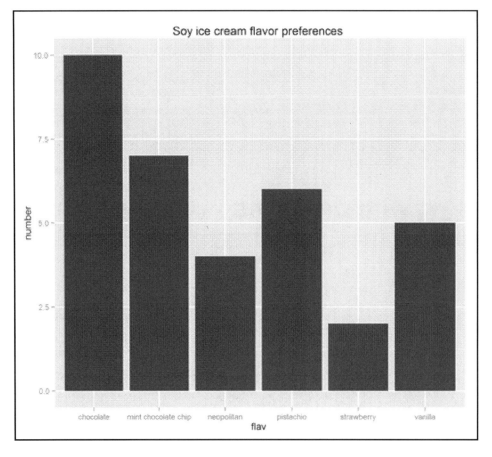

Figure 1.1: Soy ice cream flavor preferences

You're all wrong, Mint Chocolate Chip is way better!

Don't worry about the syntax of the ggplot function yet. We'll get to it in good time.

You will be installing some more packages as you work through this text. In the meantime, if you want to play around with a few more packages, you can install the `gdata` and `foreign` packages that allow you to directly import Excel spreadsheets and SPSS data files, respectively, directly into R.

Exercises

You can practice the following exercises to help you get a good grasp of the concepts learned in this chapter:

- Write a function called `simon.says` that takes in a character string and returns that string in all uppercase after prepending the string *Simon says:* to the beginning of it.
- Write a function that takes two matrices as arguments and returns a logical value representing whether the matrices can be matrix multiplied.
- Find a free dataset on the web, download it, and load it into R. Explore the structure of the dataset.
- Reflect upon how Hester Prynne allowed her scarlet letter to be decorated with flowers by her daughter in the novel, The Scarlet Letter: A Romance. To what extent is this indicative of Hester's recasting of the scarlet letter as a positive part of her identity? Back up your thesis with excerpts from the book.

Summary

In this chapter, you learned about the world's greatest analytics platform, R. We started from the beginning and built a foundation, and will now explore R further, based on the knowledge gained in this chapter. By now, you have become well-versed in the basics of R (which, paradoxically, is the hardest part). You now know how to:

- Use R as a big ol' calculator to do arithmetic
- Make vectors, operate on them, and subset them expressively
- Load data from disk
- Install packages

You have by no means finished learning about R; indeed, we have gone over mostly just the basics. However, we have enough to continue ahead, and you'll pick up more along the way. Onward to statistics land!

2
The Shape of Data

Welcome back! Now that we have enough knowledge about R under our belts, we can finally move on to applying it. Let us go then, you and I, into statistics-land...

Univariate data

In this chapter, we are going to deal with univariate data, which is a fancy way of saying *samples of one variable*--the kind of data that goes into a single R vector. Analysis of univariate data isn't concerned with the why questions—causes, relationships, or anything like that; the purpose of univariate analysis is simply to describe.

In univariate data, one variable—let's call it x—can represent categories such as soy ice cream flavors, heads or tails, names of cute classmates, the roll of a die, and so on. In cases like these, we call x a categorical variable.

```
categorical.data <- c("heads", "tails", "tails", "heads")
```

Categorical data is represented, in the preceding statement, as a vector of character type. In this particular example, we could further specify that this is a binary or dichotomous variable because it only takes on two values, namely, `heads` and `tails`.

Our variable *x* could also represent a number such as air temperature, the prices of financial instruments, and so on. In such cases, we call this a continuous variable.

```
contin.data <- c(198.41, 178.46, 165.20, 141.71, 138.77)
```

Univariate data of a continuous variable is represented, as seen in the preceding statement, as a vector of numeric type. This data is the stock prices of a hypothetical company that offers a hypothetical commercial statistics platform inferior to R.

You might come to the conclusion that if a vector contains character types, it is a categorical variable, and if it contains numeric types, it is a continuous variable. Not quite! Consider the case of data that contains the results of the roll of a six-sided die. A natural approach to storing this would be using a numeric vector. However, this isn't a continuous variable because each result can only take on six distinct values: 1, 2, 3, 4, 5, and 6. This is a **discrete numeric variable**. Other discrete numeric variables can be the number of bacteria in a petri dish or the number of love letters to cute classmates.

The mark of a continuous variable is that it could take on any value between a theoretical minimum and maximum. The range of values in a case of a die roll have a minimum of 1 and a maximum of 6, but it can never be 2.3. Contrast this with, say, the example of the stock prices, which could be zero, zillions, or anything in between.

On occasion, we are unable to neatly classify non-categorical data as either continuous or discrete. In some cases, discrete variables may be treated as if there is an underlying continuum. Additionally, continuous variables can be discretized, as we'll soon see.

Frequency distributions

A common way of describing univariate data is with a frequency distribution. We've already seen an example of a frequency distribution when we looked at the preferences for soy ice cream at the end of the last chapter. For each flavor of ice cream (categorical variable), it depicted the count or frequency of the occurrences in the underlying dataset.

To demonstrate examples of other frequency distributions, we need to find some data. Fortunately, for the convenience of useRs everywhere, R comes preloaded with almost one hundred datasets. You can view a full list if you execute `help (package="datasets")`. There are also hundreds more available from add-on packages.

The first dataset that we are going to use is `mtcars`--data on the design and performance of 32 automobiles, which was extracted from the 1974 Motor Trend US magazine. (To find out more information about this dataset, execute `?mtcars`).

Take a look at the first few lines of this dataset using the `head` function:

```
head(mtcars)
                   mpg cyl disp  hp drat    wt  qsec vs am gear carb
Mazda RX4         21.0   6  160 110 3.90 2.620 16.46  0  1    4    4
Mazda RX4 Wag     21.0   6  160 110 3.90 2.875 17.02  0  1    4    4
Datsun 710        22.8   4  108  93 3.85 2.320 18.61  1  1    4    1
Hornet 4 Drive    21.4   6  258 110 3.08 3.215 19.44  1  0    3    1
Hornet Sportabout 18.7   8  360 175 3.15 3.440 17.02  0  0    3    2
Valiant           18.1   6  225 105 2.76 3.460 20.22  1  0    3    1
```

Check out the `carb` column, which represents the number of carburetors; by now, you should recognize this as a discrete numeric variable, though we can (and will!) treat this as a categorical variable for now.

Running the `carb` vector through the `unique` function yields the distinct values that this vector contains:

```
unique(mtcars$carb)
[1] 4 1 2 3 6 8
```

We can see that there must be repeats in the `carb` vector, but how many? An easy way to perform a frequency tabulation in R is to use the `table` function:

```
table(mtcars$carb)

 1  2  3  4  6  8
 7 10  3 10  1  1
```

From the result of the preceding function, we can tell that there are 10 cars with 2 carburetors and 10 with 4, and there is one car each with 6 and 8 carburetors. The value with the most occurrences in a dataset (in this example, the `carb` column is our whole dataset) is called the **mode**. In this case, there are two such values, 2 and 4, so this dataset is bimodal. (There is a package in R, called `modeest`, to find modes easily.)

Frequency distributions are more often depicted as a chart or plot than as a table of numbers. When the univariate data is categorical, it is commonly represented as a bar chart, as shown in the following graph:

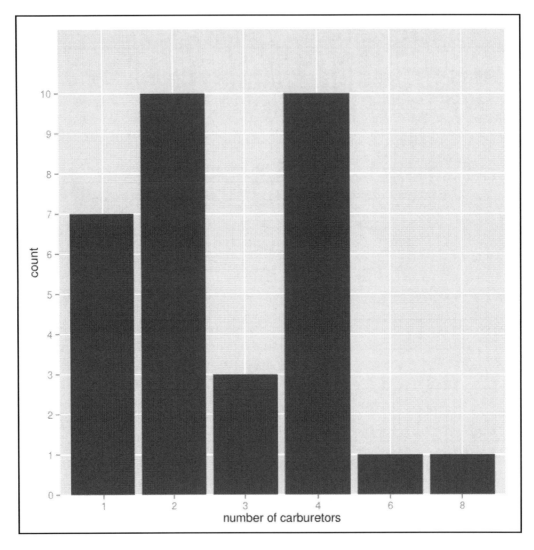

Figure 2.1: Frequency distribution of number of carburetors in a mtcars dataset

The other dataset that we are going to use to demonstrate a frequency distribution of a continuous variable is the `airquality` dataset, which holds the daily air quality measurements from May to September in NY. Take a look at it using the `head` and `str` functions. The univariate data that we will be using is the `Temp` column, which contains the temperature data in degrees Fahrenheit.

It would be useless to take the same approach to frequency tabulation as we did in the case of the car carburetors. If we did so, we would have a table containing the frequencies for each of the 40 unique temperatures--and there would be far more if the temperature wasn't rounded to the nearest degree. Additionally, who cares that there was one occurrence of 63 degrees and two occurrences of 64? I sure don't! What we do care about is the approximate temperature.

Our first step toward building a frequency distribution of the temperature data is to bin the data, which means that we divide the range of values of the vector into a series of smaller intervals. This binning is a method of discretizing a continuous variable. We then count the number of values that fall into this interval.

Choosing the size of bins to use is tricky. If there are too many bins, we run into the same problem as we did with the raw data and have an unwieldy number of columns in our frequency tabulation. If we make too few, however, we lose resolution and may lose important information. Choosing the right number of bins is more art than science, but there are certain commonly used heuristics that often produce sensible results.

We can have R construct *n* number of equally-spaced bins for us using the `cut` function which, in its simplest use case, takes a vector of data and the number of bins to create:

```
cut(airquality$Temp, 9)
```

We can then feed this result into the `table` function for a far more manageable frequency tabulation:

```
table(cut(airquality$Temp, 9))

 (56,60.6]  (60.6,65.1]  (65.1,69.7]  (69.7,74.2]  (74.2,78.8]
         8           10           14           16           26
 (78.8,83.3]  (83.3,87.9]  (87.9,92.4]   (92.4,97]
         35           22           15            7
```

Rad!

Remember when we used a bar chart to visualize the frequency distributions of categorical data? The common method to visualize the distribution of discretized continuous data is using a histogram, as seen in the following graph:

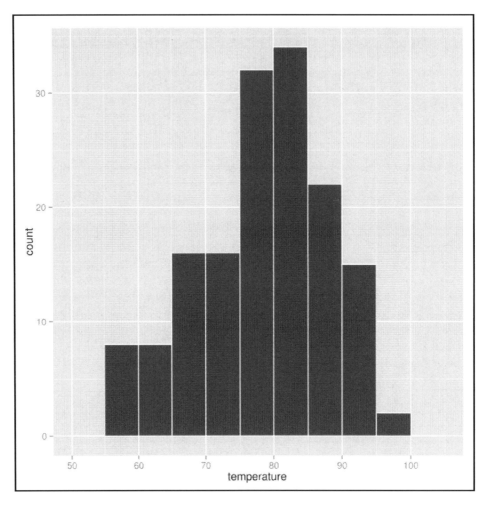

Figure 2.2: Daily temperature measurements from May to September in NYC

Central tendency

One very popular question to ask about univariate data is, *What is the typical value?* or *What's the value around which the data are centered?* To answer these questions, we have to measure the central tendency of a set of data.

We've seen one measure of central tendency already: the mode. The `mtcars$carburetors` data subset was bimodal, with a two and four carburetor setup being the most popular. The mode is the central tendency measure that is applicable to categorical data.

The mode of a discretized continuous distribution is usually considered to be the interval that contains the highest frequency of data points. This makes it dependent on the method and parameters of the binning. Finding the mode of data from a non-discretized continuous distribution is a more complicated procedure, which we'll see later.

Perhaps the most famous and commonly used measure of central tendency is the mean. The mean is the sum of a set of numerics divided by the number of elements in that set. This simple concept can also be expressed as a complex-looking equation:

$$\bar{x} = \frac{\sum x}{n}$$

Here, $\bar{x}$ (pronounced *x bar*) is the mean, which is the summation of the elements in the dataset, and *n* is the number of elements in the set. (As an aside, if you are intimidated by the equations in this book, don't be! None of them are beyond your grasp--just think of them as sentences of a language you're not proficient in yet.)

The mean is represented as when we are talking about the mean of a sample (or subset) of a larger population and μ when we are talking about the mean of the population. A population may have too many items to compute the mean directly. When this is the case, we rely on statistics applied to a sample of the population to estimate its parameters.

Another way to express the preceding equation using R constructs is as follows:

```
sum(nums)/length(nums)    # nums would be a vector of numerics
```

As you might imagine, though, the mean has an eponymous R function that is built-in already:

```
mean(c(1,2,3,4,5))
[1] 3
```

The mean is not defined for categorical data; remember that mode is the only measure of central tendency that we can use with categorical data.

The mean--occasionally referred to as the arithmetic mean to contrast with the far less often used geometric, harmonic, and trimmed means--while extraordinarily popular is not a very robust statistic. This is because the statistic is unduly affected by outliers (atypically distant data points or observations). A paradigmatic example where the robustness of the mean fails is its application to the different distributions of income.

Imagine the wages of employees in a company called *Marx & Engels, Attorneys at Law*, where the typical worker makes $40,000 a year, while the CEO makes $500,000 a year. If we compute the mean of the salaries based on a sample of ten that contains just the exploited class, we will have a fairly accurate representation of the average salary of a worker at this company. If, however, by the luck of the draw, our sample contains the CEO, the mean of the salaries will skyrocket to a value that is no longer representative or very informative.

More specifically, robust statistics are statistical measures that work well when thrown at a wide variety of different distributions. The mean works well with one particular type of distribution, the normal distribution, and, to varying degrees, fails to accurately represent the central tendency of other distributions as shown in the following image:

Figure 2.3: A normal distribution

The normal distribution (also called the **Gaussian distribution**, if you want to impress people) is frequently referred to as the **bell curve** because of its shape. As seen in the preceding image, the vast majority of the data points lie within a narrow band around the center of the distribution, which is the mean. As you get further and further from the mean, the observations become less and less frequent. It is a symmetric distribution, meaning that the side that is to the right of the mean is a mirror image of the left side of the mean.

Not only is the usage of the normal distribution extremely common in statistics, but it is also ubiquitous in real life, where it can model anything from people's heights to test scores; a few will fare lower than average and a few fare higher than average, but most are around average.

The utility of the mean as a measure of central tendency becomes strained as the normal distribution becomes more and more skewed, or asymmetrical.

If the majority of the data points fall on the left side of the distribution, with the right side tapering off moreslowly than the left, the distribution is considered **positively skewed or right-tailed**. If the longer tail is on the left side and the bulk of the distribution is hanging out to the right, it is called **negatively skewed or left-tailed**.

A negatively skewed distribution and positively skewed distribution is clearly discernible from the following graphs:

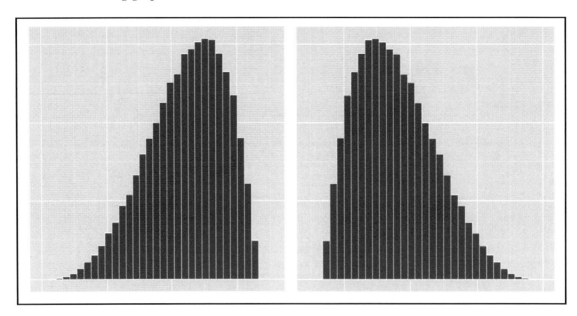

Figure 2.4: Positively and negatively skewed distributions

Luckily, for cases of skewed distributions, or other distributions for which the mean is inadequate to describe, we can use the median instead.

The median of a dataset is the middle number in the set after it is sorted. Less concretely, it is the value that cleanly separates the higher-valued half of the data and the lower-valued half.

The median of the set of numbers {1, 3, 5, 6, 7} is 5. In the set of numbers with an even number of elements, the mean of the two middle values is taken to be the median. For example, the median of the set {3, 3, 6, 7, 7, 10} is 6.5. The median is the 50th percentile, meaning that 50 percent of the observations fall below that value.

```
median(c(3, 7, 6, 10, 3, 7))
   [1] 6.5
```

Consider the example of *Marx & Engels, Attorneys at Law* that we referred to earlier. Remember that if the sample of employees' salaries included the CEO, it would give our mean a non-representative value. The median solves our problem beautifully. Let's say our sample of 10 employees' salaries was (*41,000, 40,300, 38,000, 500,000, 41,500, 37,000, 39,600, 42,000, 39,900, 39,500*). Given this set, the mean salary is $85,880 but the median is $40,100-- way more in line with the salary expectations of the proletariat at the law firm.

In symmetric data, the mean and median are often very close to each other in value, if not identical. In asymmetric data, this is not the case. It is telling when the median and the mean are very discrepant. In general, if the median is less than the mean, the dataset has a large right tail or outliers/anomalies/erroneous data to the right of the distribution. If the mean is less than the median, it tells the opposite story. The degree of difference between the mean and the median is often an indication of the degree of skewness.

This property of the median--resistance to the influence of outliers--makes it a robust statistic. In fact, the median is the most outlier-resistant metric in statistics.

As great as the median is, it's far from perfect for describing data just on its own. To see what I mean, check out the three distributions in the following image:

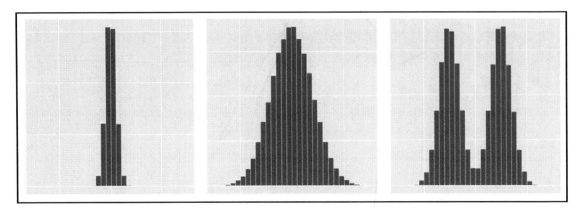

Figure 2.5: Three distributions with the same mean and median

All three have the same mean and median, yet all three are very different distributions.

Clearly, we need to look to other statistical measures to describe these differences.

 Before going on to the next chapter, check out the `summary` function in R.

Spread

Another very popular question regarding univariate data is, *How variable are the data points?* or *How spread out or dispersed are the observations?* To answer these questions, we have to measure the spread, or dispersion, of a data sample.

The simplest way to answer this question is to take the smallest value in the dataset and subtract it by the largest value. This will give you the range. However, this suffers from a problem similar to the issue of the mean. The range in salaries at the law firm will vary widely depending on whether the CEO is included in the set. Further, the range is just dependent on two values, the highest and lowest, and therefore, can't speak of the dispersion of the bulk of the dataset.

One tactic that solves the first of these problems is to use the **interquartile range**.

What about measures of spread for categorical data?

 The measures of spread that we talk about in this section are only applicable to numeric data. There are, however, measures of spread or the diversity of categorical data. In spite of the usefulness of these measures, this topic goes unmentioned or blithely ignored in most data analysis and statistics texts. This is a long and venerable tradition that we will, for the most part, adhere to in this book. If you are interested in learning more about this, search for 'entropy' or 'Diversity Indices' on the Web.

Remember when we said that the median split a sorted dataset into two equal parts, and that it was the 50th percentile because 50 percent of the observations fell below its value? In a similar way, if you were to divide a sorted dataset into four equal parts, or quartiles, the three values that make these divides would be the first, second, and third quartiles respectively. These values can also be called the 25th, 50th, and 75th percentiles. Note that the second quartile, the 50th percentile, and the median are all equivalent.

The interquartile range is the difference between the third and first quartiles. If you apply the interquartile range to a sample of salaries at the law firm that includes the CEO, the enormous salary will be discarded with the highest 25 percent of the data. However, this still only uses two values and doesn't speak to the variability of the middle 50 percent.

Well, one way we can use all the data points to inform our spread metric is by subtracting each element of a dataset from the mean of the dataset. This will give us the deviations, or *residuals*, from the mean. If we add up all these deviations, we will arrive at the *sum of the deviations from the mean*. Try to find the sum of the deviations from the mean in this set: {1, 3, 5, 6, 7}.

If we try to compute this, we notice that the positive deviations are cancelled out by the negative deviations. In order to cope with this, we need to take the absolute value, or the magnitude of the deviation, and sum them.

This is a great start, but note that this metric keeps increasing if we add more data to the set. Due to this, we may want to take the average of these deviations. This is called the **average deviation**.

For those having trouble following the description in words, the formula for average deviation from the mean is the following:

$$\frac{1}{N} \sum_{i=1}^{N} (xi - \mu)$$

Here, μ is the mean, N is the number elements of the sample, and x_i is the ith element of the dataset. It can also be expressed in R as follows:

```
sum(abs(x - mean(x))) / length(x)
```

Though average deviation is an excellent measure of spread in its own right, its use is commonly--and sometimes unfortunately--supplanted by two other measures.

Instead of taking the absolute value of each residual, we can achieve a similar outcome by squaring each deviation from the mean. This, too, ensures that each residual is positive (so that there is no canceling out). Additionally, squaring the residuals has the sometimes desirable property of magnifying larger deviations from the mean, while being more forgiving of smaller deviations. The sum of the squared deviations is called (you guessed it!) the sum of squared deviations from the mean or, simply, sum of squares. The average of the sum of squared deviations from the mean is known as the variance and is denoted by σ^2:

$$\sigma^2 = \frac{1}{N} \sum_{i=1}^{N} (xi - \mu)^2$$

When we square each deviation, we also square our units. For example, if our dataset held measurements in meters, our variance would be expressed in terms of meters squared. To get back our original units, we have to take the square root of the variance:

$$\sigma = \sqrt{\frac{1}{N} \sum_{i=1}^{N} (xi - \mu)^2}$$

This new measure, denoted by σ, is the **standard deviation**, and it is one of the most important measures in this book. It is worth going through again to make sure it's fully understood.

Note that we switched from referring to the mean as $\bar{x}$ to referring it as μ. This was not a mistake.

Remember that $\overline{x}$ was the sample mean and μ represented the population mean. The preceding equations use μ to illustrate that these equations are computing the spread metrics on the population dataset and not on a sample. If we want to describe the variance and standard deviation of a sample, we use the symbols s^2 and s instead of σ and σ^2 respectively, and our equations change slightly:

$$s^2 = \frac{1}{n-1} \sum_{i=1}^{n}(x_i - \overline{x})^2$$

$$s = \sqrt{\frac{1}{n-1} \sum_{i=1}^{n}(x_i - \overline{x})^2}$$

Instead of dividing our sum of squares by the number of elements in the set, we are now dividing it by *n-1*. What gives?

To answer this question, we have to learn a little bit about populations, samples, and estimation.

Populations, samples, and estimation

One of the core ideas of statistics is that we can use a subset of a group, study it, and then make inferences or conclusions about that much larger group.

For example, let's say we wanted to find the average (mean) weight of all the people in Germany. One way do to this is to visit all the 81 million people in Germany, record their weights, and then find the average. However, it is a far more sane endeavor to take down the weights of only a few hundred Germans, and use these to deduce the average weight of all Germans. In this case, the few hundred people we do measure is the sample, and the entirety of the people in Germany is called the **population**.

Now, there are Germans of all shapes and sizes: some heavier, some lighter. If we only pick a few Germans to weigh, we run the risk of, by chance, choosing a group of primarily underweight Germans or overweight ones. We might then come to an inaccurate conclusion about the weight of all Germans. However, as we add more Germans to our sample, these chance variations tend to balance themselves out.

All things being equal, it would be preferable to measure the weights of all Germans so that we can be absolutely sure that we have the right answer, but this just isn't feasible. If we take a large enough sample, though, and are careful that our sample is well-representative of the population, not only can we get extraordinarily close to the actual average weight of the population, but we can also quantify our uncertainty. The more Germans we include in our sample, the less uncertain we are about our estimate of the population.

In the preceding case, we are using the sample mean as an estimator of the population mean, and the actual value of the sample mean is called our **estimate**. It turns out that the formula for the population mean is a great estimator of the mean of the population when applied to only a sample. This is why we make no distinction between the population and sample means, except to replace the μ with $\bar{x}$. Unfortunately, no perfect estimator for the standard deviation of a population for all population types exists. There will always be some systematic difference in the expected value of the estimator and the real value of the population. This means that there is some bias in the estimator. Fortunately, we can partially correct it.

Note that the two differences between the population and the sample standard deviation are that the μ is replaced by $\bar{x}$ in the sample standard deviation, and the divisor n is replaced by *n-1*.

In the case of the standard deviation of the population, we know the mean μ. In the case of the sample, however, we don't know the population mean; we only have an estimate of the population mean based on the sample mean. This must be taken into account and corrected in the new equation. No longer can we divide by the number of elements in the dataset--we have to divide by the **degrees of freedom**, which is *n-1*.

What in the world are degrees of freedom? Why is it *n-1*?

Let's say we were gathering a party of six to play a board game. In this board game, each player controls one of six colored pawns. People start to join in at the board. The first person at the board gets their pick of their favorite colored pawn. The second player has one less pawn to choose from, but she still has a choice in the matter. By the time the last person joins in at the game table, she doesn't have a choice in what pawn she uses; she is forced to use the last remaining pawn. The concept of degrees of freedom is a little like this.

If we have a group of five numbers, but hold the mean of those numbers fixed, all but the last number can vary, because the last number must take on the value that will satisfy the fixed mean. We only have four degrees of freedom in this case.

More generally, the degrees of freedom is the sample size minus the number of parameters estimated from the data. When we are using the mean estimate in the standard deviation formula, we are effectively keeping one of the parameters of the formula fixed so that only *n-1* observations are free to vary. This is why the divisor of the sample standard deviation formula is *n-1*; it is the degrees of freedom that we are dividing by, not the sample size.

If you thought that the last few paragraphs were heady and theoretical, you're right. If you are confused, particularly by the concept of degrees of freedom, you can take solace in the fact that you are not alone; degrees of freedom, bias, and subtleties of population versus sample standard deviation are notoriously confusing topics for newcomers to statistics. But you only have to learn it once!

Probability distributions

Up until this point, when we spoke of distributions, we were referring to frequency distributions. However, when we talk about distributions later in the book--or when other data analysts refer to them--we will be talking about probability distributions, which are much more general.

It's easy to turn a categorical, discrete, or discretized frequency distribution into a probability distribution. As an example, refer to the frequency distribution of carburetors in the first image in this chapter. Instead of asking *What number of cars have n number of carburetors?*, we can ask, *What is the probability that, if I choose a car at random, I will get a car with n carburetors?*

We will talk more about probability (and different interpretations of probability) in `Chapter 4`, *Probability*, but for now, probability is a value between 0 and 1 (or 0 percent and 100 percent) that measures how likely an event is to occur. To answer the question, *What's the probability that I will pick a car with 4 carburetors?*, the equation is as follows:

$$P(I \ will \ pick \ a \ 4 \ carb \ cars) = \frac{\# \ of \ 4 \ carb \ cars}{number \ of \ 4 \ total \ cars}$$

You can find the probability of picking a car with any one particular number of carburetors as follows:

```
table(mtcars$carb) / length(mtcars$carb)
      1       2       3       4       6       8
0.21875 0.31250 0.09375 0.31250 0.03125 0.03125
```

Instead of making a bar chart of the frequencies, we can make a bar chart of the probabilities.

This is called a **probability mass function** (**PMF**). It looks the same, but now it maps from carburetors to probabilities, not frequencies. *Figure 2.6a* represents this.

Just as it is with the bar chart, we can easily tell that 2 and 4 are the number of carburetors most likely to be chosen at random.

We could do the same with discretized numeric variables as well. The following graph is a representation of the temperature histogram as a probability mass function:

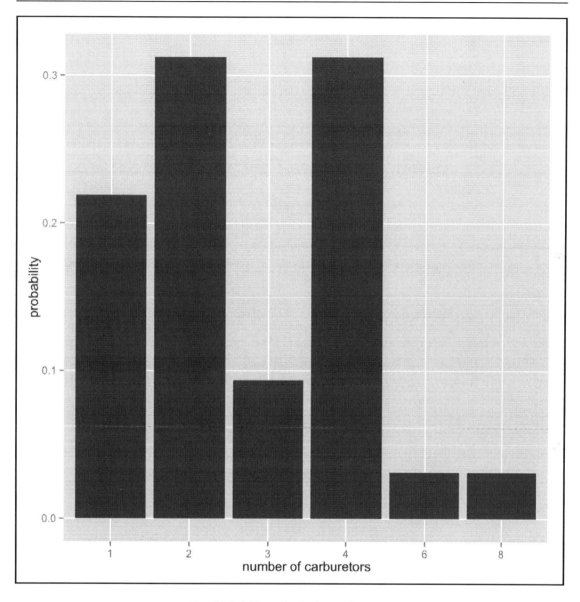

Figure 2.6a: Probability mass function of number of carburetors

The probability mass function of daily temperature measurements from May to September in NY is as follows:

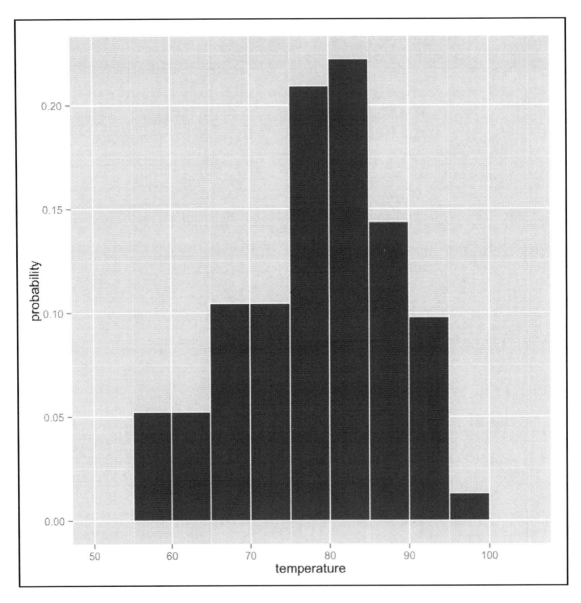

Figure 2.6b: Probability mass function of daily temperature measurements from May to September in NY

Note that this PMF only describes the temperatures of NYC in the data that we have.

There's a problem here, though: this PMF is completely dependent on the size of bins (our method of discretizing the temperatures). Imagine that we constructed the bins such that each bin held only one temperature within a degree. In this case, we wouldn't be able to tell very much from the PMF at all, as each specific degree only occurs a few times, if any, in the dataset. The same problem--but worse!--happens when we try to describe continuous variables with probabilities without discretizing them at all. Imagine trying to visualize the probability (or the frequency) of the temperatures if they were measured to the thousandth place (for example, {90.167, 67.361, ..}). There would be no visible bars at all!

What we need here is a **probability density function** (PDF). A probability density function will tell us the relative likelihood that we will experience a certain temperature. The next image shows a PDF that fits the temperature data that we've been playing with; it is analogous to, but better than, the histogram we saw in the beginning of the chapter and the PMF in the preceding figure.

The first thing you'll notice about this new plot is that it is smooth, not jagged or boxy like the histogram and PMFs. This should intuitively make more sense, because temperatures are a continuous variable and there are likely to be no sharp cut offs in the probability of experiencing temperatures from one degree to the next:

Figure 2.7: Probability density function of temperature measurements

The second thing you should notice is that the units and the values on the *y* axis have changed. The *y* axis no longer represents probabilities--it now represents probability densities. Though it may be tempting, you can't look at this function and answer the question, *What is the probability that it will be exactly 80 degrees?* Technically, the probability of it being 80.0000 exactly is microscopically small, almost zero. But that's okay! Remember, we don't care what the probability of experiencing a temperature of 80.0000 is--we just care about the probability of a temperature around there.

We can answer the question, *What's the probability that the temperature will be between a particular range?* The probability of experiencing a temperature, say 80 to 90 degrees, is the area under the curve from 80 to 90. Those of you unfortunate readers who know calculus will recognize this as the integral, or anti-derivative, of the PDF evaluated over the range:

$$\int_{80}^{90} f(x)dx$$

Here, *f(x)* is the probability density function.

The following image shows the area under the curve for this range in pink:

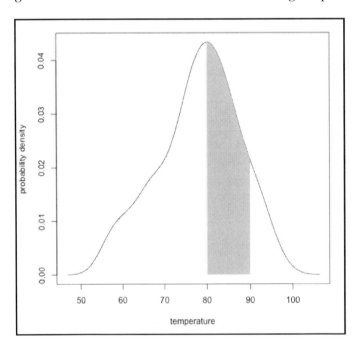

Figure 2.8: PDF with highlighted interval

You can immediately see that the region covers a lot of area--perhaps one third. According to R, it's about 34 percent:

```
# don't worry about memorizing this
temp.density <- density(airquality$Temp)
pdf <- approxfun(temp.density$x, temp.density$y, rule=2)
integrate(pdf, 80, 90)
    0.3422287 with absolute error < 7.5e-06
```

We don't get a probability density function from the sample for free. The PDF has to be estimated. The PDF isn't so much trying to convey the information about the sample we have, as attempting to model the underlying distribution that gave rise to this sample.

To do this, we use a method called **kernel density estimation**. The specifics of kernel density estimation are beyond the scope of this book, but you should know that the density estimation is heavily governed by a parameter that controls the smoothness of the estimation. This is called the **bandwidth**.

How do we choose the bandwidth? Well, it's just like choosing the size to make the bins in a histogram: there's no right answer. It's a balancing act between reducing chance or noise in the model and not losing important information by smoothing over pertinent characteristics of the data. This is a trade-off we will see time and time again throughout this text.

Anyway, the great thing about PDFs is that you don't have to know calculus to interpret PDFs. Not only are PDFs a useful tool analytically, but they also make for a top-notch visualization of the shape of data.

 Remember when we were talking about modes and I said that finding the mode of non-discretized continuously distributed data is a more complicated procedure than for discretized or categorical data? The mode for these types of univariate data is the peak of the PDF. So, in the temperature example, the mode is around 80 degrees.

The following image shows three different bandwidths used on the same data:

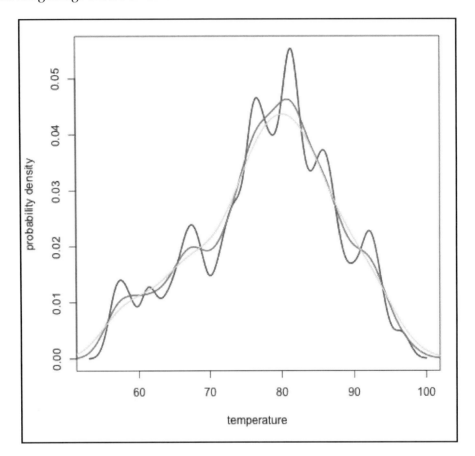

Figure 2.9: Three different bandwidths used on the same data

Visualization methods

In an earlier image, we saw three very different distributions, all with the same mean and median. I said then that we need to quantify variance to tell them apart. In the following image, there are three very different distributions, all with the same mean, median, and variance:

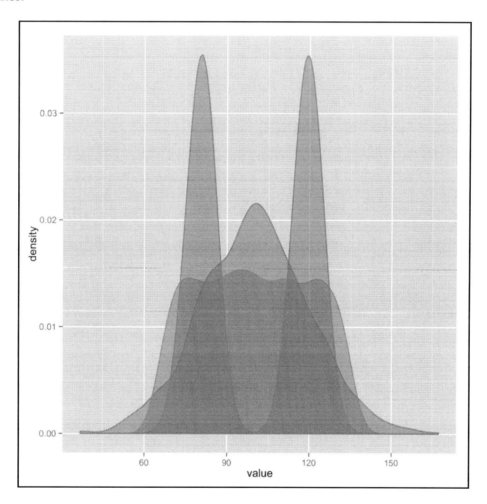

Figure 2.10: Three PDFs with the same mean, median, and standard deviation

If you just rely on basic summary statistics to understand univariate data, you'll never get the full picture. It's only when we visualize it that we can clearly see, at a glance, whether there are any clusters or areas with a high density of data points, the number of clusters there are, whether there are outliers, whether there is a pattern to the outliers, and so on. When dealing with univariate data, the shape is the most important part. (That's why this chapter is called *Shape of Data*!)

We will be using ggplot2's `qplot` function to investigate these shapes and visualize this data. `qplot` (for quick plot) is the simpler cousin of the more expressive `ggplot` function. `qplot` makes it easy to produce handsome and compelling graphics using consistent grammar. Additionally, much of the skills, lessons, and know-how from `qplot` are transferable to `ggplot` (for when we have to get more advanced).

What's ggplot2? Why are we using it?

There are a few plotting mechanisms for R, including the default one that comes with R (called **base R**). However, ggplot2 seems to be a lot of people's favorite. This is not unwarranted, given its wide use, excellent documentation, and consistent grammar.

As the base R graphics subsystem is what I learned to wield first, I've become adept at using it. There are certain types of plots that I produce faster using base R, so I still use it on a regular basis. (*Figures 2.8* to *Figure 2.10* were made using base R!)

Though we will be using ggplot2 for this book, feel free to go your own way when making your very own plots.

Most of the graphics in this section are going to take the following form:

```
qplot(column, data=dataframe, geom=...)
```

Here, `column` is a particular column of the data frame `dataframe`, and the `geom` keyword argument specifies a geometric object--it will control the type of plot that we want. To visualize univariate data, we don't have many options for `geom`. The three types that we will be using are `bar`, `histogram`, and `density`. Making a bar graph of the frequency distribution of the number of carburetors couldn't be easier:

```
library(ggplot2)
qplot(factor(carb), data=mtcars, geom="bar")
```

We get the following output:

Figure 2.11: Frequency distribution of the number of carburetors

Using the `factor` function on the `carb` column makes the plot look better in this case.

We could, if we wanted to, make an unattractive and distracting plot by coloring all the bars a different color, as follows:

```
qplot(factor(carb),
      data=mtcars,
      geom="bar",
      fill=factor(carb),
      xlab="number of carburetors")
```

We get the following graph:

2.12: With color and label modification

We also relabeled the *x* axis (which is automatically set by `qplot`) to more informative text.

It's just as easy to make a histogram of the temperature data; the main difference is that we switch `geom` from `bar` to `histogram`:

```
qplot(Temp, data=airquality, geom="histogram")
```

We get the following histogram:

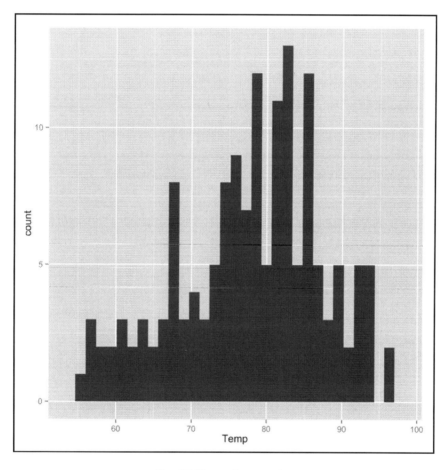

Figure 2.13: Histogram of temperature data

Why doesn't it look like the first histogram in the beginning of the chapter, you ask? Well, that's because of two reasons:

- I adjusted the bin width (size of the bins)
- I added color to the outline of the bars

The code I used for the first histogram looked as follows:

```
qplot(Temp, data=airquality, geom="histogram",
  binwidth=5, color=I("white"))
```

Making plots of the approximation of the PDF is similarly simple:

```
qplot(Temp, data=airquality, geom="density")
```

We the plot as follows:

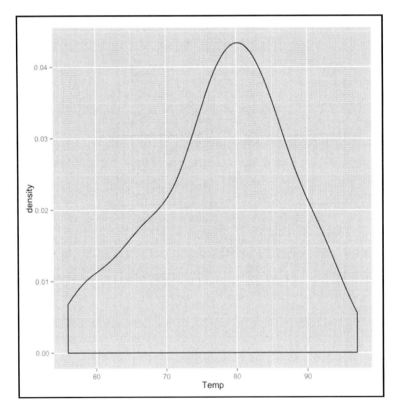

Figure 2.14: PDF of temperature data

By itself, I think the preceding plot is rather unattractive. We can give it a little more flair by doing the following:

- Filling the curve pink
- Adding a little transparency to the fill

```
qplot(Temp, data=airquality, geom="density",
    adjust=.5,          # changes bandwidth
    fill=I("pink"),
    alpha=I(.5),        # adds transparency
    main="density plot of temperature data")
```

The density plot is as follows:

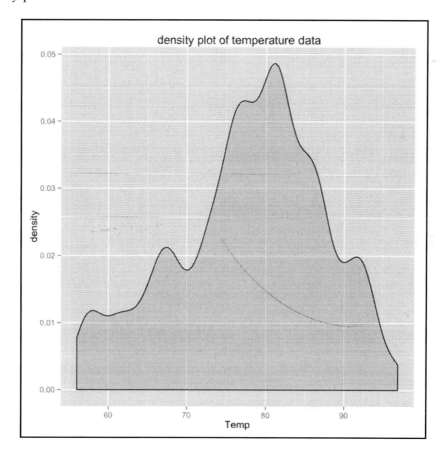

Figure 2.15: Figure 2.14 with modifications

Now that's a handsome plot!

Notice that we also made the bandwidth smaller than the default (1, which made the PDF more squiggly) and added a title to the plot with the `main` parameter.

Exercises

Here are a few exercises for you to revise the concepts learned in this chapter:

- Write an R function to compute the interquartile range.
- Learn about windorized, geometric, harmonic, and trimmed means. To what extent do these metrics solve the problem of the non-robustness of the arithmetic mean?
- Craft an assessment of Virginia Woolf's impact on feminine discourse in the 20th century. Be sure to address both prosaic and lyrical forms in your response.

Summary

One of the hardest things about data analysis is statistics, and one of the hardest things about statistics (not unlike computer programming) is that the beginning is the toughest hurdle because the concepts are so new and unfamiliar. As a result, some might find this to be one of the more challenging chapters in this text.

However, hard work during this phase pays enormous dividends; it provides a sturdy foundation on which to pile on and organize new knowledge.

To recap, in this chapter, you learned about univariate data. You also learned about:

- The types of univariate data
- How to measure the central tendency of this data
- How to measure the spread of this data
- How to visualize the shape of this data

Along the way, we also discussed a little bit about probability distributions and population/sample statistics.

I'm glad you made it through! Relax, make yourself a mocktail, and I'll see you in Chapter 3, *Describing Relationships* shortly!

Describing Relationships 3

Is there a relationship between smoking and lung cancer? Do people who care for dogs live longer? Is your university's admissions department sexist?

Tackling these exciting questions is only possible when we take a step beyond simply describing univariate datasets—one step beyond!

We will be covering the following topics in this chapter:

- Multivariate data
- Relationships between a categorical and continuous variable
- Relationships between two categorical variables
- Visualization methods

Multivariate data

In this chapter, we are going to describe relationships and begin working with multivariate data, which is a fancy way of saying *samples containing more than one variable*.

The troublemaker reader might remark that all the datasets that we've worked with thus far (`mtcars` and `airquality`) have contained more than one variable. This is technically true but only technically. The fact of the matter is that we've only been working with one of the dataset's variables at any one time. Note that multivariate analytics is not the same as doing univariate analytics on more than one variable—multivariate analyses and describing relationships involve several variables at the same time.

To put this more concretely, in the last chapter we described the shape of, say, the temperature readings in the `airquality` dataset:

```
head(airquality)
  Ozone Solar.R Wind Temp Month Day
1    41     190  7.4   67     5   1
2    36     118  8.0   72     5   2
3    12     149 12.6   74     5   3
4    18     313 11.5   62     5   4
5    NA      NA 14.3   56     5   5
6    28      NA 14.9   66     5   6
```

In this chapter, we will be exploring whether there is a relationship between temperature and the month in which the temperature was taken. (Spoiler alert: there is!)

The kind of multivariate analysis you perform is heavily influenced by the type of data that you are working with. There are three broad classes of bivariate (or two variable) relationships:

- The relationship between one categorical variable and one continuous variable
- The relationship between two categorical variables
- The relationship between two continuous variables

We will get into all of these in the next three sections. In the section after that, we will touch on describing the relationships between more than two variables. Finally, following in the tradition of the previous chapter, we will end with a section on how to create your own plots to capture the relationships that we'll be exploring.

Relationships between a categorical and continuous variable

Describing the relationship between categorical and continuous variables is perhaps the most familiar of the three broad categories.

When I was in the fifth grade, my class had to participate in an area-wide science fair. We were to devise our own experiment, perform it, and then present it. For some reason, in my experiment, I chose to water some lentil sprouts with tap water and some with alcohol to see if they grew differently.

When I measured the heights and compared the measurements of the teetotaler lentils versus the drunken lentils, I was pointing out a relationship between a categorical variable (alcohol/no-alcohol) and a continuous variable (heights of the seedlings).

Note:

I wasn't trying to make a broader statement about how alcohol affects plant growth. In the grade-school experiment, I was just summarizing the differences in the heights of those plants—the ones that were in the experiment. In order to make statements or draw conclusions about how alcohol affects plant growth in general, we would be exiting the realm of exploratory data analysis and entering the domain of inferential statistics, which we will discuss in the next unit.

The alcohol could have made the lentils grow faster (it didn't), grow slower (it did), or grow at the same rate as the tap water lentils. All three of these possibilities constitute a relationship: greater than, less than, or equal to.

To demonstrate how to uncover the relationship between these two types of variables in R, we will be using the `iris` dataset that is conveniently built right into R:

```
head(iris)
  Sepal.Length Sepal.Width Petal.Length Petal.Width Species
1          5.1         3.5          1.4         0.2  setosa
2          4.9         3.0          1.4         0.2  setosa
3          4.7         3.2          1.3         0.2  setosa
4          4.6         3.1          1.5         0.2  setosa
5          5.0         3.6          1.4         0.2  setosa
6          5.4         3.9          1.7         0.4  setosa
```

This is a famous dataset and is used today primarily for teaching purposes. It gives the lengths and widths of the petals and sepals (another part of the flower) of 150 Iris flowers. Of the 150 flowers, it has 50 measurements each from three different species of Iris flowers: setosa, versicolor, and virginica.

By now, we know how to take the mean of all the petal lengths:

```
mean(iris$Petal.Length)
[1] 3.758
```

We could also take the mean of the petal lengths of each of the three species to see if there is any difference in the means.

Naively, one might approach this task in R as follows:

```
mean(iris$Petal.Length[iris$Species=="setosa"])
   [1] 1.462
mean(iris$Petal.Length[iris$Species=="versicolor"])
   [1] 4.26
mean(iris$Petal.Length[iris$Species=="virginica"])
   [1] 5.552
```

As you might imagine, there is a far easier way to do this:

```
by(iris$Petal.Length, iris$Species, mean)
iris$Species: setosa
[1] 1.462
------------------------------------------------
iris$Species: versicolor
[1] 4.26
------------------------------------------------
iris$Species: virginica
[1] 5.552
```

The `by` function is a handy function that applies a function to split the subsets of data. In this case, the `Petal.Length` vector is divided into three subsets for each species, and then the `mean` function is called on each of these subsets. It appears as if the setosas in this sample have way shorter petals than the other two species, with the virginica sample's petal length beating out versicolor's by a smaller margin.

Although means are probably the most common statistic to be compared between categories, it is not the only statistic we can use to compare. If we had reason to believe that the virginicas have a more widely varying petal length than the other two species, we could pass the `sd` function to the `by` function as follows:

```
by(iris$Petal.Length, iris$Species, sd)
```

Most often, though, we want to be able to compare many statistics between groups at one time. To this end, it's very common to pass in the `summary` function:

```
by(iris$Petal.Length, iris$Species, summary)
iris$Species: setosa
   Min. 1st Qu.  Median   Mean 3rd Qu.    Max.
  1.000   1.400   1.500  1.462   1.575   1.900
------------------------------------------------
iris$Species: versicolor
   Min. 1st Qu.  Median   Mean 3rd Qu.    Max.
   3.00    4.00    4.35   4.26    4.60    5.10
------------------------------------------------
iris$Species: virginica
```

Min.	1st Qu.	Median	Mean	3rd Qu.	Max.
4.500	5.100	5.550	5.552	5.875	6.900

As common as this idiom is, it still presents us with a lot of dense information that is difficult to make sense of at a glance. It is more common still to visualize the differences in continuous variables between categories using a box-and-whisker plot:

Figure 3.1: A box-and-whisker plot depicting the relationship between the petal lengths of the different iris species in the iris dataset

A box-and-whisker plot (or simply, a box plot if you have places to go and you're in a rush) displays a stunningly large amount of information in a single chart. Each categorical variable has its own box and whiskers. The bottom and top ends of the box represent the first and third quartile respectively, and the black band inside the box is the median for that group, as shown in the following figure:

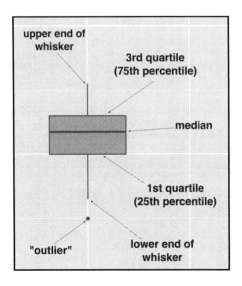

Figure 3.2: The anatomy of a box plot

Depending on whom you talk to and what you use to produce your plots, the edges of the whiskers can mean a few different things. In my favorite variation (called **Tukey's variation**), the bottom of the whiskers extend to the lowest datum within 1.5 times the interquartile range below the bottom of the box. Similarly, the very top of the whisker represents the highest datum 1.5 interquartile ranges above the third quartile (remember: interquartile range is the third quartile minus the first). This is, coincidentally, the variation that `ggplot2` uses.

The great thing about box plots is that not only do we get a great sense of the central tendency and dispersion of the distribution within a category, but we can also immediately spot the important differences between each category.

From the box plot in the previous image, it's easy to tell what we already know about the central tendency of the petal lengths between species: that the setosa in this sample have the shortest petals; that the virginica have the longest on average; and that versicolor are in the middle, but are closer to the virginica.

In addition, we can see that the setosas have the thinnest dispersion, and that the virginica have the highest—when you disregard the outlier.

Remember, we are not saying anything or drawing any conclusions yet about Iris flowers in general. In all of these analyses, we are treating all the data we have as the population of interest; in this example, the 150 flowers measured are our population of interest.

Before we move on to the next broad category of relationships, let's look at the `airquality` dataset, treat the month as the categorical variable, the temperature as the continuous variable, and see if there is a relationship between the average temperature across months:

```
by(airquality$Temp, airquality$Month, mean)
airquality$Month: 5
[1] 65.54839
------------------------------------------------
airquality$Month: 6
[1] 79.1
------------------------------------------------
airquality$Month: 7
[1] 83.90323
------------------------------------------------
airquality$Month: 8
[1] 83.96774
------------------------------------------------
airquality$Month: 9
[1] 76.9
```

This is precisely what we would expect from a city in the Northern hemisphere:

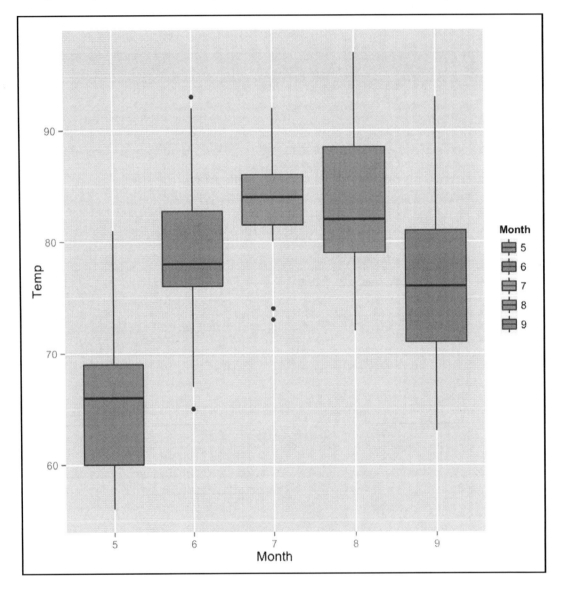

Figure 3.3: A box plot of NYC temperatures across months (May to September)

Relationships between two categorical variables

Describing the relationships between two categorical variables is done somewhat less often than the other two broad types of bivariate analyses, but it is just as fun (and useful)!

To explore this technique, we will be using the UCBAdmissions dataset, which contains the data on graduate school applicants to the **University of California Berkeley (UCB)** in 1973.

Before we get started, we have to wrap the dataset in a call to data.frame to coerce it into a data frame type variable—I'll explain why, soon:

```
ucba <- data.frame(UCBAdmissions)
head(ucba)
    Admit Gender Dept Freq
1 Admitted   Male    A  512
2 Rejected   Male    A  313
3 Admitted Female    A   89
4 Rejected Female    A   19
5 Admitted   Male    B  353
6 Rejected   Male    B  207
```

Now, what we want is a count of the frequencies of number of students in each of the following four categories:

- Accepted female
- Rejected female
- Accepted male
- Rejected male

Do you remember the frequency tabulation at the beginning of the last chapter? This is similar—except that now we are dividing the set by one more variable. This is known as **cross-tabulation** or **cross tab**. It is also sometimes referred to as a contingency table. The reason we had to coerce UCBAdmissions into a data frame is because it was already in the form of a cross tabulation (except that it further broke the data down into the different departments of the grad school). Check it out by typing UCBAdmissions at the prompt.

We can use the `xtabs` function in R to make our own cross-tabulations:

```
# the first argument to xtabs (the formula) should
# be read as: frequency *by* Gender and Admission
cross <- xtabs(Freq ~ Gender+Admit, data=ucba)
cross
          Admit
Gender    Admitted Rejected
   Male       1198     1493
   Female      557     1278
```

Here, at a glance, we can see that there were 1198 males that were admitted, 557 females that were admitted, and so on.

Is there a gender bias in UCB's graduate admissions process? Perhaps, but it's hard to tell from just looking at the 2 x 2 contingency table. Sure, there are fewer females accepted than males, but there are also, unfortunately, far fewer females that applied to UCB in the first place.

To aid us in either implicating UCB of a sexist admissions machine or exonerating them, it would help to look at a proportions table. Using a proportions table, we can easily compare the proportion of the total number of males who were accepted versus the proportion of the total number of females who were accepted. If the proportions are more or less equal, we can conclude that gender does not constitute a factor in UCB's admissions process. If this is the case, gender and admission status is said to be conditionally independent:

```
prop.table(cross, 1)
          Admit
Gender     Admitted  Rejected
   Male    0.4451877 0.5548123
   Female  0.3035422 0.6964578
```

Why did we supply 1 as an argument to `prop.table`? Look up the documentation at the R prompt. When would we want to use `prop.table(cross, 2)`?

Here, we can see that while 45 percent of the males who applied were accepted, only 30 percent of the females who applied were accepted. This is evidence that the admissions department is sexist, right? Not so fast, my friend!

This is precisely what a lawsuit lodged against UCB purported. When the issue was looked into further, it was discovered that, at the department level, women and men actually had similar admissions rates. In fact, some of the departments appeared to have a small but significant bias in favor of women. Check out department A's proportion table, for example:

```
cross2 <- xtabs(Freq ~ Gender + Admit, data=ucba[ucba$Dept=="A",])
prop.table(cross2, 1)
        Admit
 Gender    Admitted  Rejected
    Male  0.6206061 0.3793939
  Female  0.8240741 0.1759259
```

If there were any bias in admissions, this data didn't prove it. This phenomenon, where a trend that appears in combined groups of data disappears or reverses when broken down into groups, is known as **Simpson's Paradox**. In this case, it was caused by the fact that women tended to apply to departments that were far more selective.

This is probably the most famous case of Simpson's Paradox, and it is also why this dataset is built into R. The lesson here is to be careful when using pooled data and look out for hidden variables.

The relationship between two continuous variables

Do you think that there is a relationship between women's heights and their weights? If you said yes, congratulations, you're right!

We can verify this assertion using the data in R's built-in dataset, women, which holds the height and weight of 15 American women from ages 30 to 39:

```
head(women)
  height weight
1     58    115
2     59    117
3     60    120
4     61    123
5     62    126
6     63    129
nrow(women)
[1] 15
```

Specifically, this relationship is referred to as a positive relationship, because as one of the variable increases, we expect an increase in the other variable.

The most typical visual representation of the relationship between two continuous variables is a scatterplot.

A scatterplot is displayed as a group of points whose position along the *x* axis is established by one variable, and the position along the *y* axis is established by the other. When there is a positive relationship, the dots, for the most part, start in the lower-left corner and extend to the upper-right corner, as shown in the following figure. When there is a negative relationship, the dots start in the upper-left corner and extend to the lower-right one. When there is no relationship, it will look as if the dots are all over the place:

Figure 3.4: Scatterplot of women's heights and weights

The more the dots look like they form a straight line, the stronger is the relationship between two continuous variables; the more diffuse the points, the weaker is the relationship. The dots in the preceding figure look almost exactly like a straight line—this is pretty much as strong a relationship as they come.

These kinds of relationships are colloquially referred to as correlations.

Covariance

As always, visualizations are great—necessary even—but on most occasions, we are going to quantify these correlations and summarize them with numbers.

The simplest measure of correlation that is widely used is covariance. For each pair of values from the two variables, the differences from their respective means are taken. Then, those values are multiplied. If they are both positive (that is, both the values are above their respective means), then the product will be positive too. If both the values are below their respective means, the product is still positive, because the product of two negative numbers is positive. Only when one of the values is above its mean will the product be negative:

$$\mathrm{cov}_{xy} = \frac{\sum(x - \bar{x})(y - \bar{y})}{(n - 1)}$$

Remember, in sample statistics, we divide by the degrees of freedom and not the sample size.

Note:
This means that the covariance is only defined for two vectors that have the same length.

We can find the covariance between two variables in R using the `cov` function. Let's find the covariance between the heights and weights in the dataset, women:

```
cov(women$weight, women$height)
  [1] 69
  # the order we put the two columns in
  # the arguments doesn't matter
cov(women$height, women$weight)
  [1] 69
```

The covariance is positive, which denotes a positive relationship between the two variables.

The covariance, by itself, is difficult to interpret. It is especially difficult to interpret in this case, because the measurements use different scales: inches and pounds. It is also heavily dependent on the variability in each variable.

Consider what happens when we take the covariance of the weights in pounds and the heights in centimeters:

```
# there are 2.54 centimeters in each inch
# changing the units to centimeters increases
# the variability within the height variable
 cov(women$height*2.54, women$weight)
  [1] 175.26
```

Semantically speaking, the relationship hasn't changed, so why should the covariance?

Correlation coefficients

A solution to this quirk of covariance is to use Pearson's correlation coefficient instead. Outside its colloquial context, when the word correlation is uttered—especially by analysts, statisticians, or scientists—it usually refers to *Pearson's correlation*.

Pearson's correlation coefficient is different from covariance in that, instead of using the sum of the products of the deviations from the mean in the numerator, it uses the sum of the products of the number of standard deviations away from the mean. These number-of-standard-deviations-from-the-mean are called **z-scores**. If a value has a z-score of 1.5, it is 1.5 standard deviations above the mean; if a value has a z-score of -2, then it is 2 standard deviations below the mean.

Pearson's correlation coefficient is usually denoted by *r* and its equation is given as follows:

$$r = \frac{\sum (x - \bar{x})(y - \bar{y})}{(n-1) s_x s_y}$$

This is the covariance divided by the product of the two variables' standard deviation.

An important consequence of using standardized z-scores instead of the magnitude of distance from the mean is that changing the variability in one variable does not change the correlation coefficient. Now you can meaningfully compare values using two different scales or even two different distributions. The correlation between weight/height in inches and weight/height in centimeters will now be identical, because multiplication with 2.54 will not change the z-scores of each height:

```
cor(women$height, women$weight)
  [1] 0.9954948
cor(women$height*2.54, women$weight)
  [1] 0.9954948
```

Another important and helpful consequence of this standardization is that the measure of correlation will always range from -1 to 1. A Pearson correlation coefficient of 1 will denote a perfectly positive (linear) relationship, an *r* of -1 will denote a perfectly negative (linear) relationship, and an *r* of 0 will denote no (linear) relationship.

Why is the linear qualification in parentheses, though?

Intuitively, the correlation coefficient shows how well two variables are described by the straight line that fits the data most closely; this is called a **regression** or **trend line**. If there is a strong relationship between two variables, but the relationship is not linear, it cannot be represented accurately by Pearson's *r*. For example, the correlation between 1 to 100 and 100 to 200 is 1 (because it is perfectly linear), but a cubic relationship is not:

```
xs <- 1:100
cor(xs, xs+100)
  [1] 1
cor(xs, xs^3)
  [1] 0.917552
```

It is still about 0.92, which is an extremely strong correlation, but not the 1 that you should expect from a perfect correlation.

So Pearson's *r* assumes a linear relationship between two variables. There are, however, other correlation coefficients that are more tolerant of nonlinear relationships. Probably the most common of these is Spearman's rank coefficient, also called **Spearman's rho**.

Spearman's rho is calculated by taking the Pearson correlation not of the values, but of their ranks.

What's a rank?

When you assign ranks to a vector of numbers, the lowest number gets 1, the second lowest gets 2, and so on. The highest datum in the vector gets a rank that is equal to the number of elements in that vector.

In rankings, the magnitude of the difference in values of the elements is disregarded. Consider a race to a finish line involving three cars. Let's say that the winner in the first place finished at a speed three times that of the car in the second place, and the car in the second place beat the car in the third place by only a few seconds. The driver of the car that came first has a good reason to be proud of herself, but her rank, 1st place, does not say anything about how she effectively cleaned the floor with the other two candidates.

Try using R's `rank` function on the vector c(8, 6, 7, 5, 3, 0, 9). Now try it on the vector c(8, 6, 7, 5, 3, -100, 99999). The rankings are the same, right?

When we use ranks instead, the pair that has the highest value on both the *x* and *y* axes will be `c(1,1)`, even if one variable is a nonlinear function (cubed, squared, logarithmic, and so on) of the other. The correlations that we just tested will both have Spearman rhos of 1, because cubing a value will not change its rank:

```
xs <- 1:100
cor(xs, xs+100, method="spearman")
 [1] 1
cor(xs, xs^3, method="spearman")
 [1] 1
```

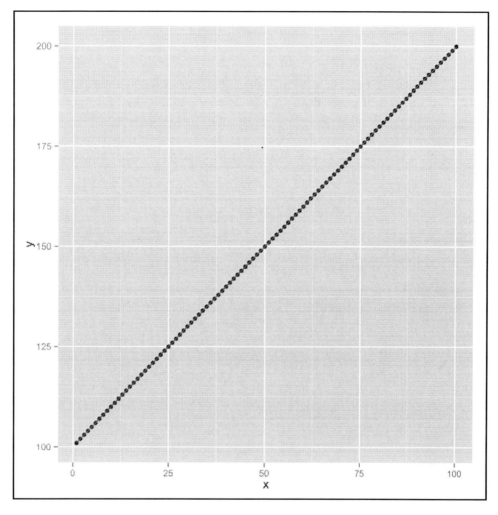

Figure 3.5: Scatterplot of *y=x + 100* with regression line; *r* and rho are both 1

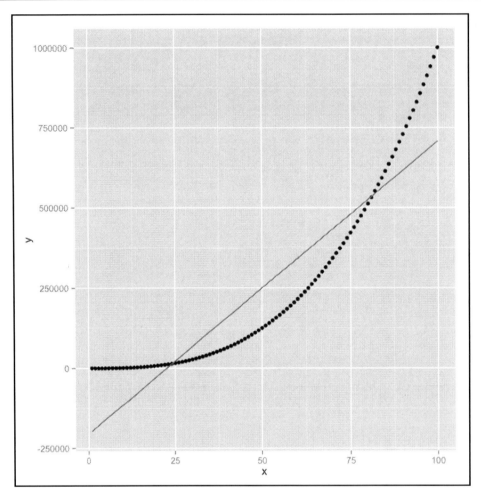

Figure 3.6: Scatterplot of with regression line. r is .92, but rho is 1

Let's use what we've learned so far to investigate the correlation between the weight of a car and the number of miles it gets to the gallon. Do you predict a negative relationship (the heavier the car, the lower the miles per gallon)?

```
cor(mtcars$wt, mtcars$mpg)
[1] -0.8676594
```

The output plot is as follows:

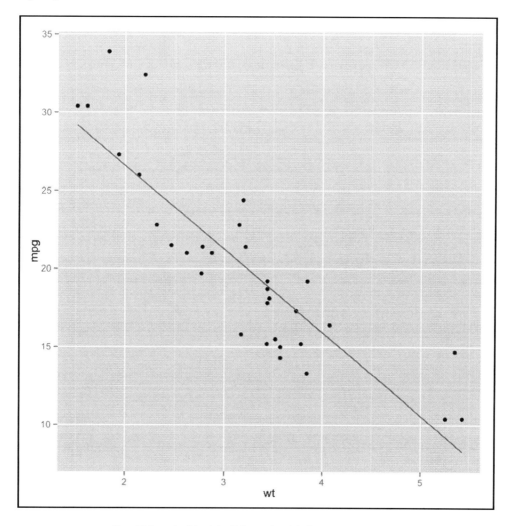

Figure 3.7: Scatterplot of the relationship between the weight of a car and its miles per gallon

This is a strong negative relationship. Although, in the preceding figure, note that the data points are more diffuse and spread around the regression line than in the other plots; this indicates a somewhat weaker relationship than we have seen thus far.

For an even weaker relationship, check out the correlation between wind speed and temperature in the `airquality` dataset:

```
cor(airquality$Temp, airquality$Wind)
 [1] -0.4579879
cor(airquality$Temp, airquality$Wind, method="spearman")
 [1] -0.4465408
```

The preceding co-relation when executed will result in the following graph:

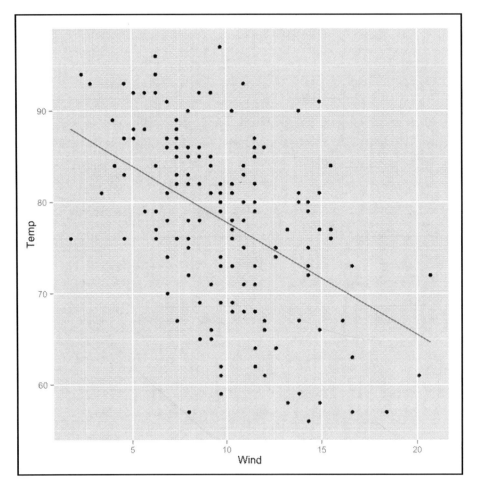

Figure 3.8: Scatterplot of the relationship between wind speed and temperature

Comparing multiple correlations

Armed with our new standardized coefficients, we can now effectively compare the correlations between different pairs of variables directly.

In data analysis, it is common to compare the correlations between all the numeric variables in a single dataset. We can do this with the `iris` dataset using the following R code snippet:

```
# have to drop 5th column (species is not numeric)
iris.nospecies <- iris[, -5]
cor(iris.nospecies)
             Sepal.Length Sepal.Width Petal.Length Petal.Width
Sepal.Length    1.0000000  -0.1175698    0.8717538   0.8179411
Sepal.Width    -0.1175698   1.0000000   -0.4284401  -0.3661259
Petal.Length    0.8717538  -0.4284401    1.0000000   0.9628654
Petal.Width     0.8179411  -0.3661259    0.9628654   1.0000000
```

This produces a correlation matrix (when it is done with the covariance, it is called a **covariance matrix**). It is square (the same number of rows and columns) and symmetric, which means that the matrix is identical to its transposition (the matrix with the axes flipped). It is symmetrical, because there are two elements for each pair of variables on either side of the diagonal line of ones. The diagonal line is all ones, because every variable is perfectly correlated with itself. Which are the most highly (positively) correlated pairs of variables? What about the most negatively correlated?

Visualization methods

We are now going to see how we can create these kinds of visualizations on our own.

Categorical and continuous variables

We have seen that box plots are a great way of comparing the distribution of a continuous variable across different categories. As you might expect, box plots are very easy to produce using `ggplot2`.

The following snippet produces the box-and-whisker plot that we saw earlier, depicting the relationship between the petal lengths of the different iris species in the `iris` dataset:

```
library(ggplot)
qplot(Species, Petal.Length, data=iris, geom="boxplot",
        fill=Species)
```

First, we specify the variable on the *x* axis (the iris species) and then the continuous variable on the *y* axis (the petal length). Finally, we specify that we are using the iris dataset, that we want a box plot, and that we want to fill the boxes with different colors for each iris species.

Another fun way of comparing distributions between the different categories is using an overlapping density plot:

```
qplot(Petal.Length, data=iris, geom="density", alpha=I(.7),
      fill=Species)
```

Here, we only need to specify the continuous variable, as the `fill` parameter will break down the density plot by species. The `alpha` parameter adds transparency to show more clearly the extent to which the distributions overlap:

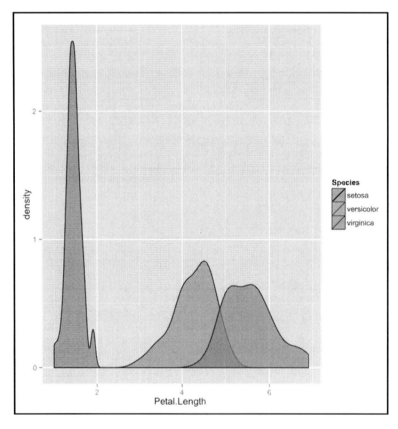

Figure 3.9: Overlapping density plot of petal length of iris flowers across species

If it is not the distribution you are trying to compare but some kind of single-value statistic (like standard deviation or sample counts), you can use the by function to get that value across all categories, and then build a bar plot where each category is a bar and the heights of the bars represent that category's statistic. For the code to construct a bar plot, refer back to the last section in Chapter 1, *Refresher*.

Two categorical variables

The visualization of categorical data is a grossly understudied domain and, in spite of some fairly powerful and compelling visualization methods, these techniques remain relatively unpopular.

My favorite method for graphically illustrating contingency tables is to use a mosaic plot. To make mosaic plots, we will need to install and load the **VCD** (**Visualizing Categorical Data**) package:

```
install.packages("vcd")
library(vcd)

ucba <- data.frame(UCBAdmissions)
mosaic(Freq ~ Gender + Admit, data=ucba,
        shade=TRUE, legend=FALSE)
```

After loading the preceding package the output obtained will be as follows:

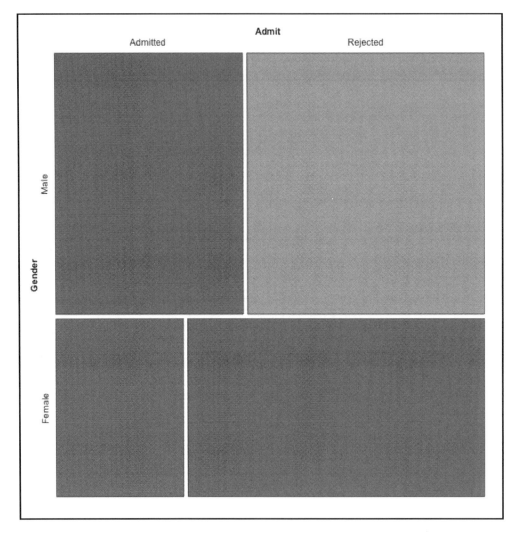

Figure 3.10: A mosaic plot of the UCBAdmissions dataset (across all departments)

The first argument to the mosaic function is a formula. This formula is meant to be read as: *display frequency broken down by gender and whether the applicant was admitted.* `shade=TRUE` adds a little life to the plot by adding colors to the boxes. The colors are actually very meaningful, as is the legend we opted not to show with the final parameter—but its meaning is beyond the scope of this section.

The mosaic plot represents each cell of a 2 x 2 contingency table as a tile; the area of the box is proportional to the number of observations in that cell. From this plot, we can easily tell that (a) more men applied to UCB than women, (b) more applicants were rejected than accepted, and (c) women were rejected at a higher proportion than male applicants.

You remember how this was misleading, right? Let's look at the mosaic plot for only department A:

```
mosaic(Freq ~ Gender+Admit, data=ucba[ucba$Dept=="A",],
        shade=TRUE, legend=FALSE)
```

The mosaic plot for department A after executing the preceding code will be as follows:

Figure 3.11: A mosaic plot of the UCBAdmissions dataset for department A

Hopefully, this plot makes the treachery of Simpson's paradox more apparent. Notice how there were far fewer female applicants than males, but the admission rates for the female applicants were much higher. Try visualizing the mosaic plots for the other departments by yourself!

Two continuous variables

The canonical way of displaying relationships between two continuous variables is via scatterplots. The scatterplot for the women's heights and weights that we saw earlier in this chapter was produced with the following R code snippet:

```
qplot(height, weight, data=women, geom="point")
```

Whether you put `height` and `weight` first depends on which variable you want tied to the *x* axis.

What about that fancy regression line?!, you ask frantically. `ggplot2` gracefully provides this feature with just a few extra characters. The scatterplot of the relationship between the weight of a car and its miles per gallon was produced as follows:

```
qplot(wt, mpg, data=mtcars, geom=c("point", "smooth"),
        method="lm", se=FALSE)
```

Here, we are specifying that we want two kinds of geometric objects, `point` and `smooth`. The latter is responsible for the regression line. `method="lm"` tells `qplot` that we want to use a linear model to create the trend line.

If we leave out the method, `ggplot2` will choose a method automatically; in this case, it would default to a method of drawing a nonlinear trend line called **LOESS**:

```
qplot(wt, mpg, data=mtcars, geom=c("point", "smooth"), se=FALSE)
```

The output obtained will be as follows:

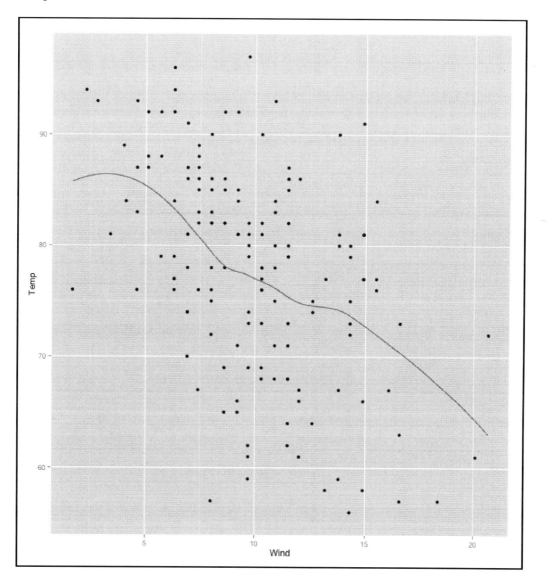

Figure 3.12: A scatterplot of the relationship between the weight of a car and its miles per gallon, and a trend-line smoothed with LOESS

The se=FALSE directive instructs ggplot2 not to plot the estimates of the error. We will get to what this means in a later chapter.

More than two continuous variables

Finally, there is an excellent way to visualize correlation matrices like the one we saw with the `iris` dataset in the section, *Comparing multiple correlations*. To do this, we have to install and load the `corrgram` package as follows:

```
install.packages("corrgram")
library(corrgram)

corrgram(iris, lower.panel=panel.conf, upper.panel=panel.pts)
```

After installing the `corrgram`:

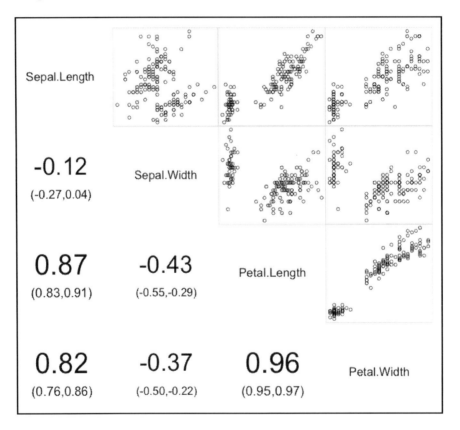

Figure 3.13: A corrgram of the iris dataset's continuous variables

With corrgrams, we can exploit the fact that correlation matrices are symmetrical by packing in more information. On the lower left panel, we have the Pearson correlation coefficients (never mind the small ranges beneath each coefficient for now). Instead of repeating these coefficients for the upper right panel, we can show a small scatterplot there instead.

We aren't limited to showing the coefficients and scatterplots in our `corrgram`, though; there are many other options and configurations available:

```
corrgram(iris, lower.panel=panel.pie, upper.panel=panel.pts,
         diag.panel=panel.density,
         main=paste0("corrgram of petal and sepal ",
                     "measurements in iris data set"))
```

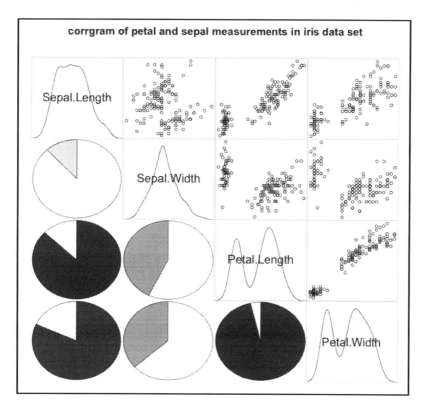

Figure 3.14: Another corrgram of the iris dataset's continuous variables

Notice that this time, we can overlay a density plot wherever there is a variable name (on the diagonal) just to get a sense of the variables' shapes. More saliently, instead of text coefficients, we have pie charts in the lower-left panel. These pie charts are meant to graphically depict the strength of the correlations.

If the color of the pie is blue (or any shade thereof), the correlation is positive; the bigger the shaded area of the pie, the stronger the magnitude of the correlation. If, however, the color of the pie is red or a shade of red, the correlation is negative, and the amount of shading on the pie is proportional to the magnitude of the correlation.

To top it all off, we added the main parameter to set the title of the plot. Note the use of `paste0` so that I could split the title up into two lines of code.

To get a better sense of what `corrgram` is capable of, you can view a live demonstration of examples if you execute the following at the prompt:

```
example(corrgram)
```

Exercises

Try out the following exercises to revise the concepts learned so far:

- Look at the documentation on cor with `help("cor")`. You can see, in addition to `"pearson"` and `"spearman"`, there is an option for `"kendall"`. Learn about *Kendall's tau*. Why, and under what conditions, is it considered better than Spearman's rho?
- For each species of iris, find the correlation coefficient between the sepal length and width. Are there any differences? How did we just combine two different types of the broad categories of bivariate analyses to perform a complex multivariate analysis?
- Download a dataset from the web, or find another built-into-R dataset that suits your fancy (using `library(help = "datasets")`). Explore relationships between the variables that you think might have some connection.
- Gustave Flaubert is well understood to be a classist misogynist and this, of course, influenced how he developed the character of Emma Bovary. However, it is not uncommon for the readers to identify and empathize with her, and they are often devastated by the book's conclusion. In fact, translator Geoffrey Wall asserts that Emma *dies in a pain that is exactly adjusted to the intensity of our preceding identification*.

How can the fact that some sympathize with Emma be reconciled with Flaubert's apparent intention? In your response, assume a post-structuralist approach to authorial intent.

Summary

There were many new ideas introduced in this chapter, so kudos to you for making it through! You're well on the way to being able to tackle some extraordinarily interesting problems on your own!

To summarize, in this chapter, you learned that the relationships between two variables can be broken down into three broad categories.

For categorical/continuous variables, you learned how to use the by function to retrieve the statistics on the continuous variable for each category. We also saw how we can use box-and-whisker plots to visually inspect the distributions of the continuous variable across categories.

For categorical/categorical configurations, we used contingency and proportions tables to compare frequencies. We also saw how mosaic plots can help spot interesting aspects of the data that might be difficult to detect when just looking at the raw numbers.

For categorical/continuous data we discovered the concepts of covariance and correlations, and explored different correlation coefficients with different assumptions about the nature of the bivariate relationship. You also learned how these concepts could be expanded to describe the relationship between more than two continuous variables. Finally, you learned how to use scatterplots and corrgrams to visually depict these relationships.

With this chapter, we've concluded the unit on exploratory data analysis, and we'll be moving on to *confirmatory data analysis* and *inferential statistics*.

4
Probability

It's time for us to put descriptive statistics down for the time being. It was fun for a while, but we're no longer content just determining the properties of observed data; now we want to start making deductions about data we haven't observed. This leads us to the realm of inferential statistics. In data analysis, probability is used to quantify uncertainty of our deductions about unobserved data. In the land of inferential statistics, probability reigns queen. Many regard her as a harsh mistress, but that's just a rumor.

Basic probability

Probability measures the likeliness that a particular event will occur. When mathematicians (us, for now!) speak of an event, we are referring to a set of potential outcomes of an experiment, or trial, to which we can assign a probability of occurrence.

Probabilities are expressed as a number between 0 and 1 (or as a percentage out of 100). An event with a probability of 0 denotes an impossible outcome, and a probability of 1 describes an event that is certain to occur.

The canonical example of probability at work is a coin flip. In the coin flip event, there are two outcomes: the coin lands on heads or the coin lands on tails. Pretending that coins never land on their edge (they almost never do), those two outcomes are the only ones possible. The sample space (the set of all possible outcomes), therefore, is {heads, tails}. As the entire sample space is covered by these two outcomes, they are said to be collectively exhaustive.

The sum of the probabilities of collectively exhaustive events is always 1. In this example, the probability that the coin flip will yield heads or yield tails is 1; it is certain that the coin will land on one of those. In a fair and correctly balanced coin, each of those two outcomes is equally likely. Therefore, we split the probability equally among the outcomes: in the event of a coin flip, the probability of obtaining heads is *0.5*, and the probability of tails is *0.5* as well. This is usually denoted as follows:

$$P(heads) = 0.5$$

The probability of a coin flip yielding either *heads* or *tails* looks like this:

$$P(heads \bigcup tails) = 1$$

The probability of a coin flip yielding both *heads* and *tails* is denoted as follows:

$$P(heads \bigcap tails) = 0$$

The two outcomes, in addition to being collectively exhaustive, are also mutually exclusive. This means that they can never co-occur. This is why the probability of *heads* and *tails* is *0*; it just can't happen.

The next obligatory application of beginner probability theory is in the case of rolling a standard six-sided die. In the event of a die roll, the sample space is (1, 2, 3, 4, 5, 6). With every roll of the die, we are sampling from this space. In this event too, each outcome is equally likely, except now we have to divide the probability across six outcomes. In the following equation, we denote the probability of rolling a *1* as *P(1)*:

$$P(1) = 1/6$$

Rolling a *1* or rolling a *2* is not collectively exhaustive (we can still roll a 3, 4, 5, or 6), but they are mutually exclusive; we can't roll a *1* and 2. If we want to calculate the probability of either one of two mutually exclusive events occurring, we add the probabilities:

$$P(1 \bigcup 2) = P(1) + P(2) = 1/3$$

While rolling a 1 or rolling a 2 aren't mutually exhaustive, rolling 1 and not rolling a 1 are. This is usually denoted in this manner:

$$P(1 \bigcup \neg 1) = 1$$

These two events—and all events that are both collectively exhaustive and mutually exclusive—are called complementary events.

Our last pedagogical example in the basic probability theory is using a deck of cards. Our deck has 52 cards—4 for each number from 2 to 10 and 4 each of Jack, Queen, King, and Ace (no Jokers!). Each of these four cards belong to one suit, either a Heart, Club, Spade, or Diamond. There are, therefore, 13 cards in each suit. Further, every Heart and Diamond card is colored red, and every Spade and Club is black. From this, we can deduce the following probabilities for the outcome of randomly choosing a card:

$$P(Ace) = \frac{4}{52}$$

$$P(Queen \bigcup King) = \frac{8}{52}$$

$$P(Black) = \frac{26}{52}$$

$$P(Club) = \frac{13}{52}$$

$$P(Club \bigcup Heart \bigcup Spade) = \frac{39}{52}$$

$$P(Club \bigcup Heart \bigcup Spade \bigcup Diamond) = 1 (collectively\ exhaustive)$$

What, then, is the probability of getting a black card and an Ace? Well, these events are conditionally independent, meaning that the probability of either outcome does not affect the probability of the other. In cases like these, the probability of event A and event B is the product of the probability of A and the probability of B:

$$P(Black \bigcap Ace) = 26/52 * 4/52 = 2/52$$

Intuitively, this makes sense, because there are two black Aces out of a possible 52.

What about the probability that we choose a red card and a Heart? These two outcomes are not conditionally independent, because knowing that the card is red has a bearing on the likelihood that the card is also a Heart. In cases like these, the probability of event *A* and *B* is denoted as follows:

$$P(A \bigcap B) = P(A)P(B|A) \text{ or } P(B)P(A|B)$$

Here, *P(A|B)* means the probability of A given B. For example, if we represent *A* as drawing a Heart and *B* as drawing a red card, *P(A | B)* means *what's the probability of drawing a heart if we know that the card we drew was red?*. As a red card is equally likely to be a Heart or a Diamond, *P(A|B)* is 0.5:

$$P(Heart \bigcap Red) = P(Red)P(Heart|Red) = \frac{26}{52} \times \frac{1}{2} = \frac{1}{4}$$

In the preceding equation, we used the form, *P(B) P(A|B)*. Had we used the form, *P(A) P(B|A)*, we would have got the same answer:

$$P(Heart \bigcap Red) = P(Red)P(Heart|Red) = \frac{26}{52} \times \frac{1}{2} = \frac{1}{4}$$

So, these two forms are equivalent:

$$P(Heart \bigcap Red) = P(Heart)P(Red|Heart) = \frac{13}{52} \times 1 = \frac{13}{52} = \frac{1}{4}$$

For kicks, let's divide both sides of the equation by *P(B)*. This yields the following equivalence:

$$P(A|B) = \frac{P(A)P(B|A)}{P(B)}$$

This equation is known as **Bayes' Theorem**. This equation is very easy to derive, but its meaning and influence is profound. In fact, it is one of the most famous equations in all of mathematics.

Bayes' Theorem has been applied to and proven useful in an enormous amount of different disciplines and contexts. It was used to help crack the German Enigma code during World War II, saving the lives of millions. It was also used recently, and famously, by Nate Silver to help correctly predict the voting patterns of 49 states in the 2008 US presidential election.

At its core, Bayes' Theorem tells us how to update the probability of a hypothesis in light of new evidence. Due to this, the following formulation of Bayes' Theorem is often more intuitive:

$$P(H|E) = \frac{P(E|H)P(H)}{P(E)}$$

Here, H is the hypothesis and E is the evidence.

Let's see an example of Bayes' Theorem in action!

There's a hot new recreational drug on the scene called **Allighate** (or **Ally** for short). It's named as such because it makes its users go wild and act like an alligator. As the effect of the drug is so deleterious, very few people actually take the drug. In fact, only about one in every thousand people (0.1%) take it.

Frightened by fear-mongering late-night news, Daisy Girl, Inc., a technology consulting firm, ordered an Allighate testing kit for all of its 200 employees so that it could offer treatment to any employee who has been using it. Not sparing any expense, they bought the best kit on the market; it had 99% sensitivity and 99% specificity. This means that it correctly identified drug users 99 out of 100 times, and only falsely identified a non-user as a user once in every 100 times.

When the results finally came back, two employees tested positive. Though the two denied using the drug, their supervisor, Ronald, was ready to send them off to get help. Just as Ronald was about to send them off, Shanice, a clever employee from the statistics department, came to their defense.

Ronald incorrectly assumed that each of the employees who tested positive were using the drug with 99% certainty and, therefore, the chances that both were using it was 98%. Shanice explained that it was actually far more likely that neither employee was using Allighate.

How so? Let's find out by applying Bayes' theorem!

Let's focus on just one employee right now; let H be the hypothesis that one of the employees is using Ally and E represent the evidence that the employee tested positive:

$$P(Ally\ User|Positive\ Test) = \frac{P(Positive\ Test|Ally\ User)P(Ally\ User)}{P(Testing\ positive,\ in\ general)}$$

We want to solve the left side of the equation, so let's plug in values. The first part of the right side of the equation, *P(Positive Test | Ally User)*, is called the **likelihood**. The probability of testing positive if you use the drug is 99%; this is what tripped up Ronald—and most other people when they first heard of the problem. The second part, *P(Ally User)*, is called the **prior**. This is our belief that any one person has used the drug before we receive any evidence. As we know that only 1% of people use Ally, this would be a reasonable choice for a prior. Finally, the denominator of the equation is a normalizing constant, which ensures that the final probability in the equation will add up to one of all possible hypotheses. Finally, the value we are trying to solve, *P(Ally user | Positive Test)*, is called the *posterior*. It is the probability of our hypothesis updated to reflect new evidence:

$$P(Ally\ User | Positive\ Test) = \frac{.99 * .001}{P(Testing\ positive, in\ general)}$$

In many practical settings, computing the normalizing factor is very difficult. In this case, because there are only two possible hypotheses—being a user or not—the probability of finding the evidence of a positive test is given as follows:

$$P(Testing\ positive | Ally\ User)P(Ally\ User) + P(Testing\ positive | Not\ an\ Ally\ User)P(Not\ an\ Ally\ User)$$

Which is:

$$(.99 * .001) + (.01 * .999) = 0.01098$$

Plugging this into the denominator, our final answer is calculated as follows:

$$P(Ally\ User | Positive\ Test) = \frac{.99 * .001}{0.01098} = 0.090164$$

Note that the new evidence, which favored the hypothesis that the employee was using Ally, shifted our prior belief from *.001* to *.09*. Even so, our prior belief about whether an employee was using Ally was so extraordinarily low, it would take some very very strong evidence indeed to convince us that an employee was an Ally user.

Ignoring the prior probability in cases like these is known as **base-rate fallacy**. Shanice assuaged Ronald's embarrassment by assuring him that it was a very common mistake.

Now to extend this to two employees: the probability of any two employees both using the drug is, as we now know, .01 squared, or 1 million to one. Squaring our new posterior yields, we get `.0081`. The probability that both employees use Ally, even given their positive results, is less than 1%. So, they are exonerated.

Sally is a different story, though. Her friends noticed her behavior had dramatically changed as of late—she snaps at co-workers and has taken to eating pencils. Her concerned cubicle-mate even followed her after work and saw her crawl into a sewer, not to emerge until the next day to go back to work.

Even though Sally passed the drug test, we know that it's likely (almost certain) that she uses Ally. Bayes' theorem gives us a way to quantify this probability!

Our prior is the same, but now our likelihood is pretty much as close to 1 as you can get—after all, how many non-Ally users do you think eat pencils and live in sewers?

A tale of two interpretations

Though it may seem strange to hear, there is actually a hot philosophical debate about what probability really is. Though there are others, the two primary camps into which virtually all mathematicians fall are the frequentist camp and the Bayesian camp.

The frequentist interpretation describes probability as the relative likelihood of observing an outcome in an experiment when you repeat the experiment multiple times. Flipping a coin is a perfect example; the probability of heads converges to 50% as the number of times it is flipped goes to infinity.

The frequentist interpretation of probability is inherently objective; there is a true probability out there in the world, which we are trying to estimate.

The Bayesian interpretation, however, views probability as our degree of belief about something. Because of this, the Bayesian interpretation is subjective; when evidence is scarce, there are sometimes wildly different degrees of belief among different people.

Described in this manner, Bayesianism may scare many people off, but it is actually quite intuitive. For example, when a meteorologist describes the probability of rain as 70%, people rarely bat an eyelash. However, this estimation only really makes sense within a Bayesian framework because exact meteorological conditions are not repeatable, as is required by frequentist probability.

Not simply a heady academic exercise, these two interpretations lead to different methodologies in solving problems in data analysis. Many times, both approaches lead to similar results. We will see examples of using both approaches to solve a problem later in this book.

Though practitioners may strongly align themselves with one side over another, good statisticians know that there's a time and a place for both approaches.

Though Bayesianism as a valid way of looking at probability is debated, Bayes' theorem is a fact about probability and is undisputed and non-controversial.

Sampling from distributions

Observing the outcome of trials that involve a random variable, a variable whose value changes due to chance, can be thought of as sampling from a probability distribution—one that describes the likelihood of each member of the sample space occurring.

That sentence probably sounds much scarier than it needs to be. Take a die roll for example:

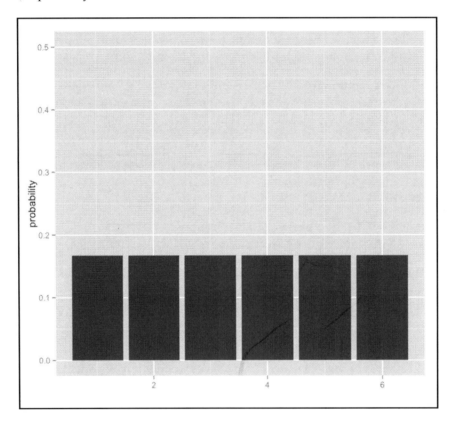

Figure 4.1: Probability distribution of outcomes of a die roll

Each roll of a die is like sampling from a discrete probability distribution for which each outcome in the sample space has a probability of 0.167 or 1/6. This is an example of a uniform distribution, because all the outcomes are uniformly as likely to occur. Further, there are a finite number of outcomes, so this is a discrete uniform distribution (there also exist continuous uniform distributions).

Flipping a coin is like sampling from a uniform distribution with only two outcomes. More specifically, the probability distribution that describes coin-flip events is called a **Bernoulli distribution**—it's a distribution describing only two events.

Parameters

We use probability distributions to describe the behavior of random variables because they make it easy to compute with and give us a lot of information about how a variable behaves. Before we perform computations with probability distributions, we have to specify the parameters of these distributions. These parameters will determine exactly what the distribution looks like and how it will behave.

For example, the behavior of both a 6-sided die and a 12-sided die is modeled with a uniform distribution. Even though the behavior of both the dice is modeled as uniform distributions, the behavior of each is a little different. To further specify the behavior of each distribution, we detail its parameter; in the case of the (discrete) uniform distribution, the parameter is called n. A uniform distribution with parameter n has n equally likely outcomes of probability $1 / n$. The n for a 6-sided die and a 12-sided die is 6 and 12 respectively.

For a Bernoulli distribution, which describes the probability distribution of an event with only two outcomes, the parameter is p. Outcome 1 occurs with probability p and the other outcome occurs with probability $1 - p$, because they are collectively exhaustive. The flip of a fair coin is modeled as a Bernoulli distribution with p = 0.5.

Imagine a six-sided die with one side labeled 1 and the other five sides labeled 2. The outcome of the die roll trials can be described with a Bernoulli distribution, too! This time, p = 0.16 (1/6). Therefore, the probability of not rolling a 1 is 5/6.

The binomial distribution

The binomial distribution is a fun one. Like our uniform distribution described in the previous section, it is discrete.

When an event has two possible outcomes, success or failure, this distribution describes the number of successes in a certain number of trials. Its parameters are n, the number of trials, and p, the probability of success.

Concretely, a binomial distribution with n=1 and p=0.5 describes the behavior of a single coin flip-if we choose to view heads as successes (we could also choose to view tails as successes). A binomial distribution with n=30 and p=0.5 describes the number of heads we should expect:

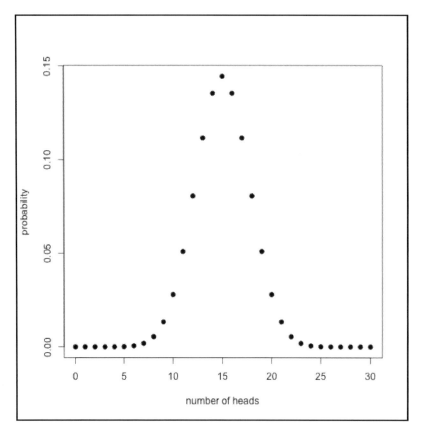

Figure 4.2: A binomial distribution (n=30, p=0.5)

On average, of course, we would expect to have 15 heads. However, randomness is the name of the game, and seeing more or fewer heads is totally expected.

How can we use the binomial distribution in practice?, you ask. Well, let's look at an application.

Larry the Untrustworthy Knave—who can only be trusted some of the time—gives us a coin that he alleges is fair. We flip it 30 times and observe 10 heads.

It turns out that the probability of getting exactly 10 heads on 30 flips is about 2.8%*. We can use R to tell us the probability of getting 10 *or fewer* heads using the `pbinom` function:

```
pbinom(10, size=30, prob=.5)
[1] 0.04936857
```

It appears as if the probability of this occurring, in a correctly balanced coin, is roughly 5%. Do you think we should take Larry at his word?

By the way... if you're interested:
The way we determined the probability of getting exactly 10 heads is using the probability formula for Bernoulli trials. The probability of getting *k* successes in *n* trials is equal to the following:

$$\binom{n}{k} p^k (1-p)^{n-k}$$

Here, *p* is the probability of getting one success:

$$\binom{n}{k} = \frac{n!}{k!(n-k)!}$$

If your palms are getting sweaty, don't worry. You don't have to memorize this in order to understand any later concepts in this book.

The normal distribution

Do you remember in `Chapter 2`, *The Shape of Data*, when we described the normal distribution and how ubiquitous it is? The behavior of many random variables in real life is very well described by a normal distribution with certain parameters.

The two parameters that uniquely specify a normal distribution are μ (*mu*) and σ (*sigma*). μ, the mean, describes where the distribution's peak is located and σ, the standard deviation, describes how wide or narrow the distribution is.

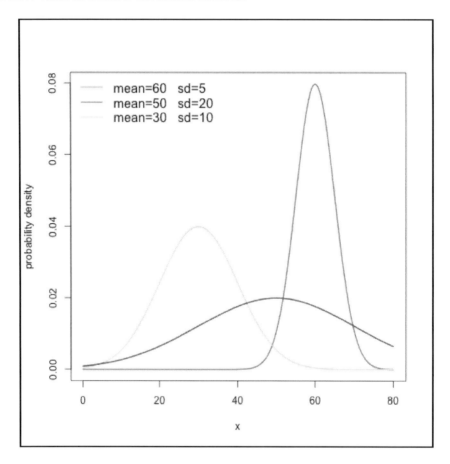

Figure 4.3: Normal distributions with different parameters

The distribution of heights of American females is approximately normally distributed with parameters μ= 65 inches and σ= 3.5 inches:

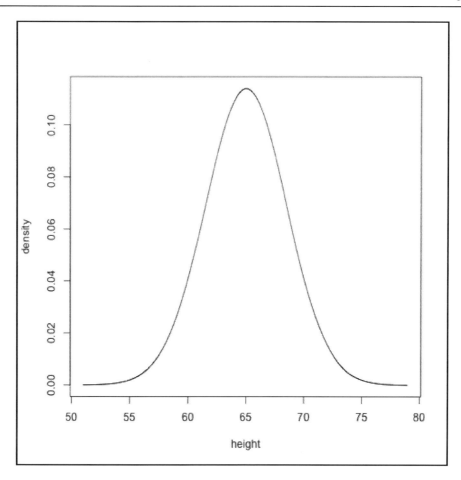

Figure 4.4: Normal distributions with different parameters

With this information, we can easily answer questions about how probable it is to choose, at random, US women of certain heights.

As mentioned earlier in Chapter 2, *The Shape of Data*, we can't really answer the question, *What is the probability that we choose a person who is exactly 60 inches?*, because virtually no one is exactly 60 inches. Instead, we answer questions about how probable it is that a random person is within a certain range of heights.

What is the probability that a randomly chosen woman is 70 inches or taller? If you recall, the probability of a height within a range is the area under the curve, or the integral over that range. In this case, the range we will integrate looks like this:

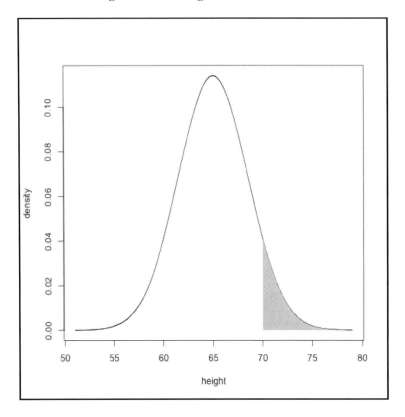

Figure 4.5: Area under the curve of the height distribution from 70 inches to positive infinity

```
> f <- function(x){ dnorm(x, mean=65, sd=3.5) }
> integrate(f, 70, Inf)
0.07656373 with absolute error < 2.2e-06
```

The preceding R code indicates that there is a 7.66% chance of randomly choosing a woman who is 70 inches or taller.

Luckily for us, the normal distribution is so popular and well studied that there is a function built into R, so we don't need to use integration ourselves:

```
> pnorm(70, mean=65, sd=3.5)
[1] 0.9234363
```

The `pnorm` function tells us the probability of choosing a woman who is shorter than 70 inches. If we want to find P (> 70 inches), we can either subtract this value by 1 (which gives us the complement) or use the optional argument `lower.tail=FALSE`.

The three-sigma rule and using z-tables

When dealing with a normal distribution, we know that it is more likely to observe an outcome that is close to the mean than it is to observe one that is distant—but just how much more likely? Well, it turns out that roughly 68% of all the values drawn from a random distribution lie within one standard deviation, or one z-score, away from the mean. Expanding our boundaries, we find that roughly 95% of all values are within two z-scores from the mean. Finally, about 99.7% of normal deviates are within three standard deviations from the mean. This is called the three-sigma rule.

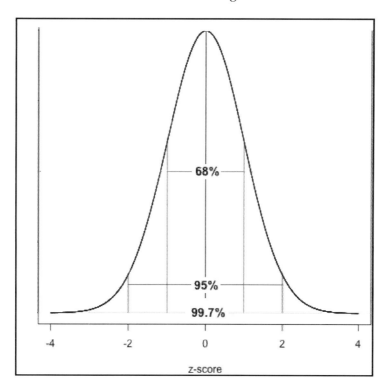

Figure 4.6: The three-sigma rule

Before computers came on the scene, finding the probability of ranges associated with random deviates was a little more complicated. To save mathematicians from having to integrate the Gaussian (normal) function by hand (eww!), they used a z-table, or standard normal table. Though using this method today is, strictly speaking, unnecessary, and it is a little more involved, understanding how it works is important at a conceptual level. Not to mention that it gives you street cred as far as statisticians are concerned!

Formally, the z-table tells us the values of cumulative distribution function at different z-scores of a normal distribution. Less abstractly, the z-table tells us the area under the curve from negative infinity to certain z-scores. For example, looking up -1 on a z-table will tell us the area to the left of one standard deviation below the mean (15.9%).

Z-tables only describe the cumulative distribution function (area under the curve) of a standard normal distribution-one with a mean of 0 and a standard deviation of 1. However, we can use a z-table on normal distributions with any parameters, μ and σ. All you need to do is convert a value from the original distribution into a z-score. This process is called **standardization** :

$$Z = \frac{(X - \mu)}{\sigma}$$

To use a z-table to find the probability of choosing a US woman at random who is taller than 70 inches, we first have to convert this value into a z-score. To do this, we subtract the mean (65 inches) from 70 and then divide that value by the standard deviation (3.5 inches).

$$\frac{(70 - 65)}{3.5} = 1.43$$

Then, we find 1.43 on the z-table; on most z-table layouts, this means finding the row labeled 1.4 (the z-score up to the tenths place) and the column .03 (the value in the hundredths place). The value at this intersection is .9236, which means that the complement (someone taller than 70 inches) is *1-.9236 = 0.0764*. This is the same answer we got when we used integration and the `pnorm` function.

Exercises

Practice the following exercises to reinforce the concepts learned in this chapter:

- Recall the drug testing at Daisy Girl, Inc. earlier in the chapter. We used .1% as our prior probability that the employee was using the drug. Why should this prior have been even lower? Using a subjective Bayesian interpretation of probability, estimate what the prior should have been given that the employee was able to hold down a job and no one saw her/him act like an alligator.
- Hark back to the example of the coin from Larry the Untrustworthy Knave. We would expect the proportion of heads in a fair coin that is flipped many times to be around 50%. In Larry's coin, the proportion was 2/3, which is unlikely to occur. The probability of 20 heads in 30 flips was 2.1%. However, find the probability of getting 40 heads in 60 flips. Even though the proportions are the same, why is the probability of observing 40 heads in 60 flips so significantly less probable? Understanding the answer to this question is key to understanding sampling theory and inferential data analysis.
- Use the binomial distribution and `pbinom` to calculate the probability of observing 10 or fewer 1s when rolling a fair 6-sided die 50 times. View rolling a 1 as a success and not rolling 1 as a failure. What is the value of the parameter, `p`?
- Use a z-table to find the probability of choosing a US woman at random who is 60 inches or shorter. Why is this the same probability as choosing one who is 70 inches or taller?
- Suppose a trolley is coming down the tracks and its brakes are not working. It is poised to run over five people who are hanging out on the tracks ahead of it. You are next to a lever that can change the tracks that the trolley is riding on. However, the second set of tracks has one person hanging out on it, too.

  Is it morally wrong to not pull the lever so that only one person is hurt, rather than five? How would a utilitarian respond? Next, what would Thomas Aquinas say about this? Back up your thesis by appealing to the Doctrine of the Double Effect in *Summa Theologica*. Also, what would Kant say? Back up your response by appealing to the categorical imperative introduced in the *Foundation of the Metaphysic of Morals*.

Summary

In this chapter, we took a detour through probability land. You learned some basic laws of probability, sample spaces, and conditional independence. You also learned how to derive Bayes' Theorem and learned that it provides the recipe to update hypotheses in the light of new evidence.

We also touched on the two primary interpretations of probability. In future chapters, we will be employing techniques from both these approaches.

We concluded with an introduction to sampling from distributions and used two—binomial and normal—distributions to answer interesting non-trivial questions about probability.

This chapter laid the important foundation that supports confirmatory data analysis. Making and checking inferences based on data is all about probability and, at this point, we know enough to move on to have a great time testing hypotheses with data!

Using Data To Reason About The World

5

In Chapter 4, *Probability*, we mentioned that the mean height of US females is 65 inches. Now pretend we didn't know this fact—how could we find out what the average height is?

We can measure every US female, but that's untenable; we would run out of money, resources, and time before we even finished with a small city!

Inferential statistics gives us the power to answer this question using a very small sample of all US women. We can use the sample to tell us something about the population we drew it from. We can use observed data to make inferences about unobserved data. By the end of this chapter, you too will be able to go out and collect a small amount of data and use it to reason about the world!

Estimating means

In the example that is going to span this entire chapter, we are going to be examining how we would estimate the mean height of all US women using only samples. Specifically, we will be estimating the population parameters using samples means as an estimator.

I am going to use the vector all.us.women to represent the population. For simplicity's sake, let's say there are only 10,000 US women:

```
> # setting seed will make random number generation reproducible
> set.seed(1)
> all.us.women <- rnorm(10000, mean=65, sd=3.5)
```

We have just created a vector of 10,000 normally distributed random variables with the same parameters as our population of interest using the `rnorm` function. Of course, at this point, we can just call `mean` on this vector and call it a day—but that's cheating! We are going to see that we can get really really close to the population mean without actually using the entire population.

Now, let's take a random sample of ten from this population using the `sample` function and compute the mean:

```
> our.sample <- sample(all.us.women, 10)
> mean(our.sample)
[1] 64.51365
```

Hey, not a bad start!

Our sample will, in all likelihood, contain some short people, some normal people, and some tall people. There's a chance that when we choose a sample, we choose one that contains predominately short people or a disproportionate number of tall people. Because of this, our estimate will not be exactly accurate. However, as we choose more and more people to include in our sample, those chance occurrences—imbalanced proportions of the short and tall—tend to balance each other out.

Note that as we increase our sample size, the sample mean isn't always closer to the population mean, but it will be closer to average.

We can test this assertion ourselves! Study the following code carefully and try running it yourself:

```
> population.mean <- mean(all.us.women)
> for(sample.size in seq(5, 30, by=5)){
+    # create empty vector with 1000 elements
+    sample.means <- numeric(1000)
+    for(i in 1:1000){
+      sample.means[i] <- mean(sample(all.us.women, sample.size))
+    }
+    distances.from.true.mean <- abs(sample.means - population.mean)
+    mean.distance.from.true.mean <- mean(distances.from.true.mean)
+    print(mean.distance.from.true.mean)
+ }
[1] 1.245492
[1] 0.8653313
[1] 0.7386099
[1] 0.6355692
[1] 0.5458136
[1] 0.5090788
```

For each sample size from 5 to 30 (going up by 5), we will take 1,000 different samples from the population, calculate their mean, take the differences from the population mean, and average them:

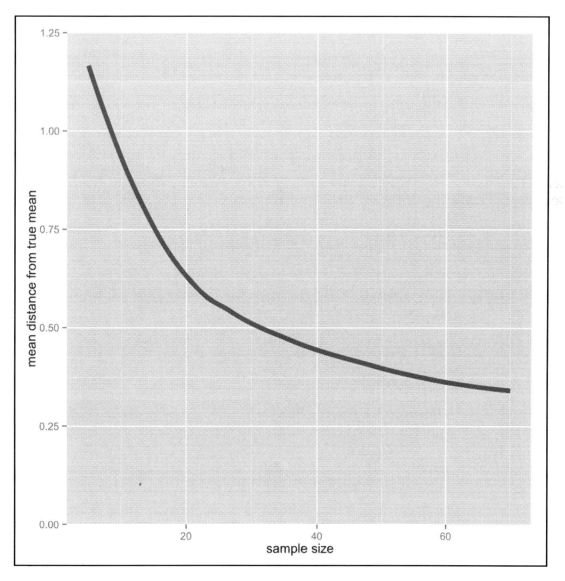

Figure 5.1: Accuracy of sample means as a function of sample size

As you can see, increasing the sample size gets us closer to the population mean. Increasing the sample size also reduces the standard deviation between the means of the samples:

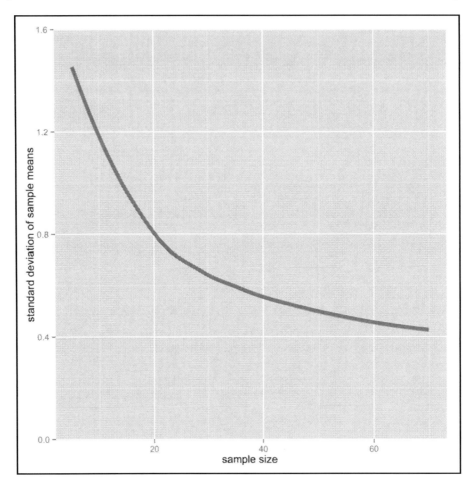

Figure 5.2: The variability of sample means as a function of sample size

Knowing that, with all other things being equal, larger samples are preferable to smaller ones, let's work with a sample size of 40 for right now. We'll take our sample and estimate our population mean as follows:

```
mean(our.new.sample)
[1] 65.19704
```

The sampling distribution

So, we have estimated that the true population mean is about 65.2; we know the population mean isn't exactly `65.19704`—but by just how much might our estimate be off?

To answer this question, let's take repeated samples from the population again. This time, we're going to take samples of size 40 from the population 10,000 times and plot a frequency distribution of the means:

```
> means.of.our.samples <- numeric(10000)
> for(i in 1:10000){
+    a.sample <- sample(all.us.women, 40)
+    means.of.our.samples[i] <- mean(a.sample)
+ }
```

We get the distribution as follows:

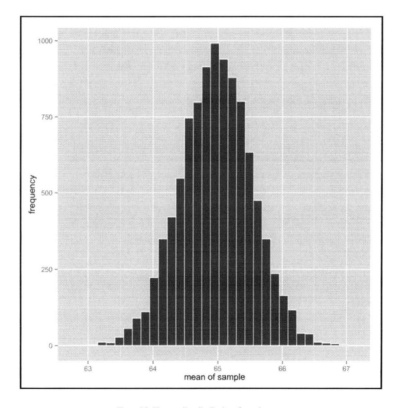

Figure 5.3: The sampling distribution of sample means

This frequency distribution is called a **sampling distribution**. In particular, as we used sample means as the value of interest, this is called the sampling distribution of the sample means (whew!). You can create a sampling distribution of any statistic (median, variance, and so on), but when we refer to sampling distributions throughout this chapter, we will be specifically referring to the sampling distribution of sample means.

Check it out: the sampling distribution looks like a normal distribution, and that's because it is a normal distribution.

For a large enough sample size, the sampling distribution of any population will be approximately normal with a mean equal to the population mean, μ, and a standard deviation as follows:

$$\frac{\sigma}{\sqrt{N}}$$

Here, N is the sample size and σ is the population standard deviation. This is one of the main tenets of the **central limit theorem**, and it is among the most important theorems in all of statistics.

Look back at the equation. Convince yourself that sample size is proportional to the narrowness of the sampling distribution by noting that the sample size is in the denominator.

The standard deviation of the sampling distribution tells us how variable a sample of a certain size's mean can be from sample to sample. It also tells us how much we expect certain samples means to vary from the true population mean. The standard deviation of the sampling distribution is called the **standard error**, and we can use it to quantify our uncertainty about our estimate of the population mean.

If the standard error is small, an estimate from one sample is likely to be closer to the true mean (because the sampling distribution is narrow). If our standard error is big, the mean of any one particular sample is likely to be farther away from the true mean, on average.

Okay, so I've convinced you that the standard error is a great statistic to use—but how do we get it? Up until now, I've said that you can calculate it by either one of the following:

- Taking many samples from the population and taking the standard deviation of the sample means
- Dividing the standard deviation of the population by the square root of the sample size

However, in practice, this isn't good enough: we don't want to take repeated samples from the population for the same reason that we can't measure the heights of all US women (because it would take too long and cost too much). In the case of using the population standard deviation to get the standard error—well, we don't know the population standard deviation—if we did, we would have already had to calculate the population mean and we wouldn't have to be estimating it with sampling!

Ideally, we want to find the standard error using only one sample. Well, it turns out that for sufficiently large samples, using the sample standard deviation, *s*, in the standard error formula (instead of the population standard deviation, σ) is a good enough approximation. Similarly, the mean of the sampling distribution is equal to the population mean, but we can use our samples mean as an estimate of that.

To reiterate, for a sample of sufficient size, we can pretend that the sampling distribution of the sample means has a mean equal to the samples mean and a standard deviation of the samples standard deviation divided by the square root of the sample size. This standard deviation of the sampling distribution is called the standard error, and it is a very important number to quantify the uncertainty of our estimation of the population mean from the sample mean.

For a concrete example, let's use our sample of 40, `our.new.sample`:

```
> mean(our.new.sample)
[1] 65.19704
> sd(our.new.sample)
[1] 3.588447
> sd(our.new.sample) / sqrt(length(our.new.sample))
[1] 0.5673833
```

Our samples mean and standard deviation is *65.2* and *3.59* respectively. The standard error of the mean is `0.567`.

This means that the sampling distribution of the sample means would look something like this:

Figure 5.4: Estimated sampling distribution of sample means based on one sample

Interval estimation

Again, we care about the standard error (the standard deviation of the sampling distribution of sample means) because it expresses the degree of uncertainty we have in our estimation. Due to this, it's not uncommon for statisticians to report the standard error along with their estimate.

What's more common, though, is for statisticians to report a range of numbers to describe their estimates; this is called **interval estimation**. In contrast, when we were just providing the sample mean as our estimate of the population mean, we were engaging in *point estimation*.

One common approach to interval estimation is to use *confidence intervals*. A confidence interval gives us a range over which a significant proportion of the sample means would fall when samples are repeatedly drawn from a population and their means are calculated. Concretely, a 95 percent confidence interval is the range that would contain 95 percent of the sample means if multiple samples were taken from the same population. 95 percent confidence intervals are very common, but 90 percent and 99 percent confidence intervals aren't rare.

Think about this for a second: if a 95 percent confidence interval contains 95 percent of the sample means, this means that the 95 percent confidence interval covers 95 percent of the area of the sampling distribution:

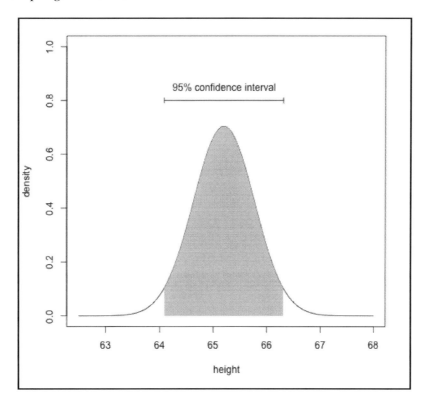

Figure 5.5: The 95 percent confidence interval of our estimate of the sample mean (64.085 to 66.31) covers 95 percent of the area in the our estimated sampling distribution

Okay, so how do we find the bounds of the confidence interval? Think back to the *three-zs* rule from the previous chapter on probability. Recall that about 95 percent of a normal distribution's area is within two standard deviations of the mean. Well, if the bounds of a confidence interval cover 95 percent of the sampling distribution, then the bounds must be two standard deviations away from the mean on both sides! As the standard deviation of the distribution of interest (the sampling distribution of sample means) is the standard error, the bounds of the confidence interval are the mean minus two times the standard error and the mean plus two times the standard error.

In reality, two standard deviations (or two z-scores) away from the mean contain a little bit more than 95 percent of the area of the distribution. To be more precise, the range between *-1.96* z-scores and *1.96* z-scores contains 95 percent of the area. Therefore, the bounds of a 95 percent confidence interval are as follows:

$$\bar{x} - (1.96s) \quad and \quad \bar{x} + (1.96s)$$

Here, $\bar{x}$ is the sample mean and *s* is the sample standard deviation.

In our example, our bounds are as follows:

```
> err <- sd(our.new.sample) / sqrt(length(our.new.sample))
> mean(our.new.sample) - (1.96*err)
[1] 64.08497
> mean(our.new.sample) + (1.96*err)
[1] 66.30912
```

How did we get 1.96?

You can get this number yourself using the qnorm function.

The qnorm function is a little like the opposite of the pnorm function that we saw in the previous chapter. That function started with a p because it gave us a probability—the probability that we would see a value equal to or below it in a normal distribution. The q in qnorm stands for **quantile**. A quantile, for a given probability, is the value at which the probability will be equal to or below that probability.

I know that was confusing! stated differently, but equivalently, a quantile for a given probability is the value such that if we put it in the `pnorm` function, we get back that same probability:

```
> qnorm(.025)
[1] -1.959964
> pnorm(-1.959964)
[1] 0.025
```

We showed earlier that 95 percent of the area under a curve of a probability distribution is within `1.9599` z-scores away from the mean. We put `.025` in the `qnorm` function, because if the mean is right smack in the middle of the 95 percent confidence interval, then there is 2.5 percent of the area to the left of the bound and 2.5 percent of the area to the right of the bound. Together, this lower 2.5 percent and upper 2.5 percent make up the missing 5 percent of the area.

Don't feel limited to the 95 percent confidence interval, though. You can figure out the bounds of a 90 percent confidence interval using just the same procedure. In an interval that contains 90 percent of the area of a curve, the bounds are the values for which 5 percent of the area is to the left and 5 percent of the area is to the right of (because 5 percent and 5 percent make up the missing 10 percent) the curve.

```
> qnorm(.05)
[1] -1.644854
> qnorm(.95)
[1] 1.644854
> # notice the symmetry?
```

This means that, for this example, the 90 percent confidence interval is 65.2 and 66.13 or *65.197 +(- 0.933).*

A warning about confidence intervals.

There are many misconceptions about confidence intervals floating about. The most pervasive is the misconception that 95 percent confidence intervals represent the interval such that there is a 95 percent chance that the population mean is in the interval. This is false. Once the bounds are created, it is no longer a question of probability; the population mean is either in there or it's not.

To convince yourself of this, take two samples from the same distribution and create 95 percent confidence intervals for both of them. They are different, right? Create a few more. How could it be the case that all of these intervals have the same probability of including the population mean?

Using a Bayesian interpretation of probability, it is possible to say that there exists intervals for which we are 95 percent certain that it encompasses the population mean, since Bayesian probability is a measure of our certainty, or degree of belief, in something. This Bayesian response to confidence intervals is called credible intervals, and you will learn about them in `Chapter 7`, *Hypothesis Testing with Resampling Methods*. The procedure for their construction is very different to that of the confidence interval.

Smaller samples

Remember when I said that the sampling distribution of sample means is approximately normal for a large enough sample size? This caveat means that for smaller sample sizes (usually considered to be below 30), the sampling distribution of the sample means is not well approximated by a normal distribution. It is, however, well approximated by another distribution: the t-distribution.

A bit of history...

The t-distribution is also known as the **Student's t-distribution**. It gets its name from the 1908 paper that introduces it, by William Sealy Gosset writing under the pen name Student. Gosset worked as a statistician at the Guinness Brewery and used the t-distribution and the related t-test to study small samples of the quality of the beer's raw constituents. He is thought to have used a pen name at the request of Guinness so that competitors wouldn't know that they were using the t statistic to their advantage.

The t-distribution has two parameters, the mean and the degrees of freedom (or df). For our purposes here, the *degrees of freedom* is equal to our sample size, – 1. For example, if we have a sample of 10 from some population and the mean is 5, then a t-distribution with parameters mean=5 and df=9 describes the sampling distribution of sample means with that sample size.

The t-distribution looks a lot like the normal distribution at first glance. However, further examination will reveal that the curve is more flat and wide. This wideness accounts for the higher level of uncertainty we have in regard to a smaller sample:

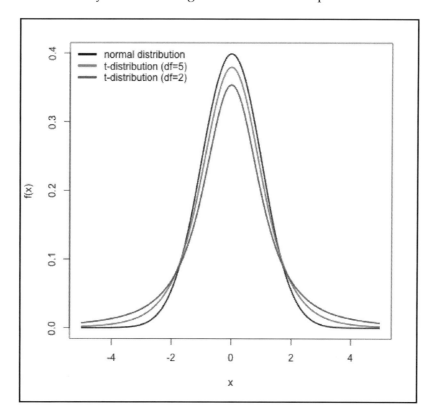

Figure 5.6: The normal distribution and two t-distributions with different degrees of freedom

Notice that as the sample size (degrees of freedom) increases, the distribution gets narrower. As the sample size gets higher and higher, it gets closer and closer to a normal distribution. By 29 degrees of freedom, it is very close to a normal distribution indeed. This is why 30 is considered a good rule of thumb for what constitutes a good cut-off between large sample sizes and small sample sizes and, thus, when deciding whether to use a normal distribution or a t-distribution as a model for the sampling distribution.

Let's say that we could only afford taking the heights of 15 US women. What, then, is our 95 percent interval estimation?

```
> small.sample <- sample(all.us.women, 15)
>  mean(small.sample)
[1] 65.51277
> qt(.025, df=14)
[1] -2.144787
> # notice the difference
> qnorm(.025)
[1] -1.959964
```

Instead of using the qnorm function to get the correct multiplier to the standard error, we want to find the quantile of the t-distribution at .025 (and .975). For this, we use the qt function, which takes a probability and number of degrees of freedom. Note that the quantile of the t-distribution is larger than the quantile of the normal distribution, which will translate to larger confidence interval bounds; again, this reflects the additional uncertainty we have in our estimate due to a smaller sample size.

```
> err <- sd(small.sample) / sqrt(length(small.sample))
> mean(small.sample) - (2.145 * err)
[1] 64.09551
> mean(small.sample) + (2.145 * err)
[1] 66.93003
```

In this case, the bounds of our 95 percent confidence interval are 64.1 and 66.9.

Exercises

Practice the following exercises to revise the concepts learned in this chapter:

- Write a function that takes a vector and returns the 95 percent confidence interval for that vector. You can return the interval as a vector of length two: the lower bound and the upper bound. Then, parameterize the confidence coefficient by letting the user of your function choose their own confidence level, but keep 95 percent as the default. Hint: the first line will look like this:

```
conf.int <- function(data.vector, conf.coeff=.95){
```

- Back when we introduced the central limit theorem, I said that the sampling distribution from any distribution would be approximately normal. Don't take my word for it! Create a population that is uniformly distributed using the `runif` function and plot a histogram of the sampling distribution using the code from this chapter and the histogram-plotting code from Chapter 2, *The Shape of Data*. Repeat the process using the beta distribution with parameters ($a=0.5$, $b=0.5$). What does the underlying distribution look like? What does the sampling distribution look like?

- A formal and rigorous definition of knowledge and what constitutes knowledge is still an open problem in epistemology. Since Plato and his dialogues, a popular definition of knowledge is the **Justified True Belief** (**JTB**) account. In this account, an agent can be said to know something, p, if (a) p is true, (b) the agent believes that p is true, and (c) the agent is justified in believing that p is true. In a 1963 paper, Edmund Gettier introduced examples that seem to satisfy these conditions, but appear not to be true cases of knowledge. Read Gettier's paper. Can the JTB account of knowledge be modified to account for *Gettier problems*? Should we reject the JTB account of knowledge and start from scratch?

Summary

The central idea of this chapter is that making the leap from sample to population carries a certain amount of uncertainty with it. In order to be good, honest analysts, we need to be able to express and quantify this uncertainty.

The example we chose to illustrate this principle was estimating population mean from a sample's mean. You learned that the uncertainty associated with inferring the population mean from sample means is modeled by the sampling distribution of the sample means. The central limit theorem tells us the parameters we can expect of this sampling distribution. You learned that we could use these parameters on their own, or in the construction of confidence intervals, to express our level of uncertainty about our estimate.

I want to congratulate you for getting this far. The topics introduced in this chapter are very often considered the most difficult to grasp in all of introductory data analysis.

Your tenacity will be greatly rewarded, though; we have laid enough of a foundation to be able to get into some real, practical topics. I promise the next chapter is a lot of fun, and it is filled with interesting examples that you can start applying to real-life problems right away!

6
Testing Hypotheses

The salt-and-pepper of inferential statistics is the estimation and testing hypotheses. In the last chapter, we talked about estimation and making certain inferences about the world. In this chapter, we will be talking about how to test the hypotheses on how the world works and evaluate the hypotheses using only sample data.

In the previous chapter, I promised that this would be a very practical chapter and I'm a man of my word; this chapter goes over a broad range of the most popular methods in modern data analysis at a relatively high level. Even so, this chapter might have a little more detail than the lazy and impatient would want. At the same time, it will have way too little detail than what the extremely curious and mathematically inclined want. In fact, some statisticians would have a heart attack at the degree to which I skip over the math involved with these subjects—but I won't tell if you don't!

Nevertheless, certain complicated concepts and math are beyond the scope of this book. The good news is that once you, dear reader, have the general concepts down, it is easy to deepen your knowledge of these techniques and their intricacies, and I advocate that you do that before making any major decisions based on the tests introduced in these chapters.

The null hypothesis significance testing framework

For better or worse, **Null Hypothesis Significance Testing** (**NHST**) is the most popular hypothesis testing framework in modern use. So, even though there are competing approaches that at least in some cases are better, you need to know this stuff up and down!

Okay,Null Hypothesis Significance Testing these are a bunch of big words. What do they mean?

NHST is a lot like being a prosecutor in the United States' or Great Britain's justice system. In these two countries, and a few others, the person being charged is presumed innocent, and the burden of *proving* the defendant's guilt is placed on the prosecutor. The prosecutor then has to argue that the evidence is inconsistent with the defendant being innocent. Only after it is shown that the extant evidence is unlikely if the person is innocent, does the court rule a guilty verdict. If the extant evidence is weak, or is likely to be observed even if the dependent is innocent, then the court rules not guilty. That doesn't mean the defendant is innocent (the defendant may very well be guilty!), it means that either the defendant was guilty or there was not sufficient evidence to prove guilt.

With simple NHST, we are testing two competing hypotheses: the *null* and the *alternative* hypotheses. The *default* hypothesis is called the null hypothesis—it is the hypothesis that our observation occurred from chance alone. In the justice system analogy, this is the hypothesis that the defendant is innocent. The alternative hypothesis is the opposite (or complementary) hypothesis; this would be like the prosecutor's hypothesis.

The *null hypothesis* terminology was introduced by a statistician named R. A. Fischer in regard to the curious case of Muriel Bristol: a woman who claimed that she could discern, just by tasting it, whether milk was added before tea in a teacup or whether the tea was poured before the milk. She is more commonly known as the *lady tasting tea*.

Her claim was put to the test! The lady tasting tea was given eight cups; four had milk added first, and four had tea added first. Her task was to correctly identify the four cups that had tea added first. The null hypothesis was that she couldn't tell the difference and would choose a random four teacups. The alternative hypothesis is, of course, that she had the ability to discern wither the tea or milk was poured first.

It turned out that she correctly identified the four cups. The chances of randomly choosing the correct four cups is 70 to 1, or about 1.4%. In other words, the chances of that happening under the null hypothesis is 1.4%. Given that it is so very unlikely to have occurred under the null hypothesis, we may choose to *reject* the null hypothesis. If the null and alternative hypotheses are mutually exclusive and collectively exhaustive, then a rejection of the null hypothesis is tantamount to an acceptance of the alternative hypothesis.

We can't say anything for certain, but we can work with probabilities. In this example, we wanted to prove or disprove the lady tasting tea's claims. We did not try to evaluate the probability that the lady could tell the difference; we assumed that she could not and tried to show that it was unlikely that she couldn't, given her stellar performance on the assessment.

So, here's the basic idea behind NHST as we know it so far:

- Assume the opposite of what you are testing.
- (Try to) show that the results you receive are unlikely given that assumption.
- Reject the assumption.

We have heretofore been rather *hand-wavy* about what constitutes sufficient *unlikelihood* to reject the null hypothesis and how we determine the probability in the first place. We'll discuss this now.

In order to quantify how likely or unlikely the results we receive are, we need to define a *test statistic*—some measure of the sample. The sampling distribution of the test statistic will tell us which test statistics are most likely to occur by chance (under the null hypothesis) with repeated trials of the experiment. Once we know what the sampling distribution of the test statistic looks like, we can tell what the probability of getting a result as extreme as we got is. This is called a *p-value*. If it is equal to or below some pre-specified boundary, called an *alpha level* (α level), we decide that the null hypothesis is a bad hypothesis and embrace the alternative hypothesis. Largely, as a matter of tradition, an alpha level of .05 is used most often, though other levels are occasionally used as well. So, if the observed result would only occur 5% or less of the time (p-value < .05), we consider it a sufficiently unlikely event and reject the null hypothesis. If the .05 cut-off sounds rather arbitrary, it's because it is.

So, here's our updated and expanded *basic idea* behind NHST:

1. Formulate a set of two hypotheses: a null hypothesis (often denoted as H0) and an alternative hypothesis (often denoted H1):
   - H_0: There is no effect
   - H_1: There is an effect

2. Compute the test statistic.

3. Given the sampling distribution of the test statistic under the null hypothesis, you can calculate the probability of obtaining a test statistic equal to or more extreme than the one you calculated. This is the *p-value*. Find it.

4. If the probability of obtaining a test statistic being equal to or more extreme than the one you calculated is sufficiently unlikely (equal to or less than your alpha level), then you may reject the null hypothesis.

5. If the null and alternative hypotheses are collectively exhaustive, you may embrace the alternative hypothesis.

The illustrative example that's going to make sense out of all of this is none other than the gambit of Larry the Untrustworthy Knave that we met in Chapter 4, *Probability*. If you recall, Larry, who can only be trusted some of the time, gave us a coin that he alleges is fair. We flip it 30 times and observe 10 heads. Let's hypothesize that the coin is unfair; let's formalize our hypotheses:

- **H_0 (null hypothesis)**: The probability of obtaining heads on this coin is 0.5
- **H_1 (alternative hypothesis)**: The probability of obtaining heads on this coin is not 0.5

Let's just use the number of heads in our sample as the test statistic. What is the sampling distribution of this test statistic? In other words, if the coin was fair, and you repeated the flipping-30-times experiment many times, what is the relative frequency of observing particular numbers of heads? We've seen it already! It's the *binomial distribution*. A binomial distribution with parameters n=30 and p=0.5 describes the number of *heads* we should expect in 30 flips.

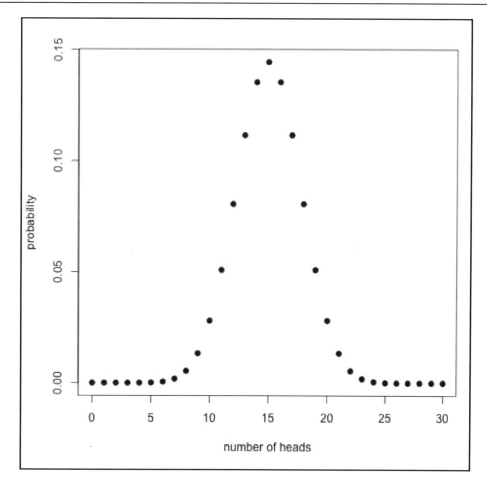

Figure 6.1: The sampling distribution of our coin-flip test statistic (the number of heads)

As you can see, the outcome that is the most likely is getting 15 heads (as you might imagine). Can you see what the probability of getting 10 heads is? Fairly unlikely, right?

So, what's the p-value, and is it less than our pre-specified alpha level? Well, we have already worked out the probability of observing 10 or fewer heads in Chapter 4, *Probability*, as follows:

```
> pbinom(10, size=30, prob=.5)
[1] 0.04936857
```

It's less than .05. We can conclude the coin is unfair, right? Well, yes and no. Mostly no. Allow me to explain.

One and two-tailed tests

You may reject the null hypothesis if the test statistic falls within a region under the curve of the sampling distribution that covers 5% of the area (if the alpha level is .05). This is called the *critical region*. Do you remember, in the last chapter, we constructed 95% confidence intervals that covered 95% percent of the sampling distribution? Well, the 5% critical region is like the opposite of this. Recall that, in order to make a symmetric 95% of the area under the curve, we had to start at the .025 quantile and end at the *.975* quantile, leaving 2.5% percent on the left tail and 2.5% of the right tail uncovered.

Similarly, in order for the critical region of a hypothesis test to cover 5% of the most extreme areas under the curve, the area must cover everything from the left of the .025 quantile and everything to the right of the .975 quantile.

So, in order to determine that the 10 heads out of 30 flips is statistically significant, the probability that you would observe 10 or fewer heads has to be less than .025.

There's a function built right into R, called `binom.test`, which will perform the calculations that we have, until now, been doing by hand. In the most basic incantation of `binom.test`, the first argument is the number of *successes* in a Bernoulli trial (the number of heads), and the second argument is the number of trials in the sample (the number of coin flips):

```
> binom.test(10,30)
          Exact binomial test
 data:   10 and 30
 number of successes = 10, number of trials = 30, p-value = 0.09874
 alternative hypothesis: true probability of success is not equal to
 0.5
 95 percent confidence interval:
  0.1728742 0.5281200
 sample estimates:
 probability of success
          0.3333333
```

If you study the output, you'll see that the p-value does not cross the significance threshold.

Now, suppose that Larry said that the coin was not biased toward tails. To see if Larry was lying, we only want to test the alternative hypothesis that the probability of heads is less than 0.5. In that case, we would set up our hypotheses like this:

- H_0: The probability of heads is greater than or equal to 0.5
- H_1: The probability of heads is less than 0.5

This is called a *directional hypothesis,* because we have a hypothesis that asserts that the deviation from chance goes in a particular direction. In this hypothesis suite, we are only testing whether the observed probability of heads falls into a critical region on only one side of the sampling distribution of the test statistic. The statistical test that we would perform in this case is, therefore, called a *one tailed test* the critical region only lies on one tail. As the area of the critical region no longer has to be divided between the two tails (like in the *two tailed* test we performed earlier), the critical region only contains the area to the *left* of the .05 quantile. The following figure shows the 3 hypotheses:

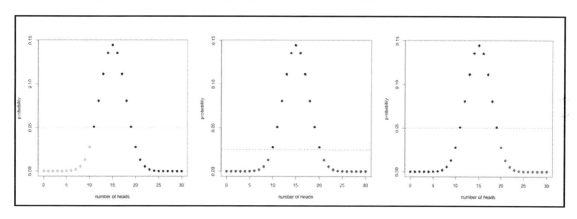

Figure 6.2: The three panels, from left to right, depict the critical regions of the left (*lesser*) one-tailed, two-tailed, and right (*greater*) alternative hypotheses. The dashed horizontal line is meant to show that, for the two-tailed tests, the critical region starts below p=.025, because it is being split between two tails. For the one tailed tests, the critical region is below the dashed horizontal line at *p=.05.*

As you can see from the figure, for the directional alternative hypothesis that heads has a probability less than 0.5, 10 heads is now included in the green critical region.

We can use the `binom.test` function to test this directional hypothesis, too. All we have to do is specify the optional parameter alternative and set its value to `"less"` (its default is `"two.sided"` for a two-tailed test):

```
> binom.test(10,30, alternative="less")
        Exact binomial test
data:  10 and 30
number of successes = 10, number of trials = 30, p-value = 0.04937
alternative hypothesis: true probability of success is less than 0.5
95 percent confidence interval:
 0.0000000 0.4994387
sample estimates:
probability of success
              0.3333333
```

If we wanted to test the directional hypothesis that the probability of heads was greater than 0.5, we would use `alternative="greater"`.

Take note of the fact that the p-value is now less than 0.05. In fact, it is identical to the probability we got from the `pbinom` function.

Errors in NHST

Certainty is a card rarely seen in the deck of a data analyst. As we make judgments and inferences based on probabilities, mistakes happen. In particular, there are two types of mistakes that are possible in NHST: *Type I errors* and *Type II errors*:

- A *Type I* error is when a hypothesis test concludes that there is an effect (rejects the null hypothesis) when, in reality, n o such effect exists
- A *Type II* error occurs when we fail to detect a real effect in the world and fail to reject the null hypothesis even if it is false

Check the following table for errors encountered in the coin example:

Coin type	Failure to reject null hypothesis (conclude no detectable effect)	Reject the null hypothesis (conclude that there is an effect)
Coin is fair	Correct positive identification	Type I error (false positive)
Coin is unfair	Type II error (false negative)	Correct identification

In the criminal justice system, Type I errors are considered especially heinous. Legal theorist William Blackstone is famous for his quote: *it is better that ten guilty persons escape than one innocent suffer*. This is why the court instructs jurors (in the United States, at least) to only convict the defendant if the jury believes the defendant is guilty beyond a reasonable doubt. The consequence is that if the jury favors the hypothesis that the defendant is guilty, but only by a little bit, the jury must give the defendant the benefit of the doubt and acquit.

This line of reasoning holds for hypothesis testing as well. Science would be in a sorry state if we accepted alternative hypotheses on rather flimsy evidence willy-nilly; it is better that we are on the side of caution when making claims about the world, even if that means that we make fewer discoveries of *honest to goodness*, real-world phenomena because our statistical tests failed to reach significance.

This sentiment underlies that decision to use an alpha level like .05. An alpha level of .05 means that we will only commit a Type I error (false positive) 5% of the time. If the alpha level were higher, we would make fewer Type II errors, but at the cost of making more Type I errors, which are more dangerous in most circumstances.

There is a similar metric to the alpha level, and it is called the *beta level* (β level). The beta level is the probability that we would fail to reject the null hypothesis if the alternative hypothesis were true. In other words, it is the probability of making a Type II error.

The complement of the beta level, 1 minus the beta level, is the probability of correctly detecting a true effect if one exists. This is called *power*. This varies from test to test. Computing the power of a test, a technique called power analysis, is a topic beyond the scope of this book. For our purposes, it will suffice to say that it depends on the type of test being performed, the sample size being used, and on the size of the effect that is being tested (*the effect size*). Greater effects, like the average difference in height between women and men, are far easier to detect than small effects, like the average difference in the length of earthworms in Carlisle and in Birmingham. Statisticians like to aim for a power of at least 80% (a beta level of .2). A test that doesn't reach this level of power (because of a small sample size or small effect size, and so on) is said to be underpowered.

A warning about significance

It's perhaps regrettable that we use the term *significance* in relation to null-hypothesis testing. When the term was first used to describe hypothesis tests, the word "significance" was chosen because it signified something. When I was writing this chapter, I checked the thesaurus for the word *significant,* and it indicated that synonyms include notable, worthy of attention, and important. This is misleading in that it is not equivalent to its intended, vestigial meaning. One thing that really confuses people is that they think statistical significance is of great importance in and of itself. This is sadly untrue; there are a few ways to achieve statistical significance without discovering anything of significance, in the colloquial sense.

As we'll see later in the chapter, one way to achieve non-significant statistical significance is by using a very large sample size. Very small differences, that make little to no difference in the real world, will nevertheless be considered statistically significant if there is a large enough sample size.

For this reason, many people make the distinction between statistical significance and practical significance or clinical relevance. Many hold the view that hypothesis testing should only be used to answer the question, *is there an effect?* or, *is there a discernible difference?*, and that the follow-up question, *is it important?* or *does it make a real difference?* should be addressed separately. I subscribe to this point of view.

To answer the follow-up questions, many use effect sizes, which, capture the magnitude of an effect in the real world. We will see an example of determining the effect size in a test later in this chapter.

A warning about p-values

P-values are, by far, the most talked about metric in NHST. P-values are also notorious for lending themselves to misinterpretation. Of the many criticisms of NHST (of which there are many, in spite of its ubiquity), the misinterpretation of p-values ranks highly. The following are two of the most common misinterpretations:

1. *Myth: A p-value is the probability that the null hypothesis is true.* This is not the case. Someone misinterpreting the p-value from our first binomial test might conclude that the chances of the coin being fair are around 10%. This is false. The p-value does not tell us the probability of the *hypothesis' truth or falsity*. In fact, the test assumes that the null hypothesis is correct. It tells us the proportion of trials for which we would receive a result as extreme or more extreme than the one we did if the null hypothesis was correct.

   I'm ashamed to admit it, but I made this mistake during my first college introductory statistics class. In my final project for the class, after weeks of collecting data, I found my p-value had not passed the barrier of significance—it was something like .07. I asked my professor if, after the fact, I could change my alpha level to .1 so my results would be positive. In my request, I appealed to the fact that it was still more probable than not that my alternative hypothesis was correct—after all, if my p-value was .07, then there was a 93% chance that the alternative hypothesis was correct. He smiled and told me to read the relevant chapter of our text again. I appreciate him for his patience and restraint in not smacking me right in the head for making such a stupid mistake. Don't be like me.

2. *Myth: A p-value is a measure of the size of an effect.* This is also incorrect, but its *wrongness* is more subtle than the first misconception. In research papers, it is common to attach phrases like *highly significant* and *very highly significant* to p-values that are much smaller than .05 (like .01 and .001). It is common to interpret p-values such as these, and statements such as these, as signaling a bigger effect than p-values that are only modestly less than .05. This is a mistake; this is conflating statistical significance with practical significance. In the previous section, we explained that you can achieve significant p-values (sometimes *very highly significant* ones) for an effect that is, for all intents and purposes, small and unimportant. We will see a very salient example of this later in this chapter

Testing the mean of one sample

An illustrative and fairly common statistical hypothesis test is the *one sample t-test*. You use it when you have one sample and you want to test whether that sample likely came from a population by comparing the mean against the known population mean. For this test to work, you have to know the population mean.

In this example, we'll be using R's built-in `precip` dataset that contains precipitation data from 70 US cities, using the code given below:

```
> head(precip)
      Mobile        Juneau       Phoenix  Little Rock  Los Angeles
        67.0          54.7           7.0         48.5         14.0
   Sacramento
        17.2
```

Don't be fooled by the fact that there are city names in there—this is a regular old vector—it's just that the elements are labeled. We can directly take the mean of this vector, just like a normal one:

```
> is.vector(precip)
[1] TRUE
> mean(precip)
[1] 34.88571
```

Let's pretend that we, somehow, know the mean precipitation of the rest of the world and is the US' precipitation significantly different to the rest of the world's precipitation?

Remember, in the last chapter, I said that the sampling distribution of sample means for sample sizes under 30 were best approximated by using a t-distribution. Well, this test is called a *t-test* because, in order to decide whether our samples' mean is consistent with the population whose mean we are testing against, we need to see where our mean falls in relation to the sampling distribution of population means. If this is confusing, reread the relevant section from the previous chapter.

In order to use the t-test in general cases, regardless of the scale, instead of working with the sampling distribution of sample means, we work with the sampling distribution of the t-statistic.

Remember z-scores from Chapter 3, *Describing Relationships*? The t-statistic is like a z-score in that it is a scale-less measure of distance from some mean. In the case of the t-statistic, though, we divide by the standard error instead of the standard deviation (because the standard deviation of the population is unknown). As the t-statistic is *standardized*, any population with any mean using any scale will have a sampling distribution of the t-statistic that is exactly the same (at the same sample size, of course).

The equation to compute the t-statistic is this:

$$t = \frac{\bar{x} - \mu}{s/\sqrt{N}}$$

Here, $\bar{x}$ is the sample mean, μ is the population mean, s is the sample standard deviation, and N is the sample size.

Let's see for ourselves what the sampling distribution of the t-statistic looks like by taking 10,000 samples of size 70 (the same size as our precip dataset) and plotting the results:

```
> # function to compute t-statistic
t.statistic <- function(thesample, thepopulation){
  numerator <- mean(thesample) - mean(thepopulation)
  denominator <- sd(thesample) / sqrt(length(thesample))
  t.stat <- numerator / denominator
  return(t.stat)
}

# make the pretend population normally distributed
# with a mean of 38
population.precipitation <- rnorm(100000, mean=38)
t.stats <- numeric(10000)
for(i in 1:10000){
  a.sample <- sample(population.precipitation, 70)
```

```
    t.stats[i] <- t.statistic(a.sample, population.precipitation)
}

# plot
library(ggplot2)
tmpdata <- data.frame(vals=t.stats)
qplot(vals, data=tmpdata, geom="histogram",
      color=I("white"),
      xlab="sampling distribution of t-statistic",
      ylab="frequency")
```

The image given below shows the sampling distribution of the t-statistic:

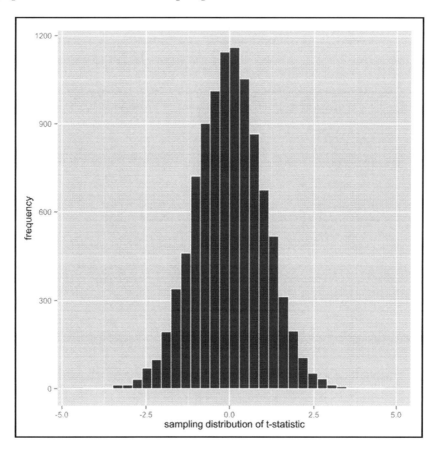

Figure 6.3: The sampling distribution of the t-statistic

Ah, there's that familiar shape again!

Fortunately, the sampling distribution of the `t-statistic` is well known, so we don't have to create our own. In fact, the sampling distribution for many test statistics are well known, so we won't be running our own simulations of them anymore. Lucky us!

Okay, so how does our sample's t-statistic compare to the t-distribution? Our t-statistic, using our function from the last code-snippet, is as follows:

```
> t.statistic(precip, population.precipitation)
[1] -1.901225
```

You can work this out for yourself easily. The t-distribution with 69 degrees of freedom. The t-statistic of our sample is shown as the dashed line in the image given below:

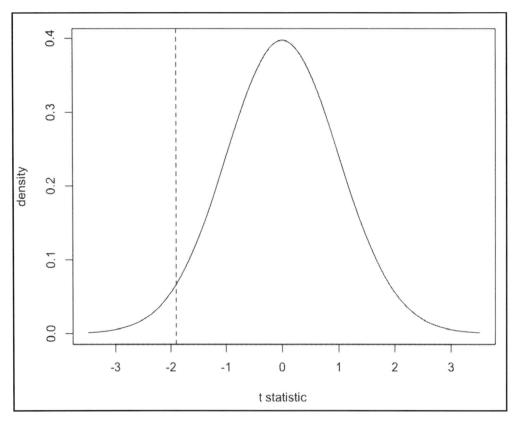

Figure 6.4: The t-distribution with 69 degrees of freedom. The t-statistic of our sample is shown as the dashed line

Hmm, it looks like a pretty unlikely occurrence to me, but is it statistically significant? First, let's formally define our hypotheses, as shown below:

- H0: The average (mean) precipitation in the US is equal to the known average precipitation in the rest of the world
- H1: The average (mean) precipitation in the US is different than the known average precipitation in the rest of the world

Then, we pre-specify an alpha level of .05, as is customary.

As our hypothesis is non-directional (we only hypothesize that the precipitation in the US is different than the world, not less or more), we define our critical region to cover 5% of the area on each side of the curve, as follows:

```
qt(.025, df=69)
[1] -1.994945
# the critical region is less than -1.995 and more than +1.995
```

So, how does it look like now? it resembles the previous figure with the critical region for non-directional hypothesis highlighted, as shown in the following image:

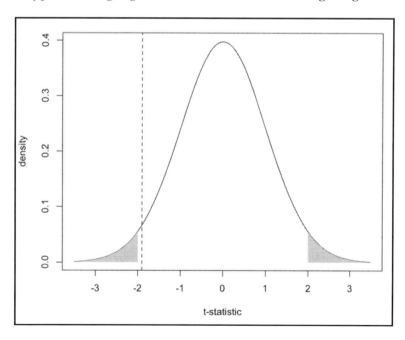

Figure 6.5: The previous figure with the critical region for non-directional hypothesis highlighted

Oh, too bad! It looks like our sample mean falls just out of the critical region. So, we fail to reject the null hypothesis.

The cruel truth if we, for some reason, hypothesized that the US precipitation was *less* than the average world precipitation is as follows:

- H_0: Mean US precipitation >= mean world precipitation
- H_1: Mean US precipitation < mean world precipitation

We would have achieved significance at `alpha = .05`.

The image given below shows the graph with directional critical region highlighted:

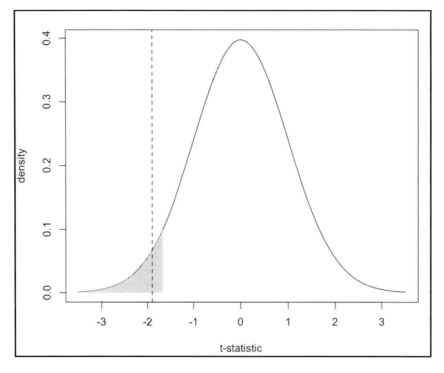

Figure 6.6: Figure 6.4 with directional critical region highlighted

Of course, we have no reason to think that US precipitation was less or more than the world's average. To change our hypothesis now would be cheating. You're not a cheater, are you?

Now that we know what we're doing, we won't be manually calculating our test statistics anymore; we'll just be using the test functions that R provides.

Let's use the function that R provides now. The one sample t-test can be performed by the `t.test` function. In its most basic form, it takes a vector of sample observations as its first argument and the population mean as its second argument:

```
> t.test(precip, mu=38)
        One Sample t-test
data:  precip
t = -1.901, df = 69, p-value = 0.06148
alternative hypothesis: true mean is not equal to 38
95 percent confidence interval:
 31.61748 38.15395
sample estimates:
mean of x
 34.88571
```

Among other things, this test tells us that the t-statistic is 1.9 (just like we calculated ourselves), the degrees of freedom were 69 (the sample size minus 1), and the p-value, which is 0.06148. Like our plot with the two-tailed critical regions showed, this p-value is greater than our pre-specified alpha level of 0.05. We fail to reject the null hypothesis.

Just for kicks, let's run the *one-tailed hypothesis test*:

```
> t.test(precip, mu=38, alternative="less")
        One Sample t-test
data:  precip
t = -1.901, df = 69, p-value = 0.03074
alternative hypothesis: true mean is less than 38
95 percent confidence interval:
     -Inf 37.61708
sample estimates:
mean of x
 34.88571
```

Now our p-value is < .05. C'est la vie.

Note that the R output indicates that the alternative hypothesis which is the true mean is less than 38. Compare this with the last t-test output.

Assumptions of the one sample t-test

There are two main assumptions of the one sample t-test are as follows:

- The data is sampled from a normal distribution. This actually has more to do with the sampling distribution of sample means being approximately normal than the actual population. As we know, the sampling distribution of sample means for sufficiently large sample sizes will always be normally distributed, even if the population is not. In reality, this assumption can be violated somewhat and the results will be valid, especially for sample sizes of over 30. We have nothing to worry about here. Usually, people check this assumption by plotting the sample means and making sure it's kind-of normal, though there are more formal ways of doing this, which we will see later. If the assumption of normality is in question, we may want to use an alternative test, like a *non-parametric test*; we'll see some examples at the end of this chapter.
- Independence of samples: Had we tested whether the US precipitation likely came from the population of the entire world's precipitation, we would have been violating this assumption. Why? As we know that the US is a member of the set (it is indeed 'in the world'), so of course it was drawn from that population. This is why we tested whether the US precipitation was on par with the rest of the world's precipitation. In other examples of the one sample t-tests, this assumption basically requires that the sample be random.

Testing two means

An even more common hypothesis test is the independent samples t-test. You would use this to check the equality of two samples' means. Concretely, an example of using this test would be if you have an experiment where you are testing to see if a new drug lowers blood pressure. You would give one group a placebo and the other group the real medication. If the mean improvement in blood pressure was significantly greater than the improvement with the placebo, you might infer that the blood pressure medication works. Outside of more academic uses, web companies use this test all the time to test the effectiveness of, for example, different internet ad campaigns; they expose random users to either one of two types of ads and test if one is more effective than the other. In web-business parlance, this is called an A-B test, but that's just business-ese for *controlled experiment*.

The term *independent* means that the two samples are separate, and that data from one sample doesn't affect data in the other. For example, if, instead of having two different groups in the blood pressure trial, we used the same participants to test both the conditions (randomizing the order we administer the placebo and the real medication), we would violate independence.

The dataset we will be using for this is the mtcars dataset that we first met in Chapter 2, *The Shape of Data*, and saw again in Chapter 3, *Describing Relationships*. Specifically, we are going to test the hypothesis that the mileage is better for manual cars than it is for cars with automatic transmission. Let's compare the means and produce a boxplot:

```
> mean(mtcars$mpg[mtcars$am==0])
[1] 17.14737
> mean(mtcars$mpg[mtcars$am==1])
[1] 24.39231
> mtcars.copy <- mtcars
> # make new column with better labels
> mtcars.copy$transmission <- ifelse(mtcars$am==0,
+                                     "auto", "manual")
> mtcars.copy$transmission <- factor(mtcars.copy$transmission)
```

```
> qplot(transmission, mpg, data=mtcars.copy,
+       geom="boxplot", fill=transmission) +
+       # no legend
+       guides(fill=FALSE)
```

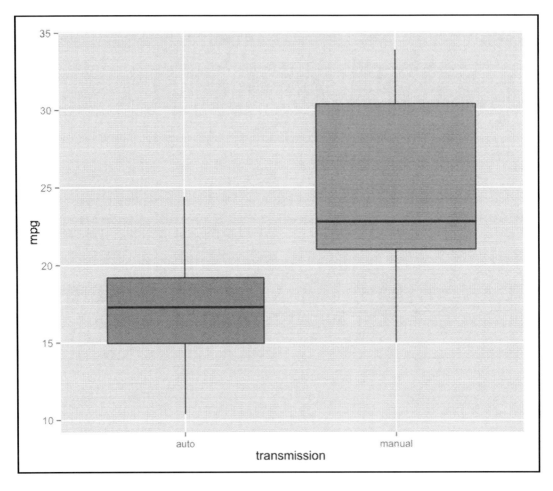

Figure 6.7: boxplot of the miles per gallon ratings for automatic cars and cars with manual transmission

Hmm, looks different... but let's check that hypothesis formally. Our hypotheses are as follows:

- H0: Mean of sample1 - mean of sample2 >= 0

- H1: Mean of sample1 - mean of sample2 < 0

To do this, we use the `t.test` function; only this time, we provide two vectors: one for each sample. We also specify our directional hypothesis in the same way:

```
> automatic.mpgs <- mtcars$mpg[mtcars$am==0]
> manual.mpgs <- mtcars$mpg[mtcars$am==1]
> t.test(automatic.mpgs, manual.mpgs, alternative="less")
        Welch Two Sample t-test
data:   automatic.mpgs and manual.mpgs
t = -3.7671, df = 18.332, p-value = 0.0006868
alternative hypothesis: true difference in means is less than 0
95 percent confidence interval:
        -Inf -3.913256
sample estimates:
mean of x mean of y
 17.14737  24.39231


> # p < .05. Yipee!
```

There is an easier way to use the t-test for independent samples that doesn't require us to make two vectors:

```
> t.test(mpg ~ am, data=mtcars, alternative="less")
```

This reads, roughly, perform a t-test of the `mpg` column grouping by the `am` column in the data frame `mtcars`. Confirm for yourself that these incantations are equivalent.

Don't be fooled!

Remember when I said that statistical significance was not synonymous with *important* and that we can use very large sample sizes to achieve statistical significance without any *clinical* relevance? Check out this snippet:

```
> set.seed(16)
> t.test(rnorm(1000000,mean=10), rnorm(1000000, mean=10))
        Welch Two Sample t-test
data:   rnorm(1e+06, mean = 10) and rnorm(1e+06, mean = 10)
t = -2.1466, df = 1999998, p-value = 0.03183
alternative hypothesis: true difference in means is not equal to 0
95 percent confidence interval:
 -0.0058104638 -0.0002640601
sample estimates:
mean of x mean of y
 9.997916 10.000954
```

Here, two vectors of one million normal deviates each are created with a mean of 10. When we use a t-test on these two vectors, it should indicate that the two vectors' means are not significantly different, right?

Well, we got a p-value of less than .05, why? If you look carefully at the last line of the R output, you might see why; the mean of the first vector is 9.997916, and the mean of the second vector is 10.000954. This tiny difference, a meager .003, is enough to tip the scale into *significant* territory. However, I can think of very few applications of statistics where .003 of anything is noteworthy even though it is, technically, statistically significant.

The larger point is that the t-test tests for equality of means, and if the means aren't exactly the same in the population, the t-test will, with enough power, detect this. Not all tiny differences in population means are important, though, so it is important to frame the results of a t-test and the p-value in context.

As mentioned earlier in the chapter, a salient strategy to put the differences in context is to use an effect size. The effect size commonly used in association with the t-test is *Cohen's d*. Cohen's d is, conceptually, pretty simple: it is a ratio of the variance explained by the "effect" and the variance in the data itself. Concretely, Cohen's d is the difference in means divided by the sample standard deviation. A high d indicates that there is a big effect (difference in means) relative to the internal variability of the data.

I mentioned that to calculate d, you have to divide the difference in means by the sample standard deviation, but which one? Although Cohen's d is conceptually straightforward (even elegant!), it is also sometimes a pain to calculate by hand, because the sample standard deviation from both samples has to be *pooled*. Fortunately, there's an R package that lets us calculate Cohen's d, and other effect size metrics, to boot, quite easily. Let's use it on the auto versus manual transmission example, as shown in the code below:

```
> install.packages("effsize")
> library(effsize)
> cohen.d(automatic.mpgs, manual.mpgs)
Cohen's d
d estimate: -1.477947 (large)
95 percent confidence interval:
      inf         sup
-2.3372176 -0.6186766
```

Cohen's d is -1.478, which is considered a very large effect size. The cohen.d function even tells you this using canned interpretations of effect sizes. If you try this with the two million element vectors from earlier, the cohen.d function will indicate that the *effect* was negligible.

Although these canned interpretations were on target these two times, make sure that you evaluate your own effect sizes in context.

Assumptions of the independent samples t-test

Homogeneity of variance (or homoscedasticity, a scary sounding word), in this case, simply means that the variance in the miles per gallon of the automatic cars is the same as the variance in miles per gallon of the manual cars. In reality, this assumption can be violated as long as you use a *Welch's T-test* like we did, instead of the *Student's T-test*. You can still use the Student's T-test with the `t.test` function, like by specifying the optional parameter `var.equal=TRUE`. You can test for this formally using `var.test` or `leveneTest` from the `car` package. If you are sure that the assumption of homoscedasticity is not violated, you may want to do this because it is a more powerful test (fewer Type II errors). Nevertheless, I usually use Welch's T-test to be on the safer side. Also, always use Welch's test if the two samples' sizes are different:

- *The sampling distribution of the sample means is approximately normal*: Again, with a large enough sample size, it always is. We don't have a terribly large sample size here, but in reality, this formulation of the t-test works even if this assumption is violated a little. We will see alternatives in due time.

- *Independence*: Like I mentioned earlier, as the samples contain completely different cars, we're okay on this front. For tests that, for example, use the same participants for both conditions, you would use a *Dependent Samples T-test* or *Paired Samples T-test* , which we will not discuss in this book. If you are interested in running one of these tests after some research, use `t.test(<vector1>, <vector2>, paired=TRUE)`.

Testing more than two means

Another really common situation requires testing whether three or more means are significantly discrepant. We would find ourselves in this situation if we had three experimental conditions in the blood pressure trial: one groups gets a placebo, one group gets a low dose of the real medication, and one groups gets a high dose of the real medication.

Hmm, for cases like these, why don't we just do a series of t-tests? For example, we can test the directional alternative hypotheses:

- The low dose of blood pressure medication lowers BP significantly more than the placebo

- The high dose of blood pressure medication lowers BP significantly more than the low dose

Well, it turns out that doing this first is pretty dangerous business, and the logic goes like this: if our alpha level is 0.05, then the chances of making a Type I error for one test is 0.05; if we perform two tests, then our chances of making a Type I error is suddenly .09025 (near 10%). By the time we perform 10 tests at that alpha level, the chances of us having making a Type I error is 40%. This is called the multiple testing problem or multiple comparisons problem.

To circumvent this problem, in the case of testing three or more means, we use a technique called **ANalysis Of VAriance**, or **ANOVA**. A significant result from an ANOVA leads to the inference that at least one of the means is significantly discrepant from one of the other means; it does not lend itself to the inference that all the means are significantly different. This is an example of an *omnibus* test, because it is a global test that doesn't tell you exactly where the differences are, just that there are differences.

You might be wondering why a test of equality of means has a name called "Analysis of Variance"; it's because it does this by comparing the variance between cases to the variance within cases. The general intuition behind an ANOVA is that the higher the ratio of variance between the different groups than within the different groups, the less likely that the different groups were sampled from the same population. This ratio is called an *F ratio*.

For our demonstration of the simplest species of ANOVA (the one-way ANOVA), we are going to be using the `WeightLoss` dataset from the car package. If you don't have the `car` package, install it. The code for creating the Weightloss dataset using car package is shown below:

```
> library(car)
> head(WeightLoss)
    group wl1 wl2 wl3 se1 se2 se3
1 Control   4   3   3  14  13  15
2 Control   4   4   3  13  14  17
3 Control   4   3   1  17  12  16
4 Control   3   2   1  11  11  12
5 Control   5   3   2  16  15  14
6 Control   6   5   4  17  18  18
> table(WeightLoss$group)
Control    Diet   DietEx
     12      12       10
```

The `WeightLoss` dataset contains pounds lost and self esteem measurements for three weeks for three different groups: a control group, one group just on a diet, and one group that dieted and exercised. We will be testing the hypothesis that states the means of the weight loss at week 2 are not all equal. We will define our hypothesis as follows:

- H0: The mean weight loss at week 2 between the control, diet group, and diet and exercise group are equal

- H1: At least two of the means of weight loss at week 2 between the control, diet group, and diet and exercise group are not equal

Before the test, let's check out a boxplot of the means, using the code given below:

```
> qplot(group, wl2, data=WeightLoss, geom="boxplot", fill=group)
```

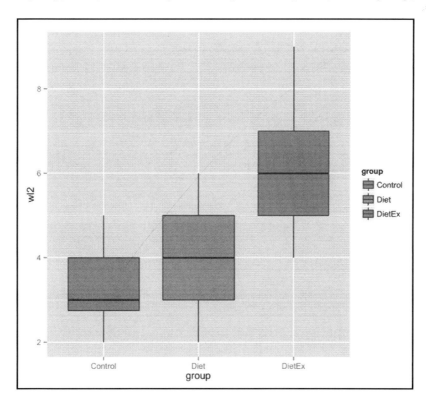

Figure 6.8: Boxplot of weight lost in week 2 of trial for three groups: control, diet, and diet & exercise

And now, we will use the following code for the ANOVA:

```
> the.anova <- aov(wl2 ~ group, data=WeightLoss)
> summary(the.anova)
            Df Sum Sq Mean Sq F value   Pr(>F)
group        2  45.28  22.641   13.37 6.49e-05 ***
Residuals   31  52.48   1.693
—
Signif. codes:  0 '***' 0.001 '**' 0.01 '*' 0.05 '.' 0.1 ' ' 1
```

Oh, snap! The p-value (`Pr(>F)`) is `6.49e-05`, which is .000065 if you haven't learned scientific notation yet.

As I said before, this just means that at least one of the comparisons between means was significant and there are four ways that this could occur:

- The means of *diet* and *diet and exercise* are different

- The means of *diet* and *control* are different

- The means of *control* and *diet and exercise* are different

- The means of *control*, *diet*, and *diet and exercise* are all different

In order to investigate further, we perform a *post-hoc test*. Quite often, the post-hoc test that analysts perform is a suite of t-tests comparing each pair of means (*pairwise t-tests*).

But wait, didn't I say that was dangerous business? I did, but it's different now, because:

- We have already performed an honest-to-goodness omnibus test at the alpha level of our choosing. Only after we achieve significance, we perform pairwise t-tests.

- We have made the corrections for the problem of multiple comparisons.

The easiest multiple comparison correcting procedure to understand is **Bonferroni correction.** In its simplest version, it simply changes the alpha value by dividing it by the number of tests being performed. It is considered the most conservative of all the multiple comparison correction methods. In fact, many consider it to be too conservative and I'm inclined to agree. Instead, I suggest using a correcting procedure called **Holm-Bonferroni correction**. R uses this by default. The code for implementing the Holm-Bonferroni correction is given below:

```
pairwise.t.test(WeightLoss$wl2, as.vector(WeightLoss$group))
        Pairwise comparisons using t tests with pooled SD
data:   WeightLoss$wl2 and as.vector(WeightLoss$group)
        Control Diet
Diet    0.28059 -
DietEx  7.1e-05 0.00091
P value adjustment method: holm
```

This output indicates that the difference in means between the *Diet* and *Diet and exercise* groups is p < .001. Additionally, it indicates that the difference between *Diet and exercise* and *Control* is p < .0001 (look at the cell where it says 7.1e-05). The p-value of the comparison of just diet and the control is .28, so we fail to reject the hypothesis that they have the same mean.

Assumptions of ANOVA

The standard one-way ANOVA makes three main assumptions:

- The observations are independent

- The distribution of the residuals (the distances between the values within the groups to their respective means) is approximately normal

- Homogeneity of variance; if you suspect that this assumption is violated, you can use R's oneway.test instead

Testing independence of proportions

Remember the University of California Berkeley dataset that we first saw when discussing the relationship between two categorical variables in chapter 3, *Describing Relationships*? Recall that UCB was sued because it appeared as though the admissions department showed preferential treatment to male applicants. Also recall that we used cross-tabulation to compare the proportion of admissions across categories.

If admission rates were, say 10%, you would expect about one out of every ten applicants to be accepted regardless of gender. If this is the case that gender has no bearing on the proportion of admits, then gender is independent.

Small deviations from this 10% proportion are, of course, to be expected in the real world and not necessarily indicative of a sexist admissions machine. However, if a test of independence of proportions is significant, that indicates that a deviation as extreme as the one we observed is very unlikely to occur if the variable were truly independent.

A test statistic that captures divergence from an idealized, perfectly independent cross-tabulation is the *chi-squared statistic, x^2 statistic)*, and its sampling distribution is known as a *chi-square distribution*. If our chi-square statistic falls into the critical region of the chi-square distribution with the appropriate degrees of freedom, then we reject the hypothesis that gender is an independent factor in admissions.

Let's perform one of these chi-square tests on the whole UCB Admissions dataset, using the code given below:

```
> # The chi-square test function takes a cross-tabulation
> # which UCBAdmissions already is. I am converting it from
> # and back so that you, dear reader, can learn how to do
> # this with other data that isn't already in cross-tabulation
> # form
> ucba <- as.data.frame(UCBAdmissions)
> head(ucba)
     Admit Gender Dept Freq
1 Admitted   Male    A  512
2 Rejected   Male    A  313
3 Admitted Female    A   89
4 Rejected Female    A   19
5 Admitted   Male    B  353
6 Rejected   Male    B  207
> # create cross-tabulation
> cross.tab <- xtabs(Freq ~ Gender+Admit, data=ucba)
>
> chisq.test(cross.tab)
        Pearson's Chi-squared test with Yates' continuity correction
  data:  cross.tab
  X-squared = 91.6096, df = 1, p-value < 2.2e-16
```

The proportions are almost certainly not independent ($p < .0001$). Before you conclude that the admission's department is sexist, remember *Simpson's Paradox*? If you don't, reread the relevant section in Chapter 3, *Describing Relationships*.

As the chi-square independence of proportion test can be (and is often used) to compare a whole mess of proportions, it's sometimes referred to an omnibus test, just like the ANOVA. It doesn't tell us what proportions are significantly discrepant, only that some proportions are.

What if my assumptions are unfounded?

The t-test and ANOVA are both considered *parametric statistical tests*. The word *parametric* is used in different contexts to signal different things but, essentially, it means that these tests make certain assumptions about the parameters of the population distributions from which the samples are drawn. When these assumptions are met (with varying degrees of tolerance to violation), the inferences are accurate, powerful (in the statistical sense), and are usually quick to calculate. When those parametric assumptions are violated, though, parametric tests can often lead to inaccurate results.

We've spoken about two main assumptions in this chapter: *normality* and *homogeneity of variance*. I mentioned that, even though you can test for homogeneity of variance with the leveneTest function from the car package, the default t.test in R removes this restriction. I also mentioned that you could use the oneway.test function in lieu of aov if you don't have to have to adhere to this assumption when performing an ANOVA. Due to these affordances, I'll just focus on the assumption of normality from now on.

In a t-test, the assumption that the sample is an approximately normal distribution can be visually verified, to a certain extent. The naïve way is to simply make a histogram of the data. A more proper approach is to use a **QQ-plot (quantile-quantile plot)**. You can view a QQ-plot in R using the qqPlot function from the car package.

Let's use it to evaluate the normality of the miles per gallon vector in `mtcars`:

```
> library(car)
> qqPlot(mtcars$mpg)
```

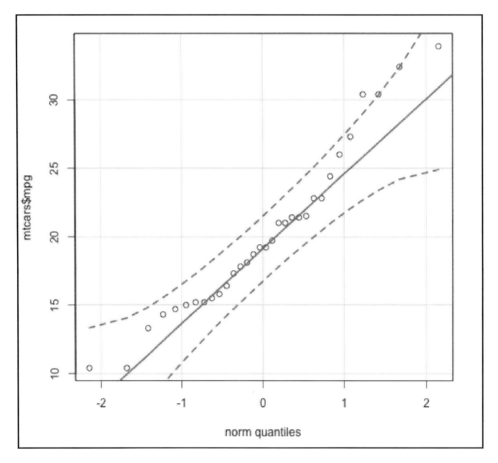

Figure 6.9: A QQ-plot of the mile per gallon vector in mtcars

A QQ-plot can actually be used to compare any sample from any theoretical distribution, but it is most often associated with the normal distribution. The plot depicts the quantiles of the sample and the quantiles of the normal distribution against each other. If the sample were perfectly normal, the points would fall on the solid red diagonal line—its divergence from this line signals a divergence from normality. Even though it is clear that the quantiles for mpg don't precisely comport with the quantiles of the normal distribution, its divergence is relatively minor.

The most powerful method to evaluate adherence to the assumption of normality is to use a *statistical test*. We are going to use the *Shapiro-Wilk test*, because it's my favorite, though there are a few others:

```
> shapiro.test(mtcars$mpg)

        Shapiro-Wilk normality test

 data:  mtcars$mpg
 W = 0.9476, p-value = 0.1229
```

This non-significant result indicates that the deviations from normality are not statistically significant.

For ANOVAs, the assumption of normality applies to the residuals, not the actual values of the data. After performing the ANOVA, we can check the normality of the residuals quite easily, using the code given below:

```
> # I'm repeating the set-up
> library(car)
> the.anova <- aov(wl2 ~ group, data=WeightLoss)
> shapiro.test(the.anova$residuals)
        Shapiro-Wilk normality test
 data:  the.anova$residuals
 W = 0.9694, p-value = 0.4444
```

We're in the clear!

What if we do violate our parametric assumptions!? In cases like these, many analysts will fall back on using non-parametric tests.

Many statistical tests, including the t-test and ANOVA, have non-parametric alternatives. The appeal of these tests is, of course, that they are resistant to violations of parametric assumptions, that they are robust. The drawback is that these tests are usually less powerful than their parametric counterparts. In other words, they have a somewhat diminished capacity to detect an effect if there truly is one to detect. For this reason, if you are going to use NHST, you should use the more powerful tests by default and switch only if your assumptions are violated.

The non-parametric alternative to the independent t-test is called the **Mann-Whitney U test**, though it is also known as the *Wilcoxon rank-sum test*. As you might expect by now, there is a function to perform this test in R. Let's use it on the auto versus manual transmission example:

```
> wilcox.test(automatic.mpgs, manual.mpgs)
```

```
        Wilcoxon rank sum test with continuity correction
data:   automatic.mpgs and manual.mpgs
W = 42, p-value = 0.001871
alternative hypothesis: true location shift is not equal to 0
```

Simple!

The non-parametric alternative to the one-way ANOVA is called the *Kruskal-Wallis test*. Can you see where I'm going with this? The following is an example that illustrates how this test can be performed in R.

```
kruskal.test(wl2 ~ group, data=WeightLoss)
        Kruskal-Wallis rank sum test
data:   wl2 by group
Kruskal-Wallis chi-squared = 14.7474, df = 2, p-value = 0.0006275
```

Super!

Exercises

Here are a few exercises for you to practise and revise the concepts learned in this chapter:

- Read about data-dredging and *p-hacking*. Why is it dangerous not to formulate a hypothesis, set an alpha level, and set a sample size *before* collecting data and analyzing results?

- Use the `library(help="datasets")` command to find a list of datasets that R has already inbuilt. Pick a few interesting ones and form a hypothesis about each one. Rigorously define your null and alternative hypotheses before you start. Test those hypotheses even if it means learning about other statistical tests.

- How you might quantify the effect size of a one-way ANOVA? Look up *eta-squared* if you get stuck.

- In ethics, the doctrine of moral relativism holds that there are no universal moral truths, and that moral judgments are dependent upon one's culture or period in history. How can moral progress (the abolition of slavery, fairer trading practices) be reconciled with a relativistic view of morality? If there is no objective moral paradigm, how can criticisms be leveled against the current views of morality? Why replace existing moral judgments with others if there is no standard to which to compare them to and, therefore, no reason to prefer one over the other?

Summary

We covered huge ground in this chapter. By now, you should be up to speed on some of the most common statistical tests. More importantly, you should have a solid grasp of the theory behind NHST and why it works. This knowledge is far more valuable than mechanically memorizing a list of statistical tests and clues for when to use each.

You learned that NHST has its origin in testing whether a weird lady's claims about tasting tea were true or not. The general procedure for NHST is to define your null and alternative hypotheses, define and calculate your test statistic, determine the shape and parameters of the sampling distribution of that test statistic, measure the probability that you would observe a test statistic as or more extreme than the one we observed (this is the p-value), and determine whether to reject or fail to reject the null hypothesis based on the whether the p-value was below or above the alpha level.

You then learned about one-tailed tests versus two-tailed tests, Type I and Type II errors, and got some warnings about terminologies and common NHST misconceptions.

Then, you learned a litany of statistical tests, we saw that the one sample t-test is used in scenarios where we want to determine if a sample's mean is significantly discrepant from some known population mean; we saw that independent samples t-tests are used to compare the means of two distinct samples against each other; we saw that we use one-way ANOVAs to test multiple means, why it's inappropriate to just perform a bunch of t-tests, and some methods of controlling Type I error rate inflation. Finally, you learned how the chi-square test is used to check the independence of proportions.

We then directly applied what you learned to real, fun data and tested real, fun hypotheses. They were fun... right!?

Lastly, we discussed parametric assumptions, how to verify that they were met, and one option to circumvent their violation at the cost of power: non-parametric tests. You learned that the non-parametric alternative to the independent samples t-test is available in R as `wilcox.test,` and the non-parametric alternative to the one-way ANOVA is available in R using the `kruskal.test` function.

In the next chapter, we will also be discussing mechanisms to test hypotheses, but this time, we will be using an attractive alternative to NHST based on the famous theorem by Reverend Thomas Bayes that you learned about in `Chapter 4`, *Probability*. You'll see how this other method of inference addresses some of the shortcomings (deserved or not) of NHST, and why it's gaining popularity in modern applied data analysis. See you there!

7
Bayesian Methods

Suppose I claim that I have a pair of magic rainbow socks. I allege that whenever I wear these special socks, I gain the ability to predict the outcome of coin tosses, using fair coins, better than chance would dictate. Putting my claim to the test, you toss a coin 30 times, and I correctly predict the outcome 20 times. Using a directional hypothesis with the binomial test, the null hypothesis would be rejected at alpha-level 0.05. Would you invest in my special socks?

Why not? If it's because you require a larger burden of proof on absurd claims, I don't blame you. As a grandparent of Bayesian analysis Pierre-Simon Laplace (who independently discovered the theorem that bears Thomas Bayes' name) once said: *The weight of evidence for an extraordinary claim must be proportioned to its strangeness.* Our prior belief-my absurd hypothesis-is so small that it would take much stronger evidence to convince the skeptical investor, let alone the scientific community.

Unfortunately, if you'd like to easily incorporate your prior beliefs into NHST, you're out of luck. Or suppose you need to assess the probability of the null hypothesis; you're out of luck there, too; NHST assumes the null hypothesis and can't make claims about the probability that a particular hypothesis is true. In cases like these (and in general), you may want to use Bayesian methods instead of frequentist methods. This chapter will tell you how. Join me!

The big idea behind Bayesian analysis

If you recall from `Chapter 4`, *Probability*, the Bayesian interpretation of probability views probability as our degree of belief in a claim or hypothesis, and Bayesian inference tells us how to update that belief in the light of new evidence. In that chapter, we used Bayesian inference to determine the probability that employees of Daisy Girl, Inc. were using an illegal drug. We saw how the incorporation of prior beliefs saved two employees from being falsely accused and helped another employee get the help she needed even though her drug screen was falsely negative.

In a general sense, Bayesian methods tell us how to dole out credibility to different hypotheses, given prior belief in those hypotheses and new evidence. In the drug example, the hypothesis suite was discrete: *drug user* or *not drug user*. More commonly, though, when we perform Bayesian analysis, our hypothesis concerns a continuous parameter, or many parameters. Our posterior (or updated beliefs) was also discrete in the drug example, but Bayesian analysis usually yields a continuous posterior called a *posterior distribution*.

We are going to use Bayesian analysis to put my magical rainbow socks claim to the test. Our parameter of interest is the proportion of coin tosses that I can correctly predict wearing the socks; we'll call this parameter θ, or *theta*. Our goal is to determine what the most likely values of theta are and whether they constitute proof of my claim.

Refer back to the section on Bayes' theorem in `Chapter 4`, *Probability*. Recall that the posterior was the *prior* times the *likelihood* divided by a normalizing constant. This normalizing constant is often difficult to compute. Luckily, since it doesn't change the shape of the posterior distribution, and we are comparing relative likelihoods and probability densities, Bayesian methods often ignore this constant. So, all we need is a probability density function to describe our prior belief and a likelihood function that describes the likelihood that we would get the evidence we received given different parameter values.

The likelihood function here is a *binomial function*, as it describes the behavior of Bernoulli trials; the binomial likelihood function for this evidence is shown in the following figure:

Figure 7.1: The likelihood function of theta for 20 out of 30 successful Bernoulli trials

For different values of theta, there are varying relative likelihoods. Note that the value of theta that corresponds to the maximum of the likelihood function is 0.667, which is the proportion of successful Bernoulli trials. This means that in the *absence of any other information*, the most likely proportion of coin flips that my magic socks allow me to predict is 67%. This is called the **Maximum Likelihood Estimate** (**MLE**).

So, we have the likelihood function; now we just need to choose a prior. We will be crafting a representation of our prior beliefs using a type of distribution called a beta distribution, for reasons that we'll see very soon.

Since our posterior is a blend of the prior and likelihood function, it is common for analysts to use a prior that doesn't much influence the results and allows the likelihood function to *speak for itself*. To this end, one may choose to use a *non-informative prior* that assigns equal credibility to all values of theta. This type of non-informative prior is called a *flat* or *uniform prior*.

The beta distribution has two hyper-parameters, α (or *alpha*) and β (or *beta*). A beta distribution with hyper-parameters α = β = 1 describes such a *flat prior*. We will call this `prior #1`.

These are usually referred to as the beta distribution's parameters. We call them *hyper-parameters* here to distinguish them from our parameter of interest, theta.

The following figure shows the flat prior on the value of theta:

Figure 7.2: A flat prior on the value of theta. This beta distribution, with alpha and beta = 1, confers an equal level of credibility to all possible values of theta, our parameter of interest.

This prior isn't really indicative of our beliefs, is it? Do we really assign as much probability to my socks giving me perfect coin-flip prediction powers as we do to the hypothesis that I'm full of baloney?

The prior that a skeptic might choose in this situation is one that looks more like the one depicted in *figure 7.3*, a beta distribution with hyper-parameters `alpha = beta = 50`. This, rather appropriately, assigns far more credibility to values of theta that are concordant with a universe without magical rainbow socks. As good scientists, though, we have to be open-minded to new possibilities, so this doesn't rule out the possibility that the socks give me special powers-the probability is low, but not zero, for extreme values of theta. We will call this `prior #2`:

Figure 7.3: A skeptic's prior

Before we perform the Bayesian update, I need to explain why I chose to use the beta distribution to describe my priors.

The Bayesian update-getting to the posterior-is performed by multiplying the prior with the likelihood. In the vast majority of applications of Bayesian analysis, we don't know what that posterior looks like, so we have to sample from it many times to get a sense of its shape. We will be doing this later in this chapter.

For cases like this, though, where the likelihood is a binomial function, using a beta distribution for our prior guarantees that our posterior will also be in the beta distribution family. This is because the beta distribution is a *conjugate prior* with respect to a binomial likelihood function. There are many other cases of distributions being self-conjugate with respect to certain likelihood functions, but it doesn't often happen in practice that we find ourselves in a position to use them as easily as we can for this problem. The beta distribution also has the nice property that it is naturally confined from 0 to 1, just like the proportion of coin flips I can correctly predict.

The fact that we know how to compute the posterior from the prior and likelihood by just changing the beta distribution's hyper-parameters makes things really easy in this case. The hyper-parameters of the posterior distribution are:

new α= old α+number of successes
new β= old β+number of failures

That means the posterior distribution using `prior #1` will have hyper-parameters `alpha=1+20` and `beta=1+10`. This is shown in *figure 7.4*:

Figure 7.4: The result of the Bayesian update of the evidence and prior #1. The interval depicts the 95% credible interval (the densest 95% of the area under the posterior distribution). This interval overlaps slightly with theta = 0.5.

A common way of summarizing the posterior distribution is with a *credible interval*. The credible interval on the plot in the above figure is the 95% credible interval and contains 95% of the densest area under the curve of the posterior distribution.

Do not confuse this with a confidence interval. Though it may look like it, this credible interval is very different than a confidence interval. Since the posterior directly contains information about the probability of our parameter of interest at different values, it is admissible to claim that there is a 95% chance that the correct parameter value is in the credible interval. We could make no such claim with confidence intervals. Please do not mix up the two meanings, or people will laugh you out of town.

Observe that the 95% most likely values for theta contain the theta value 0.5, if only barely. Due to this, one may wish to say that the evidence does not rule out the possibility that I'm full of baloney regarding my magical rainbow socks, but the evidence was suggestive.

To be clear, the end result of our Bayesian analysis is the posterior distribution depicting the credibility of different values of our parameter. The decision to interpret this as sufficient or insufficient evidence for my outlandish claim is a decision that is separate from the Bayesian analysis proper. In contrast to NHST, the information we glean from Bayesian methods-the entire posterior distribution-is much richer. Another thing that makes Bayesian methods great is that you can make intuitive claims about the probability of hypotheses and parameter values in a way that frequentist NHST does not allow you to do.

What does that posterior using `prior #2` look like? It's a beta distribution with `alpha = 50 + 20` and `beta = 50 + 10` as shown in the following code:

```
> curve(dbeta(x, 70, 60),         # plot a beta distribution
+        xlab="θ",                # name x-axis
+        ylab="posterior belief", # name y-axis
+        type="l",                # make smooth line
+        yaxt='n')                # remove y axis labels
> abline(v=.5, lty=2)             # make line at theta = 0.5
```

The following figure shows the Posterior distribution of theta using prior #2:

Figure 7.5: Posterior distribution of theta using prior #2

Choosing a prior

Notice that the posterior distribution looks a little different depending on what prior you use. The most common criticism leveled against Bayesian methods is that the choice of prior adds an unsavory subjective element to analysis. To a certain extent, they're right about the added subjective element, but their allegation that it is unsavory is way off the mark.

To see why, check out the following figure, which shows both posterior distributions (from priors #1 and #2) in the same plot. Notice how priors #1 and #2-two very different priors-given the evidence, produce posteriors that look more similar to each other than the priors did:

Figure 7.6: The posterior distributions from prior #1 and #2

Now direct your attention to the following figure, which shows the posterior of both priors if the evidence included 80 out of 120 correct trials:

Figure 7.7: The posterior distributions from prior #1 and #2 with more evidence

Note that the evidence still contains 67% correct trials, but there is now more evidence. The posterior distributions are now far more similar. Notice that now both of the posteriors' credible intervals do not contain `theta = 0.5`; with 80 out of 120 trials correctly predicted, even the most obstinate skeptic has to concede that something is going on (though they will probably disagree that the power comes from the socks!).

Take notice also of the fact that the credible intervals, in both posteriors, are now substantially narrowing, illustrating more confidence in our estimate.

Finally, imagine the case where I correctly predicted 67% of the trials, but out of 450 total trials. The posteriors derived from this evidence are shown in the following figure:

Figure 7.8: The posterior distributions from prior #1 and #2 with even more evidence

The posterior distributions are looking very similar-indeed, they are becoming identical. Given enough trials-given enough evidence-these posterior distributions will be exactly the same. When there is enough evidence available such that the posterior is dominated by it compared to the prior, it is called *overwhelming the prior*.

As long as the prior is reasonable (that is, it doesn't assign a probability of 0 to theoretically plausible parameter values), given enough evidence, everybody's posterior belief will look very similar.

There is nothing unsavory or misleading about an analysis that uses a subjective prior; the analyst just has to disclose what her prior is. You can't just pick a prior willy-nilly; it has to be justifiable to your audience. In most situations, a prior may be informed by prior evidence like scientific studies and can be something that most people can agree on. A more skeptical audience may disagree with the chosen prior, in which case the analysis can be re-run using their prior, just like we did in the magic socks example. *It is sometimes okay for people to have different prior beliefs, and it is okay for some people to require a little more evidence in order to be convinced of something.*

The belief that frequentist hypothesis testing is more objective, and therefore more correct, is mistaken insofar as it causes all parties to have a hold on the same potentially bad assumptions. The assumptions in Bayesian analysis, on the other hand, are stated clearly from the start, made public, and are auditable.

To recap, there are three situations you can come across. In all of these, it makes sense to use Bayesian methods, if that's your thing. I have summed up the situations for your reference:

- You have a lot of evidence, and it makes no real difference which prior any reasonable person uses, because the evidence will overwhelm it.
- You have very little evidence, but have to make an important decision given the evidence. In this case, you'd be foolish to not use all available information to inform your decisions.
- You have a medium amount of evidence, and different posteriors illustrate the updated beliefs from a diverse array of prior beliefs. You may require more evidence to convince the extremely skeptical, but the majority of interested parties will be come to the same conclusions.

Who cares about coin flips

Who cares about coin flips? Well, virtually no one. However, (a) *coin flips are a great simple application to get the hang of Bayesian analysis*; (b) *the kinds of problems that a beta prior and a binomial likelihood function solve go way beyond assessing the fairness of coin flips*. We are now going to apply the same technique to a real life problem that I actually came across in my work.

For my job, I had to create a career recommendation system that asked the user a few questions about their preferences and spat out some careers they may be interested in. After a few hours, I had a working prototype. In order to justify putting more resources into improving the project, I had to prove that I was on to something and that my current recommendations performed better than chance.

In order to test this, we got 40 people together, asked them the questions, and presented them with two sets of recommendations. One was the true set of recommendations that I came up with, and one was a control set-the recommendations of a person who answered the questions randomly. If my set of recommendations performed better than chance would dictate, then I had a good thing going, and could justify spending more time on the project.

Simply performing better than chance is no great feat on its own-I also wanted really good estimates of how much better than chance my initial recommendations were.

For this problem, I broke out my Bayesian toolbox! The parameter of interest is the proportion of the time my recommendations performed better than chance. If .05 and lower were very unlikely values of the parameter, as far as the posterior depicted, then I could conclude that I was on to something.

Even though I had strong suspicions that my recommendations were good, I used a uniform beta prior to preemptively thwart criticisms that my prior biased the conclusions. As for the likelihood function, it is the same function family we used for the coin flips (just with different parameters).

It turns out that 36 out of the 40 people preferred my recommendations to the random ones (three liked them both the same, and one weirdo liked the random ones better). The posterior distribution, therefore, was a beta distribution with parameters 37 and 5. The code for the same as following:

```
> curve(dbeta(x, 37, 5), xlab="θ",
+       ylab="posterior belief",
+       type="l", yaxt='n')
```

Figure 7.9: The posterior distribution of the effectiveness of my recommendations using a uniform prior

Again, the end result of the Bayesian analysis proper is the posterior distribution that illustrates credible values of the parameter. The decision to set an arbitrary threshold for concluding that my recommendations were effective or not is a separate matter.

Let's say that, before the fact, we stated that if .05 or lower were not among the 95% most credible values, we would conclude that my recommendations were effective. How do we know what the credible interval bounds are?

Even though it is relatively straightforward to determine the bounds of the credible interval analytically, doing so ourselves computationally will help us understand how the posterior distribution is summarized in the examples given later in this chapter.

To find the bounds, we will sample from a beta distribution with hyper-parameters 37 and 5 thousands of times and find the quantiles at .025 and .975. The code for the same is as follows:

```
> samp <- rbeta(10000, 37, 5)
>  quantile(samp, c(.025, .975))
      2.5%      97.5%
 0.7674591 0.9597010
```

Neat! With the previous plot already up, we can add lines to the plot indicating this 95% credible interval, as shown in the following code:

```
> # horizontal line
> lines(c(.767, .96),  c(0.1, 0.1))
> # tiny vertical left boundary
> lines(c(.767, .769), c(0.15, 0.05))
> # tiny vertical right boundary
> lines(c(.96, .96),   c(0.15, 0.05))
```

If you plot this yourself, you'll see that even the lower bound is far from the decision boundary-it looks like my work was worth it after all!

The technique of sampling from a distribution many many times to obtain numerical results is known as **Monte Carlo simulation**.

Enter MCMC – stage left

As mentioned earlier, we started with the coin flip examples because of the ease of determining the posterior distribution analytically-primarily because of the beta distribution's self-conjugacy with respect to the binomial likelihood function.

It turns out that most real-world Bayesian analyses require a more complicated solution. In particular, the hyper-parameters that define the posterior distribution are rarely known. What can be determined is the probability density in the posterior distribution for each parameter value. The easiest way to get a sense of the shape of the posterior is to sample from it many thousands of times. More specifically, we sample from all possible parameter values and record the probability density at that point.

How do we do this? Well, in the case of just one parameter value, it's often computationally tractable to just randomly sample willy-nilly from the space of all possible parameter values. For cases where we are using Bayesian analysis to determine the credible values for two parameters, things get a little more hairy.

The posterior distribution for more than one parameter value is a called a *joint distribution*; in the case of two parameters, it is, more specifically, a *bivariate distribution*. One such bivariate normal distribution can be seen in the *figure 7.10*:

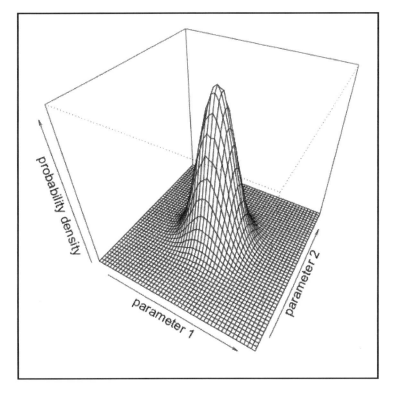

Figure 7.10: A bivariate normal distribution

To picture what it is like to sample a bi-variate posterior, imagine placing a bell jar on top of a piece of graph paper (be careful to make sure Ester Greenwood isn't under there!). Pretend we don't know the shape of the bell jar but we can, for each intersection of the lines in the graph paper, find the height of the bell jar over that exact point. Clearly, the smaller the grid on the graph paper, the higher resolution our estimate of the posterior distribution is.

Note that in the uni-variate case, we were sampling from n points, in the bi-variate case, we are sampling from n^2 points (n points for each axis). For models with more than two parameters, it is simply intractable to use this random sampling method. Luckily, there's a better option than just randomly sampling the parameter space: **Markov chain Monte Carlo (MCMC)**.

I think the easiest way to get a sense of what MCMC is, is by likening it to the game *hot and cold*. In this game-which you may have played as a child-an object is hidden and a searcher is blindfolded and tasked with finding this object. As the searcher wanders around, the other player tells the searcher whether she is *hot* or *cold*; *hot* if she is near the object, *cold* when she is far from the object. The other player also indicates whether the movement of the searcher is getting her closer to the object (getting *warmer*) or further from the object (getting *cooler*).

In this analogy, warm regions are areas were the probability density of the posterior distribution is high, and cool regions are the areas were the density is low. Put in this way, random sampling is like the searcher teleporting to random places in the space where the other player hid the object and just recording how hot or cold it is at that point. The guided behavior of the player we described before is far more efficient at exploring the areas of interest in the space.

At any one point, the blindfolded searcher has no memory of where she has been before. Her next position only depends on the point she is at currently (and the feedback of the other player). A memory-less transition process whereby the next position depends only upon the current position, and not on any previous positions, is called a *Markov chain*.

The technique for determining the shape of high-dimensional posterior distributions is therefore called Markov Chain Monte Carlo, because it uses Markov chains to intelligently sample many times from the posterior distribution (Monte Carlo simulation).

The development of software to perform MCMC on commodity hardware is, for the most part, responsible for a *Bayesian renaissance* in recent decades. Problems that were, not too long ago, completely intractable are now possible to be performed on even relatively low-powered computers.

There is far more to know about MCMC then we have the space to discuss here. Luckily, we will be using software that abstracts some of these deeper topics away from us. Nevertheless, if you decide to use Bayesian methods in your own analyses (and I hope you do!), I'd strongly recommend consulting resources that can afford to discuss MCMC at a deeper level. There are many such resources, available for free, on the web.

Before we move on to examples using this method, it is important that we bring up this one last point: Mathematically, an infinitely long MCMC chain will give us a perfect picture of the posterior distribution. Unfortunately, we don't have all the time in the world (universe [?]), and we have to settle for a finite number of MCMC samples. The longer our chains, the more accurate the description of the posterior. As the chains get longer and longer, each new sample provides a smaller and smaller amount of new information (economists call this *diminishing marginal returns*). There is a point in the MCMC sampling where the description of the posterior becomes sufficiently stable, and for all practical purposes, further sampling is unnecessary. It is at this point that we say the chain *converged*. Unfortunately, there is no perfect guarantee that our chain has achieved convergence. Of all the criticisms of using Bayesian methods, this is one of the most legitimate-but only slightly.

There are really effective heuristics for determining whether a running chain has converged, and we will be using a function that will automatically stop sampling the posterior once it has achieved convergence. Further, convergence can be all but perfectly verified by visual inspection, as we'll see soon.

For the simple models in this chapter, none of this will be a problem, anyway.

Using JAGS and runjags

Although it's a bit silly to break out MCMC for the single-parameter career recommendation analysis that we discussed earlier, applying this method to this simple example will aid in understanding its usage for more complicated models.

In order to get started, you need to install a software program called JAGS, which stands for **Just Another Gibbs Sampler** (a Gibbs sampler is a type of MCMC sampler). This program is independent of R, but we will be using R packages to communicate with it. After installing JAGS, you will need to install the R packages `rjags`, `runjags`, and `modeest`. As a reminder, you can install all three with this command:

```
> install.packages(c("rjags", "runjags", "modeest"))
```

To make sure everything is installed properly, load the `runjags` package, and run the function `testjags()`. My output looks something like this:

```
> library(runjags)
> testjags()
You are using R version 3.2.1 (2015-06-18) on a unix machine,
with the RStudio GUI
The rjags package is installed
JAGS version 3.4.0 found successfully using the command
'/usr/local/bin/jags'
```

The first step is to create the model that describes our problem. This model is written in an R-like syntax and stored in a string (character vector) that will get sent to JAGS to interpret. For this problem, we will store the model in a string variable called `our.model`, and the model looks like this:

```
our.model <- "model {
  # likelihood function
  numSuccesses ~ dbinom(successProb, numTrials)

  # prior
  successProb ~ dbeta(1, 1)

  # parameter of interest
  theta <- numSuccesses / numTrials
}"
```

Note that the JAGS syntax allows for R-style comments, which I included for clarity.

In the first few lines of the model, we are specifying the likelihood function. As we know, the likelihood function can be described with a binomial distribution. The binomial distribution function can be defined using the following code:

```
> numSuccesses ~ dbinom(successProb, numTrials)
```

The above code says that the variable `numSuccesses` is distributed according to the binomial function with hyper-parameters given by variable `successProb` and `numTrials`.

In the next relevant line, we are specifying our choice of the prior distribution. In keeping with our previous choice, this line reads, roughly: the `successProb` variable (referred to in the previous relevant line) is distributed in accordance with the beta distribution with hyper-parameters 1 and 1.

In the last line, we are specifying that the parameter we are really interested in is the proportion of successes (*number of successes divided by the number of trials*). We are calling that *theta*. Notice that we used the *deterministic assignment* operator (<–) instead of the *distributed according to* operator (~) to assign theta.

The next step is to define the `successProb` and `numTrials` variables for shipping to JAGS. We do this by stuffing these variables in an R list. We do this as follows:

```
our.data <- list(
  numTrials = 40,
  successProb = 36/40
)
```

Great! We are all set to run the MCMC, using the following code:

```
> results <- autorun.jags(our.model,
+                           data=our.data,
+                           n.chains = 3,
+                           monitor = c('theta'))
```

The function that runs the MCMC sampler and automatically stops at convergence is `autorun.jags`. The first argument is the string specifying the JAGS model. Next, we tell the function where to find the data that JAGS will need. After this, we specify that we want to run 3 independent MCMC chains; this will help guarantee convergence and, if we run them in parallel, drastically cut down on the time we have to wait for our sampling to be done. (To see some of the other options available, as always, you can run `?autorun.jags`.) Lastly, we specify that we are interested in the variable 'theta'.

After this is done, we can directly plot the `results` variable where the results of the MCMC are stored.

```
> plot(results,
+       plot.type=c("histogram", "trace"),
+       layout=c(2,1))
```

The output of this command is shown in the following figure:

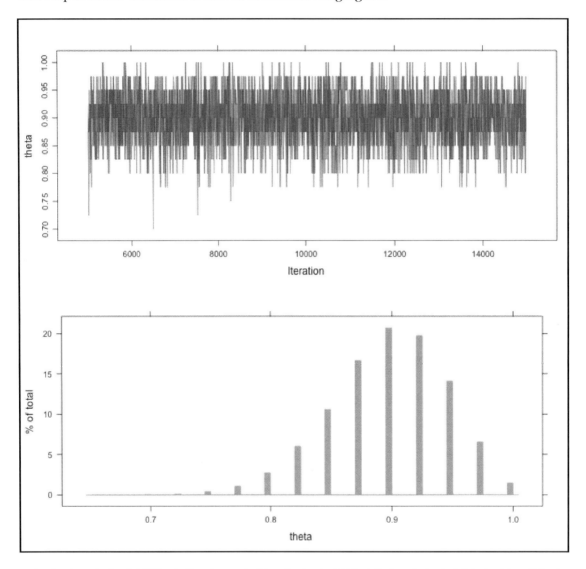

Figure 7.11: Output plots from the MCMC results. The top is a trace plot of theta values along the chain's length. The bottom is a bar plot depicting the relative credibility of different theta values.

The first of these plots is called a *trace plot*. It shows the sampled values of theta as the chain got longer. The fact that all three chains are overlapping around the same set of values is, at least in this case, a strong guarantee that all three chains have converged. The bottom plot is a bar plot that depicts the relative credibility of different values of theta. It is shown here as a bar plot, and not a smooth curve, because the binomial likelihood function is discrete. If we want a continuous representation of the posterior distribution, we can extract the sample values from the results and plot it as a density plot with a sufficiently large bandwidth, using the following code:

```
> # mcmc samples are stored in mcmc attribute
> # of results variable
> results.matrix <- as.matrix(results$mcmc)
>
> # extract the samples for 'theta'
> # the only column, in this case
> theta.samples <- results.matrix[,'theta']
>
> plot(density(theta.samples, adjust=5))
```

And we can add the bounds of the 95% credible interval to the plot as before, as shown in the following code:

```
> quantile(theta.samples, c(.025, .975))
 2.5% 97.5%
0.800 0.975
> lines(c(.8, .975), c(0.1, 0.1))
> lines(c(.8, .8), c(0.15, 0.05))
> lines(c(.975, .975), c(0.15, 0.05))
```

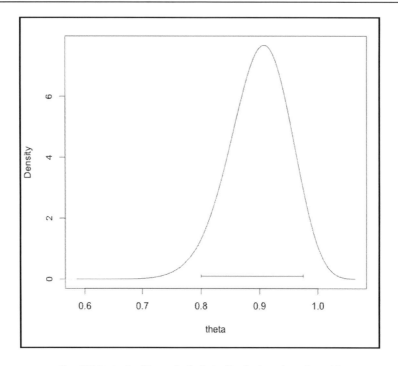

Figure 7.12: Density plot of the posterior distribution. Note that the x-axis starts here at 0.6

Rest assured that there is only a disagreement between the two credible intervals' bounds in this example because the MCMC could only sample discrete values from the posterior since the likelihood function is discrete. This will not occur in the other examples in this chapter. Regardless, the two methods seem to be in agreement about the shape of the posterior distribution and the credible values of theta. It is all but certain that my recommendations are better than chance. Go me!

Fitting distributions the Bayesian way

In this next example, we are going to be fitting a normal distribution to the precipitation dataset that we worked with in the previous chapter. We will wrap up with Bayesian analogue to the *one sample t-test*.

The results we want from this analysis are credible values of the true population mean of the precipitation data. Refer back to the previous chapter to recall that the *sample mean* was 34.89. In addition, we will also be determining credible values of the standard deviation of the precipitation data. Since we are interested in the credible values of two parameters, our posterior distribution is a joint distribution.

Our model will look a little differently now:

```
the.model <- "
model {
  mu ~ dunif(0, 60)          # prior
  stddev ~ dunif(0, 30)      # prior
  tau <- pow(stddev, -2)

  for(i in 1:theLength){
    samp[i] ~ dnorm(mu, tau)    # likelihood function
  }
}"
```

This time, we have to set two priors, one for the mean of the Gaussian curve that describes the precipitation data (`mu`), and one for the standard deviation (`stddev`). We also have to create a variable called `tau` that describes the precision (inverse of the variance) of the curve, because `dnorm` in JAGS takes the mean and the precision as hyper-parameters (and not the mean and standard deviation, like R). We specify that our prior for the `mu` parameter is uniformly distributed from 0 inches of rain to 60 inches of rain-far above any reasonable value for the population precipitation mean. We also specify that our prior for the standard deviation is a flat one from 0 to 30. If this were part of any meaningful analysis and not just a pedagogical example, our priors would be informed in part by precipitation data from other regions like the US or my precipitation data from previous years. JAGS comes chock full of different families of distributions for expressing different priors.

Next, we specify that the variable `samp` (which will hold the precipitation data) is distributed normally with unknown parameters `mu` and `tau`.

Then, we construct an R list to hold the variables to send to JAGS, using the following code:

```
the.data <- list(
  samp = precip,
  theLength = length(precip)
)
```

Cool, let's run it! On my computer, this takes 5 seconds:

```
> results <- autorun.jags(the.model,
+                          data=the.data,
+                          n.chains = 3,
+                          # now we care about two parameters
+                          monitor = c('mu', 'stddev'))
```

Let's plot the results directly like before, while being careful to plot both the *trace* plot and *histogram* from *both* parameters by increasing the `layout` argument in the call to the `plot` function, as shown in the following code:

```
> plot(results,
+       plot.type=c("histogram", "trace"),
+       layout=c(2,2))
```

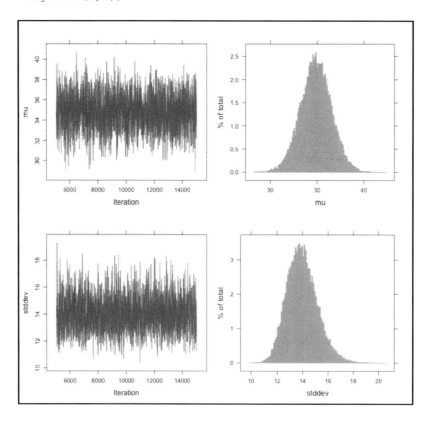

Figure 7.13: Output plots from the MCMC result of fitting a normal curve to the built-in precipitation data set.

The following shows the distribution of credible values of the `mu` parameter without reference to the `stddev` parameter. This is called a *marginal distribution*:

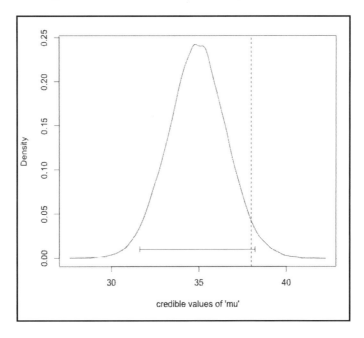

Figure 7.14: Marginal distribution of posterior for parameter 'mu'. Dashed line shows hypothetical population mean within 95% credible interval

Remember when, in the last chapter, we wanted to determine whether the US' mean precipitation was significantly discrepant from the (hypothetical) known population mean precipitation of the rest of the world of 38 inches. If we take any value outside the 95% credible interval to indicate *significance*, then, just like when we used the NHST t-test, we have to reject the hypothesis that there is significantly more or less rain in the US than in the rest of the world.

Before we move on to the next example, you may be interested in credible values for both the mean and the standard deviation at the same time. A great type of plot for depicting this information is a *contour plot*, which illustrates the shape of a three-dimensional surface by showing a series of lines for which there is equal height. The code for creating a contour plot is as follows:

```
> results.matrix <- as.matrix(results$mcmc)
>
> library(MASS)
> # we need to make a kernel density
> # estimate of the 3-d surface
```

```
> z <- kde2d(results.matrix[,'mu'],
+            results.matrix[,'stddev'],
+            n=50)
>
> plot(results.matrix)
> contour(z, drawlabels=FALSE,
+         nlevels=11, col=rainbow(11),
+         lwd=3, add=TRUE)
```

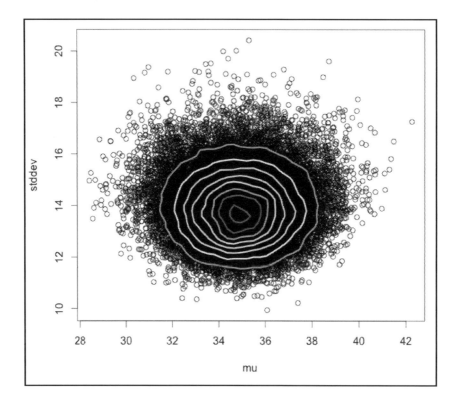

Figure 7.15: Contour plot of the joint posterior distribution. The purple contour corresponds to the region with the highest probability density.

The purple contours (the inner-most contours) show the region of the posterior with the highest probability density. These correspond to the most likely values of our two parameters. As you can see, the most likely values of the parameters for the normal distribution that best describes our present knowledge of US precipitation are a mean of a little less than 35 and a standard deviation of a little less than 14. We can corroborate the results of our visual inspection by directly printing the `results` variable:

```
> print(results)

JAGS model summary statistics from 30000 samples (chains = 3; adapt+burnin
= 5000):
        Lower95 Median Upper95    Mean     SD    Mode
mu       31.645 34.862  38.181  34.866 1.6639  34.895
stddev   11.669 13.886  16.376  13.967 1.2122  13.773
           MCerr MC%ofSD SSeff       AC.10    psrf
mu      0.012238     0.7 18484    0.002684  1.0001
stddev 0.0093951     0.8 16649   -0.0053588 1.0001

Total time taken: 5 seconds
```

This also shows other summary statistics from our MCMC samples and some information about the MCMC process.

The Bayesian independent samples t-test

For our last example in the chapter, we will be performing a sort-of Bayesian analogue to the two-sample t-test using the same data and problem from the corresponding example in the previous chapter-testing whether the means of the gas mileage for automatic and manual cars are significantly different.

 There is another popular Bayesian alternative to NHST, which uses something called *Bayes factors* to compare the likelihood of the null and alternative hypotheses.

As before, let's specify the model using non-informative flat priors, as shown in the following code:

```
the.model <- "
model {
  # each group will have a separate mu
  # and standard deviation
  for(j in 1:2){
    mu[j] ~ dunif(0, 60)        # prior
    stddev[j] ~ dunif(0, 20)    # prior
    tau[j] <- pow(stddev[j], -2)
  }
  for(i in 1:theLength){
    # likelihood function
    y[i] ~ dnorm(mu[x[i]], tau[x[i]])
  }
}"
```

Notice that the construct that describes the likelihood function is a little different now; we have to use nested subscripts for the mu and `tau` parameters to tell JAGS that we are dealing with two different versions of mu and `stddev`.

Next, we will define the data as follows:

```
the.data <- list(
  y = mtcars$mpg,
  # 'x' needs to start at 1 so
  # 1 is now automatic and 2 is manual
  x = ifelse(mtcars$am==1, 1, 2),
  theLength = nrow(mtcars)
)
```

Finally, let's roll!

```
> results <- autorun.jags(the.model,
+                         data=the.data,
+                         n.chains = 3,
+                         monitor = c('mu', 'stddev'))
```

Let's extract the samples for both mu's and make a vector that holds the differences in the mu samples between each of the two groups:

```
> results.matrix <- as.matrix(results$mcmc)
> difference.in.means <- (results.matrix[,1] -
+                         results.matrix[,2])
```

Figure 7.16 shows a plot of the credible differences in means. The likely differences in means are far above a difference of zero. We are all but certain that the means of the gas mileage for automatic and manual cars are significantly different:

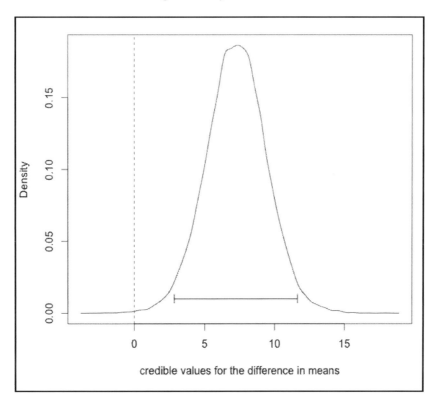

Figure 7.16: Credible values for the difference in means of the gas mileage between automatic and manual cars. The dashed line is at a difference of zero.

Notice that the decision to mimic the independent samples t-test made us focus on one particular part of the Bayesian analysis and didn't allow us to appreciate some of the other very valuable information the analysis yielded. For example, in addition to having a distribution illustrating credible differences in means, we have the posterior distribution for the credible values of both the means and standard deviations of both samples. The ability to make a decision on whether the samples' means are significantly different is nice-the ability to look at the posterior distribution of the parameters is better.

Exercises

Practice the following exercises to reinforce the concepts learned in this chapter:

- Write a function that will take a vector holding MCMC samples for a parameter and plot a density curve depicting the posterior distribution and the 95% credible interval. Be careful of different scales on the y-axis.

- Fitting a normal curve to an empirical distribution is conceptually easy, but not very robust. For distribution fitting that is more robust to outliers, it's common to use a *t-distribution* instead of the normal distribution, since the t has heavier *tails*. View the distribution of the `shape` attribute of the built-in `rock` dataset. Does this look normally distributed? Find the parameters of a normal curve that is a fit to the data. In JAGS, `dt`, the t-distribution density function, takes three parameters: the mean, the precision, and the degrees of freedom that controls the heaviness of the tails. Find the parameters after fitting a t-distribution to the data. Are the means similar? Which estimate of the mean do you think is more representative of central tendency?

- In Theseus' paradox, a wooden ship belonging to Theseus has decaying boards, which are removed and replaced with new lumber. Eventually, all the boards in the original ship have been replaced, so that the ship is made up of completely new matter. Is it still *Theseus' ship*? If not, at what point did it become a different ship?

  What would Aristotle say about this? Appeal to the doctrine of the *Four Causes*. Would Aristotle's stance still hold up if-as in Thomas Hobbes' version of the paradox-the original decaying boards were saved and used to make a complete replica of Theseus' original ship?

Summary

Although most introductory data analysis texts don't even broach the topic of Bayesian methods, you, dear reader, are versed enough in this matter to start applying these techniques to real problems.

We discovered that Bayesian methods could—at least for the models in this chapter-not only allow us to answer the same kinds of questions we might use the binomial, one sample t-test, and the independent samples t-test for, but provide a much richer and more intuitive depiction of our uncertainty in our estimates.

If these approaches interest you, I urge you to learn more about how to extend these to supersede other NHST tests. I also urge you to learn more about the mathematics behind MCMC.

As with the last chapter, we covered much ground here. If you made it through, congratulations!

8
The Bootstrap

In the kind of statistician networks I participate in, there's a huge debate on whether introductory statistics curricula need a profound overhaul. In the *particular* circles I run in, there's a big movement to shift away from the NHST methods I spoke about in Chapter 6, *Testing Hypotheses*, in favor of either the Bayesian methods we discussed in the previous chapter, or *resampling* methods such as the *bootstrap* that we'll be discussing in this chapter.

In spite of my personal ideas on the matter, preferences, and current workflow tendencies, I strongly felt that I would be doing you, dear reader, an enormous disservice leaving out such staples of data analysis as ANOVA and the Student's t-test, especially if you want to make a career of this. For better or worse, the vast majority of new research in science still makes strong use of the techniques stressed by the traditional curriculum. Additionally, these are the type of techniques that are most likely going to be asked about in an interview for a new position, especially if your interviewers are not statisticians by training.

Perhaps the most overlooked point of all: in the debate about where statistics pedagogy should move towards, the proponents of a radical departure, as cogent as their arguments may be, rely heavily on *comparison* between Bayesian methods/resampling, and the conventional toolset in their apologetics for the former. That is to say, they take knowledge of the more traditional techniques as a given, because it serves as the comparison point. Therefore, to make the most informed decision about what personally feels right for you to spend most of your energy continuing your learning journey about, a knowledge of all available options is essential.

As stated earlier, this chapter is going to be all about a technique that I personally make heavy use of in my work, *the bootstrap*. We are going to be learning about what makes it so cool, how to perform it in R, and, as always, bust some common misconceptions for a nuanced, thorough, and fair view of the landscape of the wonderful world of modern data analysis techniques.

¡Que se abra el talón!

What's... uhhh... the deal with the bootstrap?

You may be pleased to hear that you, dear reader, are already set up for a keen understanding of the bootstrap based on the material in `Chapter 5`, *Using Data to Reason about the World*. Specifically, recall how the subject of sampling distributions of sample means was broached (if you need to refer back to the section, please do!). In our very hands-on creation of our first sampling distribution of sample means, we created a vector of 10,000 normally distributed (mean of 65, and standard deviation of 3.5) values representing a *population* of the heights of US women in inches. We then took 10,000 samples of size 40 from this population, took means of those samples, and plotted this distribution.

Call to mind that this sampling distribution had a mean equal to the population mean, and a standard deviation of population standard deviation divided by the square root of the sample size. Recall that the standard deviation of the sampling distribution was called the *standard error*. It was this standard error that we used in the creation of confidence intervals.

Recall, too, two more things:

- Because we created this *population* ourselves, we had an unrestricted ability to sample from it. In real life, of course, we have to make do with the sample we are given, or, at least, the sample that we are able to go out and get for ourselves.
- In order to account for the condition of only having access to the information of a *sample* of the population, we noted that we can *pretend* our sampling distribution has a mean equal to the *sample* mean, and a standard deviation of our *sample* standard deviation divided by the square root of our sample size. Our ability to substitute these values is sometimes known as the *plug-in principle*, and it is this principle that is exploited by the bootstrap.

In the `Chapter 6`, *Testing Hypotheses*, we drove home the point that sampling distributions of statistics lies at the heart of significance testing. We capitalized on how we knew in advance what the sampling distributions of certain statistics were going to look like in order to justify the use of the easy significance tests in R, like the `t.test` function. Our assumptions about how the sampling distributions were going to look like, or, more specifically, the value of the *parameters* that define those sampling distributions, made these class of tests *parametric statistical tests*.

In short, our interval estimation and null-hypothesis significance testing relied on:

- Getting the statistic of interest from a sample of the population
- Using that statistic and some information about the sample to estimate the sampling distribution of that statistic

But, *what if* - and bear with me here - we treated our sample *as if it were* a population, and took *samples* from it in order to construct sampling distributions *empirically*? This would absolve us of the need to make assumptions about the parameters of the sampling distribution.

What would this approach to *non-parametric* estimation/testing look like? And how do we sample from the *sample itself*? The answer: a massive amount of **sampling with replacement**.

What is sampling with replacement?

Imagine, me, knowing you were a big fan of oatmeal raisin cookies to the exclusion of all other types, told you that I had a cookie jar containing cookies of different types that included some of *your* favorite type.

If you took a cookie, one by one from the jar, and set them aside looking for your special treat, you'd be sampling from the jar (with a sample size of one) *without replacement*. If, on the other hand, you weren't thinking very clearly, and each time you took a cookie out to inspect it, you put it *back* into the jar before you picked up a new one, you would be sampling the jar *with replacement*.

An interesting consequence of sampling the jar with replacement is that you can sample the jar infinitely many times, since the number of cookies in the jar never decreases between samples.

Although sampling with replacement is... not such a great way to find the oatmeal raisin cookie you're looking for, sampling with replacement is used a lot in mathematics, and is an indispensable part of the bootstrap procedure.

By the way, they were all oatmeal raisin cookies! I got them for you because I know how much you like them!

Enough talking... let's get our hands dirty with some R code demonstrating the bootstrap procedure. Specifically, we are going to use the *population* of the heights of US women (from `Chapter 5`, *Using Data To Reason About The World*), take a sample of 40 from this population, and construct a sampling distribution of the sample means by *sampling with replacement* from the sample we have. Each time we compute our statistic of interest (in this case, the mean) with a new bootstrap sample, it is called a *bootstrap replication*. We will perform 10,000 of these bootstrap replications.

This sampling distribution, arrived at not by assuming the parameters of the sampling distribution, but rather by direct simulation via the bootstrapping procedure, will heretofore be referred to as the **bootstrap distribution.** The following code illustrates the bootstrap procedure:

```
> # setting seed will make random number generation reproducible
> set.seed(1)
> all.us.women <- rnorm(10000, mean=65, sd=3.5)
> our.sample <- sample(all.us.women, 40)
> bootstrap.replicates <- numeric(10000)
> for(i in 1:10000){
+    a.sample <- sample(our.sample, 40, replace=TRUE)
+    bootstrap.replicates[i] <- mean(a.sample)
> }
> hist(bootstrap.replicates
```

Take a look at the histogram produced by the code depicted in the preceding graph (*Figure 8.1*):

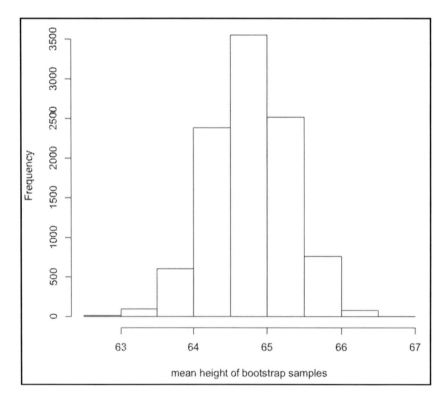

Figure 8.1: A histogram of the bootstrap distribution

What do you notice about it? The first thing that jumps out to me is that it looks a lot like the sampling distribution sample means that we got in Chapter 5, *Using Data To Reason About The World*, by sampling the *population* 10,000 times. This property, and others, are better illustrated by the following plot:

Figure 8.2: Probability density plot of (a) the sampling distribution from the population [red, solid], (b) the bootstrap distribution [blue, dashed], and t-distribution [green, dashed].

This plot depicts three different probability densities. The solid red line is the sampling distribution of sample means using samples of size 40 from the *population* (this is the same information from *Figure 5.3* in Chapter 5, *Using Data To Reason About The World*). The dashed blue line is the bootstrap distribution, as shown in *Figure 8.1*. The dashed green line is the t-distribution whose parameters are dictated by our sample. You may not be able to discriminate the two dashed lines from each other, but I promise that both are there!

There are two very important pieces of information to glean from this plot:

- The first is that the shape and locations of the sampling distribution from the population and the bootstrap distribution are almost identical. In fact, the only perceivable difference is that the peak of the bootstrap distribution is shifted about 0.22 inches to the left. This is because the mean of our sample of 40 from the population, by chance, was 0.22 inches fewer than the mean of the population. Otherwise, the two sampling distributions in this example are, for all practical purposes, completely identical.
- The second is that, in this particular example, the t-distribution we would have assumed using the parameters of our sample is, literally, indistinguishable from our bootstrap distribution. This provides very compelling evidence that we are onto something with this whole *bootstrap* business.

It is important to note that, for many applications and examples, the bootstrap distribution and the assumed parametric distribution (if one even exists), while similar, will be a little different. This is a *feature* (not a bug) of the bootstrap. The differences between the bootstrap distribution and it's parametric cousin is one of the reasons you might *prefer* to use the bootstrap.

By the way, even *if* the bootstrap distribution of sample means and the t-distribution were always identical, this *still* wouldn't mean that the bootstrap is an unnecessary technique in our toolbox. We will see why this is the case a little later in this chapter.

Performing the bootstrap in R (more elegantly)

One of the beautiful things about the bootstrap technique is that it can be performed easily using only the level of R programming that we reached by the conclusion of Chapter 1, *RefresheR* however, there is, and as you might imagine, a more automated way of doing this in R. We will be using the boot package for this, so make sure you install it:

```
btobj <- boot(our.sample, function(x, i){mean(x[i])}, 10000,
              parallel="multicore", ncpus=3)
```

That looks simple enough, but let's take a closer look at this code:

- As the first argument, the `boot` function takes the sample that we are using the bootstrap procedure on; in our case, we are passing it our sample of 40 that we took earlier.
- The second argument is a function that, itself, takes two arguments: an indexable R object (like a vector), and a list of *indices* that we will use to subset this object. The result of using these indices on the object will give us our bootstrap sample.
- The third argument is how many many bootstrap replications to perform. This brings us to an important question that it seems that we've been avoiding: how many bootstrap replications is enough? For more on this, see the info box with the same name. For our purposes with *this* example, we are using 10,000.

The final two arguments are optional, but a nice-to-have if you are using a computer with multiple cores. Since each bootstrap replication is completely independent of any of the others, each core can do it's own set of replications, and all the results can be pooled at the end. This often results in a running time that is decreased by a factor of the number of cores you are using. If you are first getting your feet wet with the bootstrap, though, perhaps it is better that you leave these options out until you are more comfortable with optional niceties. For further information, see the help page for the boot function (`help("boot")` or `?boot`).

Finally, we are assigning the output of this function (an object of class `boot`) to a variable called `btobj`.

This object has manifold associated methods; one such method is `plot`:

```
plot(btobj)
```

Finally, our `boot` object contains a few attributes that you might want to inspect:

```
str(btobj)
```

Most likely, the attribute that you'd be most interested in is the `t` attribute, which stores the bootstrap statistic for each of the replications. For example, you can get a histogram of the bootstrap distribution with the following incantation:

```
hist(btobj$t)
```

Although I promised at the start of this section that we would be performing the bootstrap more elegantly than we had when we manually filled `bootstrap.replicates` with our bootstrap statistics earlier in the chapter, you might find the code directly above to be more obtuse. Even if you do, I ask that you stick to this new procedure, since:

- The returned object is rich in information and methods that we'll be using further in this chapter
- This function allows for greater capabilities for more advanced bootstrap techniques

How many bootstrap replications should I perform?
Short answer? As many as you can.

Less glib answer? The more bootstrap replications are performed, the closer our bootstrap distribution will be to its theoretical *most accurate*, and the more accurate/reliable any assessment using the bootstrap procedure will be. Of course, they are diminishing marginal returns, and no one is asking any application of the bootstrap that a beginner or intermediate learner of statistics is likely to perform to take days or weeks (or even hours, or more than five minutes on modern hardware); but, in my experience, more is always better.

For the above example, 10,000 replications is enough (perhaps more than enough), and doesn't take more than a quarter of a second on my machine. More is certainly welcome, though.

It is always difficult to give a rule of thumb in statistics, because the bootstrap is applicable to so many problems, and each of these applications requires a different number of replications to *converge* onto an *acceptable* approximation of its theoretically complete bootstrap distribution. For the applications in this chapter, use the following rule of thumb: 10,000 is good, but 100,000 is better.

Confidence intervals

Now that we have this new, empirically determined sampling distribution (the bootstrap distribution), we can provide interval estimates of population parameters in much the same idea as we can with parametrically determined sampling distributions.

For both the parametric sampling distribution of sample means and the bootstrap distribution of sample means, the range of values from the 2.5% quantile and the 97.5% quantile of the sampling distribution represent the range of values for which 95% of the sample means would lie if repeated samples were taken from the population.

> Note that the bootstrap, at least as introduced thus far, is a *frequentist* technique, and therefore does not use *credible intervals* like those of the last chapter.

In Chapter 5, *Using Data To Reason About The World*, we saw that we can get 95% confidence intervals by getting the quantile of the t-distribution of our particular sample size, and using this to multiply with the standard error. With the bootstrap, there are many procedures available, but all of them are easier, even if they do take more computation time.

Our first approach might be just to take the quantiles using the quantile function:

```
> quantile(btobj$t, prob=0.025)
> quantile(btobj$t, prob=0.975)
```

An easier method for doing this is provided by the boot.ci function:

```
> boot.ci(btobj, conf=0.95, type="perc")
BOOTSTRAP CONFIDENCE INTERVAL CALCULATIONS
Based on 10000 bootstrap replicates
CALL :
boot.ci(boot.out = btobj, conf = 0.95, type = "perc")
Intervals :
Level Percentile
95% (63.7, 65.8 )
Calculations and Intervals on Original Scale
```

This function takes an object returned by the boot function we used earlier, and does the *hard* work for us. We explicitly specified that we wanted 95% confidence intervals using the conf argument, though this is the default value, so we will be leaving it out in the next example.

But wait... what's this type="perc" thing about? Well, as it turns out, the method of getting the bounds of the confidence interval by taking quantiles of the bootstrap distribution (referred to by boot.ci, as *perc* or *percentile* intervals) is just one way of expressing the confidence intervals of a population parameter using the bootstrap; however, it is *not* the method that we are going to be using from here on out.

The percentile method for determining confidence interval bounds works fine when the bootstrap distribution is symmetric and normal-distribution-shaped; when it isn't, we can often do much better...

The **bias-corrected and accelerated** confidence interval (**BCa**) is one such improved approach, and, incidentally, both the one I use in my personal work and the one we will be using here. In brief, attempts to correct for bias in the bootstrap distribution by performing transformations on it. The intervals it yields, in my experience, are always at least as good as those given by the percentile method, and, quite often, much better:

```
> boot.ci(btobj, type="bca")
BOOTSTRAP CONFIDENCE INTERVAL CALCULATIONS
Based on 10000 bootstrap replicates
CALL :
boot.ci(boot.out = btobj, type = "bca")
Intervals :
Level BCa
95% (63.67, 65.77 )
Calculations and Intervals on Original Scale
```

For this example, all of the approaches bear nearly identical intervals.

A one-sample test of means

We finally have enough knowledge under our belts to perform a null-hypothesis significance test using the bootstrap. In fact, given what we already learned, it can scarcely be easier!

As a note, I prefer to use the the bootstrap mainly as a method of generating confidence intervals and illustrating uncertainty in population parameter estimates, and *not* as a tool for NHST. But, at least as a demonstration, we'll see a few examples of it being used for hypothesis testing here.

For ease of comparison, let's repeat the one sample test that we performed in Chapter 6, *Testing Hypotheses*. Recall, that the precip built-in dataset contained the precipitation (in inches) of a sample of US cities. We wanted to know if the mean of the population US precipitation was significantly discrepant from the precipitation average of the rest of the world – a value that we, quite unjustifiably, and arbitrarily, said to be 38 inches.

The one sample t-test was performed thusly:

```
> t.test(precip, mu=38)
One Sample t-test
data: precip
t = -1.901, df = 69, p-value = 0.06148
alternative hypothesis: true mean is not equal to 38
95 percent confidence interval:
  31.61748 38.15395
sample estimates:
mean of x
  34.88571
```

Instead, using the bootstrap, we will simply construct the 95% confidence interval of the mean of US precipitation, and note if the confidence interval includes 38 inches. Let's use 300,000 bootstrap replications this time, as construction of accurate confidence intervals is greatly aided by an increased number of bootstrap samples (though 300,000 would generally be considered *overkill* for this application):

```
> set.seed(1)
> btobj <- boot(precip, function(x, i){mean(x[i])}, 300000)
> boot.ci(btobj, type="bca")
BOOTSTRAP CONFIDENCE INTERVAL CALCULATIONS
Based on 300000 bootstrap replicates
CALL :
boot.ci(boot.out = btobj, type = "bca")
Intervals :
Level BCa
95% (31.60, 37.98 )
Calculations and Intervals on Original Scale
```

In contrast to our results from the one-sample t-test, the 95% does *not* contain 38. This would lead us to reject the null hypothesis (at least at the 0.05 alpha level).

Interestingly, the percentile approach to confidence interval estimation *does* contain 38. Welcome to the wonderful world of statistics.

In a case like this, if we were researchers trying to test this hypothesis, say, for a research paper, the only acceptable and ethical *modus operandi* is to, before analyzing *any* of the data, explicitly state which statistical test and approach we are going to use to test our hypothesis. The test we chose *and no others* should be the ones we appeal to in our *results* section. That is to say, *do not* set out to use, for example, a parametric t-test, and then test the same hypothesis using the bootstrap; get a result you want, and then pretend that it was the approach you were going to take all along. Don't be a cheater.

By the way, I did not - all the way back in `Chapter 6`, *Testing Hypotheses*, arbitrarily state that the population precipitation to 38 inches in order show the incongruence between the results of the bootstrap and the t-test. As a matter of fact, I couldn't have done this, because this chapter is new in the second edition, and I didn't know that I was going to eventually use the bootstrap to test this back then; however, I am quite pleased to be able to demonstrate this result. This "happy accident" further illustrates the limitations of NHST (the bootstrap included) relative to estimation of effect sizes and/or Bayesian techniques. It seems silly that a simple choice of statistical test should make the difference between a publishable result and a non-publishable result, and, by extension, the increased possibility of tenure, and not.

A one-tailed test using the bootstrap, at least as we've introduced it thus far, is a more hairy affair than a two-tailed test of means. My recommendation, for now, is to not attempt to perform a one-tailed test using the bootstrap for a problem type like this.

If the bootstrap is so cool, why isn't it mentioned more in the classic statistics tests?

 The simple answer to this question is that, before the introduction of computers was powerful enough, bootstrapping was just intractable. Comparing the ease with a t-test can be performed (using the computation of just *one* sample mean and an old-fashioned lookup table) with the computation of 10,000 sample means, let alone the estimation of confidence interval bounds!

Now that bootstrapping is a tractable problem even on low-powered commodity hardware, there are no excuses for the bootstrap not being more popular. Well, besides for cultural inertia.

Bootstrapping statistics other than the mean

In the conclusion of the section *What's... uhhh... the deal with the bootstrap?*, I briefly touched on two important points. The first was an ominous and unexplained implication that a parametric distribution describing the sampling distribution of a statistic of interest may not exist. The second was a promise that even if, for example, the bootstrap distribution of means were *identical* to the t-distribution in all cases, there would still be great merit in learning how to wield the bootstrap. In this section, I hope to make clear these two points.

First, let's think back to all the tests of means we performed in `Chapter 6`, *Testing Hypotheses*. Let's ask ourselves *why* we wanted to test equality of *means*. It is certainly true that the arithmetic mean is one of the most common, if not *the* most common measures of central tendency and, indeed, in all of statistics. But why is it that we are *always* testing means? May it not be useful to ask (and test), for example, if the *medians* of two groups are significantly discrepant? Remember *Marx and Engels*, the law office from `Chapter 2`, *The Shape of Data*, where the typical employee made $40,000 a year, but the arithmetic mean of salaries was grossly inflated by the CEO fat cat's salary of $500,000. If we wanted to conduct a test of whether the typical employee's salary was significantly different between two law firms, would it not make a good deal of sense to compare the median salaries, instead?

The answer is, of course, *yes*. In that case, why didn't we?

The answer is very simple. Recall that at the foundation of interval estimation and the null-hypothesis significance tests of `Chapter 6`, *Testing Hypotheses*, is the concept of the sampling distribution of a test statistic. Specifically, all tests we used in that chapter took it for granted that we can determine the parameters of the sampling distribution of our statistic of interest. And, because we chose certain well-behaved statistics, we always could. For example, the sampling distribution of sample means will always have a t-distribution. This makes hypothesis testing with the mean very easy.

Here's the thing, though: the sampling distribution of a test statistic only plays nice for certain types of statistics. As an example, although we can determine the sampling distribution of sample *medians* analytically (as opposed to via simulation), the math is awkward, and the subject is rarely broached in statistics texts.

As a result, we are often left, quite tacitly, with the idea that testing for equality of means is our only option for testing for the equality of measures of central tendency; however, this is not the case.

 More than anything else, I think that the greatest thing about the bootstrap is the ease with which we can create sampling distributions for a whole range of statistics that are simply ignored in other texts.

In our illustrative example, we will compute, using the bootstrap, a sampling distribution of sample means, sample medians, and sample trimmed means (trimming off the most extreme 5% of values in each sample), and plot their distributions.

Let's make a pretend sample of salaries of the workers of the aforementioned law office:

```
> set.seed(1)
> law.salaries <- c(c(rnorm(70, mean=40000, sd=7000)), 500000, 400000,
350000)
```

Here, we create a vector containing 70 normally distributed values around $40,000, but include three salaries from big shots at the company who command a salary a full order of magnitude higher.

Let's do the the bootstrapping, and compute the confidence intervals. To save space, I'm going to include the intervals in the comments beside each call to boot.ci. Feel free to check these values yourself:

```
> btobj.mean <- boot(law.salaries, function(x, i){mean(x[i])}, 300000)
> btobj.median <- boot(law.salaries, function(x, i){median(x[i])}, 300000)
> btobj.tmean <- boot(law.salaries, function(x, i){mean(x[i], trim=0.05)},
300000)
> boot.ci(btobj.mean, type="bca")     # 44989 - 84084
> boot.ci(btobj.median, type="bca")   # 39607 - 42926
> boot.ci(btobj.tmean, type="bca")    # 39993 - 57715
```

Here's a plot of the probability densities for each of the bootstrap distributions:

Figure 8.3: The probability density functions of the bootstrap distributions of (a) sample means [solid blue], (b) sample medians [dashed red], and (c) sample trimmed means [shorter-dashed green]

The bootstrap distribution of sample means (depicted as the solid blue line) is very dispersed. This is not a surprise, given that the salaries in the law firm can vary quite wildly. The bootstrap distribution of sample *medians*, in contrast (shown as the dashed red line) are very densely packed around $40,000. Finally, the trimmed means (shown as the green line with shorter dashes) look a lot like the sample medians at first, but have a much heavier right tail. This is precisely what we would expect given that the tail of distribution of actual salaries is so positively skewed, though the tail of the trimmed mean bootstrap distribution is greatly attenuated by the trimming procedure.

Now, imagine the workers of the law office start to gain class consciousness. They somehow figure out that the trimmed mean of the population of workers in all other law offices is $70,000. Using only a sample of the salaries within their ranks, can they figure out whether they have a strong case for striking?

The answer is, *of course!* In fact, we are already most of the way there. We noted that the upper limit of the 95% confidence interval of the trimmed mean is $57,715. Since $70,000 falls way outside the range of this interval, it looks like the workers of Marx & Engels have some organizing to do!

Also... ha! Try doing a test of trimmed means using a parametric hypothesis test!

Are there still *other* statistics we can bootstrap?

Yes! Some other very common applications of the bootstrap are constructing bootstrap distributions and confidence intervals for standard deviations, measures of entropy, correlation coefficients, and regression coefficients, which we will learn about in the next chapter!

It should be noted, though, that we can't just bootstrap *everything* under the sun. A classic example is a *sample maximum value* (or *minimum*). Statistics like these, that vary wildly from sample to sample, make for extremely unstable bootstrap distributions, and are unsuitable for making inferences. When in doubt, stick to bootstrapping statistics that you've seen in the scientific literature

Busting bootstrap myths

There are two very prevalent myths regarding the bootstrap that we will briefly address in this section.

The first is that the bootstrap is a panacea for small sample sizes. I think at least part of this myth is due to the name *the bootstrap,* which conjures of images of some rugged person pulling themselves up by the bootstraps and making something from nothing. Unfortunately, the bootstrap does *not* make something from nothing, nor does it even make more out of less. The important thing to remember is that the accuracy of your bootstrap distribution is completely dependent on the representativeness of your original sample. Refer back to *Figure 8.1.* Notice that, although the bootstrap distribution and the sampling distribution of sample means have the same shape, the bootstrap distribution was shifted slightly to the left because, by chance, the sample we got had a mean slightly less than the population mean. This will happen. And, of course, the smaller the sample size, the more often these types of mis-estimations will occur. No amount of resampling, no amount of bootstrap replications, can correct for a bias in our *sample*.

You can, of course, explore data by using bootstrap procedures to your heart's content, but I would strongly advise against drawing important conclusions from the bootstrap with an *n* fewer than 25, and many others would put that number *much* higher.

The second biggest myth surrounding the bootstrap is that it is an *assumption-free* technique. No assumptions! We can let the data speak completely for itself! Right?

Well, no. The data does speak completely for itself, and this is, no doubt, a *very* attractive property of the technique, but it is misleading to say that the bootstrap makes no assumptions.

The biggest and most obvious assumption of the bootstrap is that data points that are outside the set of discrete values in our sample are impossible to encounter. The consequence of this assumption is very subtle, and not readily apparent when bootstrapping, for example, sample means; however, construct for yourself a bootstrap distribution of sample *medians*, particularly for a sample less than 20. Plot this distribution. Notice anything weird? This distribution is jagged, and quite unattractive. This is because the bootstrap replications can only contain values that have been included in our sample. As a consequence, our bootstrap distribution isn't nice and smooth like before, and this has deleterious consequences regarding the reliability of our confidence intervals. (It is for this reason, by the way, that I generally prefer to use the bootstrap on *trimmed means*, as opposed to *medians*.)

What have we left out?

What have we left out? Both the good news and bad news is: quite a bit. The bootstrap is a wonderful tool, but there is a lot to know about it. There are heavy tomes written on just this topic, and statisticians who devote their whole careers on studying it. Even I, for example, spend a non-trivial amount of time doing original research on this technique.

The content of this chapter, I hope, serves as a substantial introduction to the method, and that the example applications we have seen are immediately usable by you, dear reader, in your research. I would, however, be doing you an injustice if I:

- Didn't encourage you to seek out more information on this topic
- Didn't mention some of the subjects we had to leave out of this chapter for brevity

The first of the subjects heretofore unmentioned are that there are quite a few variations of the bootstrap. For example, the method of resampling of the sample we used here is not the only method we could have used. Technically speaking, the approach we took to resampling is called **Monte Carlo case resampling**. In another approach, called the *smooth bootstrap*, conceptually-speaking, samples are drawn not from the sample we have, but from a kernel-density estimation of the probability distribution that gave rise to the data. This has the attractive quality of circumventing the perils of the big assumption of the bootstrap that we explained in the last section. Of course, this approach is not without it's own assumptions and drawbacks as well.

In another approach, called the *parametric bootstrap*, a parametric model of the data is built and the resamples are sampled from this distribution. This, of course, is *not* a non-parametric application of the bootstrap.

Other approaches to the bootstrap include the *block bootstrap*, the *wild bootstrap*, and even the *Bayesian bootstrap*.

The final thing that we didn't cover here is that there are other resampling methods besides the bootstrap. One such other method is *the jackknife,* which can be thought of as an approximation of the bootstrap. Another method, called *permutation tests*, is generally considered to be superior to the bootstrap for hypothesis testing. Intrigued readers – and non-intrigued readers, too, I guess – are strongly encouraged to read up on this tool.

Exercises

- One of the great things about the bootstrap is how conceptually simple and flexible the procedure is. This makes it very easy to do our own research on it. In this exercise, we will be doing simulations of simulations. Specifically, to see for ourselves the deterioration of the reliability of bootstrap results as sample sizes get smaller, make samples of a normal distribution of a fixed mean, 30 or 50 times, with sample sizes of 100 to 5, going down by 5 each time. For each of these 30 to 50 times, perform the bootstrap procedure (with a sensible number of replications), and find out which proportion of the time the BCa confidence interval contains the mean we chose. Is it 95%, like we would expect? Repeat the procedure with other types of distributions. Does the reliability of the results differ?

- Learn about the other approaches to the bootstrap that we mentioned in the last section. How does the smooth bootstrap solve the problem of the assumption of the non-existence of data points not in our sample that the traditional bootstrap posits? On the other hand, how does it annul one of the key advantages of the Monte Carlo non-parametric bootstrap method?

- Let's turn our attention to the philosophy of art. Marcel Duchamp's *Fountain* was revolutionary in the art world for positing that context, rather than content, determines what is and isn't art. The rest of this exercise is intentionally left blank.

Summary

To review, in this chapter we explored another powerful method for interval estimation and, to a certain extent, hypothesis testing. First, we put this technique in context to be appealing to the similarity with the resampling simulations we performed in earlier chapters. We learned that the bootstrap is a lot like building sampling distributions from population data, but by sampling with replacement from our sample data instead.

We saw examples of the results from the bootstrap procedure, and noted that it is often congruent with results from parametric interval estimation techniques. In spite of this, we learned about what makes the bootstrap different from other alternatives, what makes it special, and an honest look at some of its drawbacks.

After performing the bootstrap manually, to get a thorough handle on how the procedure works, we learned how to perform it in a more elegant and extensible fashion using the `boot` package. We saw that the objects returned from the `boot` function can give us access to improved interval estimates that correct for bias. We also saw the flexibility of this function by swapping out the function for computing our previous statistic of interest (mean) for the median and trimmed mean. We noted that this was one of the main benefits of this procedure.

Finally, as we do often, we busted some common myths about the bootstrap, so we can make the most informed decision we can for which interval estimation technique is most suitable for our own problems at hand.

This concludes the chapter on confirmatory data analysis and inferential statistics. In the next chapter, we will be concerned less with estimating parameters, and more interested in prediction. Last one, there is a rotten egg!

9
Predicting Continuous Variables

Now that we've fully covered introductory inferential statistics, we're now going to shift our attention to one of the most exciting and practically useful topics in data analysis: *predictive analytics*. Throughout this chapter, we are going to introduce concepts and terminology from a closely related field called **statistical learning** or, as it's more commonly referred to, **machine learning**.

Whereas in the last unit we were using data to make inferences about the world, this unit is primarily about using data to make inferences (or predictions) about other data. On the surface, this might not sound more appealing, but consider the fruits of this area of study: if you've ever received a call from your credit card company asking to confirm a suspicious purchase that you, in fact, did not make, it's because sophisticated algorithms *learned* your purchasing behavior and were able to detect deviation from that pattern.

Since this is the first chapter leaving inferential statistics and delving into predictive analytics, it's only natural that we would start with a technique that is used for both ends: **linear regression**.

At the surface level, linear regression is a method that is used both to predict the values that continuous variables take on, and to make inferences about how certain variables are related to a continuous variable. These two procedures, prediction and inference, rely on the information from *statistical models* as their foundation. Statistical models are idealized representations of a theory meant to illustrate and explain a process that generates data. A model is usually an equation, or series of equations, with some number of parameters.

Throughout this chapter, remember the quote (generally attributed to) George Box:

All models are wrong but some are useful.

A model airplane or car might not be the real thing, but it can help us learn and understand some pretty powerful properties of the object that is being modeled.

Although linear regression is, at a high level, conceptually quite simple, it is absolutely indispensable for modern applied statistics, and a thorough understanding of linear models will pay enormous dividends throughout your career as an analyst.

Linear models

A small baking outfit in upstate New York called *No Scone Unturned* keeps careful records of the baked goods it produces. The left panel of *Figure 9.1* is a scatterplot of diameters and circumferences (in centimeters) of No Scone Unturned's cookies, and depicts their relationship:

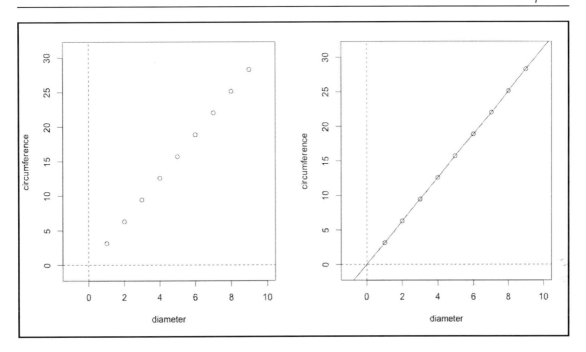

Figure 9.1: A scatterplot of diameters and circumferences of No Scone Unturned's cookies (left); the same plot with a best fit regression line plotted over the data points (right)

A straight line is the perfect thing to represent this data. After fitting a straight line to the data, we can make predictions about the circumferences of cookies that we haven't observed, such as 11 or 0.7 (if you weren't playing truant in grade school, you'd know there's a consistent and predictable relationship between the diameter of a circle and the circle's circumference, namely π, but we'll ignore that for now).

You may have learned that the equation that describes a line in a Cartesian plane is:

$$y = mx + b$$

b is the y-intercept (the place where the line intersects with the vertical line at $x=0$), and m is the slope (describing the direction and steepness of the line).
In linear regression, the equation describing y as a function of x is written as:

$$y = b_0 + b_1 x$$

b_0 (sometimes β_0) is the y-intercept, and $b1$(sometimes β_1) is the slope. Collectively, the b's are known as the *beta coefficients*.

The equation of the line that best describes this data is:

$$y = 0 + 3.1415x$$

b_0 and b_1 are 0 and π respectively.

Knowing this, it is easy to predict the circumferences of cookies that we haven't measured yet. The circumference of the cookie with a diameter of 11 centimeters is 0 + 3.1415(11) or 34.558, and a cookie of 0.7 centimeters is 0 + 3.1415(0.7) or 2.2.

In predictive analytics's parlance, the variable that we are trying to predict is called the *dependent* (or, sometimes, *target*) variable, because its values are dependent on other variables. The variables that we use to predict the dependent variable are called *independent* (or, sometimes, *predictor*) variables.

Before moving onto a less silly example, it is important to understand the proper interpretation of the slope: it describes how much the dependent variable increases (or decreases) for each unit increase of the independent variable. In this case, for every centimeter increase in a cookie's diameter, the circumference increases by π centimeters. In contrast, a negative indicates that as the independent variable increases, the dependent variable *decreases*.

Simple linear regression

Onto a substantially less trivial example; let's say No Scone Unturned has been keeping careful records of how many raisins (in grams) they have been using for their famous oatmeal raisin cookies. They want to construct a linear model describing the relationship between the area of a cookie (in centimeters squared) and how many raisins they use, on average.

In particular, they want to use linear regression to predict how many grams of raisins they will need for a 1-meter long oatmeal raisin cookie. Predicting a continuous variable (grams of raisins) from other variables sounds like a job for regression! In particular, when we use just a single predictor variable (the area of the cookies), the technique is called *simple linear regression*.

The left panel of *Figure 9.2* illustrates the relationship between the area of cookies and the amount of raisins it used. It also shows the best-fit regression line:

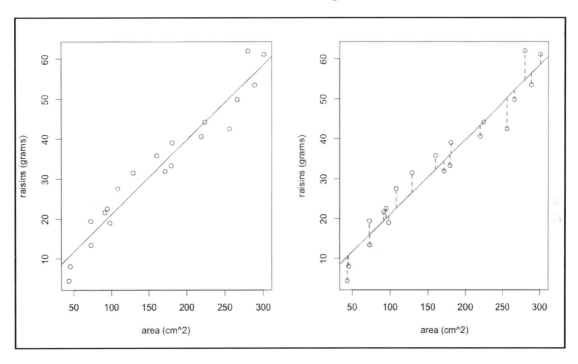

Figure 9.2: A scatterplot of areas and grams of raisins in No Scone Unturned's cookies with a best-fit regression line(left); the same plot with highlighted residuals (right)

Note that, in contrast to the last example, virtually none of the data points actually rest *on* the best-fit line; there are now errors. This is because there is a random component to how many raisins are used.

The right panel of *Figure 9.2* draws dashed red lines between each data point and what the best-fit line would predict is the amount of raisins necessary. These dashed lines represent the error in the prediction, and these errors are called **residuals**.

So far, we haven't discussed *how* the best-fit line is determined. In essence, the line of the best fit will minimize the amount of *dashed line*. More specifically, the residuals are squared and added up—this is called the **Residual Sum of Squares** (**RSS**). The line that is the best fit will minimize the RSS. This method is called *ordinary least squares*, or OLS.

Look at the two plots in *Figure 9.3*. Notice how the regression lines are drawn in ways that clearly do not minimize the amount of *red line*. The RSS can be further minimized by increasing the slope in the first plot, and decreasing it in the second plot:

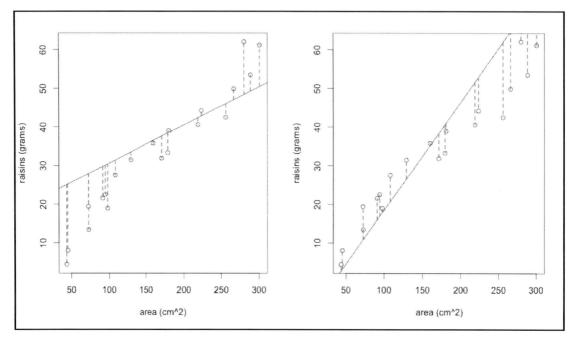

Figure 9.3: Two regression lines that do not minimize the RSS

Now that there are differences between the observed values and the predicted values—as there will be in every real-life linear regression you perform—the equation that describes y, the dependent variable, changes slightly:

$$y = b_0 + b_1 x + \varepsilon$$

The equation without the residual term only describes our prediction, $\hat{y}$, pronounced *y hat* (because it looks like is wearing a little hat):

$$\hat{y} = b_0 + b_1 x$$

Our error term is, therefore, the difference between the value that our model predicts and the actual empirical value for each observation i:

$$\varepsilon_i = y_i - \hat{y}_i$$

Formally, the RSS is:

$$RSS = \sum_{i=1}^{n} \varepsilon_i^2 = \sum_{i=1}^{n} \left(y_i - \hat{y}_i \right)^2$$

Recall that this is the term that gets minimized when finding the best-fit line.

If the RSS is the sum of the squared residuals (or error terms), the mean of the squared residuals is known as the **Mean Squared Error** (**MSE**), and is a very important measure of the accuracy of a model.

Formally, the MSE is:

$$MSE = \frac{1}{n} \sum_{i=1}^{n} \varepsilon_i^2$$

Occasionally, you will encounter the **Root Mean Squared Error** (**RMSE**) as a measure of model fit. This is just the square root of the MSE, put in the same units as the dependent variable (instead of the units of the dependent variable squared). The difference between the MSE and RMSE is like the difference between variance and standard deviation, respectively. In fact, in both these cases (the MSE/RMSE and variance/standard-deviation), the error terms have to be squared for the very same reason; if they were not, the positive and negative residuals would cancel each other out.

Now that we have a bit of the requisite math, we're ready to perform a simple linear regression ourselves, and to interpret the output. We will be using the venerable `mtcars` dataset, and will try to predict a car's gas mileage (`mpg`) with the car's weight (`wt`). We will also be using R's base graphics system (not `ggplot2`) in this section, because the visualization of linear models is arguably simpler in base R.

First, let's plot the cars' gas mileage as a function of their weights:

```
plot(mpg ~ wt, data=mtcars)
```

Here we employ the *formula* syntax that we were first introduced to in Chapter 3, *Describing Relationships* and that we used extensively in Chapter 6, *Testing Hypotheses*. We will be using it heavily in this chapter as well. As a refresher, mph ~ wt roughly reads mpg as a function of wt.

Next, let's run a simple linear regression with the lm function, and save it to a variable called model:

```
model <- lm(mpg ~ wt, data=mtcars)
```

Now that we have the model saved, we can, very simply, add a plot of the linear model to the scatterplot we have already created:

```
abline(model)
```

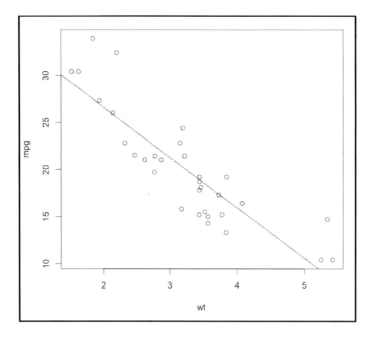

Figure 9.4: The result of plotting output from lm

Finally, let's view the result of fitting the linear model using the `summary` function, and interpret the output:

```
summary(model)
Call:
lm(formula = mpg ~ wt, data = mtcars)
Residuals:
    Min      1Q  Median      3Q     Max
-4.5432 -2.3647 -0.1252  1.4096  6.8727
Coefficients:
            Estimate Std. Error t value Pr(>|t|)
(Intercept)  37.2851     1.8776  19.858  < 2e-16 ***
wt           -5.3445     0.5591  -9.559 1.29e-10 ***
---
Signif. codes:  0 '***' 0.001 '**' 0.01 '*' 0.05 '.' 0.1 ' ' 1
Residual standard error: 3.046 on 30 degrees of freedom
Multiple R-squared:  0.7528,  Adjusted R-squared:  0.7446
F-statistic: 91.38 on 1 and 30 DF,  p-value: 1.294e-10
```

The first block of text reminds us how the model was built syntax-wise (which can actually be useful in situations where the `lm` call is performed dynamically).

Next, we see a five-number summary of the residuals. Remember that this is in units of the dependent variable. In other words, the data point with the highest residual is 6.87 miles per gallon.

In the next block, labeled `Coefficients`, direct your attention to the two values in the `Estimate` column; these are the beta coefficients that minimize the RSS. Specifically, b_0=37.285 and $b1$=-5.345. The equation that describes the best-fit linear model, then, is:

$$y = 37.285 + (-5.345)x$$

Remember, the way to interpret the b_1 coefficient is that for every unit increase of the independent variable (it's in units of 1,000 pounds), the dependent variable goes *down* (because it's negative) 5.345 units (which are miles per gallon). The b_0 coefficient indicates, rather nonsensically, that a car that weighs nothing would have a gas mileage of 37.285 miles per gallon. Recall that all models are wrong, but some are useful.

If we wanted to predict the gas mileage of a car that weighed 6,000 pounds, our equation would yield an estimate of 5.125 miles per gallon. Instead of doing the math by hand, we can use the `predict` function as long as we supply it with a data frame that holds the relevant information for new observations that we want to predict:

```
predict(model, newdata=data.frame(wt=6))
       1
5.218297
```

Interestingly, we would predict a car that weighs 7,000 pounds would get -0.126 miles per gallon. Again, all models are wrong, but some are useful. For most reasonable car weights, our very simple model yields reasonable predictions.

If we were only interested in prediction—and only interested in this particular model—we would stop here. But, as I mentioned in this chapter's preface, linear regression is also a tool for inference, and a pretty powerful one at that. In fact, we will soon see that many of the statistical tests we were introduced to in Chapter 6, *Testing Hypotheses*, can be equivalently expressed and performed as a linear model.

When viewing linear regression as a tool of inference, it's important to remember that our coefficients are actually just *estimates*. The cars observed in `mtcars` represent just a small sample of all extant cars. If somehow we observed all cars and built a linear model, the beta coefficients would be *population coefficients*. The coefficients that we asked R to calculate are best guesses based on our sample, and, just like our other estimates in previous chapters, they can undershoot or overshoot the population coefficients. Their accuracy is a function of factors such as the sample size, the representativeness of our sample, and the inherent volatility or noisiness of the system we are trying to model.

As estimates, we can quantify our uncertainty in our beta coefficients using *standard error*, as introduced in Chapter 5, *Using Data to Reason about the World*. The column of values directly to the right of the `Estimate` column, labeled `Std. Error`, gives us these measures. The estimates of the beta coefficients also have a sampling distribution and, therefore, confidence intervals could be constructed for them.

Finally, because the beta coefficients have well-defined sampling distributions (as long as certain simplifying assumptions hold true), we can perform hypothesis tests on them. The most common hypothesis test performed on beta coefficients asks whether they are significantly discrepant from zero. Semantically, if a beta coefficient is significantly discrepant from zero, it is an indication that the independent variable has a significant impact on the prediction of the dependent variable. Remember the long-running warning in Chapter 6, *Testing Hypotheses*, though: just because something is *significant* doesn't mean it is important.

The hypothesis tests compares the coefficients to zero yield p-values; those p-values are depicted in the final column of the Coefficients section, labeled Pr(>|t|). We usually don't care about the significance of the intercept coefficient (b0), so we can ignore that. Rather importantly, the p-value for the coefficient belonging to the wt variable is near zero, indicating that the weight of a car has some predictive power on the gas mileage of that car.

Getting back to the summary output, direct your attention to the entry called Multiple R-squared. R-squared—also R^2 or *coefficient of determination*—is, like MSE, a measure of how good of a fit the model is. In contrast to the MSE though, which is in the units of the dependent variable, R^2 is always between 0 and 1, and thus can be interpreted more easily. For example, if we changed the units of the dependent variable from miles per gallon to miles per liter, the MSE would change, but the R^2 would not.

An R^2 of 1 indicates a perfect fit with no residual error, and an R^2 of 0 indicates the worst possible fit—the independent variable doesn't help predict the dependent variable at all:

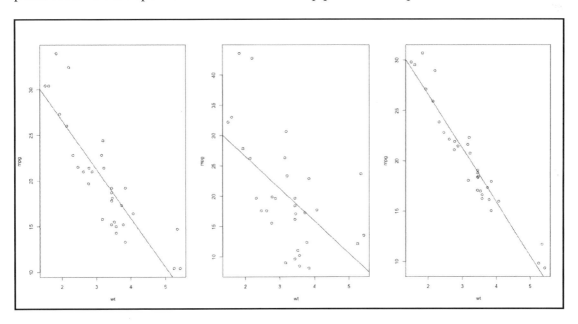

Figure 9.5: Linear models (from left to right) with s of 0.75, 0.33, and 0.92

Helpfully, the R^2 is directly interpretable as the amount of variance in the dependent variable that is explained by the independent variable. In this case, for example, the weight of a car explains about 75.3% of the variance of the gas mileage. Whether 75% constitutes a good R^2 depends heavily on the domain, but in my field (the behavioral sciences), an R^2 of 75% is really good.

We will have to come back to the rest of information in the `summary` output in the section about multiple regression.

 Take note of the fact that the p-value of the F-statistic in the last line of the output is the same as the p-value of the t-statistic of the only non-intercept coefficient.

Simple linear regression with a binary predictor

One of the coolest things about linear regression is that we are not limited to using predictor variables that are continuous. For example, in the last section, we used the continuous variable `wt` (weight) to predict miles per gallon. But linear models are adaptable to using categorical variables, such as `am` (automatic or manual transmission) as well.

Normally, in a simple linear regression equation, $\hat{y} = b_0 + b_1 x$, x will hold the actual value of the predictor variable. In the case of a simple linear regression with a binary predictor (such as `am`), x will hold a *dummy variable* instead. Specifically, when the predictor is automatic, x will be 0, and when the predictor is manual, x will be 1.

More formally:

$$\hat{y} = b_0 + b_1 0 \qquad \textit{if } x_i \textit{ is automatic}$$

$$\hat{y}_i = b_0 + b_1 1 \qquad \textit{if } x_i \textit{ is manual}$$

Put in this manner, the interpretation of the coefficients changes slightly, since the $b_1 x$ will be zero when the car is automatic; b_0 is the mean miles per gallon for automatic cars.

Similarly, since $b_1 x$ will be equal to b_1 when the car is manual, b_1 is equal to the mean difference in the gas mileage between automatic and manual cars.

Concretely:

```
model <- lm(mpg ~ am, data=mtcars)
summary(model)
Call:
lm(formula = mpg ~ am, data = mtcars)
Residuals:
    Min      1Q  Median      3Q     Max
-9.3923 -3.0923 -0.2974  3.2439  9.5077
Coefficients:
            Estimate Std. Error t value Pr(>|t|)
(Intercept)   17.147      1.125  15.247 1.13e-15 ***
am             7.245      1.764   4.106 0.000285 ***
---
Signif. codes:  0 '***' 0.001 '**' 0.01 '*' 0.05 '.' 0.1 ' ' 1
Residual standard error: 4.902 on 30 degrees of freedom
Multiple R-squared:  0.3598,  Adjusted R-squared:  0.3385
F-statistic: 16.86 on 1 and 30 DF,  p-value: 0.000285
mean(mtcars$mpg[mtcars$am==0])
[1] 17.14737
(mean(mtcars$mpg[mtcars$am==1]) -
 mean(mtcars$mpg[mtcars$am==0]))
[1] 7.244939
```

The intercept term b_0 is 7.15, which is the mean gas mileage of the automatic cars, and b_1 is 7.24, which is the difference of the means between the two groups.

The interpretation of the t-statistic and p-value are very special now; a hypothesis test checking to see if b_1 (the difference in group means) is significantly different from zero is tantamount to a hypothesis test testing the equality of means (the students t-test)! Indeed, the t-statistic and p-values are the same:

```
# use var.equal to choose Students t-test
# over Welch's t-test
t.test(mpg ~ am, data=mtcars, var.equal=TRUE)
   Two Sample t-test
data:  mpg by am
t = -4.1061, df = 30, p-value = 0.000285
alternative hypothesis: true difference in means is not equal to 0
95 percent confidence interval:
```

```
   -10.84837   -3.64151
sample estimates:
mean in group 0 mean in group 1
        17.14737        24.39231
```

Isn't that neat? A two-sample test of equality of means can be equivalently expressed as a linear model! This basic idea can be extended to handle non-binary categorical variables too—we'll look at this in the section on multiple regression.

Note that in `mtcars`, the `am` column was already coded as 1s (manuals) and 0s (automatics). If automatic cars were dummy coded as 1 and manuals were dummy coded as 0, the results would semantically be the same; the only difference being that b_0 would be the mean of manual cars, and b_1 would be the (negative) difference in means. The R^2 and p-values would be the same.

If you are working with a dataset that doesn't already have the binary predictor dummy coded, R's `lm` can handle this too, so long as you wrap the column in a call to `factor`. Consider the following code, for example:

```
mtcars$automatic <- ifelse(mtcars$am==0, "yes", "no")
model <- lm(mpg ~ factor(automatic), data=mtcars)
model
Call:
lm(formula = mpg ~ factor(automatic), data = mtcars)
Coefficients:
          (Intercept)   factor(automatic)yes
               24.392                 -7.245
```

Finally, note that a car being automatic or manual explains some of the variance in gas mileage, but far less than weight did; this model's R^2 is only 0.36.

A word of warning

Before we move on, a word of warning: the first part of every regression analysis should be to plot the relevant data. To convince you of this, consider Anscombe's quartet depicted in the following figure:

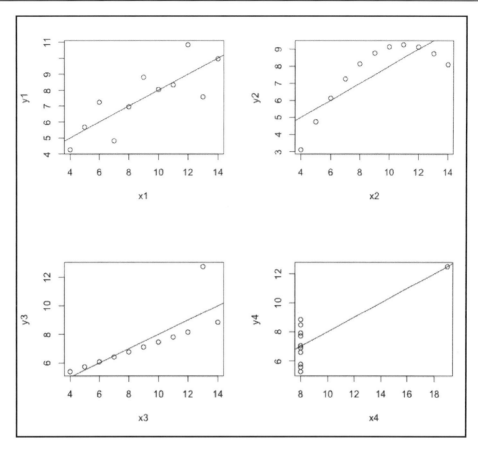

Figure 9.6: Four datasets with identical means, standard deviations, regression coefficients, and R^2

Anscombe's quartet holds four x-y pairs that have the same mean, standard deviation, correlation coefficients, linear regression coefficients, and R^2s. In spite of these similarities, all four of these data pairs are very different. It is a warning to not blindly apply statistics on data that you haven't visualized. It is also a warning to take linear regression diagnostics (which we will go over before the chapter's end) seriously.

Only two of the x-y pairs in Anscombe's quartet can be modeled with *simple* linear regression: the ones in the left column. Of particular interest is the one on the bottom left; it looks like it contains an outlier. After thorough investigation into why that datum made it into our dataset, if we decide we really should discard it, we can either (a) remove the offending row, or (b) use robust linear regression.

For a more or less drop-in replacement for `lm` that uses a robust version of OLS called **Iteratively Re-Weighted Least Squares (IWLS)**, you can use the `rlm` function from the `MASS` package, as shown in the following code:

```
library(MASS)
data(anscombe)
plot(y3 ~ x3, data=anscombe)
abline(lm(y3 ~ x3, data=anscombe),
       col="blue", lty=2, lwd=2)
abline(rlm(y3 ~ x3, data=anscombe),
       col="red", lty=1, lwd=2)
```

The following code shows the output plot like so:

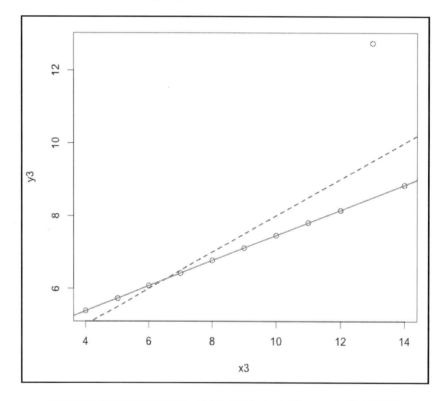

Figure 9.7: The difference between a linear regression fit with OLS and a robust linear regression fitted with IWLS

OK, one more warning. Some suggest that you should almost always use `rlm` in favor of `lm`. It's true that `rlm` is the bee's knees, but there is a subtle danger in doing this, as illustrated by the following statistical urban legend.

Some time in 1984, NASA was studying ozone concentrations from various locations. NASA used robust statistical methods that automatically discarded anomalous data points, believing most of them to be instrument errors or errors in transmission. As a result of this, some extremely low ozone readings in the atmosphere above Antarctica were removed from NASA's atmospheric models. The very next year, British scientists published a paper describing a very deteriorated ozone layer in the Antarctic. Had NASA paid closer attention to outliers, they would have been the first to discover it.

It turns out that the relevant part of this story is a myth, but the fact that it is so widely believed is a testament to how possible it is.

The point is, *outliers* should always be investigated and not simply ignored, because they may be indicative of poor model choice, faulty instrumentation, or a gigantic hole in the ozone layer. Once the outliers are accounted for, then use robust methods to your heart's content.

Multiple regression

More often than not, we want to include not just one, but *multiple* predictors (independent variables) in our predictive models. Luckily, linear regression can easily accommodate us! The technique? Multiple regression.

By giving each predictor its very own beta coefficient in a linear model, the target variable gets informed by a weighted sum of its predictors. For example, a multiple regression using two predictor variables looks like this:

$$\hat{Y} = b_0 + b_1 X_1 + b_2 X_2$$

Now, instead of estimating two coefficients (b_0 and b_1), we are estimating three: the intercept, the slope of the first predictor, and the slope of the second predictor.

Before explaining further, let's perform a multiple regression predicting gas mileage from weight and horsepower, using the following code:

```
model <- lm(mpg ~ wt + hp, data=mtcars)
summary(model)
Call:
```

```
lm(formula = mpg ~ wt + hp, data = mtcars)
Residuals:
   Min      1Q Median     3Q    Max
-3.941 -1.600 -0.182  1.050  5.854
Coefficients:
             Estimate Std. Error t value Pr(>|t|)
(Intercept) 37.22727    1.59879  23.285  < 2e-16 ***
wt          -3.87783    0.63273  -6.129 1.12e-06 ***
hp          -0.03177    0.00903  -3.519  0.00145 **
---
Signif. codes:  0 '***' 0.001 '**' 0.01 '*' 0.05 '.' 0.1 ' ' 1
Residual standard error: 2.593 on 29 degrees of freedom
Multiple R-squared:  0.8268,  Adjusted R-squared:  0.8148
F-statistic: 69.21 on 2 and 29 DF,  p-value: 9.109e-12
```

Since we are now dealing with three variables, the predictive model can no longer be visualized with a line; it must be visualized as a plane in 3D space, as seen in the following figure:

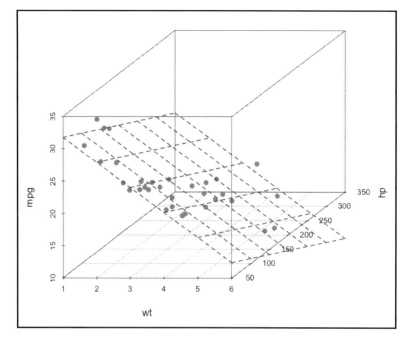

Figure 9.8: The prediction region that is formed by a two-predictor linear model is a plane

Aided by the visualization, we can see that both our predictions of mpg are informed by both wt and hp. Both of them contribute negatively to the gas mileage. You can see this from the fact that the coefficients are both negative. Visually, we can verify this by noting that the plane slopes downward as wt increases and as hp increases, although the slope for the later predictor is less dramatic.

Although we lose the ability to easily visualize it, the prediction region formed by a more-than-two predictor linear model is called a **hyperplane**, and exists in n-dimensional space where n is the number of predictor variables plus 1.

The astute reader may have noticed that the beta coefficient belonging to the wt variable is not the same as it was in the simple linear regression. The beta coefficient for hp, too, is different than the one estimated using simple regression, as shown in the following code:

```
coef(lm(mpg ~ wt + hp, data=mtcars))
(Intercept)              wt               hp
37.22727012 -3.87783074 -0.03177295
coef(lm(mpg ~ wt, data=mtcars))
(Intercept)              wt
37.285126    -5.344472
coef(lm(mpg ~ hp, data=mtcars))
(Intercept)              hp
30.09886054 -0.06822828
```

The explanation has to do with a subtle difference in how the coefficients should be interpreted now that there is more than one independent variable. The proper interpretation of the coefficient belonging to wt is not that as the weight of the car increases by 1 unit (1,000 pounds), the miles per gallon, on average, decreases by -3.878 miles per gallon. Instead, the proper interpretation is *holding horsepower constant,* as the weight of the car increases by 1 unit (1,000 pounds), the miles per gallon, on average, decreases by -3.878 miles per gallon.

Similarly, the correct interpretation of the coefficient belonging to wt is *holding the weight of the car constant*; as the horsepower of the car increases by 1, the miles per gallon, on average, decreases by -0.032 miles per gallon. Still confused?

It turns out that cars with more horsepower use more gas. It is *also* true that cars with higher horsepower tend to be heavier. When we put these predictors (weight and horsepower) into a linear model together, the model attempts to tease apart the independent contributions of each of the variables by removing the effects of the other. In multivariate analysis, this is known as *controlling* for a variable. Hence, the preface to the interpretation can be, equivalently, stated as *controlling for the effects of the weight of a car, as the horsepower...* Because cars with higher horsepower tend to be heavier, when you remove the effect of horsepower, the influence of weight goes down, and vice versa. This is why the coefficients for these predictors are both smaller than they are in simple single-predictor regression.

In controlled experiments, scientists introduce an experimental condition on two samples that are virtually the same except for the independent variable being manipulated (for example, giving one group a placebo and one group real medication). If they are careful, they can attribute any observed effect *directly* on the manipulated independent variable. In simple cases like this, statistical control is often unnecessary. But statistical control is of utmost importance in the other areas of science (especially the behavioral and social sciences) and business, where we are privy only to data from non-controlled natural phenomena.

For example, suppose someone made the claim that gum chewing causes heart disease. To back up this claim, they appealed to data showing that the more someone chews gum, the higher the probability of developing heart disease. The astute skeptic could claim that it's not the gum chewing *per se* that is causing the heart disease, but the fact that smokers tend to chew gum more often than non-smokers to mask the gross smell of tobacco smoke. If the person who made the original claim went back to the data, and included the number of cigarettes smoked per day as a component of a regression analysis, there would be a coefficient representing the *independent* influence of gum chewing, and ostensibly, the statistical test of that coefficient's difference from zero would fail to reject the null hypothesis.

In this situation, the number of cigarettes smoked per day is called a *confounding variable*. The purpose of a carefully designed scientific experiment is to eliminate confounds, but as mentioned earlier, this is often not a luxury available in certain circumstances and domains.

For example, we are so sure that cigarette smoking causes heart disease that it would be unethical to design a controlled experiment in which we take two random samples of people, and ask one group to smoke and one group to just pretend to smoke. Sadly, cigarette companies know this, and they can plausibly claim that it isn't cigarette smoking that causes heart disease, but rather that the kind of people who eventually become cigarette smokers also engage in behaviors that increase the risk of heart disease—such as eating red meat and not exercising—and that it's *those* variables that are making it appear as if smoking is associated with heart disease. Since we can't control for every potential confound that the cigarette companies can dream up, we may never be able to thwart this claim.

Anyhow, back to our two-predictor example: examine the R^2 value, and how it is different now that we've included horsepower as an additional predictor. Our model now explains more of the variance in gas mileage. As a result, our predictions will, on average, be more accurate.

Let's predict what the gas mileage of a 2,500 pound car with a horsepower of 275 (horses?) might be, with the help of the following code:

```
predict(model, newdata = data.frame(wt=2.5, hp=275))
       1
18.79513
```

Finally, we can explain the last line of the linear model summary: the one with the F-statistic and associated p-value. The F-statistic measures the ability of the entire model, as a whole, to explain any variance in the dependent variable. Since it has a sampling distribution (the F-distribution) and associated degrees, it yields a p-value, which can be interpreted as *the probability that a model would explain this much (or more) of the variance of the dependent variable if the predictors had no predictive power*. The fact that our model has a p-value lower than 0.05 suggests that our model predicts the dependent variable better than chance.

Now we can see why the p-value for the F-statistic in the simple linear regression was the same as the p-value of the t-statistic for the only non-intercept predictor: the tests were equivalent because there was only one source of predictive capability.

We can also see now why the p-value associated with our F-statistic in the multiple regression analysis output earlier is far lower than the p-values of the t-statistics of the individual predictors: the latter only captures the predictive power of each (one) predictor, while the former captures the predictive power of the model as a whole (all two).

Regression with a non-binary predictor

Back in a previous section, I promised that the same dummy-coding method that we used to regress binary categorical variables could be adapted to handle categorical variables with more than two values. For an example of this, we are going to use the same `WeightLoss` dataset as we did to illustrate ANOVA.

To review, the `WeightLoss` dataset contains pounds lost and self-esteem measurements for three weeks for three different groups: a control group, one group just on a diet, and one group that dieted and exercised. We will be trying to predict the amount of weight lost in week two by the group the participant was in.

Instead of just having one dummy-coded predictor, we now need two. Specifically:

$$X_{1_j} = 1 \text{ if participant i is in the diet only group}$$
$$X_{1_j} = 0 \qquad\qquad otherwise$$
$$and$$
$$X_{2_j} = 1 \text{ if participant i is in the diet and exercise group}$$
$$X_{2_j} = 0 \qquad\qquad otherwise$$

Consequently, the equations describing our predictive model are:

$$\hat{y}_i = b_0 + b_1 0 + b_2 0 = b_0 \qquad \text{if } x_i \text{ is control}$$
$$\hat{y}_i = b_0 + b_1 1 + b_2 0 = b_0 + b_1 \qquad \text{if } x_i \text{ is diet only}$$
$$\hat{y}_i = b_0 + b_1 0 + b_2 1 = b_0 + b_2 \qquad \text{if } x_i \text{ is diet and exercise}$$

This means that b_0 is the mean of weight lost in the control group, $b1$ is the difference in the weight lost between the control and diet only group, and $b2$ is the difference in the weight lost between the control, the diet, and the exercise group:

```
# the dataset is in the car package
library(car)
model <- lm(wl2 ~ factor(group), data=WeightLoss)
summary(model)
Call:
lm(formula = wl2 ~ factor(group), data = WeightLoss)
Residuals:
    Min      1Q Median     3Q     Max
 -2.100  -1.054  -0.100  0.900   2.900
Coefficients:
                    Estimate Std. Error t value Pr(>|t|)
(Intercept)           3.3333     0.3756   8.874 5.12e-10 ***
```

```
factor(group)Diet      0.5833     0.5312   1.098    0.281
factor(group)DietEx    2.7667     0.5571   4.966 2.37e-05 ***
---
Signif. codes:  0 '***' 0.001 '**' 0.01 '*' 0.05 '.' 0.1 ' ' 1
Residual standard error: 1.301 on 31 degrees of freedom
Multiple R-squared:  0.4632,   Adjusted R-squared:  0.4285
F-statistic: 13.37 on 2 and 31 DF,  p-value: 6.494e-05
```

As before, the p-values associated with the t-statistics are directly interpretable as a t-test of equality of means with the weight lost by the control. Observe that the p-value associated with the t-statistic of the `factor(group)Diet` coefficient is not significant. This comports with the results from the pairwise-t-test from Chapter 6, *Testing Hypotheses*.

Most magnificently, compare the F-statistic and the associated p-value in the preceding code with the one in the aov ANOVA from Chapter 6, *Testing Hypotheses*. They are the same! The F-test of a linear model with a non-binary categorical variable predictor is the same as an NHST analysis of variance!

Kitchen sink regression

When the goal of using regression is simply *predictive* modeling, we often don't care about which *particular* predictors go into our model, so long as the final model yields the best possible predictions.

A naïve (and awful) approach is to use all the independent variables available to try to model the dependent variable. Let's try this approach by trying to predict mpg from every other variable in the mtcars dataset, using the following code:

```
# the period after the squiggly denotes all other variables
model <- lm(mpg ~ ., data=mtcars)
summary(model)
Call:
lm(formula = mpg ~ ., data = mtcars)
Residuals:
    Min      1Q  Median      3Q     Max
-3.4506 -1.6044 -0.1196  1.2193  4.6271

Coefficients:
            Estimate Std. Error t value Pr(>|t|)
(Intercept) 12.30337   18.71788   0.657   0.5181
cyl         -0.11144    1.04502  -0.107   0.9161
disp         0.01334    0.01786   0.747   0.4635
```

```
hp          -0.02148    0.02177   -0.987    0.3350
drat         0.78711    1.63537    0.481    0.6353
wt          -3.71530    1.89441   -1.961    0.0633 .
qsec         0.82104    0.73084    1.123    0.2739
vs           0.31776    2.10451    0.151    0.8814
am           2.52023    2.05665    1.225    0.2340
gear         0.65541    1.49326    0.439    0.6652
carb        -0.19942    0.82875   -0.241    0.8122
---
Signif. codes:  0 '***' 0.001 '**' 0.01 '*' 0.05 '.' 0.1 ' ' 1

Residual standard error: 2.65 on 21 degrees of freedom
Multiple R-squared:  0.869,     Adjusted R-squared:  0.8066
F-statistic: 13.93 on 10 and 21 DF,  p-value: 3.793e-07
```

Hey, check out our R-squared value! It looks like our model explains 87% of the variance in the dependent variable. This is really good—it's certainly better than our simple regression models that used weight (wt) and transmission (am) with the respective R-squared values, 0.753 and 0.36.

Maybe there's something to just including everything we have in our linear models. In fact, if our only goal is to maximize our R-squared, you can always achieve this by throwing every variable you have into the mix, since the introduction of each marginal variable can only increase the amount of variance explained. Even if a newly introduced variable has absolutely no predictive power, the worst it can do is not help to explain any variance in the dependent variable—it can never make the model explain less variance.

This approach to regression analysis is often (non-affectionately) called *kitchen sink* regression, and is akin to throwing all of your variables against a wall to *see what sticks*. If you have a hunch that this approach to predictive modeling is crummy, your instinct is correct on this one.

To develop your intuition about why this approach backfires, consider building a linear model to predict a variable of only 32 observations using 200 explanatory variables, which are uniformly and randomly distributed. Just by random chance, there will very likely be some variables that correlate strongly to the dependent variable. A linear regression that includes some of these *lucky* variables will yield a model that is surprisingly (sometimes astoundingly) predictive.

Remember that when we are creating predictive models, we rarely (if ever) care about how well we can predict the data we already have. The whole point of predictive analytics is to be able to predict the behavior of data we don't have. For example, memorizing the answer key to last year's Social Studies final won't help you on this year's final, if the questions are changed—it'll only prove you can get an A+ on last year's test.

Imagine generating a new random dataset of 200 explanatory variables and one dependent variable, using the coefficients from the linear model of the first random dataset. How well do you think the model will perform?

The model will, of course, perform very poorly, because the coefficients in the model were informed solely by random noise. The model captured chance patterns in the data that it was built with and not a larger, more general pattern—mostly because there was no larger pattern to model!

In statistical learning parlance, this phenomenon is called *overfitting*, and it happens often when there are many predictors in a model. It is particularly frequent when the number of observations is less than (or not very much larger than) the number of predictor variables (like in mtcars), because there is a greater probability for the many predictors to have a spurious relationship with the dependent variable.

This general occurrence—a model performing well on the data it was built with but poorly on subsequent data—illustrates perfectly perhaps the most common complication with statistical learning and predictive analytics: the *bias-variance trade-off*.

The bias-variance trade-off

In statistical learning, the *bias* of a model refers to the error of the model introduced by attempting to model a complicated real-life relationship with an approximation. A model with no bias will never make any errors in prediction (like the cookie-area prediction problem). A model with high bias will fail to accurately predict its dependent variable.

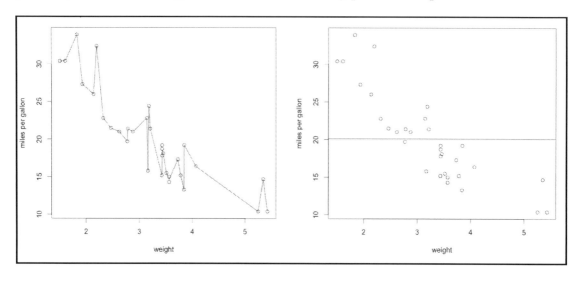

Figure 9.9: The two extremes of the bias-variance trade-off: a complicated model with essentially zero bias (on training data) but enormous variance (left), a simple model with high bias but virtually no variance (right)

The *variance* of a model refers to how sensitive a model is to changes in the data that built the model. A model with low variance would change very little when built with new data. A linear model with high variance is very sensitive to changes to the data that it was built with, and the estimated coefficients will be *unstable*.

The term bias-variance trade-off illustrates that it is easy to decrease bias at the expense of increasing variance, and vice versa. Good models will try to minimize both.

The *Figure 9.9* depicts two extremes of the bias-variance trade-off. The leftmost model depicts a complicated and highly convoluted model that passes through all the data points. This model has essentially no bias, as it has no error when predicting the data that it was built with. However, the model is clearly picking up on random noise in the dataset, and if the model were used to predict new data, there would be significant error. If the same general model were rebuilt with new data, the model would change significantly (high variance).

As a result, the model is not generalizable to new data. Models like this suffer from *overfitting*, which often occurs when overly complicated or overly flexible models are fited to data—especially when sample size is lacking.

In contrast, the model on the right panel of *Figure 9.9* is a simple model (the simplest, actually). It is just a horizontal line at the mean of the dependent variable, mpg. This does a pretty terrible job modeling the variance in the dependent variable, and exhibits high bias. This model does have one attractive property though—the model will barely change at all if fit to new data; the horizontal line will just move up or down slightly based on the mean of the mpg column of the new data.

To demonstrate that our kitchen sink regression puts us on the wrong side of the optimal point in the bias-variance trade-off, we will use a model validation and assessment technique called *cross-validation*.

Cross-validation

Given that the goal of predictive analytics is to build generalizable models that predict well for data yet unobserved, we should ideally be testing our models on data unseen, and check our predictions against the observed outcomes. The problem with that, of course, is that we don't know the outcomes of data unseen—that's why we want a predictive model. We do, however, have a trick up our sleeve, called the *validation set* approach.

The validation set approach is a technique to evaluate a model's ability to perform well on an independent dataset. But instead of waiting to get our hands on a completely new dataset, we simulate a new dataset with the one we already have.

The main idea is that we can split our dataset into two subsets; one of these subsets (called the *training set*) is used to fit our model, and then the other (the testing set) is used to test the accuracy of that model. Since the model was built before ever touching the testing set, the testing set serves as an independent data source of prediction accuracy estimates, unbiased by the model's precision attributable to its modeling of idiosyncratic noise.

To get at our predictive accuracy by performing our own validation set, let's use the sample function to divide the row indices of mtcars into two equal groups, create the subsets, and train a model on the training set:

```
set.seed(1)
train.indices <- sample(1:nrow(mtcars), nrow(mtcars)/2)
training <- mtcars[train.indices,]
testing <- mtcars[-train.indices,]
model <- lm(mpg ~ ., data=training)
```

```
summary(model)
..... (output truncated)
Residual standard error: 1.188 on 5 degrees of freedom
Multiple R-squared:  0.988,  Adjusted R-squared:  0.9639
F-statistic: 41.06 on 10 and 5 DF,  p-value: 0.0003599
```

Before we go on, note that the model now explains a whopping 99% of the variance in mpg. Any this high should be a red flag; I've never seen a legitimate model with an R-squared this high on a non-contrived dataset. The increase in R^2 is attributable primarily due to the decrease in observations (from 32 to 16) and the resultant increased opportunity to model spurious correlations.

Let's calculate the MSE of the model on the training dataset. To do this, we will be using the predict function without the newdata argument, which tells us the model it would predict on given the training data (these are referred to as the *fitted values*), as shown in the following code:

```
mean((predict(model) - training$mpg) ^ 2)
[1] 0.4408109
```

```
# Cool, but how does it perform on the validation set?
mean((predict(model, newdata=testing) - testing$mpg) ^ 2)
[1] 337.9995
```

My word!

In practice, the error on the training data is almost always a little less than the error on the testing data. However, a discrepancy in the MSE between the training and testing set as large as this is a clear-as-day indication that our model doesn't generalize.

Let's compare this model's validation set performance to a simpler model with a lower R^2 which only uses am and wt as predictors:

```
simpler.model <- lm(mpg ~ am + wt, data=training)
mean((predict(simpler.model) - training$mpg) ^ 2)
[1] 9.396091
mean((predict(simpler.model, newdata=testing) - testing$mpg) ^ 2)
[1] 12.70338
```

Notice that the MSE on the training data is much higher, but our validation set MSE is *much* lower.

If the goal is to blindly maximize the R^2, the more predictors, the better. If the goal is a generalizable and useful predictive model, the goal should be to minimize the testing set MSE.

The validation set approach outlined in the previous paragraph has two important drawbacks. For one, the model was only built using half of the available data. Secondly, we only tested the model's performance on one testing set; at the slight of a magician's hand, our testing set could have contained some bizarre hard-to-predict examples that would make the validation set MSE too large.

Consider the following change to the approach: we divide the data up, just as before, into set *a* and set *b*. Then, we train the model on set *a*, test it on set *b*, then train it on *b* and test it on *a*. This approach has a clear advantage over our previous approach, because it averages the out-of-sample MSEs of *two* testing sets. Additionally, the model will now be informed by all the data. This is called **two-fold cross validation**, and the general technique is called **k-fold cross validation**.

The coefficients of the model will, of course, be different, but the actual data model (the variables to include and how to fit the line) will be the same.

To see how *k*-fold cross validation works in a more general sense, consider the procedure to perform *k*-fold cross validation where *k*=5. First, we divide the data into five equal groups (sets *a*, *b*, *c*, *d*, and *e*), and we train the model on the data from sets *a*, *b*, *c*, and *d*. Then we record the MSE of the model against *unseen* data in set *e*. We repeat this four more times, leaving out a different set and testing the model with it. Finally, the average of our five out-of-sample MSEs is our five-fold cross validated MSE.

Your goal now should be to select a model that minimizes the *k*-fold cross validation MSE. Common choices of *k* are 5 and 10.

To perform *k*-fold cross validation, we will be using the `cv.glm` function from the `boot` package. This will also require us to build our models using the `glm` function (this stands for *generalized linear models,* which we'll learn about in the next chapter) instead of `lm`. For current purposes, it is a drop-in replacement.

```
library(boot)
bad.model <- glm(mpg ~ ., data=mtcars)
better.model <- glm(mpg ~ am + wt + qsec, data=mtcars)
bad.cv.err <- cv.glm(mtcars, bad.model, K=5)
# the cross-validated MSE estimate we will be using
# is a bias-corrected one stored as the second element
# in the 'delta' vector of the cv.err object
bad.cv.err$delta[2]
[1] 14.92426
```

```
better.cv.err <- cv.glm(mtcars, better.model, K=5)
better.cv.err$delta[2]
[1] 7.944148
```

The use of *k*-fold cross validation over the simple validation set approach has illustrated that the kitchen sink model is not as bad as we previously thought (because we trained it using more data), but it is still outperformed by the far simpler model that includes only am, wt, and qsec as predictors.

This out-performance by a simple model is no idiosyncrasy of this dataset; it is a well-observed phenomenon in predictive analytics. Simpler models often outperform overly complicated models because of the resistance of a simpler model to overfitting. Further, simpler models are easier to interpret, to understand, and to use. The idea that, given the same level of predictive power, we should prefer simpler models to complicated ones is expressed in a famous principle called *Occam's Razor*.

Finally, we have enough background information to discuss the only piece of the lm summary output we haven't touched upon yet: adjusted R-squared. Adjusted R^2 attempts to take into account the fact that extraneous variables thrown into a linear model will always increase its R^2. Adjusted R^2, therefore, takes the number of predictors into account. As such, it penalizes complex models. Adjusted R^2 will always be equal to or lower than non-adjusted R^2 (it can even be negative!). The addition of each marginal predictor will only cause an increase in adjusted if it contributes significantly to the predictive power of the model, that is, more than would be dictated by chance. If it doesn't, the adjusted R^2 will decrease. Adjusted R^2 has some great properties, and as a result, many will try to select models that maximize the adjusted R^2, but I prefer the minimization of cross-validated MSE as my main model selection criterion.

Compare for yourself the adjusted R^2 of the kitchen sink model and a model using am, wt, and qsec.

Striking a balance

As *Figure 9.10* depicts, as a model becomes more complicated/flexible—as it starts to include more and more predictors—the bias of the model continues to decrease. Along the complexity axis, as the model begins to fit the data better and better, the cross-validation error decreases as well. At a certain point, the model becomes overly complex, and begins to fit idiosyncratic noise in the training data set—it overfits!

The cross-validation error begins to climb again, even as the bias of the model approaches its theoretical minimum!

The very left of the plot depicts models with too much bias, but little variance. The right side of the plot depicts models that have very low bias, but very high variance, and thus are useless predictive models:

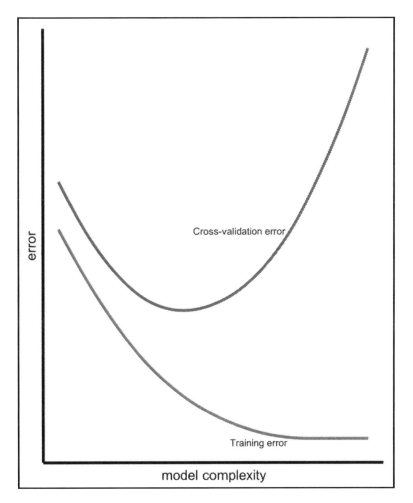

Figure 9.10: As model complexity/flexibility increases, training error (bias) tends to be reduced. Up to a certain point, the cross-validation error decreases as well. After that point, the cross-validation error starts to go up again, even as the model's bias continues to decrease. After this point, the model is too flexible and overfits

The ideal point in this bias-variance trade-off is the point where the *cross-validation error* (not the training error) is minimized.

Okay, so how do we get there?

Although there are more advanced methods that we'll touch on in the *Advanced topics* section, at this stage of the game, our primary recourse for finding our bias-variance trade-off sweet spot is *careful feature selection*. In statistical learning parlance, feature selection refers to selecting which predictor variables to include in our model (for some reason, they call predictor variables *features*).

I emphasized the word *careful* because there are plenty of dangerous ways to do this. One such method—and perhaps the most intuitive—is to simply build models containing every possible subset of the available predictors, and choose the best one as measured by adjusted R^2 or the minimization of the cross-validated error. Probably the biggest problem with this approach is that it's computationally very expensive—to build a model for every possible subset of predictors in `mtcars`, you would need to build (and cross-validate) 1,023 different models. The number of possible models rises exponentially with the number of predictors. Because of this, for many real-world modeling scenarios, this method is out of the question.

There is another approach that, for the most part, solves the problem of the computational intractability of the all-possible-subsets approach: step-wise regression.

Stepwise regression is a technique that programmatically tests different predictor combinations by adding predictors in (forward stepwise), or taking predictors out (backward stepwise) according the value that each predictor adds to the model as measured by its influence on the adjusted R^2. Therefore, like the all-possible-subsets approach, stepwise regression automates the process of feature selection.

 In case you care, the most popular implementation of this technique (the `stepAIC` function in the `MASS` package) in R doesn't maximize the adjusted R^2 but instead minimizes a related model quality measure called the **Akaike Information Criterion (AIC)**.

There are numerous problems with this approach. The *least* of these is that it is not guaranteed to find the best possible model.

One of the primary issues that people cite is that it results in lazy science by absolving us of the need to think out the problem, because we let an automated procedure make decisions for us. This school of thought usually holds that models should be informed, at least partially, by some amount of theory and domain expertise.

It is for these reasons that stepwise regression has fallen out of favor among many statisticians, and why I'm choosing not to recommend using it.

Stepwise regression is like alcohol: some people can use it without incident, but some can't use it safely. It is also like alcohol in that if you think you *need* to use it, you've got a big problem. Finally, neither can be advertised to children.

At this stage of the game, I suggest that your main approach to balancing bias and variance should be informed, theory-driven feature selection, and paying close attention to *k*-fold cross validation results. In cases where you have absolutely no theory, I suggest using *regularization*, a technique that is, unfortunately, beyond the scope of this text. The *Advanced topics* section briefly extols the virtues of regularization, if you want more information.

Linear regression diagnostics

I would be negligent if I failed to mention the boring but very critical topic of the assumptions of linear models, and how to detect violations of those assumptions. Just like the assumptions of the hypothesis tests in Chapter 6, *Testing Hypotheses*, linear regression has its own set of assumptions, the violation of which jeopardizes the accuracy of our model and any inferences derived from it to varying degrees. The checks and tests that ensure these assumptions are met are called *diagnostics*.

There are five major assumptions of linear regression:

- That the errors (residuals) are normally distributed with a mean of zero
- That the error terms are uncorrelated
- That the errors have a constant variance
- That the effect of the independent variables on the dependent variable are linear and additive
- That multi-collinearity is at a minimum

We'll briefly touch on these assumptions, and how to check for them in this section here. To do this, we will be using a residual-fitted plot, since it allows us, with some skill, to verify most of these assumptions. To view a residual-fitted plot, just call the `plot` function on your linear model object:

```
my.model <- lm(mpg ~ wt, data=mtcars)
plot(my.model)
```

This will show you a series of four diagnostic plots—the residual-fitted plot is the first. You can also opt to view just the residual-fitted plot with this related incantation:

```
plot(my.model, which=1)
```

We are also going back to Anscombe's Quartet, since the quartet's aberrant relationships collectively illustrate the problems that you might find when fitting regression models and in assumption violation. To re-familiarize yourself with the quartet, look back to *Figure 9.6*.

Second Anscombe relationship

The first relationship in Anscombe's Quartet (y1 ~ x1) is the only one that can appropriately be modeled with linear regression as is. In contrast, the second relationship (y2 ~ x2) depicts a relationship that violates the requirement of a linear relationship. It also subtly violates the assumption of normally distributed residuals with a mean of zero.

To see why, refer to *Figure 9.11*, which depicts its residual-fitted plot:

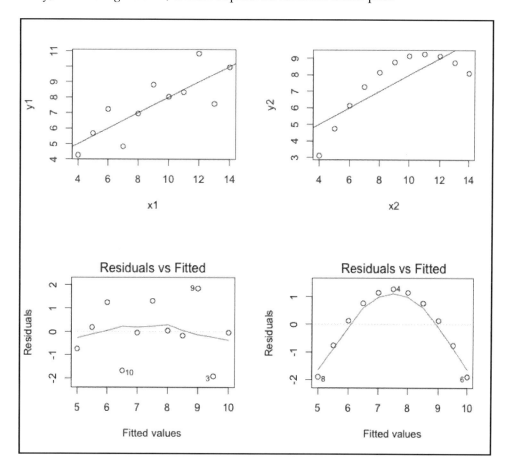

Figure 9.11: The top two panels show the first and second relationships of Anscombe's quartet, respectively. The bottom two panels depict each top panel's respective residual-fitted plot.

A non-pathological residual-fitted plot will have data points randomly distributed along the invisible horizontal line, where the y-axis equals 0. By default, this plot also contains a smooth curve that attempts to fit the residuals. In a non-pathological sample, this smooth curve should be approximately straight, and straddle the line at y=0.

As you can see, the first Anscombe relationship does this well. In contrast, the smooth curve of the second relationship is a parabola. These residuals could have been drawn from a normal distribution with a mean of zero, but it is highly unlikely. Instead, it looks like these residuals were drawn from a distribution—perhaps from a normal distribution—whose mean changed as a function of the x-axis. Specifically, it appears as if the residuals at the two ends were drawn from a distribution whose mean was negative, and the middle residuals had a positive mean.

Third Anscombe relationship

We already dug deeper into this relationship when we spoke of robust regression earlier in the chapter. We saw that a robust fit of this relationship more or less ignored the clear outlier. Indeed, the robust fit is almost identical to the non-robust linear fit after the outlier is removed.

On occasion, a data point that is an outlier in the y-axis but not the x-axis (like this one) doesn't *influence* the regression line much, meaning that its omission wouldn't cause a substantial change in the estimated intercept and coefficients.

A data point that is an outlier in the x-axis (or axes) is said to have high *leverage*. Sometimes, points with high leverage don't influence the regression line much, either. However, data points that have high leverage and are outliers very often exert high influence on the regression fit, and must be handled appropriately.

Refer to the upper-right panel of *Figure 9.12*. The aberrant data point in the fourth relationship of Anscombe's quartet has very high leverage and high influence. Note that the slope of the regression line is completely determined by the y-position of that point.

Fourth Anscombe relationship

The following image depicts some of the linear regression diagnostic plots of the fourth Anscombe relationship:

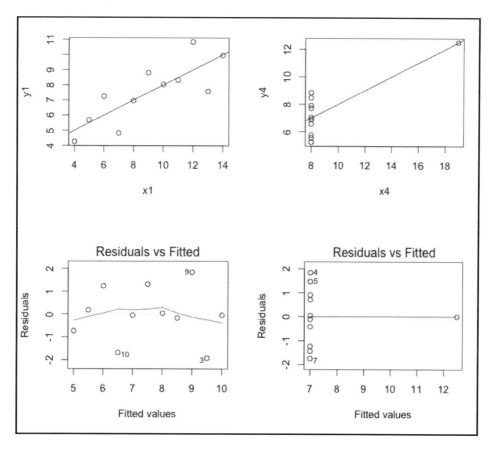

Figure 9.12: The first and the fourth Anscombe relationships and their respective residual-fitted plots

Although it's difficult to say for sure, this is probably in violation of the assumption of constant variance of residuals (also called *homogeneity of variance* or *homoscedasticity* if you're a fancy-pants).

A more illustrative example of the violation of homoscedasticity (or *heteroscedasticity*) is shown in *Figure 9.13*:

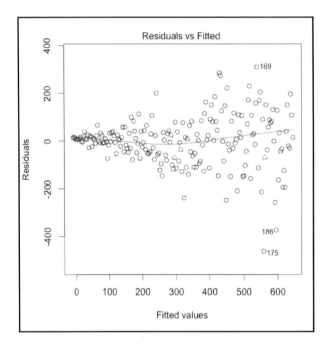

Figure 9.13: A paradigmatic depiction of the residual-fitted plot of a regression model for which the assumption of homogeneity of variance is violated

The preceding plot depicts the characteristic *funnel* shape symptomatic of residual-fitted plots of offending regression models. Notice how on the left, the residuals vary very little, but the variances grow as you go along the x-axis.

Bear in mind that the residual-fitted plot need not resemble a funnel; any residual-fitted plot that very clearly shows the variance change as a function of the x-axis violates this assumption.

Looking back on Anscombe's Quartet, you may think that the three relationships' unsuitability for linear modeling was obvious, and you may not immediately see the benefit of diagnostic plots. But before you write off the art (not science) of linear regression diagnostics, consider that these were all relationships with a single predictor. In multiple regression, with tens of predictors (or more), it is very difficult to diagnose problems by just plotting different cuts of the data. It is in this domain where linear regression diagnostics really shine.

Finally, the last hazard to be mindful of when linearly regressing is the problem of *collinearity* or *multicollinearity*. Collinearity occurs when two (or more) predictors are very highly correlated. This causes multiple problems for regression models, including highly uncertain and unstable coefficient estimates. An extreme example of this would be if we are trying to predict weight from height, and we had both height in feet and height in meters as predictors. In its most simple case, collinearity can be checked for by looking at the correlation matrix of all the regressors (using the `cor` function); any cell that has a high correlation coefficient implies two predictors that are highly correlated and, therefore, hold redundant information in the model. In theory, one of these predictors should be removed.

A more sneaky issue presents itself when there are no two *individual* predictors that are highly correlated, but there are multiple predictors that are *collectively* correlated. This is *multicollinearity*. This would occur to a small extent, for example, if instead of predicting `mpg` from other variables in the `mtcars` dataset, we were trying to predict a non-existent new variable using `mpg` and the other predictors. Since we know that `mpg` can be fairly reliably estimated from some of the other variables in `mtcars`, when it is a predictor in a regression modeling another variable, it would be difficult to tell whether the target's variance is truly explained by `mpg`, or whether it is explained by `mpg`'s *predictors*.

The most common technique to detect multicollinearity is to calculate each predictor variable's **Variance Inflation Factor (VIF)**. The VIF measures how much larger the variance of a coefficient is because of its collinearity. Mathematically, the VIF of a predictor, *a*, is:

$$VIF(a) = \frac{1}{1 + R^2_{b+c+d...}}$$

$R^2_{b+c+d...}$ is the R^2 of a linear model predicting from all other predictors (*b,c,d and so on*).

As such, the VIF has a lower bound of one (in the case that the predictor cannot be predicted accurately from the other predictors). Its upper bound is asymptotically infinite. In general, most view VIFs of more than four as a cause for concern, and VIFs of 10 or above indicative of a very high degree of multicollinearity. You can calculate VIFs for a model, post hoc, with the `vif` function from the `car` package, with the help of the following code:

```
model <- lm(mpg ~ am + wt + qsec, data=mtcars)
library(car)
vif(model)
      am        wt      qsec
2.541437 2.482952 1.364339
```

Advanced topics

Linear models are the biggest idea in applied statistics and predictive analytics. There are massive volumes written about even the smallest details of linear regression. As such, there are some important ideas that we can't go over here because of space concerns, or because it requires knowledge beyond the scope of this book. So you don't feel like you're in the dark, though, here are some of the topics we didn't cover—that I would have liked to—and why they are neat:

- **Regularization**: Regularization was mentioned briefly in the subsection about balancing bias and variance. In this context, *regularization is a technique wherein we penalize models for complexity, to varying degrees*. My favorite method of regularizing linear models is by using *elastic-net regression*. It is a fantastic technique and, if you are interested in learning more about it, I suggest you install and read the vignette of the `glmnet` package, with the help of the following code:

```
install.packages("glmnet")
library(glmnet)
vignette("glmnet_beta")
```

- **Non-linear modeling**: Surprisingly, we can model highly *non*-linear relationships using linear regression. For example, let's say we wanted to build a model that predicts how many raisins to use for a cookie using the cookie's *radius* as a predictor. The relationship between the predictor and target is no longer linear—it's quadratic. However, if we create a new predictor that is the radius squared, the target will now have a linear relationship with the new predictor, and thus can be captured using linear regression.

  This basic premise can be extended to capture relationships that are cubic (power of three), quartic (power of four), and so on; this is called *polynomial regression*. Other forms of non-linear modeling don't use polynomial features, but instead, directly fit non-linear functions to the predictors. Among these forms include regression splines and **Generalized Additive Models (GAMs)**.

- **Interaction terms**: Just like there are generalizations of linear regression that remove the requirement of linearity, so too are there generalizations of linear regressions that eliminate the need for the strictly additive and independent effects between predictors.

Take grapefruit juice, for example. Grapefruit juice is well known to block intestinal enzyme CYP3A, and drastically effect how the body absorbs certain medicines. Let's *pretend* that grapefruit juice is mildly effective at treating existential dysphoria. And suppose there is a drug called *Soma* that is highly effective at treating this condition. When alleviation of symptoms is plotted as a function of dosage, the grapefruit juice will have a very small slope, but the Soma will have a very large slope. Now, if we also pretend that grapefruit juice increases the efficiency of Soma absorption, then the relief from dysphoria of someone taking *both* grapefruit juice and Soma will be far higher than would be predicted by a multiple regression model that doesn't take into account the synergistic effects of Soma and the juice. The simplest way to model this interaction effect is to include the interaction term in the `lm` formula, as shown in the following code:

```
my.model <- lm(relief ~ soma*juice, data=my.data)
```

This builds a linear regression formula of the following form:

$$\hat{y}_i = b_0 + b_1\left(soma\right) + b_2\left(juice\right) + b_3\left(soma \times juice\right)$$

If b_3 is larger than b_1 and b_3 then there is an interaction effect that is being modeled. On the other hand, if b_3 is zero and b_1 and b_2 are positive, that suggests that the grapefruit juice completely blocks the effects of Soma (and vice versa).

- **Bayesian linear regression**: Bayesian linear regression is an alternative approach to the preceding methods that offers a lot of compelling benefits. One of the major benefits of Bayesian linear regression-which echoes the benefits of Bayesian methods as a whole-is that we obtain a posterior distribution of credible values for each of the beta coefficients. This makes it easy to make probabilistic statements about intervals in which the population coefficient is likely to lie. This makes hypothesis testing very easy.

Another major benefit is that we are no longer held hostage to the assumption that the residuals are normally distributed. If you were the good person you lay claim to being, on your online dating profiles, you would have done the exercises at the end of the last chapter. If so, you would have seen how we could use the t-distribution to make our models more robust to the influence of outliers. In Bayesian linear regression, it is easy to use a t-distributed likelihood function to describe the distribution of the residuals. Lastly, by adjusting the priors on the beta coefficients and making them sharply peaked at zero, we achieve a certain amount of shrinkage regularization for free, and build models that are inherently resistant to overfitting.

Exercises

Practice the following exercises to revise the concepts learned thus far:

- By far, the best way to become comfortable and learn the ins and outs of applied regression analysis is to actually *carry out* regression analyses. To this end, you can use some of the many datasets that are included in R. To get a full listing of the datasets in the datasets package, execute the following code:

```
help(package="datasets")
```

- There are hundreds more datasets spread across the other several thousand R packages. Even better, load your own datasets, and attempt to model them.

- Examine and plot the `pressure` dataset, which describes the relationship between the vapor pressure of mercury and temperature. What assumption of linear regression does this violate? Attempt to model this using linear regression by using `temperature` squared as a predictor, as shown in the following code:

```
lm(pressure ~ I(temperature^2), data=pressure)
```

- Compare the fit between the model that uses the non-squared `temperature` and this one. Explore cubic and quartic relationships between `temperature` and `pressure`. How accurately can you predict `pressure`? Employ cross-validation to make sure that no overfitting has occurred. Marvel at how nicely physics plays with statistics sometimes, and wish that the behavioral sciences would behave better.

- Keep an eye out for provocative news, human-interest stories, or popular culture anecdotes that claim suspect causal relationships like *gum chewing causes heart disease* or *dark chocolate promotes weight loss*. If these claims were backed up using data from *natural experiments*, try to think of potential confounding variables that invalidate the claim. Impress upon your friends and family that the media is trying to take advantage of their gullibility and non-fluency in the principles of statistics. As you become more adept at recognizing suspicious claims, you'll be invited to fewer and fewer parties. This will clear up your schedule for more studying.
- Describe some of the changes in the politics and everyday lives of Chileans during the military dictatorship of Pinochet. Economically-speaking, what were some of the changes that occurred during the implementation of the policies of the *Chicago Boys*? Ruling-style-wise, would you describe Pinochet's regime as *fascist*? Appeal to Roger Griffin's concept of *Palingenetic Ultranationalism* in your response.

Summary

Whew, we've been through a lot in this chapter, and I commend you for sticking it out. Your tenacity will be well rewarded when you start using regression analysis in your own projects or to research like a professional.

We started off with the basics: how to describe a line, simple linear relationships, and how a best-fit regression line is determined. You saw how we can use R to easily plot these best-fit lines.

We went on to explore regression analysis with more than one predictor. You learned how to interpret the loquacious `lm` summary output, and what everything meant. In the context of multiple regression, you learned how the coefficients are properly interpreted as the effect of a predictor *controlling* for all other predictors. You're now aware that controlling for and thinking about confounds is one of the cornerstones of statistical thinking.

We discovered that we weren't limited to using continuous predictors, and that, using dummy coding, we can not only model the effects of categorical variables, but also replicate the functionalities, two-sample t-test and one-way ANOVA.

You learned of the hazards of going hog-wild and including all available predictors in a linear model. Specifically, you've come to find out that reckless pursuit of R^2 maximization is a losing strategy when it comes to building interpretable, generalizable, and useful models. You've learned that it is far better to minimize an out-of-sample error using estimates from cross validation. We framed this preference for test error minimization of training error minimization in terms of the bias-variance trade-off.

Penultimately, you learned the standard assumptions of linear regression, and we touched upon some ways to determine whether our assumptions hold. You came to understand that regression diagnostics isn't an exact science.

Lastly, you learned that there's much we haven't learned about regression analysis. This will keep us humble and hungry for more knowledge.

10
Predicting Categorical Variables

Our first foray into predictive analytics began with regression techniques for predicting continuous variables. In this chapter, we will be discussing a perhaps even more popular class of techniques from statistical learning known as **classification**.

All these techniques have at least one thing in common: we train a learner on input, for which the correct classifications are known, with the intention of using the trained model on new data whose class is unknown. In this way, classification is a set of algorithms and methods to predict *categorical* variables.

Whether you know it or not, statistical learning algorithms performing classification are all around you. For example, if you've ever accidently checked the *spam* folder of your email and been horrified, you can thank your lucky stars that there are sophisticated classification mechanisms that your email is run through to automatically mark spam as such so you don't have to see it. On the other hand, if you've ever had a legitimate email sent to spam, or a spam email sneak past the spam filter into your inbox, you've witnessed the limitations of classification algorithms firsthand: since the emails aren't being audited by a human one by one, and are being audited by a computer instead, *misclassification* happens. Just like our linear regression predictions differed from our training data to varying degrees, so too do classification algorithms make mistakes. Our job is to make sure we build models that minimize these misclassifications—a task which is not always easy.

There are *many* different classification methods available in R; we will be learning about four of the most popular ones in this chapter, starting with k-Nearest Neighbors.

k-Nearest neighbors

You're at a train terminal looking for the right line to stand in to get on the train from Upstate NY to Penn Station in NYC. You've settled into what you think is the right line, but you're still not sure because it's so crowded and chaotic. Not wanting to wait in the wrong line, you turn to the person closest to you and ask them where they're going. Penn Station, says the stranger, blithely.

You decide to get some second opinions. You turn to the second closest person and the third closest person and ask them separately: *Penn Station* and *Nova Scotia* respectively. The general consensus seems to be that you're in the right line, and that's good enough for you.

If you've understood the preceding interaction, you already understand the idea behind k-Nearest Neighbors (k-NN hereafter) on a fundamental level. In particular, you've just performed k-NN, where k=3. Had you just stopped at the first person, you would have performed k-NN, where k=1.

So, k-NN is a classification technique that, for each data point we want to classify, finds the k closest training data points and returns the consensus. In traditional settings, the most common distance metric is Euclidean distance (which, in two dimensions, is equal to the distance from point a to point b given by the Pythagorean Theorem). Another common distance metric is Manhattan distance, which, in two dimensions, is equal to the sum of the length of the *legs* of the triangle connecting two data points. The following figure shows the Manhattan distance:

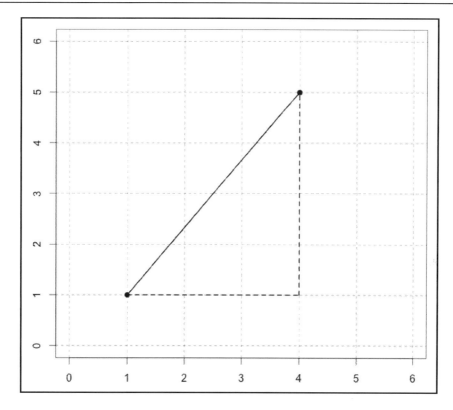

Figure 10.1: Two points on a Cartesian plane. Their Euclidean distance is 5. Their Manhattan distance is 3+4=7

k-Nearest Neighbors is a bit of an oddball technique; most statistical learning methods attempt to impose a particular model on the data and estimate the parameters of that model. Put another way, the goal of most learning methods is to learn an *objective function* that maps inputs to outputs. Once the objective function is learned, there is no longer a need for the training set.

In contrast, k-NN learns no such objective function. Rather, it lets the data *speak for itself.* Since there is no actual *learning,* per se, going on, k-NN needs to hold on to training dataset for future classifications. This also means that the *training step* is instantaneous, since there is no training to be done. Most of the time spent during the classification of a data point is spent finding its nearest neighbors. This property of k-NN makes it a *lazy learning* algorithm.

Since no particular model is imposed on the training data, k-NN is one of the most flexible and accurate classification learners there are, and it is very widely used. With great flexibility, though, comes great responsibility—it is our responsibility to ensure that k-NN hasn't overfit the training data:

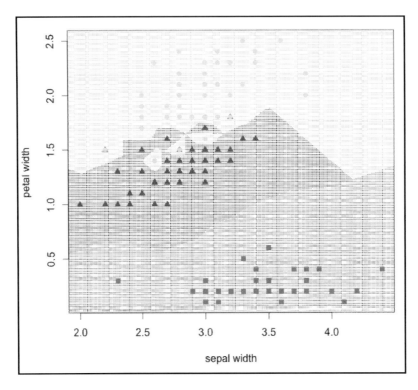

Figure 10.2: The species classification regions of the iris dataset using 1-NN

In *Figure 10.2*, we use the built-in `iris` dataset. This dataset contains four continuous measurements of iris flowers and maps each observation to one of three species: *iris setosa* (the square points), *iris virginica* (the circular points), and *iris versicolor* (the triangular points). In this example, we use only two of the available four attributes in our classification for ease of visualization: sepal width and petal width. As you can see, each species seems to occupy its own little space in our *2-D feature space*. However, there seems to be a little overlap between the *versicolor* and *virginica* data points. Because this classifier is using only one nearest neighbor, there appear to be small regions of training data-specific idiosyncratic classification behavior where *virginicas* is encroaching the *versicolor* classification region. This is what it looks like when our k-NN overfits the data. In our train station metaphor, this is tantamount to asking only one neighbor what line you're on and the misinformed (or malevolent) neighbor telling you the wrong answer.

k-NN classifiers that have overfit have traded low variance for low bias. It is common for overfit k-NN classifiers to have a 0% misclassification rate on the training data, but small changes in the training data harshly change the classification regions (high variance). Like with regression (and the rest of the classifiers we'll be learning about in this chapter), we aim to find the optimal point in the bias-variance trade-off—the one that minimizes error in an *independent testing set*, and not one that minimizes training set misclassification errors.

We do this by modifying the k in k-NN and using the consensus of more neighbors. Beware—if you ask too many neighbors, you start to take the answers of rather distant neighbors seriously, and this can also adversely affect accuracy. Finding the **sweet spot**, where k is neither too small or two large, is called *hyperparameter optimization* (because k is called a *hyperparameter* of k-NN):

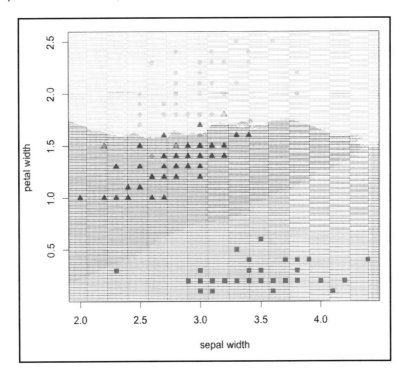

Figure 10.3: The species classification regions of the iris dataset using 15-NN. The boundaries between the classification regions are now smoother and less overfit

Compare *Figure 10.2* to *Figure 10.3*, which depicts the classification regions of the iris classification task using 15 nearest neighbors. The aberrant virginicas are no longer carving out their own territory in versicolor's region, and the boundaries between the classification regions (also called *decision boundaries*) are now smoother—often a trait of classifiers that have found the *sweet spot* in the bias-variance trade-off. One can imagine that new training data will no longer have such a drastic effect on the decision boundaries, at least not as much as with the 1-NN classifier.

In the iris flower example, and the next example, we deal with continuous predictors only. k-NN can handle categorical variables, though, not unlike how we dummy coded categorical variables in linear regression in the last chapter! Though we didn't talk about how, regression (and k-NN) handle non-binary categorical variables, too. Can you think of how this is done? Hint: we can't use just one dummy variable for a non-binary categorical variable, and the number of dummy variables needed is one less than the number of categories.

Using k-NN in R

The dataset we will be using for all the examples in this chapter is the PimaIndiansDiabetes dataset from the mlbench package. This dataset is part of the data collected from one of the numerous diabetes studies done on the Pima Indians, a group of indigenous Americans who have among the highest prevalence of Type II diabetes in the world—probably due to a combination of genetic factors and their relatively recent introduction to a heavily processed Western diet. For 768 observations, it has nine attributes, including skin fold thickness, BMI, and so on, and a binary variable representing whether the patient had diabetes. We will be using the eight predictor variables to train a classifier to predict whether a patient has diabetes or not.

This dataset was chosen because it has many observations available, has a good amount of predictor variables available, and is an interesting problem. Additionally, it is not unlike many other medical datasets that have a few predictors and a binary class outcome (for example, alive/dead, pregnant/not-pregnant, benign/malignant). Finally, unlike many classification datasets, this one has a good mixture of both class outcomes; this contains 35% diabetes positive observations. Grievously imbalanced datasets can cause a problem with some classifiers and impair our accuracy estimates.

To get this dataset, we are going to run the following commands to install the necessary package, load the data, and give the dataset a new name that is faster to type:

```
# "class" is one of the packages that implement k-NN
# "chemometrics" contains a function we need
# "mlbench" holds the dataset
install.packages(c("class", "mlbench", "chemometrics"))
library(class)
library(mlbench)
data(PimaIndiansDiabetes)
PID <- PimaIndiansDiabetes
```

Now, let's divide our dataset into a training set and a testing set using an 80/20 split, using the following code:

```
# we set the seed so that our splits are the same
set.seed(3)
ntrain <- round(nrow(PID)*4/5)
train <- sample(1:nrow(PID), ntrain)
training <- PID[train,]
testing <- PID[-train,]
```

Now we have to choose how many nearest neighbors we want to use. Luckily, there's a great function called `knnEval` from the `chemometrics` package that will allow us to graphically visualize the effectiveness of k-NN with a different k using cross-validation. Our objective measures of effectiveness will be the *misclassification rate,* or the percent of testing observations that are misclassified. The following code depicts this process:

```
resknn <- knnEval(scale(PID[,-9]), PID[,9], train, kfold=10,
                  knnvec=seq(1,50,by=1),
                  legpos="bottomright")
```

There's a lot here to explain! The first three arguments are the *predictor matrix, the variables to predict,* and the *indices of the training dataset* respectively. Note that the ninth column of the PID data frame holds the class labels—to get a matrix containing just the predictors, we can remove the ninth column by using a negative column index. The scale function that we call on the predictor matrix subtracts each value in each column from the column's mean and divides each value by their respective column's standard deviation—it converts each value to a z-score! This is usually important in k-NN in order for the distances between data points to be meaningful. For example, the distance between data points would change drastically if a column previously measured in meters was re-represented as millimeters. The scale function puts all the features in comparable ranges regardless of the original units.

Note that for the third argument, we are not supplying the function with the training dataset, but the indices that we used to construct the training dataset. If you are confused, inspect the various objects we have in our workspace with the head function.

The final three arguments indicate that we want to use a 10-fold cross-validation, check every value of k from 1 to 50, and put the legend in the lower-left corner of the plot.

The plot that this code produces is shown in *Figure 10.4*:

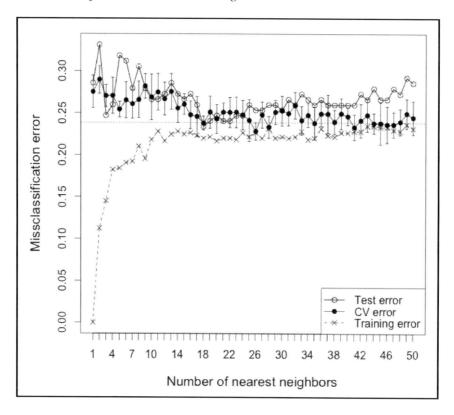

Figure 10.4: A plot illustrating test set error, the cross-validated error, and training set error as a function of k in k-NN. After about k=15, the test and CV error doesn't appear to change much

As you can see from the preceding plot, after about k=15, the test and cross-validated misclassification error don't seem to change much. Using k=27 seems like a safe bet, as measured by the *minimization of CV* error.

To see what it looks like when we underfit and use too many neighbors, check out *Figure 10.5*, which expands the x-axis of the last figure to show the misclassification error of using up to 200 neighbors. Notice that the test and CV error start off high (at 1-NN) and quickly decrease. At about 70-NN, though, the test and CV error start to rise steadily as the classifier underfits. Note also that the training error starts out at 0 for 1-NN (as we would expect), but very sharply quickly increases as we add more neighbors. This is a good reminder that our goal is not to minimize the training set error but to minimize error on an independent dataset, either a test set or an estimate using cross-validation.

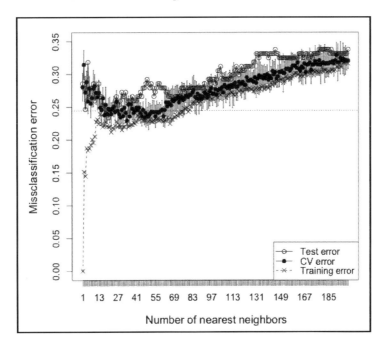

Figure 10.5: A plot illustrating a test set error, cross-validated error, and training set error, and a function of k in k-NN up to k=200. Notice how the error increases as the number of neighbors becomes too large and causes the classifier to overfit

Let's perform the k-NN!

```
predictions <- knn(scale(training[,-9]),
                   scale(testing[,-9]),
                   training[,9], k=27)
# function to give correct classification rate
accuracy <- function(predictions, answers){
```

```
    sum((predictions==answers)/(length(answers)))
  }
  accuracy(predictions, testing[,9])
[1] 0.7597403
```

It looks like using 27-NN gave us a correct classification rate of 76% (a misclassification rate of 100%—76% = 24%). Is that good? Well, let's put it in perspective.

If we randomly guessed whether each testing observation was positive for diabetes, we would expect a classification rate of 50%. But remember that the number of non-diabetes observations outnumber the number of observations of diabetes (non-diabetes observations are 65% of the total). So, if we built a classifier that just predicted *no diabetes* for every observation, we would expect a 65% correct classification rate. Luckily, our classifier performs significantly better than our naïve classifier, although perhaps not as good as we would have hoped. As we'll learn as the chapter moves on, k-NN is competitive with the accuracy of other classifiers—I guess it's just a really hard problem!

Confusion matrices

We can get a more detailed look at our classifier's accuracy via a *confusion matrix*. You can get R to give up a confusion matrix with the following command:

```
table(test[,9], preds)
      preds
        neg pos
  neg  86   9
  pos  28  31
```

The columns in this matrix represent our classifier's predictions; the rows represent the true classifications of our testing set observations. If you recall from Chapter 3, *Describing Relationships*, this means that the confusion matrix is a cross-tabulation (or *contingency table*) of our predictions and the actual classifications. The cell in the top-left corner represents observations that didn't have diabetes that we correctly predicted as non-diabetic (*true negatives*). In contrast, the cell in the lower-right corner represents *true positives*. The upper-left cell contains the count of *false positives*, observations that we incorrectly predicted as having diabetes. Finally, the remaining cell holds the number of *false negatives*, of which there are 28.

This is helpful for examining whether there is a class that we are systematically misclassifying or whether our false negatives and false positive are significantly imbalanced. Additionally, there are often different costs associated with false negatives and false positives. For example, in this case, the cost of misclassifying a patient as non-diabetic is great, because it impedes our ability to help a truly diabetic patient. In contrast, misclassifying a non-diabetic patient as diabetic, although not ideal, incurs a far less grievous cost. A confusion matrix lets us view, at a glance, just what types of errors we are making. For k-NN, and the other classifiers in this chapter, there are ways to specify the cost of each type of misclassification in order to exact a classifier optimized for a particular cost-sensitive domain, but that is beyond the scope of this book.

Limitations of k-NN

Before we move on, we should talk about some of the limitations of k-NN.

First, if you're not careful to use an optimized implementation of k-NN, classification can be slow, since it requires the calculation of the test data point's distance to every other data point; sophisticated implementations have mechanisms for partially handling this.

Second, *vanilla* k-NN can perform poorly when the amount of predictor variables becomes too large. In the iris example, we used only two predictors, which can be plotted in two-dimensional space where the Euclidean distance is just the 2-D Pythagorean theorem that we learned in middle school. A classification problem with n predictors is represented in n-dimensional space; the Euclidean distance between two points in a high-dimensional space can be very large, even if the data points are similar. This, and other complications that arise from predictive analytics techniques using a high-dimensional feature spaces, are, colloquially, known as the *curse of dimensionality*. It is not uncommon for medical, image, or video data to have hundreds or even thousands of dimensions. Luckily, there are ways of dealing with these situations. But let's not dwell on that.

Logistic regression

Remember when I said *a thorough understanding of linear models will pay enormous dividends throughout your career as an analyst* in the previous chapter? Well, I wasn't lying! This next classifier is a product of a generalization of linear regression that can act as a classifier.

What if we used linear regression on a binary outcome variable, representing diabetes as *1* and not diabetes as *0*? We know that the output of linear regression is a continuous prediction, but what if, instead of predicting the binary class (diabetes or not diabetes), we attempted to predict the *probability* of an observation having diabetes? So far, the idea is to train a linear regression on a training set where the variables we are trying to predict are dummy-coded as 0 or 1, and the predictions on an independent training set are interpreted as a continuous probability of class membership.

It turns out this idea is not quite as crazy as it sounds—the outcome of the predictions are indeed proportional to the probability of each observation's class membership. The biggest problem is that the outcome is only *proportional* to the class membership probability and can't be directly interpreted as a true probability. The reason is simple: probability is, indeed, a continuous measurement, but it is also a *constrained* measurement—it is bounded by 0 and 1. With regular old linear regression, we will often get predicted outcomes below 0 and above 1, and it is unclear how to interpret those outcomes.

But what if we had a way of taking the outcome of a linear regression (a linear combination of beta coefficients and predictors) and applying a function to it that constrains it to be between 0 and 1 so that it can be interpreted as a proper probability? Luckily, we can do this with the logistic function:

$$f(x) = \frac{1}{1 - e^{-x}}$$

The plot for this is depicted in *Figure 10.6*:

Figure 10.6: The logistic function

Note that no matter the value of x (the output of the linear regression), we use—from negative infinity to positive infinity—the y (the output of the logistic function) is always between 0 and 1. Now we can adapt linear regression to output probabilities!

The function that we apply to the linear combination of predictors to change it into the kind of prediction we want is called the *inverse link function*. The function that transforms the dependent variable into a value that can be modeled using linear regression is just called the *link function*. In logistic regression, the link function (which is the inverse of the inverse link function, the *logistic function*) is called the *logit function*:

$$\hat{Y} = b_0 + b_1 X_1 + b_2 X_2 + \cdots$$

linear regression

$$\hat{Y} = logistic\left(b_0 + b_1 X_1 + b_2 X_2 + \cdots\right)$$

Before we get started using this powerful idea on our data, there are two other problems that we must contend with. The first is that we can't use ordinary least squares to solve for the coefficients anymore, because the link function is non-linear. Most statistical software solves this problem using a technique called **Maximum Likelihood Estimation** (**MLE**) instead, though there are other alternatives.

The second problem is that an assumption of linear regression (if you remember from the last chapter) is that the error distribution is normally distributed. In the context of linear regression, this doesn't make sense, because it is a binary categorical variable. So, logistic regression models the error distribution as a Bernoulli distribution (or a binomial distribution, depending on how you look at it).

Generalized Linear Model (GLM)

If you are surprised that linear regression can be generalized enough to accommodate classification, prepare to be astonished by generalized linear models!

GLMs are a generalization of regular linear regression that allow for other link functions to map from linear model output to the dependent variable, and other error distributions to describe the residuals. In logistic regression, the link function and error distribution is the logit and binomial respectively. In regular linear regression, the link function is the identity function (a function that returns its argument unchanged), and the error distribution is the normal distribution.

Besides regular linear regression and logistic regression, there are still other species of GLM that use other link functions and error distributions. Another common GLM is Poisson regression, a technique that is used to predict/model count data (number of traffic stops, number of red cards, and so on), which uses the logarithm as the link function and the Poisson distribution as its error distribution. The use of the log link function constrains the response variable (the dependent variable) so that it is always above zero.

Remember that we expressed the t-test and ANOVA in terms of the linear model? So the GLM encompasses not only linear regression, logistic regression, Poisson regression, and the like, but it also encompasses t-tests, ANOVA, and the related technique called **ANCOVA** (**Analysis of Covariance**). Pretty cool, eh?

Using logistic regression in R

Performing logistic regression—an advanced and widely used classification method—could scarcely be easier in R. To fit a logistic regression, we use the familiar `glm` function. The difference now is that we'll be specifying our own error distribution and link function (the `glm` calls of last chapter assumed we wanted the regular linear regression error distribution and link function, by default). These are specified in the `family` argument:

```
model <- glm(diabetes ~ ., data=PID, family=binomial(logit))
```

Here, we build a logistic regression using all available predictor variables.

You may also see logistic regressions being performed where the family argument looks like `family="binomial"` or `family=binomial()`—it's all the same thing, I just like being more explicit.

Let's look at the output from calling the summary on the model, using the following code:

```
summary(model)
Call:
glm(formula = diabetes ~ ., family = binomial(logit), data = PID)
Deviance Residuals:
    Min       1Q     Median       3Q        Max
 -2.5566  -0.7274   -0.4159    0.7267     2.9297
Coefficients:
               Estimate Std. Error  z value  Pr(>|z|)
(Intercept)  -8.4046964  0.7166359  -11.728  < 2e-16  ***
pregnant      0.1231823  0.0320776    3.840  0.000123 ***
glucose       0.0351637  0.0037087    9.481  < 2e-16  ***
pressure     -0.0132955  0.0052336   -2.540  0.011072 *
   . . .
```

The output is similar to that of regular linear regression; for example, we still get estimates of the coefficients and associated p-values. The interpretation of the beta coefficients requires a little more care this time around, though. The beta coefficient of `pregnant`, `0.123`, means that a one unit increase in `pregnant` (an increase in the number of times being pregnant by one) is associated with an increase of the logarithm of the odds of the observation being diabetic. If this is confusing, concentrate on the fact that if the coefficient is positive, it has a positive impact on the probability of the dependent variable, and if the coefficient is negative, it has a negative impact on the probability of the binary outcome. Whether *positive* means *higher probability of diabetes* or *higher probability of no diabetes* depends on whether your binary dependent variable is dummy-coded.

To find the training set accuracy of our model, we can use the `accuracy` function we wrote in the last section. In order to use it correctly, though, we need to convert the probabilities into class labels, as follows:

```
predictions <- round(predict(model, type="response"))
predictions <- ifelse(predictions == 1, "pos", "neg")
accuracy(predictions, PID$diabetes)
[1] 0.7825521
```

Cool, we get 78% accuracy on the training data, but remember: if we overfit, our training set accuracy will not be a reliable estimate of performance on an independent dataset. In order to test this model's generalizability, let's perform k-fold cross-validation, just like in the previous chapter:

```
set.seed(3)
library(boot)
cv.err <- cv.glm(PID, model, K=5)
cv.err$delta[2]
[1] 0.154716
1 - cv.err$delta[2]
[1] 0.845284
```

Wow, our CV-estimated accuracy rate is 85%! This indicates that it is highly unlikely that we are overfitting. If you are wondering why we were using all available predictors after I said that doing so was dangerous business in the last chapter, it's because although they do make the model more complex, the extra predictors don't cause the model to overfit.

Finally, let's test the model on the independent test set so that we can compare this model's accuracy against k-NN's:

```
predictions <- round(predict(model, type="response",
                             newdata=test))
predictions <- ifelse(predictions == 1, "pos", "neg")
accuracy(predictions, test[,9])    # 78%
[1] 0.7792208
```

Nice! A 78% accuracy rate!

It looks like logistic regression may have given us a slight improvement over the more flexible k-NN. Additionally, the model gives us at least a little transparency as to why each observation is classified the way it is—a luxury not available to us via k-NN.

Before we move on, it's important to discuss two limitations of logistic regression:

- The first is that logistic regression proper does not handle non-binary categorical variables—variables with more than two levels. There exists a generalization of logistic regression, called multinomial regression, that can handle this situation, but this is vastly less common than logistic regression. It is, therefore, more common to see another classifier being used for a non-binary classification problem.
- The last limitation of logistic regression is that it results in a linear decision boundary. This means that if a binary outcome is not easily separated by a line, plane, or hyperplane, then logistic regression *may* not be the best route. *May* in the previous sentence is italicized because there are tricks you can use to get logistic regression to spit out a non-linear decision boundary—sometimes, a high performing one—as we'll see in the *Choosing a classifier* section.

Decision trees

We now move on to one of the easily interpretable and most popular classifiers there are out there: the decision tree. Decision trees, which look like an upside down tree with the trunk on top and the leaves on the bottom, play an important role in situations where classification decisions have to be transparent and easily understood and explained. They also handle both continuous and categorical predictors, outliers, and irrelevant predictors rather gracefully. Finally, the general idea behind the algorithms that create decision trees are quite intuitive, though the details can sometimes get hairy.

Figure 10.7 depicts a simple decision tree designed to classify motor vehicles into either motorcycles, golf carts, or sedans:

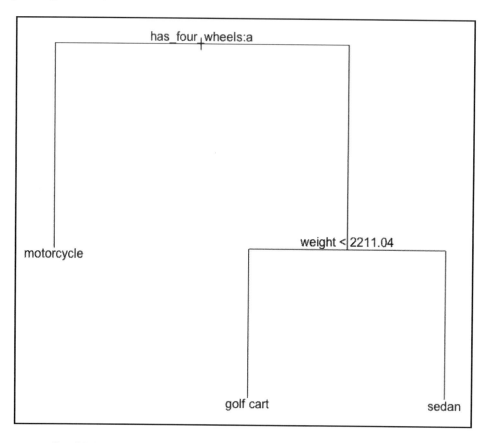

Figure 10.7: A simple and illustrative decision tree that classifies motor vehicles into either motorcycles, golf carts, or sedans

This is a rather simple decision tree with only three *leaves* (terminal nodes) and two decision points. Note that the first decision point is (a) on a binary categorical variable, and (b) results in one terminal node, *motorcycle*. The other *branch* contains the other decision point, a continuous variable with a *split point*. This split point was chosen carefully by the decision tree—creating the algorithm to result in the most informative split, the one that best classifies the rest of the observations as measured by the misclassification rate of the training data.

Actually, in most cases, the decision tree-creating algorithm doesn't choose a split that results in the lowest misclassification rate of the training data, but chooses one that minimizes either the Gini coefficient or the cross entropy of the remaining training observations. The reasons for this are two-fold: (a) both the Gini coefficient and the cross entropy have mathematical properties that make them more easily amendable to numerical optimization, and (b) it generally results in a final tree with less bias.

The overall idea of the decision tree-growing algorithm, *recursive splitting*, is simple:

1. Choose a variable and split point that results in the best classification outcomes.
2. For each of the resulting branches, check to see if some stopping criteria is met. If so, leave it alone. If not, move onto the next step.
3. Repeat Step 1 on the branches that do not meet the stopping criteria.

The stopping criterion is usually either a certain *depth*, which the tree cannot grow past, or a minimum number of observations, which a leaf node cannot further classify. Both of these are hyper-parameters (also called *tuning parameters*) of the decision tree algorithm—just like the k in k-NN—and must be fiddled with in order to achieve the best possible decision tree for classifying an independent dataset.

A decision tree, if not kept in check, can grossly overfit the data, returning an enormous and complicated tree with a minimum leaf node size of one, resulting in a nearly bias-less classification mechanism with prodigious variance. To prevent this, either the tuning parameters must be chosen carefully or a huge tree can be built and cut down to size afterward. The latter technique is generally preferred and is, quite appropriately, called *pruning*. The most common pruning technique is called *cost complexity pruning*, where complex parts of the tree that provide little in the way of classification power, as measured by improvement of the final misclassification rate, are cut down and removed.

Enough theory—let's get started! First, we'll grow a full tree using the PID dataset and plot the result:

```
library(tree)
our.big.tree <- tree(diabetes ~ ., data=training)
summary(our.big.tree)
Classification tree:
tree(formula = diabetes ~ ., data = training)
Variables actually used in tree construction:
[1] "glucose"  "age"       "mass"      "pedigree" "triceps"  "pregnant"
[7] "insulin"
Number of terminal nodes:   16
```

```
Residual mean deviance:   0.7488 = 447.8 / 598
Misclassification error rate: 0.184 = 113 / 614
plot(our.big.tree)
text(our.big.tree)
```

The resulting plot is depicted in *Figure 10.8*:

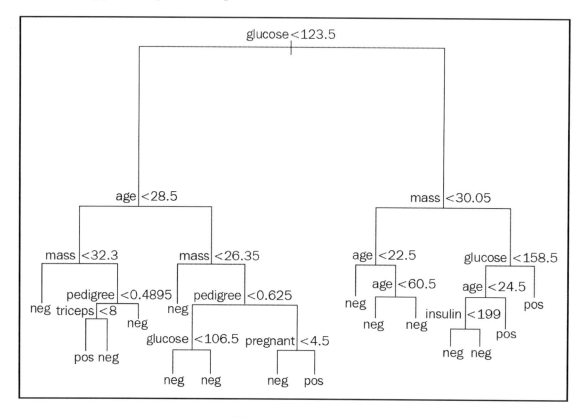

Figure 10.8: An unpruned and complex decision tree

The power of a decision tree—which is usually not competitive with other classification mechanisms, accuracy-wise—is in that the representation of the decision rules are transparent, easy to visualize, and easy to explain. This tree is rather large and unwieldy, which hinders its ability to be understood (or memorized) at a glance. Additionally, for all its complexity, it only achieves an 81% accuracy rate on *the training data* (as reported by the summary function).

We can (and will) do better! Next, we will be investigating the optimal size of the tree employing cross-validation, using the `cv.tree` function, as shown in the following code:

```
set.seed(3)
cv.results <- cv.tree(our.big.tree, FUN=prune.misclass)
plot(cv.results$size, cv.results$dev, type="b")
```

In the preceding code, we are telling the `cv.tree` function that we want to prune our tree using the misclassification rate as our objective metric. Then, we are plotting the CV error rate (`dev`) and a function of tree size (`size`):

Figure 10.9: A plot cross-validated misclassification error as a function of tree size. Observe that a tree of size one performs terribly, and that the error rate steeply declines before rising slightly as the tree is overfit and large

As you can see from the output (shown in *Figure 10.9*), the optimal size (number of terminal nodes) of the tree seems to be 5. However, a tree of size 3 is not terribly less performant than a tree of size 5; so, for ease of visualization, interpretation, and memorization, we will be using a final tree with three terminal nodes. To actually perform the pruning, we will be using the `prune.misclass` function, which takes the size of the tree as an argument:

```
pruned.tree <- prune.misclass(our.big.tree, best=3)
plot(pruned.tree)
text(pruned.tree)
# let's test its accuracy
pruned.preds <- predict(pruned.tree, newdata=test, type="class")
accuracy(pruned.preds, test[,9])     # 71%
[1] 0.7077922
```

The final tree is depicted in *Figure 10.10*:

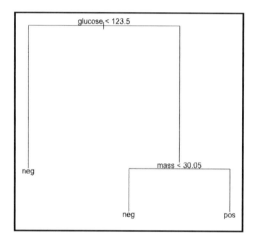

Figure 10.10: Simpler decision tree with the same testing set performance as the tree in Figure 10.8

Rad! A tree so simple it can be easily memorized by medical personnel and achieves the same testing-set accuracy as the unwieldy tree in figure 10.8: 71%! Now, the accuracy rate by itself is nothing to write home about, particularly because the naïve classifier achieves a 65% accuracy rate. Nevertheless, the fact that a significantly better classifier can be built from two simple rules—closely following the logic physicians employ anyway—is where decision trees have a huge leg up relative to other techniques. Further, we could have bumped up this accuracy rate with more samples and more careful hyper-parameter tuning.

Random forests

The final classifier that we will be discussing in this chapter is the aptly named *Random Forest* and is an example of a meta-technique called *ensemble learning*. The idea and logic behind random forests follows.

Given that (unpruned) decision trees can be nearly bias-less high variance classifiers, a method of reducing variance at the cost of a marginal increase of bias could greatly improve upon the predictive accuracy of the technique. One salient approach to reducing the variance of decision trees is to train a bunch of unpruned decision trees on different random subsets of the training data, sampling with replacement—this is called *bootstrap aggregating* or *bagging*. At the classification phase, the test observation is run through all of these trees (a forest, perhaps?), and each resulting classification casts a vote for the final classification of the whole forest. The class with the highest number of votes is the winner. It turns out that the consensus among many high-variance trees on bootstrapped subsets of the training data results in a significant accuracy improvement and vastly decreased variance.

> ### *Très bien ensemble!*
>
>
> *Bagging* is one example of an ensemble method—a meta-technique that uses multiple classifiers to improve predictive accuracy. Nearly bias-less/high-variance classifiers are the ones that seem to benefit the most from ensemble methods. Additionally, ensemble methods are easiest to use with classifiers that are created and trained rapidly, since the *ipso facto* method relies on a large number of them. Decision trees fit all of these characteristics, and this accounts for why bagged trees and random forests are the most common ensemble learning instruments.

So far, what we have chronicled describes a technique called *bagged trees*. But random forests have one more trick up their sleeves! Observing that the variance can be further reduced by forcing the trees to be less similar, random forests differ from bagged trees by forcing the tree to only use a subset of its available predictors to split on in the growing phase.

Many people become confused as to how *deliberately* reducing the efficacy of the component trees can possibly result in a more accurate ensemble. To clear this up, consider that a few very influential predictors will dominate the expression of the trees, even if the subsets contain little overlap. By constraining the number of predictors a tree can use in each splitting phase, a more diverse crop of trees is built. This results in a forest with lower variance than a forest with no constraints.

Random forests are the modern darling of classifiers, and for good reason. For one, they are often extraordinarily accurate. Second, since random forests use only two hyper-parameters (the number of trees to use in the forest and the number of predictors to use at each step of the splitting process), they are very easy to create, and require little in the way of hyper-parameter tuning. Third, it is extremely difficult for a random forest to overfit, and it doesn't happen very often at all, in practice. For example, increasing the number of trees that make up the forest does not cause the forest to overfit, and fiddling with the number of predictors hyper-parameter can't possibly result in a forest with a higher variance than that of the component tree that overfits the most.

One last awesome property of the random forest is that the training error rate that it reports is a nearly unbiased, estimator cross-validated error rate. This is because the training error rate, at least that R reports using the `predict` function on a `randomForest` with no `newdata` argument, is the average error rate of the classifier tested on all the observations that were kept out of the training sample at each stage of the bootstrap aggregation. Because these were independent observations, and not used for training, it closely approximates the CV error rate. The error rate reported on the remaining observations left out of the sample at every bagging step is called the **Out-Of-Bag** (**OOB**) error rate.

The primary drawback to random forests is that they, to some extent, revoke the chief benefit of decision trees: their interpretability. It is far harder to visualize the behavior of a random forest than it is for any of the component trees. This puts the interpretability of random forests somewhere between logistic regression (which is marginally more interpretable) and k-NN (which is largely un-interpretable).

At long last, let's use a random forest on our dataset, as shown in the following code, to classify observations as being positive or negative for diabetes:

```
library(randomForest)
forest <- randomForest(diabetes ~ ., data=training,
                        importance=TRUE,
                        ntree=2000,
                        mtry=5)
accuracy(predict(forest), training[,9])
[1] 0.7654723
predictions <- predict(forest, newdata = test)
accuracy(predictions, test[,9])
[1] 0.7727273
```

In this incantation, we set the number of trees (ntree) to an arbitrarily high number and set the number of predictors (mtry) to 5. Though it is not shown above, I used the OOB error rate to guide in the choosing of this hyper-parameter. Had we left it blank, it would have defaulted to the square root of the number of total predictors.

As you can see from the output of our accuracy function, the random forest competes with the performance of our highest performing (on this dataset, at least) classifier: logistic regression. On other datasets, with other characteristics, random forests sometimes blow the competition out of the water.

Choosing a classifier

The following figures my be indecipherable if viewed in black and white. Color versions of these figures can be found on Packt's website. Please make sure you seek these out for a full understanding of the material!

These are just four of the most popular classifiers out there, but there are many more to choose from. Although some classification mechanisms perform better on some types of datasets than others, it can be hard to develop intuition as to exactly the ones they are suitable for. In order to help with this, we will be examining the efficacy of our four classifiers on four different two-dimensional made-up datasets, each with a vastly different optimal decision boundary. In doing so, we will learn more about the characteristics of each classifier and gain a better sense of the kinds of data they might be better suited for.

The four datasets are depicted in *Figure 10.11*:

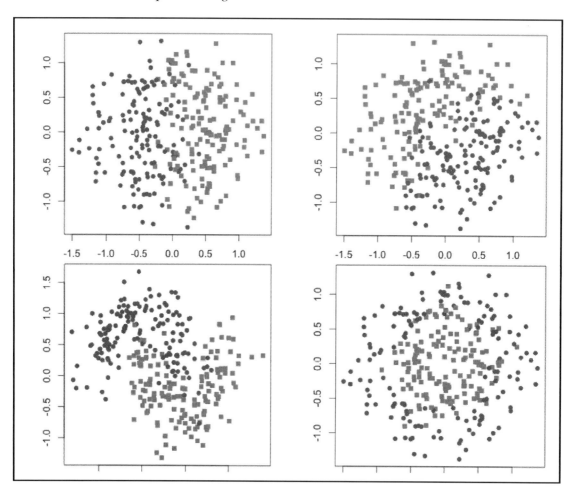

Figure 10.11: A plot depicting the class patterns of our four illustrative and contrived datasets

The vertical decision boundary

The first contrived dataset we will be looking at is the one in the top-left panel of *Figure 10.11*. This is a relatively simple classification problem because, just by visual inspection, you can tell that the optimal decision boundary is a vertical line. Let's see how each of our classifiers fair on this dataset:

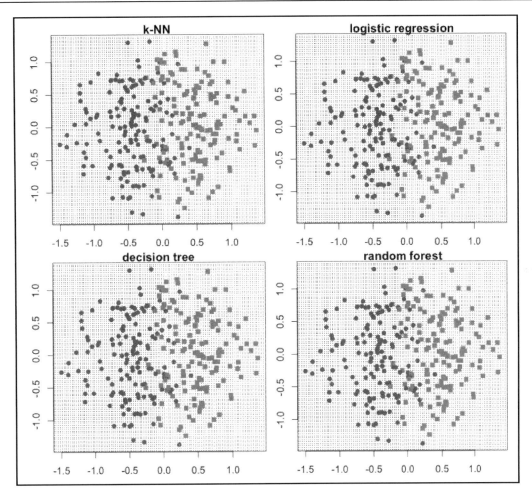

Figure 10.12: A plot of the decision boundaries of our four classifiers on our first contrived dataset

As you can see, all of our classifiers performed well on this simple dataset; all of the methods find an appropriate straight vertical line that is most representative of the class division. In general, logistic regression is great for linear decision boundaries. Decision trees also work well for straight decision boundaries, as long as the boundaries are orthogonal to the axes! Observe the next dataset.

The diagonal decision boundary

The second dataset sports an optimal decision boundary that is a diagonal line—one that is *not* orthogonal to the axes. Here, we start to see some cool behavior from certain classifiers:

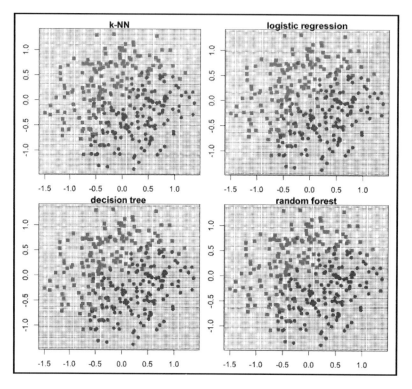

Figure 10.13: A plot of the decision boundaries of our four classifiers on our second contrived dataset

Though all four classifiers were reasonably effective in this dataset's classification, we start to see each of the classifiers' personalities come out. First, the k-NN creates a boundary that closely approximates the optimal one. The logistic regression, amazingly, throws a perfect linear boundary at the exact right spot.

The decision tree's boundary is curious; it is made up of perpendicular zig-zags. Though the optimal decision boundary is linear in the input space, the decision tree can't capture its essence. This is because decision trees only split on a function of one variable at a time. Thus, datasets with complex interactions may not be the best ones to attack with a decision tree.

Finally, the random forest, being composed of sufficiently varied decision trees, is able to capture the spirit of the optimal boundary.

The crescent decision boundary

This third dataset, depicted in the bottom-left panel of *Figure 10.11*, exhibits a very non-linear classification pattern:

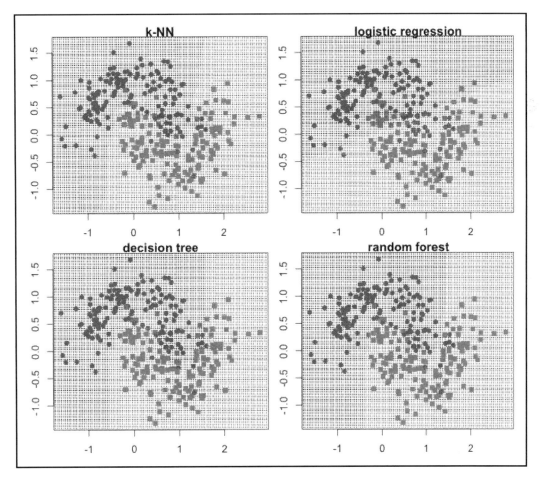

Figure 10.14: A plot of the decision boundaries of our four classifiers on our third contrived dataset

In the preceding figure, our top performers are k-NN, which is highly effective with non-linear boundaries, and random forest, which is similarly effective. The decision tree is a little too jagged to compete at the top level. But the real loser here is logistic regression. Because logistic regression returns linear decision boundaries, it is ineffective at classifying the data.

To be fair, with a little finesse, logistic regression can handle these boundaries, too, as we'll see in the last example. However, in highly non-linear situations, where the nature of the non-linear boundary is unknown or unknowable, logistic regression is often outperformed by other classifiers that natively handle these situations with ease.

The circular decision boundary

The last dataset we will be looking at, like the previous one, contains a non-linear classification pattern:

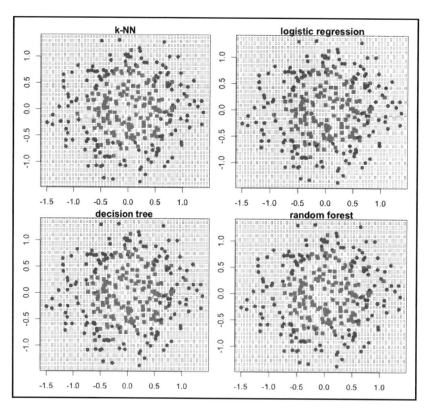

Figure 10.15: A plot of the decision boundaries of our four classifiers on our fourth contrived dataset

Again, just like in the last case, the winners are k-NN and random forest, followed by the decision tree with its jagged edges. And, again, the logistic regression unproductively throws a linear boundary at a distinctively not-linear pattern. However, stating that logistic regression is unsuitable for problems of this type is both negligent and dead wrong.

With a slight change to the incantation of the logistic regression, the whole game is changed, and logistic regression becomes the clear winner:

```
model <- glm(factor(dep.var) ~ ind.var1 +
            I(ind.var1^2) + ind.var2 + I(ind.var2^2),
            data=this, family=binomial(logit))
```

Now, let's take a look at a second-order (quadratic) logistic regression:

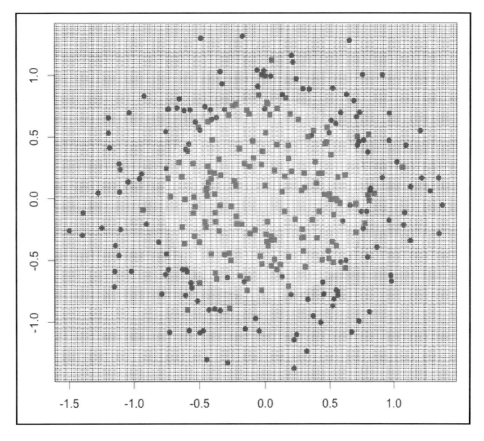

Figure 10.16: A second-order (quadratic) logistic regression decision boundary

In the preceding figure, instead of modeling the binary dependent variable (dep.var) as a linear combination of solely the two independent variables (ind.var1 and ind.var2), we model it as a function of those two variables and those two variables *squared*. The result is still a linear combination of the inputs (before the inverse link function), but now the inputs contain non-linear transformations of the other original inputs. This general technique is called *polynomial regression* and can be used to create a wide variety of non-linear boundaries. In this example, just squaring the inputs (resulting in a quadratic polynomial) outputs a classification circle that exactly matches the optimal decision boundary, as you can see in *Figure 10.16*. Cubing the original inputs (creating a cubic polynomial) suffices to describe the boundary in the previous example.

In fact, a logistic regression containing polynomial terms of arbitrarily large order can fit any decision boundary—no matter how non-linear and complicated. Careful, though! Using high-order polynomials is a great way to make sure you overfit your data.

My general advice is to only use polynomial regression in cases where you know *a priority* what polynomial form your boundaries take on, such as an ellipse! If you must experiment, keep a close eye on your cross-validated error rate to make sure you are not fooling yourself into thinking that you are doing the right thing by taking on more and more polynomial terms.

Exercises

Practise the following exercises to get a firm grasp on the concepts learned so far:

- Did you notice that I put *CV* in italics when I said that using k=27 seems like a safe bet as measured by the minimization of the CV error? Did you wonder why? I (quite deliberately) made a gaffe in choosing the k in the k-NN from *Figure 10.4*. My choice wasn't wrong, per se, but my choice of k may have been informed by data that should have been unavailable to me. How might have I committed a common but serious error in hyper-parameter tuning? How might I have done things differently?

- Remember that we spent a long time talking about the assumptions of linear regression? In contrast, we spent virtually no time discussing the assumptions of logistic regression. Although logistic regression has less stringent assumptions than its cousin, it is not assumption-free. Think about what some assumptions of logistic regression might be. Confirm your suspicions by doing research on the web. My omission of the assumptions was not out of laziness, and (again) it was quite deliberate. As you progress in your career as a data analyst, you will often come across exciting new classification methods that you will, no doubt, want to put to use right away. A trait that will set you apart from your more impulsive colleagues is one that promotes careful examination and independent research into where these techniques could go wrong.

- You may be surprised to learn that all of the classification techniques that we discussed in this chapter can be adapted for use in regression (predicting continuous variables)! The adaptation of logistic regression is obvious, but think about how you might adapt the others for use in this purpose. Do some research into it.

- Did the Foucault's *Chinese Encyclopedia* exist? To what extent does Foucault's lackadaisical approach to history undermine his project?

Summary

At a high level, in this chapter you learned about four of the most popular classifiers out there: *k-Nearest Neighbors*, *logistic regression*, *decision trees*, and *random forests*. Not only did you learn the basics and mechanics of these four algorithms, but you saw how easy they were to perform in R. Along the way, you learned about confusion matrices, hyper-parameter tuning, and maybe even a few new R incantations.

We also visited some more general ideas; for example, you've expanded your understanding of the *bias-variance trade-off*, looked at how the GLM can perform great feats, and have become acquainted with ensemble learning and bootstrap aggregation. It's also my hope that you've developed some intuition as to which classifiers to use in different situations. Finally, given that we couldn't achieve perfect classification on our diabetes dataset, I hope that you've gained an appreciation for the art and difficulty of classification. Perhaps you've even caught the statistical learning bug and want to try to beat the performance in this chapter! That would be great! There are competitions on the web for people just like you, and it is a great way to hone your skills. This, for better or worse, concludes our unit on predictive analytics. In the final chapter, we will be discussing some of the trials and tribulations of data analysis as they tend to happen in practice. Stay tuned!

Predicting Changes with Time

11

The inventory and staffing of your favorite bookstore, the telecommunications route of every important phone call you make or website you visit, policy changes with regard to climate change, your retirement portfolio, exploitative pricing models that capitalize on consumer need and scarcity under the guise of *efficient allocation of resources;* all of these, and *innumerable* others, have one thing in common. They make heavy use of the statistical approach to predicting changes with time, or *time series forecasting,* based on data from past and present.

In this chapter, we are going to go through different *methods* of forecasting but only one overarching *model* (exponential smoothing/ETS), though there exist many others (ARIMA, RBF neural networks, and so on). There are a few reasons for this:

- First, the model we'll be talking about, as we'll see, is very widely applicable to a range of different time series with a range of different properties
- Second, concentrating on one will give us a much better sense of the complexities and details of forecasting without trying, for *completeness'* sake, to cover everything in a very shallow manner

Before we start, here is something to note: the layout of the topics introduced in this chapter takes a mild departure from the usual progression seen in many introductory texts. Often, these texts are optimized for reference.

Something I've tried to underscore with only delving in to one forecasting model, is that this chapter should be read from front to back in its entirety as it follows an intuitive progression with each topic building on the fundamentals of the last. This sentiment is also echoed in the preface of this book in regard to chapter order, particularly the first several chapters. In both cases, I think this is key to *really* understanding the material.

What is a time series?

Broadly, a *time series* is a set of data points, for one or more variables, that is put in the order of the time they occurred. When we speak of time series in this chapter, we are referring specifically to regularly spaced, *fixed interval* time series. As such, the measurements can be taken yearly, every second, and everything in between and beyond, as long as there is an equal interval of time between each successive observation and measurements exist at the end of every interval.

For the purposes of statistical time series forecasting, we treat observations as realizations of random variables, much like in virtually everything we've done so far. Pointedly, observations of a time series are realizations of a *stochastic process*. Because our observations are recorded in intervals, as opposed to continuously, you can refer to time series data as a *discrete-time* stochastic process, to impress a date (update: don't do this, it will backfire)!

What is forecasting?

Before we move on, let's make a distinction between two related terms. Time series *analysis* is the description, analysis, and/or search for insights and meaning of time series data that has already happened. *Forecasting*, as we've already read in the preface, is the prediction of *future* values of a discrete-time stochastic process.

We will, incidentally, be doing some time series analysis in the process of forecasting future values but, by virtue of being in the **predictive analytics** unit of this book, we will mainly be focused on *prediction*, rather than analysis proper.

One other note: When we speak of forecasting in this chapter, we are referring specifically to *quantitative forecasting* as opposed to *judgemental* or *qualitative* forecasts (which seek to make predictions in spite of a lack or dearth of historical data, or in light of an unforeseen "shock to the system".

In contrast, quantitative forecasting is used when we have sufficient numerical values for past observations to pick up patterns, and we are comfortable making the assumption that the patterns and occurrences in the past are likely to extend, relatively unchanged, into the future.

Forecasting is all about finding *patterns* in a series. Once we identify patterns, we can extrapolate future values. The reliability of the results of a forecast is contingent on our ability to correctly identify patterns in the series (if there even are any) and distinguishing those patterns from noise.

Uncertainty

The role of (and obstacles created by) uncertainty in forecasting is difficult to understate. Even if we could identify the deterministic patterns of a series as best as theoretically possible, there is still uncertainty in our forecasts due to random noise in our observed data, which will also be present in the future. In addition, there is uncertainty surrounding our proper identification of the patterns, or *signal*, of our series and our parameter estimates.

There's a time and a place for *point forecasts*, or forecasts that predict a single value of a variable for some future time, but we would often like some kind of measure of the uncertainty of our predictions. If we think of observations in time as realizations from a stochastic model, we can describe likely – or, at least, *plausible – futures*, or *scenarios*, based on our model. Many many likely futures forecasts form a distribution, for which we can build prediction intervals. Good prediction intervals will capture uncertainty coming from the level of noise in the original series *and* uncertainty coming from uncertainty in our estimates of model parameters. This uncertainty generally increases as we move further along the forecast *horizon*, or the number of values (years, months, and so on) out we are trying to forecast.

The prediction intervals (PIs) are usually expressed in the language of confidence and credible intervals (95% prediction interval, 80% prediction interval, and so on). Bite back the urge to interpret these intervals literally. There are many different ways to derive prediction intervals, and each way warrants a different interpretation – a little like how confidence and credible intervals require vastly different interpretations. Moreover, it is well observed that PIs, most frequently, *understate* the degree of our uncertainty when we compare predictions with the actual observed values in the future. PIs are an invaluable tool in uncertainty visualization but avoid being fooled by the numbers or making quantitative statements about the probability of future values being within the bounds of a PI.

Difficulties in forecasting

The final note I'd like to make about forecasting, before we move on, is how very *hard* it is. There are several reasons for this. One of the main reasons is that humans are *extremely* adept at picking up patterns where none actually exist. For example, humans were guided by evolution to be experts in seeing faces because it is so essential to our survival. This explains why humans tend to see faces in everything (the surface of the moon, a piece of toast, the bark of a tree). Bringing it back to the topic at hand, if you show the vast majority of people a completely random time series, they will pick up *patterns* among noise and extrapolate these artificial patterns into the future. And, more often than you might think, there are just *no discernible patterns* in time series.

Another difficulty in forecasting is the inability to account for the unexpected. Now, it *isn't* the case that proper forecasting assumes that the future will not change; it *does*, however, make the assumption that the same *kinds* of changes that happen in the past will keep occurring into the future. For example, if someone were in charge of predicting the load/visitors on a David Bowie fan page on the internet, this person can legitimately be charged with identifying high-traffic periods such as weekly patterns, or spikes in traffic during fan-club meet ups, and incorporating them into a forecasting model. But say, when David Bowie quite unexpectedly (to the general public, at least) passed away, the number of visitors to the fan page took down the web server. The forecaster could (and often would) be blamed for not having somehow correctly "divined" this, even though there was absolutely nothing in the past observations that the forecaster could have extrapolated from. In much of forecasting – including all the examples in this chapter – the only thing we have to go on are the historical data.

It is very often the case that forecasters take the heat when very unexpected events change the course of time series. Just think back to enormous stock market crashes, or the unexpected final results of the 2016 US presidential election.

Forecasting, like economics, is often a dismal science.

Creating and plotting time series

A common approach in tutorials is to jump right into manipulating a plotting time series by using one of R's *many* built-in time series data sets. Here, I'd like to explain how to actually create a time series object (an R object of type ts) like you would if you were to have to perform forecasting on your *own* data.

I made available some special data sets that we'll use in this and future chapters by putting on a repository on the internet.

Let's first start by downloading one of these data sets and peering into its contents:

```
>
download.file("https://raw.githubusercontent.com/tonyfischetti/dawr/master/
forecasting/school-supplies.csv", "./school-supplies.csv")
> school <- read.csv("./school-supplies.csv")
> head(school)
  thedate hits
1 2004-01 20
2 2004-02 24
3 2004-03 19
4 2004-04 26
5 2004-05 25
6 2004-06 24
> start(schoolts)
[1] 2004 1
> end(schoolts)
[1] 2018 3
```

This is a data set that contains the number of Google searches for *school supplies* on a monthly basis from January 2004 to March 2018. You can build and download your own data sets like this by visiting the website `https://trends.google.com/trends/` and searching for a term in **Exploring Topics.**

To create a time series object from this, we use the `ts` function, like so:

```
> schoolts <- ts(school$hits, start=c(2004, 1), frequency=12)
> schoolts
     Jan Feb Mar Apr May Jun Jul Aug Sep Oct Nov Dec
2004  20  24  19  26  25  24  55  88  32  26  20  19
2005  27  24  22  19  24  22  57  82  34  21  19  19
2006  22  21  19  17  21  24  61  77  29  18  16  14
2007  22  16  17  18  21  25  56  86  27  18  16  14
2008  19  16  16  16  19  20  55  79  24  16  14  12
2009  16  16  15  13  15  19  54  85  24  14  15  11
2010  17  15  13  13  15  18  49  78  23  13  11  10
2011  15  12  11  11  12  17  53  79  22  12  12  10
...
```

The arguments to the `ts` function, in this example, are

- A vector holding the values for each observation
- A vector containing the year and the month of the first observation
- The number of observations per unit of time; since this is a monthly series, `12` is the appropriate value

To keep your attention – before creating or downloading our other time series data sets, let's plot this time series object! Plotting a `ts` object in R could scarcely be easier: just executing `plot(schoolts)` will suffice. However, the package that we will be using the most in this chapter (`forecast`) provides a method of the `ggplot2` library's generic `autoplot` function for quickly plotting time series, as well. We'll be using this method here in order to reap the other benefits of `ggplot2` over base-R graphics and produce more attractive default plots:

```
> library(ggplot2)
> library(forecast)
> autoplot(schoolts)
```

The resulting plot is shown in Figure 11.1 in the top left panel.

Let's create another time series object with different properties.

This data set contains temperature anomaly data from NASA (see the citation at the end of the chapter). Since this data set contains temperature *anomalies*, the raw temperatures are not reported; instead the data contains a metric illustrating to what extent the temperature differs from its *usual* temperature. The range of values is between -0.5 and 1. You can read more information about this by following the first citation at the end of the chapter.

The original monthly data set was transformed by aggregating at the yearly level to make it easier to work with here:

```
>
download.file("https://raw.githubusercontent.com/tonyfischetti/dawr/master/
forecasting/yearly-land-air-temp.csv", "yearly-temp.csv")
> yearlytemp <- read.csv("yearly-temp.csv")
> head(yearlytemp)
  year val
1 1880 -0.1900000
2 1881 -0.1008333
3 1882 -0.1108333
4 1883 -0.1941667
5 1884 -0.2966667
6 1885 -0.3175000
```

Since this is yearly data (starting in 1880), the number of observations per unit of time (frequency) is 1:

```
> tempts <- ts(yearlytemp$val, start=1880, frequency=1)
> autoplot(tempts)
```

The plot is shown in the top right panel of Figure 11.1.

Now, let's actually *create* a series with made up data. Specifically, we will be sampling from a normal (Gaussian) distribution of mean 100 and a standard deviation of 20 100 times and (quite arbitrarily) set the time of the first observation to 1900. This will also be yearly data:

```
> # set the seed for deterministic "randomness"
> set.seed(2)
> gausnoise <- rnorm(100, mean=100, sd=20)
> head(gausnoise)
[1] 82.06171 103.69698 131.75691 77.39249 98.39496 102.64841
> gausts <- ts(gausnoise, start=1900, frequency=1)
> autoplot(gausts)
```

The plot is shown in the bottom left panel of Figure 11.1. We'll be using this series a lot in the following sections.

Lastly, we'll use the classic `AirPassengers` data set built right into R:

```
> autoplot(AirPassengers)
```

The plot is shown in the bottom right of Figure 11.1:

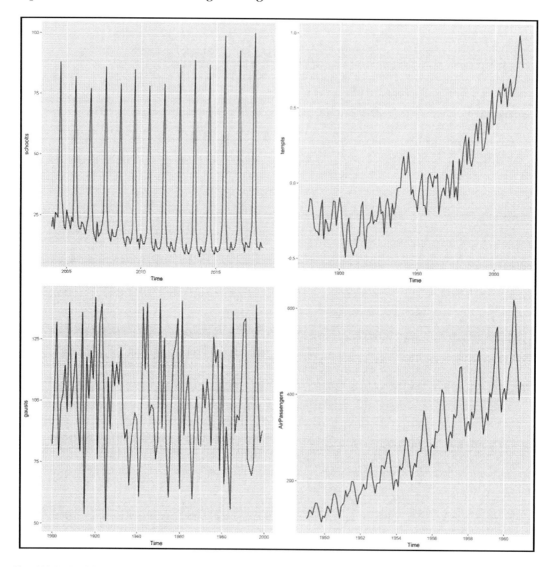

Figure 11.1: Number of Google search hits for school supplies (top left), global temperature anomalies (top right), a Gaussian white noise process (bottom left), and airline passenger data (bottom right)

Before we move on, I'd like to briefly demonstrate some of the advantages of using `ggplot2` library's `autoplot` generic on these series. As an example, check out how wild the fluctuations appear in the plot of the Google hits for the `school supplies` series.

We can set new, wider *y* axis limits, add a plot title, add a better label to the axes, and save the resulting plot to a PNG file using the same functions that we would use if this were just a regular `ggplot` construct:

```
> autoplot(schoolts) +
+    ylim(0, 200) +
+    ggtitle('google hits for "school supplies" since 2004') +
+    ggsave("school-supplies-fancy.png")
Saving 7 x 6.43 in image
```

The plot is shown as follows:

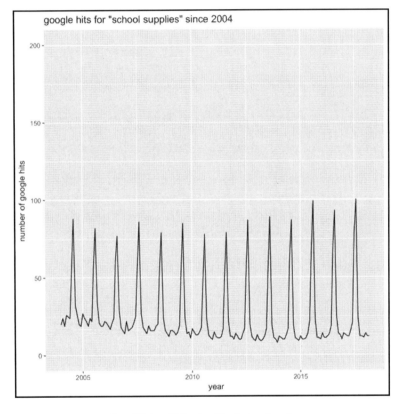

Figure 11.2: A modified version of the school supplies series

Much better!

Components of time series

It is worthwhile thinking of a time series as the combination of components, a **trend** component (**T**), a **seasonal** component (**S**), and an **error** (or *irregular*) component (**E**).

The *trend* is the long term movement of a time series. For example, both the time series in the left column of Figure 11.1 have a steady trend. The trend of the temperature anomaly data, in contrast, appears to have a slight upward trend from 1880 to around 1960, at which point the trend appears to increase at a much faster rate. This looks as if it were a *non-linear trend*.

The *seasonal* component is a pattern in the series that always occurs at a fixed, unchanging period of time. Possible periods of seasonal patterns are over every week or year. For example, our `school supplies` series has a *very* strong seasonal component, with peaks every August (often a month before the start of a school year). The `AirPassenger` data set, too, has a very strong seasonal component with peaks every summer. The seasonal period, here, is also yearly. *Seasonality* doesn't always have to occur over a fixed period of a year, though. For example, the number of riders on the New York City subway system have a strong *weekly* seasonal component, with more riders during the work week (when many people are trying to get to work) than on the weekends.

The error or irregular component, is the remainder of a series with the trend and seasonality removed. These values represent random error – remember, time series observations are realization of random variables. In our examples thus far, both the `school supplies` data and the `AirPassengers` data seem to not have a very strong error component. In contrast, the temperature data seems to have quite a bit of an irregularity about it and, finally, the normally distributed (Gaussian) noise series (on the bottom left of Figure 11.1) is *literally just* irregularity.

In the field, a fourth component – a *cyclic* component – is often spoken about. Cycles are general swings on one side of the trend line, or another, and usually last for a long time. For example, business cycles are said to occur (generally) every 7 to 11 years. In economics, it starts with an increase in production and low interest rates, then moves to crashes and firm bankruptcies, high interest rates and declining prices and economic production, to recovery again. As another example, it was observed in the mid 19th century that the number of sunspots (dark, relatively low temperature spots on the surface of the sun caused by changes in magnetic flux and, therefore, heat transfer) follow a cycle that is approximately 11 years long. This is known as the solar cycle.

It is not uncommon to confuse a cycle with either a seasonal or a trend component. For example, Figure 11.3 is a plot of an excerpt of the `sunspot` time series built right into R. At a quick glance, the solar cycles *appear* to be a seasonal pattern because they seem to occur at rather fixed intervals. A closer look, however (or some know-how in astronomy and electromagnetism, I suppose) reveals that these patterns are only *nearly* regular. As another example, there have been natural (not human-caused) climate cycles in Earth's history as far back as we can reliably measure; although, it appears that there is a drastic trend change around 1970 in our series, it could *theoretically* (but almost certainly not) be the case that it just happens to be the start of one of these natural cycles (and not due to a very large increase in total fossil carbon emissions). The main point is that, when you are only looking at a part of a series (or if that is the only part of the series available) you can sometimes confuse cyclical behavior for trends. This is a problem because cycles are *far* harder to forecast with than trends:

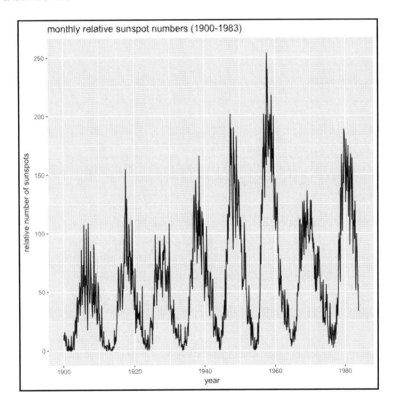

Figure 11.3: Monthly relative sunspot sightings and solar cycles

Anyway, cyclical behavior is, for many purposes and for many different reasons, lumped in this the trend component, even though they are technically distinct.

These three components (trend/cycle [T], seasonality [S], and error/irregular [E]) can be combined in two main ways to give rise to a particular series that we want to analyze.

In an *additive* formulation, the components are just added together: if we use *Y* to represent the *observed* value at a point in time in our series, and *[t]* to represent the value of a component at arbitrary time *t*, then the additive model looks like this:

$Y[t] = T[t] + S[t] + E[t]$

The *multiplicative* formulation, instead, takes the product of all the components:

$Y[t] = T[t] \times S[t] \times E[t]$

When the magnitude of the seasonal variations or variance of the trend/cycle remain relatively stable with time, an additive formulation makes a good model. In contrast, the multiplicative formulation is appropriate when the magnitudes of these components change as a function of time. The AirPassengers series, for example, is a classic example of a series where the components interact in a multiplicative fashion. This is common for other economic series as well.

Time series decomposition

The technique of *time series decomposition* seeks to separate out the components that make up a series, using various techniques. There are several reasons why someone would want to do this, but the three main motivations are usually (a) to independently view the estimated trend component, (b) to provide a series with the seasonal component removed, and (c) to study the dynamics of the seasonal component in isolation.

The school supplies series, for example, was one that we identified as having a roughly level trend and an additive seasonal and error component. We can decompose this series using the function of the same name in R:

```
> schoolcomps <- decompose(schoolts)
> autoplot(schoolcomps)
```

The plot of decomposition of an additive time series is as follows:

Figure 11.4: Decomposition of the school supplies series

As you can see, the procedure took its best guesses as to the shapes and levels of its constitute components. In the top panel, we see the actual observed data. Below, we see the error/irregular component. In the third, we have a best-guess as to how the seasonal component looks. Finally, the last panel from the top, shows the trend/cycle component. Although it may look like there is a very strong dip in the trend component, note the scale of the *y* axis. Even if there *were* a true trend, a model of this series without any trend whatsoever would not be an inappropriate one.

Contrastingly, the `AirPassengers` series is an example of a multiplicative combining of components. We can decompose this series by providing an explicit directive to the `decompose` function alerting it to use a multiplicative model:

```
> aircomps <- decompose(AirPassengers, type="multiplicative")
> autoplot(aircomps)
```

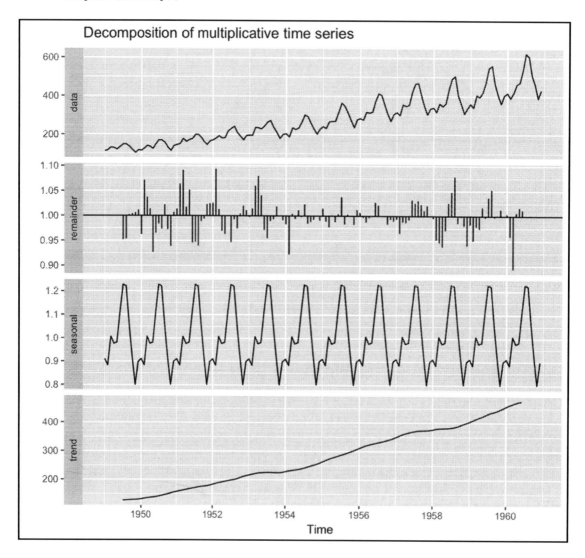

Figure 11.5: Decomposition of the AirPassengers series

The decomposition process appears to have separated a very handsome looking seasonal component and identified a rather linear trend. Note the **remainder** (error) component, though. This doesn't look great, and it is a sign that the decomposition procedure failed to be as effective as it could be. We'll see why in the following two sections.

White noise

I'd like to talk about a very special time series in this section: the *white noise* series. White noise is an important topic of physics, psychoacoustics, computer science, electronics, and even medicine. As you might expect, the concept of the white noise series is an important fundamental in time series analysis and forecasting, as well.

If you've ever turned your radio on between stations, you've heard white noise in action but what is it really?

White noise (in the strict sense of the term) is a random series whose samples are identically distributed and statistically independent. For example, the time series we made from sampling from the normal distribution 100 times was a white noise series. At every point in time, the mean of the distribution which gave rise to the samples was constant, and every sample was completely independent of the sample before it.

More specifically, the series we created from random sampling is called a **Gaussian white noise** series, since the observations came from a normal (Gaussian) distribution. Even outside of time series analysis, Gaussian noise is very common. For example, communication channels are often troubled by white noise. This noise is the sum of many different kinds of random fluctuations (photon noise, black body radiation, thermal noise) that result in signal disturbances that roughly follow a normal distribution. This is a little bit like what you hear when a radio is detuned.

But why do we care, you ask.

A Gaussian white noise series is a series with no discernible pattern that can be exploited for prediction. The only rational forecast for a series like this is the mean of the observed values.

This is the end state of the error component of a good forecast model. If our model has picked up on all systematic information in our series and modeled it, the residuals (the differences between the already-observed and predicted values) should have no information left to model. If our residuals are serially correlated, or have a non-zero mean, that means we can still improve our model by taking advantage of this information. Thus, comparison to the Gaussian white noise series (or the *properties* of a Gaussian noise series) is an important technique in forecast assessment.

In addition, working with a series of this type at various times during the remainder of this chapter will, due to its simplicity and well-understood properties, be great for practice and illustrative purposes.

Autocorrelation

As we've covered for some time now, correlation is a measure of how strongly two variables fluctuate together. *Autocorrelation* is a measure of how strongly a series correlates to *lagged* versions of itself. A series with strong autocorrelation is said to be **serially correlated**.

Let's take {8, 6, 7, 5, 3, 0, 9} to be our example series. This series lagged one observation is {NA, 8, 6, 7, 5, 3, 0}:

```
Lag 0   8   6   7  5  3  0  9
Lag 1   NA  8   6  7  5  3  0
Lag 2   NA  NA  8  6  7  5  3
```

If we take the correlation coefficient of the lag 0 (observed values) and lag 1, we get -0.06. We can repeat this correlation evaluation for all lags *n-1*, where *n* is the length of the original series. This is the series **autocorrelation function**, or **ACF**.

You can visualize a time series' autocorrelation function using the `ggAcf` function provided by the `forecast` package. (Note that this plot is sometimes called a correlogram). Let's take a look at the ACF for the `school supplies` series and see what's going on:

```
> ggAcf(schoolts)
```

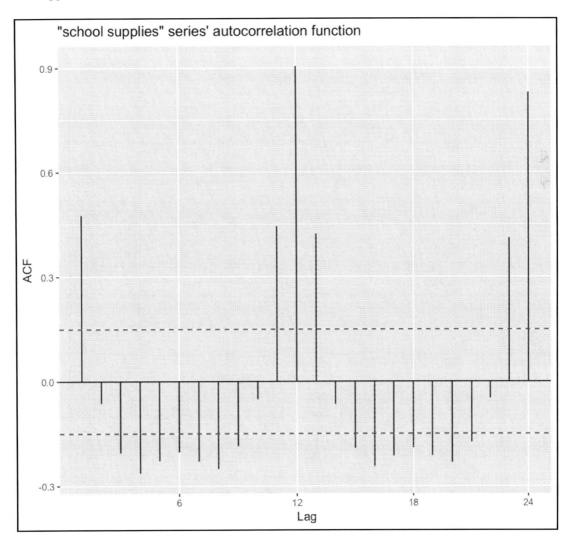

Figure 11.6: Autocorrelation function of the "school supplies series

As you work more and more with time series, you'll come to immediately identify ACF plots like the one in Figure 11.6 as classic examples of the autocorrelation dynamics of a seasonal time series. As you can see, the correlations across lags follow a *U* shape. The peak of this pattern, every 12 months is a positive correlation of a whooping 0.9. This means that the correlation between the series and the series lag by a year is almost perfect. The negative correlations in between are significant (in the colloquial sense), as well. This indicates that there is significant serial correlation in this series. In the statistical sense, any autocorrelations that pass the dashed blue horizontal bars are considered *significant*.

Let's have a look at Figure 11.7, showing the ACFs for our four example series:

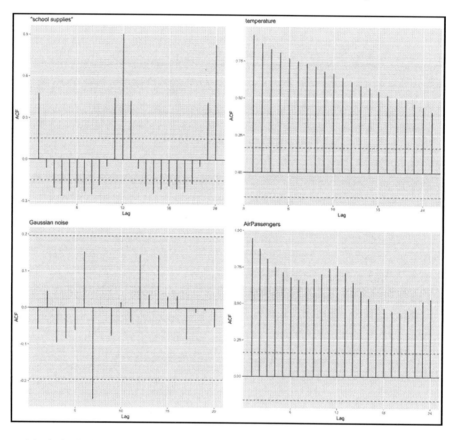

Figure 11.7: Autocorrelation plots for school supplies (top left), global temperature anomalies (top right), a Gaussian white noise process (bottom left), and airline passenger data (bottom right)

Our other series with very strong seasonality, `AirPassengers`, also has a very characteristic ACF plot. This also contains marked peaks at a yearly lag, but all autocorrelations are positive. This is due to the unwavering positive trend in the series, *independent* of the seasonal component.

The ACF plot for the temperature data is characteristic of a series with very high serial correlation, that drops off steadily – but slowly – as the lag value increases. This is a series with a strong trend and no seasonality that would lead to *spikes* in the autocorrelation function.

Probably the most important ACF plot though, is that of the Gaussian noise series. This is what the ACF plot of a non-serially correlated series looks like. Note that the correlations tend to jump around without any real pattern. Also note that all the autocorrelations (save for one) are within the dashed lines. Don't be fooled by that wayward line, though! We would expect 1 out of every 20 autocorrelations to be *statistically significant* by chance! The presence of the aberrant bar *does not* mean that our series is a serial correlation, as we'll soon see.

There's a more principled way to test if a series is serially correlated, though. We can test for serial correlation, within an NHST framework, using the `Ljung-Box` test:

```
> Box.test(schoolts, type="Ljung-Box")
Box-Ljung test
data: schoolts
X-squared = 39.472, df = 1, p-value = 0.0000000003328
```

A significant `p-value` is said to suggest a rejection of the null hypothesis that the series being tested *isn't* serially correlated. Therefore, many choose to interpret a significant `p-value` as indicating that a series *is* serially correlated. Many people would interpret the output of the preceding test as proof that the `school supplies` series has serial correlation. In this case, it incontrovertibly does, though I hope you remember what I've said about NHST in the last unit. Interpret the p-values as you will.

Let's check out the test outputs of our other series:

```
> Box.test(tempts, type="Ljung-Box")
Box-Ljung test
data: tempts
X-squared = 121.71, df = 1, p-value < 2.2e-16
>
> Box.test(gausts, type="Ljung-Box")
Box-Ljung test
data: gausts
X-squared = 0.36027, df = 1, p-value = 0.5484
>
```

```
> Box.test(AirPassengers, type="Ljung-Box")
Box-Ljung test
data: AirPassengers
X-squared = 132.14, df = 1, p-value < 2.2e-16
```

In spite of that deviant autocorrelation in the Gaussian noise series passing the "significance" guide bars, we fail to reject the null hypothesis that this series is serially correlated. In this case, we know that the series isn't and can't be serially correlated

Some forecasting procedures *require* that we transform our series into one that is not serially correlated in order to work properly. In cases like these, it is popular to use a Ljung-Box test to verify that we prepared the series correctly. Our forecasting methods, on the other hand, don't require this preparation; we *will*, though, be using a Ljung-Box test on our residuals when we assess our models.

A related concept that you will see in time series literature is *stationarity*. A *stationary* time series is one where the mean, variance and autocorrelation does not change over time. Our Gaussian noise series is the only one we've seen so far that is stationary. We can however, if we needed to, make our other series stationary by performing transformations on them, such as *differencing*, or subtracting consecutive observations from each other.

We do not focus on stationarity or differencing here, because our forecasting methods do not require it; but I wanted to bring the topic up just so you, dear reader, are not dazed and confused if you see the topic broached in other time series literature.

Smoothing

Since the removal of the irregular component and visualizing just the trend in a series is of such interest to practitioners, various methods of *smoothing*, or remove the *roughness* and noise of a series to get a better sense on the signal, have been devised.

Perhaps the simplest method of smoothing a series is to use a *simple moving average*. In this technique a *window* length is defined. Say our window is set to five observations: for each observation in the time series, then, the first two observations to the left and right (along with the current observation) are averaged; this average then becomes the new value at that point in the series.

Let's perform a simple moving average smoothing on the Gaussian noise series and visualize the results of using different window lengths. We will use the SMA function from the TTR package:

```
> library(TTR)
> sm5 <- SMA(gausnoise, n=5)
> sm10 <- SMA(gausnoise, n=10)
> sm15 <- SMA(gausnoise, n=15)
> head(sm5, n=10)
 [1] NA NA NA NA 98.66061 102.77795 104.87037
 [8] 97.56020 110.01960 109.78546
```

The plot for the smoothed Gaussian noise time series is as follows:

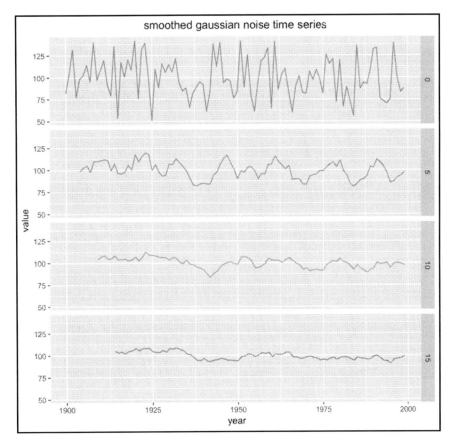

Figure 11.8: Using a simple moving average of window size 0, 5, 10, and 15 on the Gaussian noise series

This plot depicts the raw series (top panel), and the smoothed series for window lengths 5, 10, and 15 (second, third, and last panels, respectively). Notice how the series gets smoother and smoother the larger we make the window.

Note that in the simple moving average procedure:

- The only observations that have any bearing on the new calculated value are the ones within the window
- All observations in the window contribute to the new value equally. In some respects, it's a little silly to think that observations 10 intervals away should influence the new value as much as the observations 1 and 2 intervals away.

A more sophisticated procedure for smoothing allows:

- All the observations to contribute to the calculated value at each observation
- Weights closer observations more heavily influence the final smoothed value

More concretely, a particular weight is given to the closest observations, and the weights of the subsequent observations decay *exponentially* as we move further away. How much weight is given to the closest observation is controlled by the *alpha* parameter, which ranges from 0 to 1.

The following code will perform simple exponential smoothing using the `ses` function (with alpha parameters of 0, 0.1, 0.33, 0.66, and 1):

```
> se1 <- ses(gausts, alpha=.999)
> se.66 <- ses(gausts, alpha=.666)
> se.33 <- ses(gausts, alpha=.333)
> se.1 <- ses(gausts, alpha=0.1)
> se0 <- ses(gausts, alpha-0.001)
> head(fitted(se.1))
Time Series:
Start = 1900
End = 1905
Frequency = 1
[1] 102.9813 100.8894 101.1701 104.2288 101.5452 101.2301
```

Note that another benefit of exponential smoothing is that we don't lose observations at the beginning of the series, like we do with the simple moving average method.

The following plot is of an exponentially smoothed Gaussian noise series for these different alpha parameters:

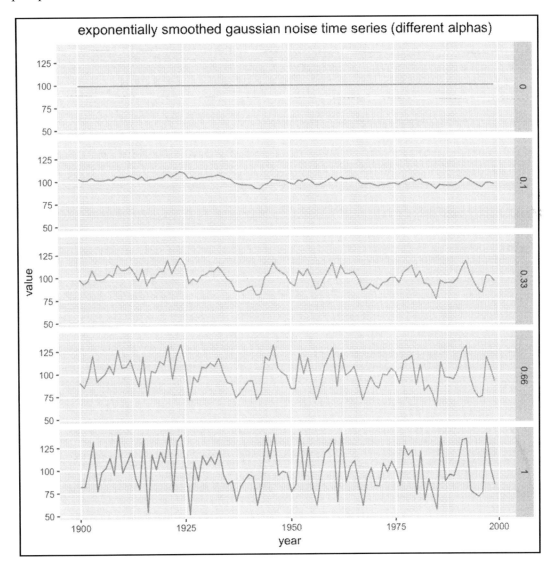

Figure 11.9: Using simple exponential smoothing with alpha parameters 0, 0.1, 0.33, 0.66, and 1 on the Gaussian noise series

Note that an alpha of 0 weights all observations equally, and results in a straight line at the mean of the overall series. An alpha of 1, on the other hand, uses only the current observation and, thus, results in a series identical to the original one. The lower the alpha parameter, the more *smooth* the new series will appear.

Be careful, though! By setting the alpha parameter too low, you may lose the ability to visualize important dynamics of the trend/cycle!

Simple exponential smoothing for forecasting

As it turns out, simple exponential smoothing can be used to forecast into the future, as well! This method is the simplest of all exponential smoothing forecast methods, and is really only to be used for trend-less series (such as the Gaussian noise series).

In this section, we will be making a forecast with this method, and see a few other very simple forecasting methods for comparison. Let's start with these simple forecasting methods.

The mean method simply forecasts future values using the mean of the historical data. Let's see it in action:

```
> mfore <- meanf(gausts, h=20)
> autoplot(mfore)
```

The meanf function (which performs the forecast and returns an object of the same name) takes a h argument, which specifies how far into the future we would like to forecast. In these examples, we will be forecasting 20 years into the future.

The second line uses the autoplot method of the forecast object to create a quite handsome default plot (depicted in the following plot):

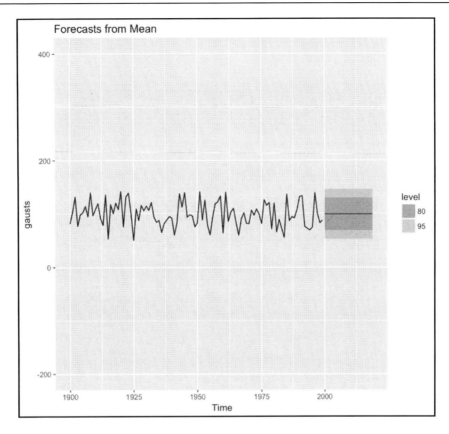

Figure 11.10: Using the mean forecasting method on the Gaussian noise series

The plot, by default, shows the historical data, the forecasts h number of intervals into the future and the 95% and 80% **prediction intervals**. Do *not* trust these intervals.

Another simple method is the **naive** method. This simply forecasts the last observed value for every future value. As dumb as this might sound, this is very often the best we can do, especially in very short term forecasts of the price of financial instruments.

Finally, there's the simple exponential smoothing forecast, which uses the same `ses` function as we used before. This also takes an h parameter (just like the naive method) and returns an object of type `forecast` which can be plotted painlessly with `autoplot`. If we do not specify the `alpha` parameter, the `ses` function will try to estimate its proper value.

Let's now perform forecasts for the same horizon using these two methods, and visualize the results of all three:

```
> nfore <- naive(gausts, h=20)
> sfore <- ses(gausts, h=20)
> # we are setting PI to false to suppress
> # plotting the prediction intervals
> autoplot(gausts) +
+    ylim(0, 200) + xlim(1900, 2010) +
+    autolayer(mfore, PI=FALSE, series="mean") +
+    autolayer(nfore, PI=FALSE, series="naive") +
+    autolayer(sfore, PI=FALSE, series="ses")
```

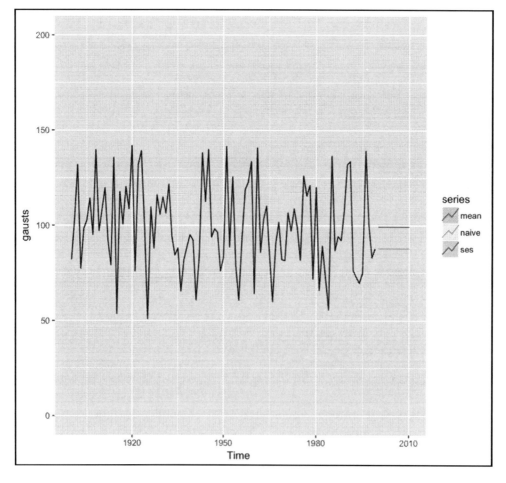

Figure 11.11: Using the mean, naive and simple exponential forecasting methods on the Gaussian noise series

As you can see, the naive method just extended the last observation 20 intervals ahead into the future.

You might ask yourself, where are the forecasts using the mean method. In this case, the mean and the simple exponential smoothing method yielded nearly identical forecasts so the former is completely eclipsed by the line of the latter. Calling summary on the sfore object will give some clue as to why this is the case:

```
> summary(sfore)
Forecast method: Simple exponential smoothing
Model Information:Simple exponential smoothing
Call:
ses(y = gausts, h = 20)
Smoothing parameters:
alpha = 0.0001
Initial states:
l = 99.3055
sigma: 23.0888
AIC AICc BIC
1094.386 1094.636 1102.202
Error measures:
ME RMSE MAE MPE MAPE MASE
Training set 0.07145194 23.08877 19.04151 -5.942264 20.89301 0.7154352
ACF1
Training set -0.05912586
Forecasts:
Point Forecast Lo 80 Hi 80 Lo 95 Hi 95
2000 99.3062 69.71675 128.8957 54.05305 144.5594
2001 99.3062 69.71675 128.8957 54.05305 144.5594
2002 99.3062 69.71675 128.8957 54.05305 144.5594
. . . .
```

This spits out quite of bit of information (some of which we will be able to interpret by this chapter's conclusion). The data that I'd like to draw your attention to now, though, is the estimate of the alpha parameter, 0.0001. For this series, the ses intelligently estimated the proper alpha level at near zero, which, as we've seen in Figure 11.9, is essentially a straight line at the mean. There are no patterns in this series we can exploit to improve upon the dead-simple mean method.

Accuracy assessment

Just like with the prediction of continuous and categorical variables in the previous two chapters, honest assessments of model accuracy is of the upmost importance.

The typical first step in the assessment of forecasts is a thorough analysis of the residuals (again, the difference between the values the model gives and the actual observed values). This often includes plotting a histogram of the residuals (to check for a zero mean and symmetric distribution) and an ACF plot (to verify that there is no serial correlation in the residuals). Additionally, a great thing to do is to run a Ljung-Box test on the residuals to more qualitatively check for serial correlation. Luckily for us, the forecast package provides a function, checkresiduals, (that takes an object of type forecast) that does all of these things for us:

```
> checkresiduals(mfore)
Ljung-Box test
data: Residuals from Mean
Q* = 12.702, df = 9, p-value = 0.1766
Model df: 1. Total lags used: 10
>
> checkresiduals(nfore)
Ljung-Box test
data: Residuals from Naive method
Q* = 58.18, df = 10, p-value = 0.000000007996
Model df: 0. Total lags used: 10
>
> checkresiduals(sfore)
Ljung-Box test
data: Residuals from Simple exponential smoothing
Q* = 12.701, df = 8, p-value = 0.1226
Model df: 2. Total lags used: 10
```

The plots for all of these calls to `checkresiduals` is shown in Figure 11.12:

Figure 11.12: The plots of the checkresiduals function on the forecast objects of the mean, naive, and the simple exponential forecasting methods on the Gaussian noise series

As is suggested by the plots (and evident from the Ljung-Box test output) the only forecast that doesn't pass our "smell test" test is the naive method, as we might have predicted.

As with the statistical learning algorithms and techniques from the previous two chapters, just testing how well our model fits the data is never enough. A model with enough parameters can *perfectly* fit our historical data, but perform very poorly when it comes to actually forecasting future values (overfitting). Therefore, we must have a way of testing the accuracy of our model on data that we haven't seen. We will use the same exact training/testing set approach as we did in the last two chapters in order to do this.

The Gaussian noise series runs from January 1900 to January 1999. Suppose we created a training set by taking an excerpt of this series from 1900 to 1980 and trying to predict the values for the subsequent 19 years.

We can, quite easily, take an *excerpt* of the series of this type using the `window` function. Then, let's fit out simple models to only the *training* series and save the results to variables with descriptive names:

```
> train <- window(gausts, start=1900, end=1980)
> nforetr <- naive(train, h=20)
> mforetr <- meanf(train, h=20)
> sforetr <- ses(train, h=20)
```

Now we can get different fit metrics by comparing the predictions of the models with the *actual* observed values that we left out of the *training* phase. To do this, we can call `forecast` function's `accuracy` function with two arguments, the `forecast object` and the full time series. The output is a whole mess of different fit metrics, but I'll only be showing the two simplest and most popular ones here, RMSE, and MAE. These are the ones we'll learn about in this section, but feel free to learn about the other ones (particularly MAPE and MASE) with supplemental self-study:

```
> accuracy(nforetr, gausts)
RMSE MAE
Training set 33.41918 26.86576
Test set 36.44798 33.16893
>
accuracy(mforetr, gausts)
RMSE MAE
Training set 22.41742 18.33581
Test set 25.96117 22.84341
>
> accuracy(sforetr, gausts)
RMSE MAE
Training set 22.41900 18.34584
Test set 26.00306 22.91065
```

The **RMSE** is the **root squared mean error**. This is exactly like the RSME that we learned about in the chapter on linear regression. To review, all the errors are squared (so positive and negative values don't cancel each other out), averaged, and then square rooted (in order to express the error in the units of the original data again). As before, the smaller the RSME, the better.

The **MAE** is the **mean absolute error**. This is simply the mean of the absolute values (positives stay positive, negatives turn positive) of the errors. As with the RSME, the smaller, the better.

As with the assessment of models in the last two chapters, we are wary of the vanilla training/testing set paradigm, in part, because we worry that we (a) are putting too much stake in the assessment of just *one* (possibly idiosyncratic testing set), and (b) that we are losing valuable observations that we can train our models with. The solution back then was cross-validation; this will also be the hero here.

Cross validation for time series works a little differently than for regression and classification methods. Say we have a time series for times 1 to *t*. We take an excerpt of our series from 1 to *k*, where *k* can be anything from 1 (theoretically but not in practice) and one less than *t*. This excerpt is used as the **training set** and a forecast for the next (untrained on) observation is made with the resultant model fit. An error metric is then calculated and recorded. In the next step, we take an excerpt of the original time series from 1 to *k+1* and forecast and evaluate the accuracy of the predicted value at *k+2*. This process is repeated until the end of the line is reached and our procedure can't take any more excerpts of the series (because *k+n* is equal to *t*). Finally, we take either the mean or the median of the recorded *t-k* error measurements. This method, as described is called *one-step ahead rolling origin forecasts*. In this context, the *origin* is the last observation in the training set or, sometimes, the first observation in the test set.

This procedure has the attractive property of allowing us to use more available data to train models and more errors measurements to average over any bizarre idiosyncrasies. Note that:

- We can't set *k too* low because there has to be enough data in order to make a reasonable forecast
- We don't have to limit ourselves to *one-step ahead* forecasts. One-step ahead forecasts are just a special case of *h-step ahead* (where *h* forecasts are made for each rolling origin) where *h=1*. Here, we'll be using *h=5*.

We can perform time series cross validation (CV) quite easily with the aptly named `tsCV` function. To use this function, we must provide:

- A time series
- A function that returns a forecast object
- A forecast horizon (*h*):

```
> tsCV(gausts, meanf, h=5)
Time Series:
Start = 1900
End = 1999
Frequency = 1
  [1]       NA       NA       NA       NA       NA 20.5866966
  [7] 21.2797482 -10.6324936 40.9624573 -1.4363504 9.0277723 18.1906911
...
```

The `tsCV` functions spits out the residuals for each origin. To make things easier to use, let's create a function as a `wrapper` around the `tsCV` function that we can call to return the RMSE using time series CV. For this function, which we'll name `ts_cv_rmse`, we'll choose a default forecast horizon of 5 which, if we really wanted to, we could override by specifying the `h` argument explicitly:

```
ts_cv_rmse <- function(thets, thefun, h=5){
    resids <- tsCV(thets, thefun, h=h)
    return(sqrt(mean(resids^2, na.rm=TRUE)))
}
```

Now, let's use our new function to evaluate our three forecast models:

```
> ts_cv_rmse(gausts, naive)
[1] 33.82626
> ts_cv_rmse(gausts, meanf)
[1] 23.75519
> ts_cv_rmse(gausts, ses)
[1] 24.00897
```

Rad!

Notice how the `mean` method (albeit, very very slightly) outperforms the (marginally) more complex simple exponential smoothing method? This is more common than you might think.

Double exponential smoothing

Where the simple (single) exponential smoothing method we've seen in the last section is only really appropriate for series with trend, *double exponential smoothing* forecasts – also known as *Holt's linear method* – can be used for series with trend (but no seasonality). Our `temperature` series would be a fine fit for this type of forecasting method.

Holt's linear method builds on simple exponential smoothing by introducing a term for the trend. So now, in addition to the alpha *smoothness* parameter for the level (trend-less series), we have a beta parameter which controls the smoothness of the *trend* component. We can perform Holt's linear method using the `holt` function from (you guessed it!) the `forecast` package. Like the alpha parameter in the `ses` function, the `holt` function will use maximum likelihood optimization to choose an appropriate *beta* parameter for us, if we leave it out of the argument list. Let's use this method to make a forecast 50 years out.

Note that we are only using a forecast horizon this long in order to better visualize the increase in uncertainty (the widening of the prediction intervals) and to better visualize how the trend changes in our second example. I don't generally recommend making forecasts 50 years into the future:

```
hwfr <- holt(tempts, h=50)
autoplot(hwfr)
```

We get the following plot of forecast from Holt's method:

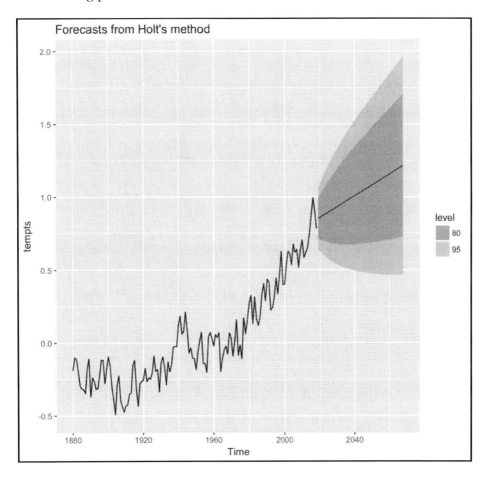

Figure 11.13: Forecast of our temperature series using Holt's linear method.

Now we've got something going on!

Note, please, how our uncertainty (as depicted by the widening prediction intervals) increase as we move further away from the forecast origin.

It is often noted that it is silly to think that a linear trend will continue indefinitely into the future. To cope with this, a variation of Holt's linear method was proposed that adds yet another parameter into the mix, *phi*. This parameter is responsible to *dampening* the linear forecast so that it levels off as we move further from the forecast origin. (This type of trend forecast is called a *damped trend*.) As you might expect, the `holt` function will intelligently choose a defensible *phi* parameter for us if we leave it out. All we have to do is tell the `holt` function that we want a *damped trend* using the `damped=TRUE` argument:

```
> hwfrd <- holt(tempts, h=50, damped=TRUE)
> autoplot(hwfrd)
```

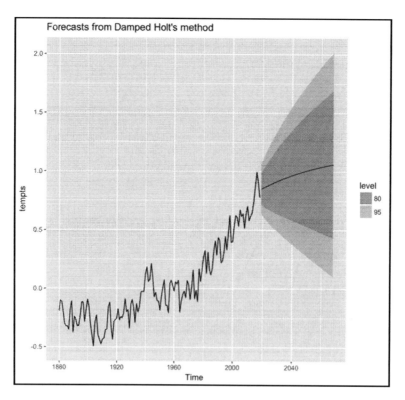

Figure 11.14: Forecast of our temperature series using Holt's linear method with a damped trend.

As you can see, this forecast scheme has the sometimes advantageous property of "leveling off" for predictions that are further and further into the future.

Note that the two trends we've forecasted in this section so far are *specifically* called **additive trend** and **additive damped trend**, respectively. The importance of this full qualification will become clear in a subsequent section. There is also a provision in the `holt` function to forecast an **exponential trend** but we will not be specifying a trend of this type (at least not manually) in this chapter.

Before we move on, let's evaluate the results of our forecasts using the assessment techniques we used in the last chapter, and use the simpler forecasting methods we've learned about to establish some sort of baseline.

Our first step, is to call `checkresiduals` on our two new forecast objects:

```
> checkresiduals(hwfr)
Ljung-Box test
data: Residuals from Holt's method
Q* = 16.666, df = 6, p-value = 0.01059
Model df: 4. Total lags used: 10
>
> checkresiduals(hwfrd)
Ljung-Box test
data: Residuals from Damped Holt's method
Q* = 17.769, df = 5, p-value = 0.00325
Model df: 5. Total lags used: 10
```

The results of the Ljung-Box tests hint that there may be serial correlation in our residuals. This suggests that we might be able to improve on this forecast by better identifying the underlying patterns.

Finally, let's compare our models with our baseline models using our `ts_cv_rmse` function:

```
> ts_cv_rmse(tempts, holt)
[1] 0.1780076
> # have to use an anonymous function in order to specify a damped trend
> ts_cv_rmse(tempts, function(x, h) holt(x, damped=TRUE, h=h))
[1] 0.1892179
> ts_cv_rmse(tempts, meanf)
[1] 0.3555613
> ts_cv_rmse(tempts, naive)
[1] 0.1631819
```

As we can plainly see (both in this output, and in Figure 11.15), the regular linear trend beats out the damped trend, and they both blow the *mean* method out of the water. It is interesting that the `naive` method appears to beat both of Holt's methods, at least according to the `cross-validated` RMSE. The cause of this strange finding turns out to be the result of the fact that much of the earlier parts of the series appear to be relatively trend-less and, for this region, both Holt methods overpredict. The `naive` method (as is made plain in Figure 11.15) is almost certainly *not* the best forecast. This underscores the importance of quantitative model evaluation *and* visualizing results and using best judgement:

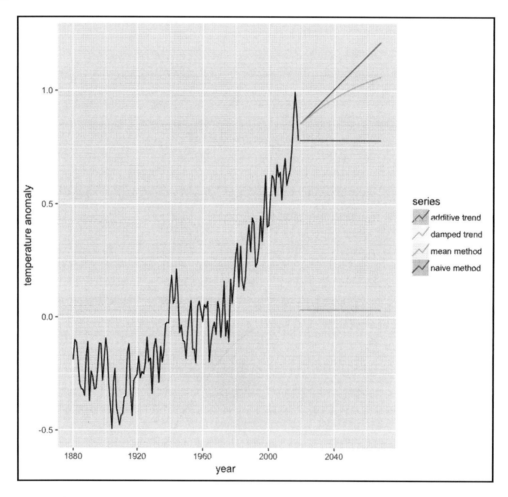

Figure 11.15: Forecast of our temperature data using an additive trend, a damped trend, the mean method, and the naive method

Triple exponential smoothing

Just as double exponential smoothing expanded on simple exponential smoothing, *triple exponential smoothing* (also commonly referred to as *Holt–Winters forecasting*) builds on and expands the capabilities of Holt's linear method. This method is finally able to cope with seasonal data. It is called triple exponential smoothing because, for series with seasonality, there are now *three* signals to be removed (error, trend, and seasonality). Holt–Winters achieves this by adding yet another parameter, *gamma*, that controls the smoothing of the seasonal component. We will be letting the hw function choose the appropriate gamma value for us.

We will be performing Holt–Winters forecasting on both of our seasonal series examples. Let's start with `school supplies`. Let's forecast 4 years (48 periods) into the future:

```
> hwfore <- hw(schoolts, h=48, seasonal="additive")
> autoplot(hwfore)
```

We get the forecast as follows:

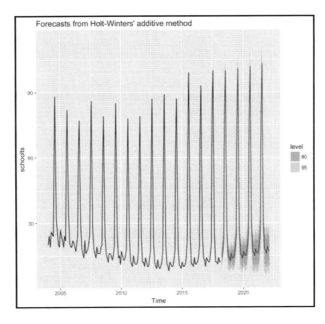

Figure 11.16: Forecast of our school supplies series using Holt–Winters (triple exponential smoothing)

Pretty cool, huh?

Note that we had to specify the type of seasonality (additive or multiplicative) in the call to the hw function.

In order to establish some kind of comparison with a simpler model, we'll contrast the forecasts from the Holt–Winters procedure with a seasonal variant of the *naive* method. This variant, instead of taking the last observation and using it as the prediction, will use the last value *at that point in the series one season ago*. Concretely, since this series follows a yearly seasonal pattern, a prediction for March of 2019 will use the observation on March 2018 as its prediction. In spite of its simplicity, this method works remarkably well for seasonal data with a small or non-existent trend component:

```
ts_cv_rmse(schoolts, function(x, h) hw(x, seasonal="additive"))
[1] 9.34646
ts_cv_rmse(schoolts, snaive)
[1] 3
```

As with last time, it *appears* as if the simpler method outperformed the more principled one, and by a large margin.

Two things:

- Remember our warning about why the naive method outperformed Holt's method in the last sections.

- Don't be thrown by what appears to be a large difference in RMSE magnitude; remember that RMSE is *scale* dependent – if the units were (nonsensically) in *tenths of a visitor* the RSME difference with be 63.4 (instead of 6.34). It's best to also visualize the forecasts in a plot, as in Figure 11.17:

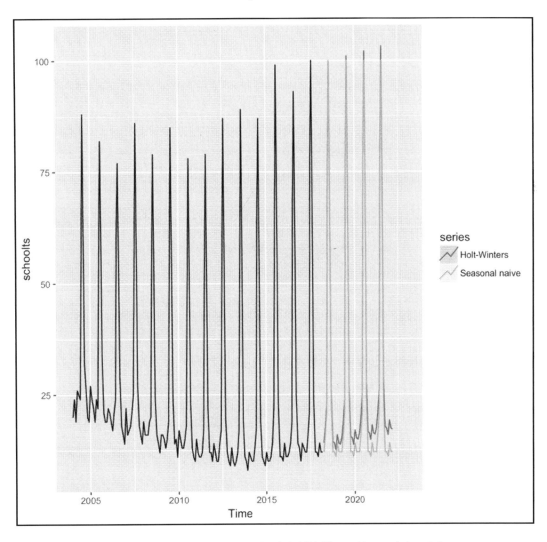

Figure 11.17: Forecast of our school supplies series using both Holt–Winters and the seasonal naive method

Run `checkresiduals` on both of these forecast objects for yourself.

Finally, let's use this method to forecast the `AirPassengers` data. If you recall from the section on decomposition, the `AirPassengers` series has a multiplicative seasonal component:

```
> hwfore <- hw(AirPassengers, h=48, seasonal="multiplicative")
> # now let's compare the simpler approaches
> snfore <- snaive(AirPassengers, h=48)
> nfore <- naive(AirPassengers, h=48)
> mfore <- meanf(AirPassengers, h=48)
> ts_cv_rmse(AirPassengers, function(x, h) hw(x,
seasonal="multiplicative"))
[1] 22.33878
> ts_cv_rmse(AirPassengers, snaive)
[1] 35.9892
> ts_cv_rmse(AirPassengers, naive)
[1] 77.16156
> ts_cv_rmse(AirPassengers, meanf)
[1] 126.4193
```

Finally, a forecast that unequivocally outperforms the simpler competition:

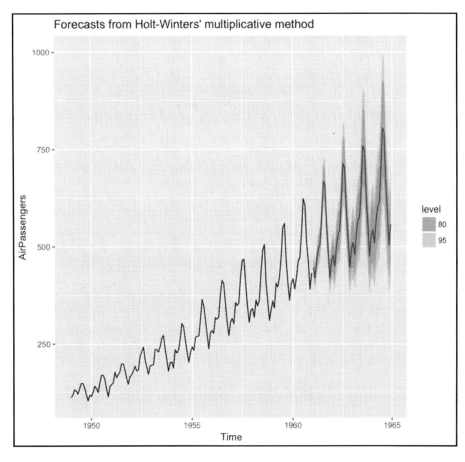

Figure 11.18: Forecast of the AirPassengers series using Holt–Winters and multiplicative seasonality

ETS and the state space model

We've seen three methods so far: simple exponential smoothing for trend-less data, double exponential smoothing (also known as Holt's linear method) for a linear or damped trend component, and triple exponential smoothing (or Holt–Winters) for additive or multiplicative seasonality.

In a taxonomy of these methods first proposed in 1969 and expanded/refined in an important 2001 paper by Rob Hyndman (the author of the `forecast` package) *et al.,* these methods can be nicely summarized in a table such as this:

Seasonal component

Trend component	None	Additive	Multiplicative
None	NN	NA	NM
Additive	AN	AA	AM
Additive Damped	DN	DA	DM
Multiplicative	MN	MA	MM

This taxonomy encompasses all popular exponential smoothing methods including all the ones we've used so far (and many that we haven't). For example, the simple exponential smoothing method we used on the white noise series is NN, the models we tried on the climate change data (linear, and damped trend) were AN, and DN, respectively, and so on.

For each of these 12, there exists a version using either additive or multiplicative errors. Therefore, in this taxonomy there are 24 methods. Any of these methods can be identified by specifying which type of **Error, Trend**, and **Seasonal** (or **ETS**) component they use. For example, an exponential smoothing method with multiplicative errors, linear trend, and a multiplicative seasonality (which is, in fact, essentially what we first used to predict future values in the `AirPassengers` series can thus be written as ETS(M, A, M).

As it turns out, *fairly* recently (at least in comparison to the age of the discipline and domain of other subjects broached in this book) it was discovered that the equations that underlie these methods can be rewritten to conform to the format of **state space models**. This was an extremely important development. Why? Well, remember when we said that these exponential smoothing methods and equations give point forecasts only. Once the parameters of the exponential smoothing methods are estimated, a series of equations (that we didn't show in this chapter) determine a single forecast value. However, when expressed in the form of a state space model (a stochastic model) we gain a principled approach to assess uncertainty and, thus, establish prediction intervals.

Prior to this, prediction intervals *were* offered (and still are in other packages) for exponential smoothing methods, but they were arrived at via approximations using *other* (non-exponential smoothing) time series models within the state space framework.

Another advantage of the state space framework for exponential smoothing forecasts is that it allows for the relatively easy and principled calculation of the model's goodness of fit. As a consequence, we now have a way to try several different species of exponential smoothing methods and *automatically* select the best, based on some criterion.

To this end, the `ets` function will try most of the methods from this taxonomy (using smart heuristics based on the series to decide which to try) and automatically select the model that yields the lowest **Akaike Information Criterion** (**AIC**). If you recall, AIC was mentioned in passing in the `Chapter 09`, *Predicting Continuous Variables*, as an alternative measure of goodness of fit, somewhat similar in principle to adjusted R-squared.

The `ets` function could scarcely be easier to use. The only thing to keep in mind, is that this function doesn't return an object of type `forecast` like the rest of the forecasting functions we've seen so far. Rather, it returns an object of class `ets` which *then* has to be used in a call to the `forecast` function to yield a `forecast` object (that can be `autoplot`ed, and so on).

Let's try to use the `ets` function to forecast:

```
> etsobj <- ets(schoolts)
> summary(etsobj)
ETS(M,A,A)
Call:
ets(y = schoolts)
Smoothing parameters:
alpha = 0.0464
beta = 0.0017
gamma = 0.3957
...
AIC AICc BIC
1107.799 1111.799 1161.207
Training set error measures:
ME RMSE MAE MPE MAPE MASE ACF1
Training set 0.3560261 3.080813 1.879578 -0.146184 7.017015 0.9028789
0.2787678
>
> etsfore <- forecast(etsobj, h=48)
```

Study the output of the call to `summary` on the `ets` object, which is rich in important information. For example, we can tell that the procedure (evinced by `ETS(M,A,A)`) chose to model the series using multiplicative errors, an additive trend, and additive seasonality. Even though it might seem weird that `ets` modeled this series as having any trend at all, this automatically chosen model actually outperforms our hand-chosen one – at least as far as AIC is concerned.

If you call `autoplot` on the `etsfore` object yourself, you'll see that the procedure yielded a forecast that looks a lot like the one we created in the last section. This time, though, we didn't have to choose for ourselves whether to use a triple exponential smoothing method, or whether to use additive or multiplicative errors: `ets` made the decision for us.

Interventions for improvement

Now, I know that so far in this book, we've approached automatic model selection techniques with a fair bit of healthy skepticism. In light of that, you might ask why I would spend time extolling the virtues of `ets` here all of a sudden.

While it's true that there's danger in automatic model selection – and we'll see an example of that later in this section – I'm more open to automated techniques for forecasting than for other domains. This is for two main reasons.

For one, in many of the sectors that employ forecasting, there is often a need to forecast estimations for *a ton* of different series, often, and at a high frequency basis. Think of an airline that has to set prices for flight tickets for hundreds of flights and update those prices on a daily (or even hourly) basis, based on projected consumer demand. Because of the intractability of hand-tuning models for each and every one of these series, many current approaches use in-house hard-coded algorithms for forecasting – sometimes decades old – using rules-of-thumb that are often outdated or that make assumptions that no longer hold. So, in addition to this intractability, it is quite obvious that very frequently there isn't the need for a very high degree of accuracy. Often, any principled approach will yield predictions that are much better than nothing.

Lastly, think back to my opposition to step-wise regression. A large part of my criticisms appealed to the fact that at least some degree of domain knowledge and principled hypothesis formulation should go into the selection of independent variables, *especially* if a linear model is used in an *analysis-proper* context, as opposed to a purely predictive context. These criticisms are often inapplicable to time series forecasting both because (a) it is frequently a purely predictive endeavor, and (b) because no principled hypotheses or explanations for vicissitudes of time series observations exist.

That being said, we'll briefly look at one example of how `ets` can sometimes go wrong or, at least, how a little bit of tinkering with the model can yield predictions that are more beneficial in certain circumstances.

As our example, let's look at the results of a hands-off, automated forecast model of our `temperature` series using `ets`:

```
> etsobj <- ets(tempts)
> summary(etsobj)
ETS(A,N,N)
Call:
ets(y = tempts)
...
> autoplot(forecast(etsobj, h=50))
```

The plot is as follows:

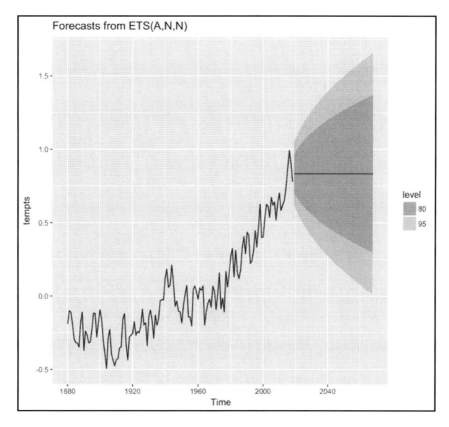

Figure 11.19: Automated forecast of the temperature time series using ets

In this instance, `ets` chose to model the series using no trend component. This is probably because of the relatively trend-less signal from 1880 to 1960. Is this an appropriate fit to the data, though? Perhaps it would be more useful to perform a forecast using an excerpt of the data starting in 1970:

```
> etsobj2 <- ets(window(tempts, start=1970))
> summary(etsobj2)
ETS(A,A,N)
Call:
ets(y = window(tempts, start = 1970))
...
> autoplot(forecast(etsobj2, h=50))
```

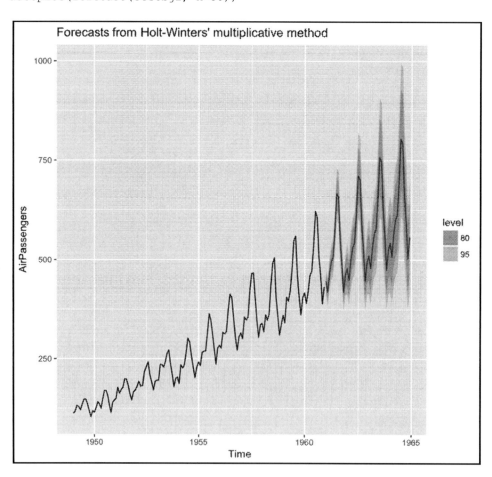

Figure 11.20: Automated forecast of the temperature series starting in 1970

Would this make a better forecast of the data? I think so. But, in line of what I said about forecasting being a dismal science, both approaches are justifiable and produce valid forecasts depending on the purpose.

By the way, you can also achieve an upward trending forecast of this series (the whole series) by passing the argument `model="ZAN"` into the `ets` function. This tells `ets` to (a) choose the best error term, (b) explicitly choose an additive trend, and (c) explicitly choose no seasonal component.

What we didn't cover

In an effort to spend more time laying a foundation and facilitating a deeper understanding of *one* of the most popular intermediate methods of forecasting (and, even as it is, I couldn't go into *nearly* as much detail as I would have liked to for want of space), we necessarily had to miss out on a few topics that would have been nice and helpful to cover. Particularly, the primary topic that comes to mind is ARIMA, or *autoregressive integrated moving average*, models.

ARIMA models, like exponential smoothing methods as of the late last and early this century, are often expressed as state space models. In addition, many of the exponential smoothing methods we used in this chapter can be translated to equivalent ARIMA models (this is, in fact, how many software programs provided prediction intervals for exponential smoothing forecasts before the state-space/ETS framework opened up the door to do it directly). Due to this *translatability* for certain popular models, I felt more at ease just concentrating on exponential smoothing methods. I would have liked to have at least introduced you, dear reader, to the general concepts and nomenclature of ARIMA models, though. I humbly urge you to dig into the topic of ARIMA, if forecasting is of particular interest to you.

Citations for the climate change data

GISTEMP Team, 2018: *GISS Surface Temperature Analysis (GISTEMP)*. NASA Goddard Institute for Space Studies. Dataset accessed 2018-03-15 at `https://data.giss.nasa.gov/gistemp/`.

Hansen, J., R. Ruedy, M. Sato, and K. Lo, 2010: `Global surface temperature change`, Rev. Geophys., 48, RG4004, doi:10.1029/2010RG000345.

Exercises

- Learn more about the other measures of accuracy provided by `forecast` function's `accuracy` function. What advantages does MAPE have over RMSE/MAE

- Learn how to interpret the alpha, beta, gamma, (and sometimes phi) parameters of an ETS object. What does it mean to have a low beta parameter? Try to explicitly specify extreme values for some of these parameters using named arguments in the `ets` function. How does it affect the quality and dynamics of your forecasts?

- The GitHub repository that we used to download some of the data sets in this chapter (and we will be using for different data sets for subsequent chapters, as well) also contains a data set containing Google searches for *Dr. Martin Luther King, Jr.*, what example series in this chapter does this most resemble? Is there seasonality in this series? If so, when do the spikes in searches occur? Why do you think that is? Take your best guess as to which particular ETS model `ets` would chose to describe this series. Try it for yourself.

- Read Dr. Martin Luther King, Jr's *Letter from a Birmingham Jail*. Pay particular attention to the passage where Dr. King expresses grave disappointment in the *White moderate* who is *more devoted to order than to justice*. Draw parallels between *A Call for Unity* (the newspaper open letter that prompted Dr. King to pen the Birmingham Jail letter) and appeals to slow down or stop modern civil rights struggles (especially non-violent protest) to the end of *not dividing the country further* and *stop all this fighting and just get along*.

Summary

We started with a discussion of what time series is before diving into forecasting and its types. We then moved towards creating and plotting time series, components of time series and time series decomposition. White noise was discussed at length, as were autocorrelation and smoothing. ETS and the state space model were also covered, as were interventions for improvement. We ended with a discussion of the topics not covered in time series and a few exercises.

12
Sources of Data

The previous two units (*Confirmatory Data Analysis and Inferential Statistics* and *Predictive Analytics*) have focused on teaching both theory and practice in ideal data scenarios, so that our more academic quests can be divorced from outside concerns about the veracity or format of the data. To this end, we deliberately stayed away from datasets not already built into R or available from add-on packages. But very few people I know get by in their careers by using R and not importing any data from sources outside of R packages. Well, we very briefly touched upon how to load data into R (the `read.*` commands) in the very first chapter of this book, did we not? So we should be all set, right?

Here's the rub: I know a few people who can get by using simple CSVs and tab-delimited text locally with the primary `read.*` commands and can get by not using outside sources of data at all! The unfortunate fact is that many introductory analytics texts largely disregard this reality. This produces many well-informed new analysts who are nevertheless stymied on their first attempt to apply their fresh knowledge to *real-world data*. In my opinion, any text that purports to be a practical resource for data analysts cannot afford to ignore this.

Luckily, due to largely undirected and unplanned personal research, I do for blog posts and my own edification using motley collections of publicly available data sources in various formats. I—although perhaps delusional—consider myself fairly adept at navigating this criminally overlooked portion of practical analytics. It is the body of lessons I've learned during these wild data adventures that I'd like to impart to you in this and the subsequent chapter, dear reader.

It's common for data sources to be not only difficult to load, for various reasons, but to be difficult to work with because of errors, *junk*, or just general idiosyncrasies. Because of this, this chapter and the next few chapters will have a lot in common. This chapter will concentrate more on getting data from outside sources and getting it into a somewhat usable form in R. The next chapters will discuss particularly common gotchas while working with data in an imperfect world.

I appreciate that not everyone has the interest or the time available to go on wild goose hunts for publicly available data to answer questions formed on a whim. Nevertheless, the techniques that we'll be discussing in this chapter should be very helpful in handling the variety of data formats that you'll have to contend with in the course of your work or research. Additionally, having the wherewithal to employ freely available data on the web can be indispensable for learning new analytics methods and technologies.

The first source of data we'll be looking at is that of the venerable relational database.

Relational databases

Perhaps the most common external source of data is from relational databases. Since this section is probably of interest to only those who work with databases—or at least plan to—some knowledge of the basics of relational databases is assumed.

One way to connect to databases from R is to use the RODBC package. This allows one to access any database that implements the ODBC common interface (for example, PostgreSQL, Access, Oracle, SQLite, DB2, and so on). A more common method, for whatever reason, is to use the DBI package and DBI-compliant drivers.

DBI is an R package that defines a generalized interface for communication between different databases and R. As with ODBC, it allows the same compliant SQL to run on multiple databases. The DBI package alone is not sufficient for communicating with any particular database from R; in order to use DBI, you must also install and load a DBI-compliant driver for your particular database. Packages exist providing drivers for many RDBMSs. Among them are RPostgreSQL, RSQLite, RMySQL, and ROracle.

In order to most easily demonstrate R/DB communication, we will be using a SQLite database. This will also most easily allow the prudent reader to create the example database and follow along. The SQL we'll be using is standard, so you can really use any DB you want, anyhow.

Our example database has two columns: `artists` and `paintings`. The `artists` table contains a unique integer ID, an artist's name, and the year they were born. The `paintings` table contains a unique integer ID, an artist ID, the name of the painting, and its completion date. The artist ID in the `paintings` table is a foreign key that references the artist ID in the `artist` table; this is how this database links paintings to their respective painters.

If you want to follow along, use the following SQL statements to create and populate the database. If you're using SQLite, name the database `art.db`:

```
CREATE TABLE artists(
  artist_id INTEGER PRIMARY KEY,
  name TEXT,
  born_on INTEGER
);

CREATE TABLE paintings(
  painting_id INTEGER PRIMARY KEY,
  painting_artist INTEGER,
  painting_name TEXT,
  year_completed INTEGER,
  FOREIGN KEY(painting_artist) REFERENCES artists(artist_id)
);

INSERT INTO artists(name, born_on)
VALUES ("Kay Sage", 1898),
("Piet Mondrian", 1872),
("Rene Magritte", 1898),
("Man Ray", 1890),
("Jean-Michel Basquiat", 1960);

INSERT INTO paintings(painting_artist, painting_name, year_completed)
VALUES (4, "Orquesta Sinfonica",  1916),
(4, "La Fortune", 1938),
(1, "Tommorow is Never", 1955),
(1, "The Answer is No", 1958),
(1, "No Passing", 1954),
```

```
(5, "Bird on Money", 1981),
(2, "Place de la Concorde", 1943),
(2, "Composition No. 10",  1942),
(3, "The Human Condition", 1935),
(3, "The Treachery of Images", 1948),
(3, "The Son of Man", 1964);
```

Confirm for yourself that the following SQL commands yield the appropriate results by typing them into the `sqlite3` command-line interface:

```
SELECT * FROM artists;
-------------------------------
1 | Kay Sage            | 1898
2 | Piet Mondrian       | 1872
3 | Rene Magritte       | 1898
4 | Man Ray             | 1890
5 | Jean-Michel Basquiat | 1960
```

```
SELECT * FROM paintings;
---------------------------------------
1  | 4 | Orquesta Sinfonica     | 1916
2  | 4 | La Fortune             | 1938
3  | 1 | Tommorow is Never      | 1955
4  | 1 | The Answer is No       | 1958
5  | 1 | No Passing             | 1954
6  | 5 | Bird on Money          | 1981
7  | 2 | Place de la Concorde   | 1943
8  | 2 | Composition No. 10     | 1942
9  | 3 | The Human Condition    | 1935
10 | 3 | The Treachery of Images | 1948
11 | 3 | The Son of Man         | 1964
```

For our first act, we load the necessary packages, choose our database driver, and connect to the database:

```
library(DBI)
library(RSQLite)
# we read the art sqlite db from the current
# working directory which can be get and set
# with getwd() and setwd(), respectively
art_db <- dbConnect(sqlite, "./art.db")
```

Again, we are using `sqlite` for this example, but this procedure is applicable to all DBI-compliant database drivers.

Let's now run a query against this database. Let's get a list of all the painting names and their respective artists' names. This will require a join operation between the two tables:

```
result <- dbSendQuery(art_db,
  "SELECT paintings.painting_name, artists.name
  FROM paintings INNER JOIN artists
  ON paintings.painting_artist=artists.artist_id;")
response <- fetch(result)
head(response)
dbClearResult(result)
```

```
---------------------------------------------

            painting_name                      name
1 Orquesta Sinfonica                        Man Ray
2           La Fortune                       Man Ray
3   Tommorow is Never                       Kay Sage
4     The Answer is No                      Kay Sage
5           No Passing                      Kay Sage
```

Here we used the dbSendQuery function to send a query to the database. Its first and second arguments were the database handle variable (from the dbConnect function) and the SQL statement, respectively. We store a handle to the result in a variable. Next, the fetch function retrieves the response from the handle. By default, it will retrieve all matches from the query, though this can be limited by specifying the n argument (see help("fetch")). The result of the fetch is then stored in the response variable. response is an R data frame like any other; we can do any of the operations we've already learned with it. Finally, we clear the result, which is good practice, because it frees resources.

For a slightly more involved query, let's try to find the average (mean) age of the artists at the age they were when each of the paintings were completed. This still requires a join, but this time we are selecting paintings.year_completed and artists.born_on:

```
result <- dbSendQuery(art_db,
  "SELECT paintings.year_completed, artists.born_on
  FROM paintings INNER JOIN artists
  ON paintings.painting_artist=artists.artist_id;")
response <- fetch(result)
head(response)
dbClearResult(result)
```

```
---------------------------
```

```
      year_completed born_on
1               1916    1890
2               1938    1890
3               1955    1898
4               1958    1898
5               1954    1898
6               1981    1960
```

At this time, row-wise subtraction and averaging can be performed simply:

```
mean(response$year_completed - response$born_on)

-----------

[1] 51.091
```

Finally, we close our connection to the database:

```
dbDisconnect(art_db)
```

Why didn't we just do that in SQL?

Why, indeed. Although this very simple example could have easily just been written into the logic of the SQL query, for more complicated data analysis this simply won't cut it. Unless you are using a really specialized database, many databases aren't prepared for certain mathematical functions with regards to numerical accuracy. More importantly, most databases don't implement advanced math functions at all. Even if they did, they almost certainly wouldn't be portable between different RDBMSs. There is great merit in having analytics logic reside in R so that if, for whatever reason, you have to switch databases, your analysis code will remain unchanged.

If SQL is your cup of tea, did you know you can use the `sqldf` package to perform arbitrary SQL queries on `data.frame`?
There is a rising interest and (to a lesser extent) need for databases that don't adhere to the relational paradigm. These so-called NoSQL databases include the immensely popular Hadoop/HDFS, MongoDB, CouchDB, Neo4j, and Redis, among many others. There are R packages for communicating to most of these, too, including one for every one of the databases mentioned here by name. Since the operation of all of these packages is idiosyncratic and heavily dependent on which species of NoSQL the database in question belongs to, your best bet for learning how to use this is to read the help pages and/or vignettes for each package.

Using JSON

Javascript Object Notation (JSON) is a standardized human-readable data format that plays an enormous role in communication between web browsers and web servers. JSON was originally borne out of a need to represent arbitrarily complex data structures in Javascript, a web scripting language, but it has since grown into a language agnostic data serialization format.

It is a common need to import and parse JSON in R, particularly when working with web data. For example, it is very common for websites to offer web services that take an arbitrary query from a web browser, and return the response as JSON. We will look at an example of this very use case later in this section.

For our first look into JSON parsing for R, we'll use the `jsonlite` package to read a small JSON string, which serializes some information about the best musical act in history, The Beatles:

```
library(jsonlite)

example.json <- '
{
  "thebeatles": {
    "formed": 1960,
    "members": [
      {
        "firstname": "George",
        "lastname": "Harrison"
      },
      {
        "firstname": "Ringo",
        "lastname": "Starr"
      },
      {
        "firstname": "Paul",
        "lastname": "McCartney"
      },
      {
        "firstname": "John",
        "lastname": "Lennon"
      }
    ]
  }
}'

the_beatles <- fromJSON(example.json)
```

```
print(the_beatles)
--------------------
$thebeatles
$thebeatles$formed
[1] 1960

$thebeatles$members
  firstname   lastname
1    George   Harrison
2     Ringo      Starr
3      Paul  McCartney
4      John     Lennon
```

We used the `fromJSON` function to read in the string. The result is an R list, whose elements/attributes can be accessed via the $ operator, or the [[double square bracket function/operator. For example, we can access the date when The Beatles formed, in R, in the following two ways:

```
the_beatles$thebeatles$formed
the_beatles[["thebeatles"]][["formed"]]
---------
[1] 1960
[1] 1960
```

> In R, a `list` is a data structure that is kind of like a vector, but allows elements of differing data types. A single list may contain numerics, strings, vectors, or even other lists!

Now that we have the very basics of handling JSON down, let's move on to using it in a non-trivial manner!

There's a music/social media platform called www.last.fm that kindly provides a web service API that's free for public use (as long as you abide by their reasonable terms). This **Application Programming Interface (API)** allows us to query various points of data about musical artists by crafting special URLs. The results of following these URLs are either a JSON or XML payload, which are directly consumable from R.

In this non-trivial example of using web data, we will be building a rudimentary recommendation system. Our system will allow us to suggest new music to a particular person based on an artist that they already like. In order to do this, we have to query the Last.fm API to gather all the *tags* associated with particular artists. These *tags* function a lot like genre classifications. The success of our recommendation system will be predicated on the assumption that musical artists with overlapping tags are more similar to each other than artists with disparate tags, and that someone is more likely to enjoy similar artists than an arbitrary dissimilar artist.

Here's an example JSON excerpt of the result of querying the API for tags of a particular artist:

```
{
  "toptags": {
    "tag": [
      {
        "count": 100,
        "name": "female vocalists",
        "url": "http://www.last.fm/tag/female+vocalists"
      },
      {
        "count": 71,
        "name": "singer-songwriter",
        "url": "http://www.last.fm/tag/singer-songwriter"
      },
      {
        "count": 65,
        "name": "pop",
        "url": "http://www.last.fm/tag/pop"
      }
    ]
  }
}
```

Here, we only care about the name of the tag, not the URL or the count of occasions Last.fm users applied each tag to the artist.

Let's first create a function that will construct the properly formatted query URL for a particular artist. The Last.fm developer website indicates that the format is:

```
http://ws.audioscrobbler.com/2.0/?method=artist.gettoptags&artist=<THE_ARTI
ST>&api_key=c2e57923a25c03f3d8b317b3c8622b43&format=json
```

In order to create these URLs based upon arbitrary input, we can use the `paste0` function to concatenate the component strings. However, URLs can't handle certain characters such as spaces; in order to convert the artist's name to a format suitable for a URL, we'll use the `URLencode` function from the (preloaded) `utils` package.

```
URLencode("The Beatles")
-------
[1] "The%20Beatles"
```

Now we have all the pieces to put this function together:

```
create_artist_query_url_lfm <- function(artist_name){
  prefix <-
"http://ws.audioscrobbler.com/2.0/?method=artist.gettoptags&artist="
  postfix <- "&api_key=c2e57923a25c03f3d8b317b3c8622b43&format=json"
  encoded_artist <- URLencode(artist_name)
  return(paste0(prefix, encoded_artist, postfix))
}

create_artist_query_url_lfm("Depeche Mode")
--------------------
[1]
"http://ws.audioscrobbler.com/2.0/?method=artist.gettoptags&artist=Depeche%
20Mode&api_key=c2e57923a25c03f3d8b317b3c8622b43&format=json"
```

Fantastic! Now we make the web request, and parse the resulting JSON. Luckily, the `fromJSON` function that we've been using can take a URL and automatically make the web request for us. Let's see what it looks like:

```
fromJSON(create_artist_query_url_lfm("Depeche Mode"))

------------------------------------------

$toptags
$toptags$tag
  count        name                                 url
1   100    electronic    http://www.last.fm/tag/electronic
2    87      new wave      http://www.last.fm/tag/new+wave
3    59           80s          http://www.last.fm/tag/80s
4    56     synth pop     http://www.last.fm/tag/synth+pop
  ........
```

Neat-o! If you take a close look at the structure, you'll see that the tag names are stored in the `name` attribute of the `tag` attribute of the `toptags` attribute (whew!). This means we can extract just the tag names with `$toptags$tag$name`. Let's write a function that will take an artist's name, and return a list of the tags in a vector:

```
get_tag_vector_lfm <- function(an_artist){
  artist_url <- create_artist_query_url_lfm(an_artist)
  json <- fromJSON(artist_url)
  return(json$toptags$tag$name)
}

get_tag_vector_lfm("Depeche Mode")

----------------------------------------

  [1] "electronic"      "new wave"        "80s"
  [4] "synth pop"       "synthpop"        "seen live"
  [7] "alternative"     "rock"            "british"
  ........
```

Next, we have to go ahead and retrieve the tags for all artists. Instead of doing this (and probably violating Last.fm's terms of service), we'll just pretend that there are only six musical artists in the world. We'll store all of these artists in a list. This will make it easy to use the `lapply` function to apply the `get_tag_vector_lfm` function to each artist in the list. Finally, we'll name all the elements in the list appropriately:

```
our_artists <- list("Kate Bush", "Peter Tosh", "Radiohead",
                     "The Smiths", "The Cure", "Black Uhuru")
our_artists_tags <- lapply(our_artists, get_tag_vector_lfm)
names(our_artists_tags) <- our_artists

print(our_artists_tags)

----------------------------------------

$`Kate Bush`
  [1] "female vocalists"  "singer-songwriter" "pop"
  [4] "alternative"       "80s"               "british"
  ........
$`Peter Tosh`
  [1] "reggae"            "roots reggae"      "Rasta"
  [4] "roots"             "ska"               "jamaican"
  ........
$Radiohead
  [1] "alternative"           "alternative rock"
  [3] "rock"                  "indie"   .
```

```
 . . . . . . . .
$`The Smiths`
 [1] "indie"           "80s"            "post-punk"
 [4] "new wave"        "alternative"    "rock"
 . . . . . . . .
$`The Cure`
 [1] "post-punk"       "new wave"       "alternative"
 [4] "80s"             "rock"           "seen live"
 . . . . . . . .
$`Black Uhuru`
 [1] "reggae"          "roots reggae"   "dub"
 [4] "jamaica"         "roots"          "jamaican"
 . . . . . . . .
```

Now that we have all the artists' tags stored as a list of vectors, we need some way of comparing the tag lists, and judging them for similarity.

The first idea that may come to mind is to count the number of tags each pair of artists have in common. Though this may seem like a good idea at first glance, consider the following scenario.

Artist A and Artist B have hundreds of tags each, and they share three tags in common; artists C and D each have two tags, both of which are mutually shared. Our naive metric for similarity suggests that artists A and B are more similar than C and D (by 50%). If your intuition tells you that C and D are more similar, though, we are both in agreement.

To make our similarity measure comport more with our intuition, we will instead use the **Jaccard index**. The Jaccard index (also *Jaccard coefficient*) between sets A and B, *J(A,B)* is given by:

$$J(A, B) = \frac{|A \cap B|}{|A \cup B|}$$

Here, $\cap$ is the set intersection (the common tags), $\cup$ is the set union (an unduplicated list of all the tags in both sets), and $|X|$ is the set X's **cardinality** (the number of elements in that set).

This metric has the attractive property that it is naturally constrained:

$$0 \leq J(A, B) \leq 1$$

Let's write a function that takes two sets, and returns the Jaccard index. We'll employ the built-in functions `intersect` and `union`:

```
jaccard_index <- function(one, two){
  length(intersect(one, two))/length(union(one, two))
}
```

Let's try it on The Cure and Radiohead:

```
jaccard_index(our_artists_tags[["Radiohead"]],
              our_artists_tags[["The Cure"]])
```

```
---------------

[1] 0.3333
```

Neat! Manual checking confirms that this is the right answer.

The next step is to construct a *similarity matrix*. This is a $n \times n$ matrix (where *n* is the number of artists) that depicts all the pairwise similarity measurements. If this explanation is confusing, look at the code output before reading the following code snippet:

```
similarity_matrix <- function(artist_list, similarity_fn) {
    num <- length(artist_list)
    # initialize a num by num matrix of zeroes
    sim_matrix <- matrix(0, ncol = num, nrow = num)
    # name the rows and columns for easy lookup
    rownames(sim_matrix) <- names(artist_list)
    colnames(sim_matrix) <- names(artist_list)

    # for each row in the matrix
    for(i in 1:nrow(sim_matrix)) {
        # and each column
        for(j in 1:ncol(sim_matrix)) {
            # calculate that pair's similarity
            the_index <- similarity_fn(artist_list[[i]],
                                       artist_list[[j]])
            # and store it in the right place in the matrix
            sim_matrix[i,j] <- round(the_index, 2)
        }
    }
    return(sim_matrix)
}

sim_matrix <- similarity_matrix(our_artists_tags, jaccard_index)
print(sim_matrix)
```

	Kate Bush	Peter Tosh	Radiohead	The Smiths	The Cure	Black Uhuru
Kate Bush	1.00	0.05	0.31	0.25	0.21	0.04
Peter Tosh	0.05	1.00	0.02	0.03	0.03	0.33
Radiohead	0.31	0.02	1.00	0.31	0.33	0.04
The Smiths	0.25	0.03	0.31	1.00	0.44	0.05
The Cure	0.21	0.03	0.33	0.44	1.00	0.05
Black Uhuru	0.04	0.33	0.04	0.05	0.05	1.00

If you're familiar with some of these bands, you'll no doubt see that the similarity matrix in the preceding output makes a lot of prima facie sense—it looks like our theory is sound!

If you noticed, the values along the diagonal (from the upper-left point to the lower-right) are all 1. This is because the Jaccard index of two identical sets is always 1, and an artist's similarity with themselves is always 1. Additionally, all the values are symmetric with respect to the diagonal; whether you look up Peter Tosh and Radiohead by column and then row, or vice versa, the value will be the same (.02). This property means that the matrix is *symmetric*. This is a property of all similarity matrices using symmetric (commutative) similarity functions.

A similar (and perhaps more common) concept is that of a *distance matrix* (or *dissimilarity matrix*). The idea is the same, but now the values that are higher will refer to more musically distant pairs of artists. Also, the diagonal will be zeroes, since an artist is the least musically different from themselves than any other artist. If all the values of a similarity matrix are between 0 and 1 (as is often the case), you can easily make it into a distance matrix by subtracting 1 from every element. Subtracting from 1 again will yield the original similarity matrix.

Recommendations can now be furnished, for listeners of one of the bands, by sorting that artist's column in the matrix in a descending order, for example, if a user likes `The Smiths`, but is unsure what other bands she should try listening to:

```
# The Smiths are the fourth column
sim_matrix[order(sim_matrix[,4], decreasing=TRUE), 4]
```

The Smiths	The Cure	Radiohead	Kate Bush	Black Uhuru
1.00	0.44	0.31	0.25	0.05
Peter Tosh				
0.03				

Of course, a recommendation of `The Smiths` for this user is nonsensical. Going down the list, it looks like a recommendation of `The Cure` is the safest bet, though `Radiohead` and `Kate Bush` may also be fine recommendations. `Black Uhuru` and `Peter Tosh` are unsafe bets if all we know about the user's a fondness for The Smiths.

XML

XML, like JSON, is an absolutely ubiquitous format for data transfer over the internet. In addition to being used on the web, XML is also a popular data format for application configuration files and the list. In fact, newer Microsoft Office documents (with the extensions `.docx` or `.xlsx`) are stored as XML files.

Here's what our simple Beatles dataset may look like in XML:

```
example_xml1 <- '
<the_beatles>
  <formed>1960</formed>
  <members>
    <member>
      <first_name>George</first_name>
      <last_name>Harrison</last_name>
    </member>
    <member>
      <first_name>Ringo</first_name>
      <last_name>Starr</last_name>
    </member>
    <member>
      <first_name>Paul</first_name>
      <last_name>McCartney</last_name>
    </member>
    <member>
      <first_name>John</first_name>
      <last_name>Lennon</last_name>
    </member>
  </members>
</the_beatles>'
```

Much like JSON, XML is stored in a tree structure; this is called a **DOM (Document Object Model)** tree in XML parlance. Each piece of information in an XML document—surrounded by names in angle brackets—is called an element or *node*. In the hierarchical structure, subnodes are called *children*. In the preceding code, `formed` is a child of `the_beatles`, and `member` is a child of `members`. Each node may have zero or more children who may have children nodes of their own. For example, the `members` node has four children, each of whom have two children, `first_name` and `last_name`. The common parent of all the elements (whether direct parent or great-great-grandparent) is the *root node*, which doesn't have a parent.

As with JSON, XML and XML import functions is an enormous topic. We'll only briefly cover some of the more common and basic know-how in this chapter. Fortunately, R has built-in help and documentation. For this package, `help(package="XML")` indicates that more documentation is available at the package's URL: `http://www.omegahat.org/RSXML`.

We will read the preceding XML with the XML package. If you don't have it already, make sure you install it:

```
library(XML)
the_beatles <- xmlTreeParse(example_xml1)
print(names(the_beatles))
```

```
-------------------
```

```
[1] "doc" "dtd"
```

```
print(the_beatles$doc)
```

```
--------------------
```

```
$file
[1] "<buffer>"

$version
[1] "1.0"

$children
$children$the_beatles
<the_beatles>
 <formed>1960</formed>
 <members>
  <member>
   <first_name>George</first_name>
   <last_name>Harrison</last_name>
```

```
  </member>
  . . . . . . . . . .
 </members>
</the_beatles>
```

```
attr(,"class")
[1] "XMLDocumentContent"
```

xmlTreeParse reads and parses the DOM, and stores it as an R list. The actual content is stored in the children attribute of the doc attribute. We can access the year The Beatles were formed like so:

```
print(xmlValue(the_beatles$doc$children$the_beatles[["formed"]]))
```

```
---------------------
```

```
[1] "1960"
```

Here, we use the xmlValue function to extract the value stored in the formed node.

If we wanted to get to the first names of all the members, we would have to store the root node of the DOM, and iterate over the children of the members node. In particular, we would use the sapply function (which applies a function to each element of a vector) over the children with a function that returns the XML value of the first_name node. Concretely:

```
root <- xmlRoot(the_beatles)
sapply(xmlChildren(root[["members"]]), function(x){
    xmlValue(x[["first_name"]])
})
```

```
-------------------------------------------
```

```
   member    member    member    member
  "George"   "Ringo"    "Paul"    "John"
```

Though it's possible to work with the DOM in this manner, it is much more common to interrogate XML using XPath.

XPath is kind of like an XML query language, like SQL, but for XML. It allows us to select nodes that match a particular pattern or location. For matching, it uses *path expressions* that identify nodes based on their name, location, or relationships with other nodes.

This powerful tool also comes with a proportionally steep learning curve. Luckily, it is somewhat easy to get started. In addition, there are a lot of great tutorials online. The excellent tutorial that taught me XPath is available at
`http://www.w3schools.com/xsl/xpath_intro.asp`.

To use XPath, we have to re-import the XML using the `xmlParse` (not `XMLTreeParse`) function, which uses a different optimized internal representation. To replicate the results of the previous code snippet using XPath, we are going to use the following XPath statement:

```
all_first_names <- "//member/first_name"
```

The preceding statement roughly translates to *for all* `member` *nodes occurring anywhere in the document, get the child node named* `first_name`:

```
the_beatles <- xmlParse(example_xml1)
getNodeSet(the_beatles, all_first_names)


--------

[[1]]
<first_name>George</first_name>

[[2]]
<first_name>Ringo</first_name>

[[3]]
<first_name>Paul</first_name>

[[4]]
<first name>John</first_name>

attr(,"class")
[1] "XMLNodeSet"
```

Equivalent XPath expressions can also be written thus:

```
getNodeSet(the_beatles, "//first_name")
getNodeSet(the_beatles, "/the_beatles/members/member/first_name")
```

And just the XML values for each node can be extracted thus:

```
sapply(getNodeSet(the_beatles, all_first_names), xmlValue)


-------------------------------

[1] "George" "Ringo"  "Paul"   "John"
```

There is more than one way to represent the same information in XML. The following XML is another way of representing the same data about The Beatles. This uses XML *attributes* instead of nodes for `formed`, `first_name`, and `last_name`:

```
example_xml2 <- '
<the_beatles formed="1990">
  <members>
    <member first_name="George" last_name="Harrison"/>
    <member first_name="Richard" last_name="Starkey"/>
    <member first_name="Paul" last_name="McCartney"/>
    <member first_name="John" last_name="Lennon"/>
  </members>
</the_beatles>'
```

In this case, retrieving a vector of all first names can be done using this snippet:

```
sapply(getNodeSet(the_beatles, "//member[@first_name]"),
       function(x){ xmlAttrs(x)[["first_name"]] })


-----------


[1] "George"   "Richard" "Paul"      "John"
```

It may help your understanding of XML processing in R to use it in a real-life example.

There is a repository of music information called MusicBrainz (`http://musicbrainz.org`). Like Last.fm, this website kindly allows custom queries against their information database, and returns the results in XML format.

We will use this service to extend the recommendation system that we created using just tags from Last.fm by combining them with tags from MusicBrainz.

To query the database for a particular artist, the format is as follows: `http://musicbrainz.org/ws/2/artist/?query=artist`.

For example, the query for *Kate Bush* is:
`http://musicbrainz.org/ws/2/artist/?query=artist:Kate%20Bush`.

If you visit that link, you'll see that it returns an XML document that contains a list of artists that match the search to varying degrees. The list contains, among others, John Bush, Shelly Bush, and Bush. Luckily, the matches are in order of descending *matchiness* and, for all the artists that we'll be working with, the correct artist is the first artist in the `artist-list` node.

In case you can't view the link yourself, the following is essentially the structure of it:

```
<metadata xmlns="http://musicbrainz.org/ns/mmd-2.0#">
  <artist-list>
    <artist>
      <name>Kate Bush</name>
      <tag-list>
        <tag count="1">
          <name>kent</name>
        </tag>
        <tag count="1">
          <name>english</name>
        </tag>
        <tag count="3">
          <name>british</name>
        </tag>
      </tag-list>
    </artist>
  <artist-list>
</metadata>
```

This means that the XPath expressions that selects all the tags (of the first artist) is given by: `//artist[1]/tag-list/tag/name`.

As with JSON/Last.fm, let's write the function that, for any given artist, returns the appropriate query URL:

```
create_artist_query_url_mb <- function(artist){
  encoded_artist <- URLencode(artist)
  return(paste0("http://musicbrainz.org/ws/2/artist/?query=artist:",
                encoded_artist))
}

create_artist_query_url_mb("Depeche Mode")
```

```
-------
```

```
[1] "http://musicbrainz.org/ws/2/artist/?query=artist:Depeche%20Mode"
```

Now, let's write the function that returns the list of tags for a particular artist.

Because nothing is ever easy, the XPath mentioned in the preceding code will not work as is. This is because the MusicBrainz XML uses an *XML namespace*. Though it makes our job (marginally) harder, an XML namespace is generally a good thing, because it eliminates ambiguity when referring to element names between different XML documents whose element names are arbitrarily defined by the developer.

As the response suggests, the namespace is given by `http://musicbrainz.org/ns/mmd-2.0#`. In order to use this in our tag extraction function and in XPath selection, we need to store and name this namespace first:

```
ns <- "http://musicbrainz.org/ns/mmd-2.0#"
names(ns)[1] <- "ns"
```

Now we have all we need to write the Music Brainz counterpart to the `get_tag_vector_lfm` function:

```
get_tag_vector_mb <- function(an_artist, ns){
  artist_url <- create_artist_query_url_mb(an_artist)
  the_xml <- xmlParse(artist_url)
  xpath <- "//ns:artist[1]/ns:tag-list/ns:tag/ns:name"
  the_nodes <- getNodeSet(the_xml, xpath, ns)
  return(unlist(lapply(the_nodes, xmlValue)))
}

get_tag_vector_mb("Depeche Mode", ns)


------------------------------------

 [1] "electronica"     "post punk"       "alternative dance"
 [4] "electronic"      "dark wave"       "britannique"
 . . . . . . . . . . .
```

Like `fromJSON`, `xmlParse` handles URLs natively.

Let's finish this up:

```
our_artists <- list("Kate Bush", "Peter Tosh", "Radiohead",
                    "The Smiths", "The Cure", "Black Uhuru")
our_artists_tags_mb <- lapply(our_artists, get_tag_vector_mb, ns)
names(our_artists_tags_mb) <- our_artists

sim_matrix <- similarity_matrix(our_artists_tags_mb, jaccard_index)
print(sim_matrix)


-------

            Kate Bush Peter Tosh Radiohead The Smiths The Cure Black Uhuru
Kate Bush       1.00      0.00       0.24      0.27      0.24      0.00
Peter Tosh      0.00      1.00       0.00      0.00      0.00      0.17
Radiohead       0.24      0.00       1.00      0.23      0.23      0.00
The Smiths      0.27      0.00       0.23      1.00      0.38      0.00
The Cure        0.24      0.00       0.23      0.38      1.00      0.00
Black Uhuru     0.00      0.17       0.00      0.00      0.00      1.00
```

```
> sim_matrix[order(sim_matrix[,4], decreasing=TRUE), 4]
```

```
--------------------------------
```

```
 The Smiths    The Cure    Kate Bush    Radiohead   Peter Tosh Black Uhuru
        1.00        0.38         0.27         0.23         0.00        0.00
```

This yields results that are quite similar to the recommendation system that uses tags from only Last.fm. Personally, I like the former better, but how about we combine both? We can do this easily by taking the set intersection of artists' tags between the two services:

```
for(i in 1:length(our_artists_tags)){
    the_artist <- names(our_artists_tags)[i]
    # the_artist now holds the current artist's name
    combined_tags <- union(our_artists_tags[[the_artist]],
                        our_artists_tags_mb[[the_artist]])
    our_artists_tags[[the_artist]] <- combined_tags
}

sim_matrix <- similarity_matrix(our_artists_tags, jaccard_index)
print(sim_matrix)
```

```
--------
```

	Kate Bush	Peter Tosh	Radiohead	The Smiths	The Cure	Black Uhuru
Kate Bush	1.00	0.04	0.29	0.24	0.19	0.03
Peter Tosh	0.04	1.00	0.01	0.03	0.03	0.29
Radiohead	0.29	0.01	1.00	0.29	0.30	0.03
The Smiths	0.24	0.03	0.29	1.00	0.40	0.05
The Cure	0.19	0.03	0.30	0.40	1.00	0.05
Black Uhuru	0.03	0.29	0.03	0.05	0.05	1.00

Super!

Other data formats

One of things that makes R great is the wealth of high-quality add-on packages. As you might expect, there are many of these add-on packages with the ability to import data in a multitude of other formats. Whether it's an arcane markup language, a proprietary binary file, Excel spreadsheet, and so on, there is almost certainly an R package out there for you to handle it. But how do you find them?

One way is to browse the community maintained CRAN Task Views (`https://cran.r-project.org/web/views/`). A Task View is a way to browse for packages related to a particular topic, domain, or special interest. The germane Task View, here, is the Web Technologies Task View (`https://cran.r-project.org/web/views/WebTechnologies.html`). You'll notice that `jsonlite` and the `XML` package are mentioned on the first page.

The easiest way to discover these packages, though, is through your favorite web browser. For example, if you are looking for a package to import YAML data (yet another data serialization format), you might search `R CRAN package yaml`. If you use a search engine that tracks you (don't fight the singularity), eventually a search of only R YAML will suffice to get you where you need to go.

Developing fast and reliable information retrieval skills (like search engine-fu) is probably one of the most valuable assets of a statistical programmer, or any programmer, for that matter. Cultivating these skills will serve you well, dear reader.

Online repositories

Look back to the Web Technologies Task View we talked about in the previous section. There are a tremendous amount of R packages specifically designed to import data directly from specialized sources on the web. Among these are packages to search for and retrieve the full text of academic articles in the *Public Library of Science* journals (`rplos`), to search for and download the full text of Wikipedia articles (`WikipediR`), to download data about Berlin from the German government (`BerlinData`), to interface with the Chromosome Counts Database (`chromer`), to download historical financial data (`quantmod`), and to access the information in the PubChem chemistry database (`rpubchem`).

These examples notwithstanding, given that there are many hundreds of immense repositories of public data, it is far too much to expect the R community to have a package specially built for every single one. Luckily, with the ability to handle many different data formats under our belt, we can just download and import the data from these repositories ourselves. The following are a few of my favorite repositories. Perhaps some of them will have dedicated R packages for handling them by the time you read this:

- `data.gov`: A huge repository of data from the US government in a variety of formats including CSV, XML, and JSON
- `data.gov.uk`: The UK's equivalent repository

- `data.worldbank.org`: A spot for data made available by the World Bank including data on climate change, poverty, and aid effectiveness.
- `archive.ics.uci.edu/ml/`: 333 (at time of writing) datasets of various lengths and widths for testing statistical learning algorithms
- `www.cdc.gov/nchs/data_access/ftp_data.htm`: Some health-related datasets made available by the US Centers for Disease Control

Exercises

Practice the following exercises to revise the concepts learned in this chapter:

- How did we waste computation in the `similarity_matrix` function?
- Both the Last.fm and the MusicBrainz API have a *count* value associated with each tag, which can be taken to represent the extent to which the tag applied to the artist. By ignoring this field, in both cases we implicitly used a count of 1 for every tag, making well-fitting tags just as important as relatively less well-fitting ones. Rewrite the code to take *count* into account, and weigh each tag proportionally to its *count* value. This will be challenging, but it will be invaluable for understanding the material. It will also boost your confidence as an R programmer once you finish. Go you!
- How else might you be able to extend and improve upon our ragtag recommender system?
- The *efficient market hypothesis* posits that since the price of financial instruments reflects all the relevant information about its value at any given time, it is impossible to consistently *beat the market*. Familiarize yourself with the *weak, semi-strong*, and *strong* formulations of this hypothesis. Which, if any, of the camps do you align with? Why? Be specific.

Summary

This chapter began with a discussion on relation databases. You've learned that the DBI package defines a standard interface on which various database drivers build upon. You then learned how to query these types of databases, and to load the results in R.

Next, you gained an appreciation for JSON and XML (right?), and how to approach the importing of data from these formats. We then put our chops to the test by wielding data provided to us by two different web service APIs.

I stealthily snuck in some fancy new R constructs in this chapter. For example, prior to this chapter, we never explicitly worked with lists before.

Finally, you learned about how to look for information beyond which this chapter can provide, and some other places from which you can get data to play around with.

In the next chapter, we won't be talking about how to load data from different sources; we'll be talking about how to deal with disorderly data that is already loaded.

13
Dealing with Missing Data

Following the advice of the last chapter, you will get a shiny new dataset from the web or a database. You get to work on it. All of a sudden, you find yourself getting warnings about missing values and odd results from tests you're running. You take a closer look at the data and notice that a good proportion of your data—in multiple columns—has NA values. Uh oh.

Desperate, you check if there were import errors; there doesn't seem to be any. *What are you going to do?*

Analysis with missing data

Missing data is another one of those topics that is largely ignored in most introductory texts. Probably part of the reason why this is the case is that many myths about analysis with missing data still abound. Additionally, some of the research into cutting-edge techniques is still relatively new. A more legitimate reason for its absence in introductory texts is that most of the more principle methodologies are fairly complicated, mathematically speaking.

Nevertheless, the incredible ubiquity of problems related to missing data in real-life data analysis necessitates some broaching of the subject. This section serves as a gentle introduction to the subject and one of the more effective techniques for dealing with it.

A common refrain on the subject is something along the lines of *the best way to deal with missing data is not to have any*. It's true that missing data is a messy subject, and there are a lot of ways to *do it wrong*. It's important not to take this advice to the extreme, though. In order to bypass missing data problems, some have not allowed survey participants, for example, to go on without answering all the questions on a form. You can coerce the participants in a longitudinal study to not drop out, too. Don't do this. Not only is it unethical, it is also prodigiously counter-productive; there are treatments for missing data, but there are no treatments for *bad* data.

The standard treatment for the problem of missing data is to replace the missing data with non-missing values. This process is called *imputation*. In most cases, the goal of imputation is not to *recreate the lost completed dataset* but to allow valid statistical estimates or inferences to be drawn from incomplete data. Because of this, the effectiveness of different imputation techniques can't be evaluated by their ability to most accurately recreate the data from a simulated missing dataset; they must instead be judged by their ability to support the same statistical inferences as would be drawn from the analysis of the complete data. In this way, filling in the missing data is only a step towards the real goal—the analysis. The imputed dataset is rarely considered the final goal of imputation.

There are many different ways that missing data is dealt with in practice—some are good, some are not so good. Some are okay under certain circumstances, but not okay in others. Some involve missing data deletion, while some involve imputation. We will briefly touch on some of the more common methods. The ultimate goal of this chapter, though, is to get you started on what is often described as the *gold-standard* of imputation techniques: multiple imputation.

Visualizing missing data

In order to demonstrate the visualizing patterns of missing data, we first have to create some missing data. This will also be the same dataset that we perform analysis on later in the chapter. To showcase how to use multiple imputation in a semi-realistic scenario, we are going to create a version of the mtcars dataset with a few missing values:

Okay, let's set the `seed` (for deterministic *randomness*), and create a variable to hold our new marred dataset, using the following code:

```
set.seed(2)
miss_mtcars <- mtcars
```

First, we are going to create seven missing values in `drat` (about 20 percent), five missing values in the `mpg` column (about 15 percent), five missing values in the `cyl` column, three missing values in `wt` (about 10 percent), and three missing values in `vs`:

```
some_rows <- sample(1:nrow(miss_mtcars), 7)
miss_mtcars$drat[some_rows] <- NA

some_rows <- sample(1:nrow(miss_mtcars), 5)
miss_mtcars$mpg[some_rows] <- NA

some_rows <- sample(1:nrow(miss_mtcars), 5)
miss_mtcars$cyl[some_rows] <- NA

some_rows <- sample(1:nrow(miss_mtcars), 3)
miss_mtcars$wt[some_rows] <- NA

some_rows <- sample(1:nrow(miss_mtcars), 3)
miss_mtcars$vs[some_rows] <- NA
```

Now we are going to create four missing values in `qsec`, but only for automatic cars, using the following code:

```
only_automatic <- which(miss_mtcars$am==0)
some_rows <- sample(only_automatic, 4)
miss_mtcars$qsec[some_rows] <- NA
```

Now, let's take a look at the dataset:

```
miss_mtcars
                   mpg cyl  disp  hp drat    wt  qsec vs am gear carb
Mazda RX4          21.0   6 160.0 110 3.90 2.620 16.46  0  1    4    4
Mazda RX4 Wag      21.0   6 160.0 110 3.90 2.875 17.02  0  1    4    4
Datsun 710         22.8   4 108.0  93 3.85   NA 18.61  1  1    4    1
Hornet 4 Drive     21.4   6 258.0 110   NA 3.215 19.44  1  0    3    1
Hornet Sportabout  18.7   8 360.0 175   NA 3.440 17.02  0  0    3    2
Valiant            18.1  NA 225.0 105   NA 3.460    NA  1  0    3    1
```

Great, now let's visualize the *missingness*.

The first way we are going to visualize the pattern of missing data is by using the md.pattern function from the mice package (which is also the package that we are ultimately going to use for imputing our missing data). If you don't have the package already, install it:

```
library(mice)
md.pattern(miss_mtcars)
    disp hp am gear carb wt vs qsec mpg cyl drat
12     1  1  1    1    1  1  1    1   1   1    1  0
4      1  1  1    1    1  1  1    1   0   1    1  1
2      1  1  1    1    1  1  1    1   1   0    1  1
3      1  1  1    1    1  1  1    1   1   1    0  1
3      1  1  1    1    1  0  1    1   1   1    1  1
2      1  1  1    1    1  1  1    0   1   1    1  1
1      1  1  1    1    1  1  1    1   0   1    0  2
1      1  1  1    1    1  1  1    0   1   0    1  2
1      1  1  1    1    1  1  0    1   1   0    1  2
2      1  1  1    1    1  1  0    1   1   1    0  2
1      1  1  1    1    1  1  1    0   1   0    0  3
       0  0  0    0    0  3  3    4   5   5    7 27
```

A row-wise missing data pattern refers to the columns that are missing for each row. This function aggregates and counts the number of rows with the same missing data pattern. This function outputs a binary (0 and 1) matrix. Cells with a 1 represent non-missing data; 0 represents missing data. Since the rows are sorted in an increasing-amount-of-missingness order, the first row always refers to the missing data pattern containing the least amount of missing data.

In this case, the missing data pattern with the least amount of missing data is the pattern containing no missing data at all. Because of this, the first row has all 1s in the columns that are named after the columns in the miss_mtcars dataset. The left-most column is a count of the number of rows that display the missing data pattern, and the right-most column is a count of the number of missing data points in that pattern. The last row contains a count of the number of missing data points in each column.

As you can see, 12 of the rows contain no missing data. The next most common missing data pattern is the one missing just the mpg; four rows fit this pattern. There are only six rows that contain more than one missing value. Only one of these rows contains more than two missing values (as shown in the second-to-last row).

As far as datasets with missing data go, this particular one doesn't contain much. It is not uncommon for some datasets to have more than 30 percent of its data missing. This dataset doesn't even hit 3 percent.

Now let's visualize the missing data pattern graphically using the VIM package. You will probably have to install this, too:

```
library(VIM)
aggr(miss_mtcars, numbers=TRUE)
```

The output will be as follows:

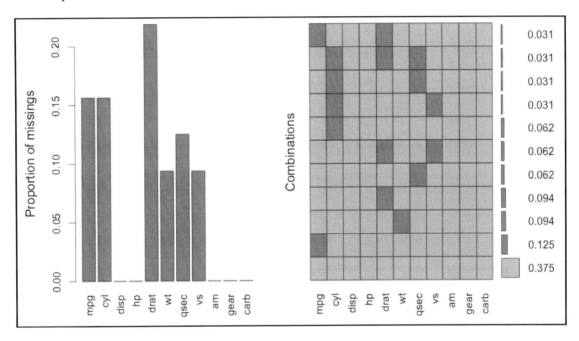

Figure 13.1: The output of VIM's visual aggregation of missing data. The left plot shows the proportion on missing values for each column. The right plot depicts the prevalence of row-wise missing data patterns, like md.pattern

At a glance, this representation shows us, effortlessly, that the drat column accounts for the highest proportion of missingness, column-wise, followed by mpg, cyl, qsec, vs, and wt. The graphic on the right shows us information similar to that of the output of md.pattern. This representation, though, makes it easier to tell if there is some systematic pattern of missingness. The blue cells represent non-missing data, and the red cells represent missing data. The numbers on the right of the figure represent the proportion of rows displaying that missing data pattern. 37.5 percent of the rows contain no missing data whatsoever.

Types of missing data

The VIM package allowed us to visualize the missing *data patterns*. A related term, the *missing data mechanism*, describes the process that determines each data point's likelihood of being missing. There are three main categories of missing data mechanisms: **Missing Completely At Random (MCAR)**, **Missing At Random (MAR)**, and **Missing Not At Random (MNAR)**. Discrimination based on missing data mechanism is crucial, since it informs us about the options for handling the missingness.

The first mechanism, MCAR, occurs when data's missingness is unrelated to the data. This would occur, for example, if rows were deleted from a database at random, or if a gust of wind took a random sample of a surveyor's survey forms off into the horizon. The mechanism that governs the missingness of drat, mpg, cyl, wt, and vs is MCAR, because we randomly selected elements to go missing. This mechanism, while being the easiest to work with, is seldom tenable in practice.

MNAR, on the other hand, occurs when a variable's missingness is related to the variable itself. For example, suppose the scale that weighed each car had a capacity of only 3,700 pounds, and because of this, the eight cars that weighed more than that were recorded as NA. This is a classic example of the MNAR mechanism—it is the weight of the observation itself that is the cause for its being missing. Another example would be if during the course of a trial of an anti-depressant drug, participants who were not being helped by the drug became too depressed to continue with the trial. At the end of the trial, when all the participants' level of depression is accessed and recorded, there would be missing values for participants whose reason for absence is related to their level of depression.

The last mechanism, *missing at random*, is somewhat unfortunately named. Contrary to what it may sound like, it means there is a systematic relationship between the missingness of an outcome variable and other observed variables, but *not* the outcome variable itself. This is probably best explained by the following example.

Suppose that in a survey, there is a question about income level that, in its wording, uses a particular colloquialism. Due to this, a large number of the participants in the survey whose native language is not English couldn't interpret the question, and left it blank. If the survey collected just the name, gender, and income, the missing data mechanism of the question on income would be MNAR. If, however, the questionnaire included a question that asked if the participant spoke English as a first language, then the mechanism would be MAR. The inclusion of the *is English your first language* variable means that the missingness of the income question can be completely accounted for.

The reason for the moniker *missing at random* is that *when you control the relationship between the missing variable and the observed variable(s) it is related to* (for example, "What is your income?" and "Is English your first language?" respectively), the data is missing at random.

As another example, there is a systematic relationship between the am and qsec variables in our simulated missing dataset: qsecs were missing only for automatic cars. But *within* the group of automatic cars, the qsec variable is missing at random. Therefore, qsec's mechanism is MAR; *controlling for transmission type*, qsec is missing at random. Bear in mind, though, if we removed am from our simulated dataset, qsec would become MNAR.

As mentioned earlier, MCAR is the easiest type to work with because of the complete absence of a systematic relationship in the data's missingness. Many unsophisticated techniques for handling missing data rest on the assumption that the data are MCAR. On the other hand, MNAR data is the hardest to work with since the properties of the missing data that caused its missingness have to be understood quantifiably, and included in the imputation model. Though multiple imputations can handle the MNAR mechanisms, the procedures involved become more complicated and far beyond the scope of this text. The MCAR and MAR mechanisms allow us not to worry about the properties and parameters of the missing data. For this reason, we may sometimes find MCAR or MAR missingness being referred to as *ignorable missingness*.

MAR data is not as hard to work with as MNAR data, but it is not as forgiving as MCAR. For this reason, though, our simulated dataset contains MCAR and MAR components; the mechanism that describes the whole data is MAR. Just one MAR mechanism makes the whole dataset MAR.

So which one is it?

You may have noticed that the place of a particular dataset in the missing data mechanism taxonomy is dependent on the variables that it includes. For example, we know that the mechanism behind qsec is MAR, but if the dataset *did not include* am, it would be MNAR. Since we are the ones that created the data, we know the procedure that resulted in qsec's missing values. If we weren't the ones creating the data—as happens in the real world—and the dataset did not contain the am column, we would just see a bunch of arbitrarily missing qsec values. This might lead us to *believe* that the data is MCAR. It isn't, though; just because the variable to which another variable's missingness is systematically related is non-observed doesn't mean that it doesn't exist.

This raises a critical question: can we ever be sure that our data is not MNAR? The unfortunate answer is *no*. Since the data that we need to prove or disprove as MNAR is *ipso facto* missing, the MNAR assumption can never be conclusively disconfirmed. It's our job, as critically thinking data analysts, to ask whether there is likely an MNAR mechanism or not.

Unsophisticated methods for dealing with missing data

Complete case analysis

This method, also called *list-wise deletion*, is a straightforward procedure that simply removes all rows or elements containing missing values prior to the analysis. In the univariate case—taking the mean of the drat column, for example—all elements of drat that are missing would simply be removed:

```
mean(miss_mtcars$drat)
[1] NA
mean(miss_mtcars$drat, na.rm=TRUE)
[1] 3.63
```

In a multivariate procedure—for example, linear regression predicting mpg from am, wt, and qsec—all rows that have a missing value in any of the columns included in the regression are removed:

```
listwise_model <- lm(mpg ~ am + wt + qsec,
                     data=miss_mtcars,
                     na.action = na.omit)
## OR
# complete.cases returns a boolean vector
comp <- complete.cases(cbind(miss_mtcars$mpg,
                            miss_mtcars$am,
                            miss_mtcars$wt,
                            miss_mtcars$qsec))
comp_mtcars <- mtcars[comp,]
listwise_model <- lm(mpg ~ am + wt + qsec,
                     data=comp_mtcars)
```

Under an MCAR mechanism, a complete case analysis produces unbiased estimates of the mean, variance/standard deviation, and regression coefficients, which means that the estimates don't systematically differ from the true values on average, since the included data elements are just a random sampling of the recorded data elements. However, inference-wise, since we lost a number of our samples, we are going to lose statistical power and generate standard errors and confidence intervals that are bigger than they need to be. Additionally, in the multivariate regression case, note that our sample size depends on the variables that we include in the regression; the more variables, the more missing data that we open ourselves up to, and the more rows that we are liable to lose. This makes comparing results across different models slightly hairy.

Under an MAR or MNAR mechanism, list-wise deletion will produce biased estimates of the mean and variance. For example, if am were highly correlated with qsec, the fact that we are missing qsec only for automatic cars would significantly shift our estimates of the mean of qsec. Surprisingly, list-wise deletion produces unbiased estimates of the regression coefficients, if the data is MNAR or MAR, as long as the relevant variables are included in the regression equations. For this reason, if there are relatively few missing values in a dataset that is to be used in regression analysis, list-wise deletion could be an acceptable alternative to more principled approaches.

Pairwise deletion

Also called *available-case analysis*, this technique is (somewhat unfortunately) common when estimating covariance or correlation matrices. For each pair of variables, it only uses the cases that are non-missing for both. This often means that the number of elements used will vary from cell to cell of the covariance/correlation matrices. This can result in absurd correlation coefficients that are above one, making the resulting matrices largely useless to methodologies that depend on them.

Mean substitution

Mean substitution, as the name suggests, replaces all the missing values with the mean of the available cases. Take a look at the following code, for example:

```
mean_sub <- miss_mtcars
mean_sub$qsec[is.na(mean_sub$qsec)] <- mean(mean_sub$qsec,
                                            na.rm=TRUE)
# etc...
```

Although this seemingly solves the problem of the loss of sample size in the list-wise deletion procedure, mean substitution has some very unsavory properties of its own. Whilst mean substitution produces unbiased estimates of the mean of a column, it produces biased estimates of the variance, since it removes the natural variability that would have occurred in the missing values had they not been missing. The variance estimates from mean substitution will therefore be, systematically, too small. Additionally, it's not hard to see that mean substitution will result in biased estimates if the data is MAR or MNAR. For these reasons, mean substitution is not recommended under virtually any circumstance.

Hot deck imputation

Hot deck imputation is an intuitively elegant approach that fills in the missing data with *donor* values from another row in the dataset. In the least sophisticated formulation, a random non-missing element from the same dataset is shared with a missing value. In more sophisticated hot deck approaches, the donor value comes from a row that is similar to the row with the missing data. The multiple imputation techniques that we will be using in a later section of this chapter borrows this idea for one of its imputation methods.

The term *hot deck* refers to the old practice of storing data in decks of punch cards. The deck that holds the donor value is *hot* because it is the one that is currently being processed.

Regression imputation

This approach attempts to fill in the missing data in a column using regression to predict likely values of the missing elements using other columns as predictors. For example, using regression imputation on the `drat` column would employ a linear regression predicting `drat` from all the other columns in `miss_mtcars`. The process would be repeated for all columns containing missing data, until the dataset is *complete*.

This procedure is intuitively appealing, because it integrates knowledge of the other variables and patterns of the dataset. This creates a set of more informed imputations. As a result, this produces unbiased estimates of the mean and regression coefficients under MCAR and MAR (so long as the relevant variables are included in the regression model).

However, this approach is not without its problems. The predicted values of the missing data lie right on the regression line but, as we know, very few data points lie *right* on the regression line—there is usually a normally distributed residual (error) term. Due to this, regression imputation underestimates the variability of the missing values. As a result, it will result in biased estimates of the variance and covariance between different columns. However, we're on the right track.

Stochastic regression imputation

As far as *unsophisticated* approaches go, stochastic regression is fairly evolved. This approach solves some of the issues of regression imputation and produces unbiased estimates of the mean, variance, covariance, and regression coefficients under MCAR and MAR. It does this by adding a random (stochastic) value to the predictions of regression imputation. This random added value is *sampled* from the residual (error) distribution of the linear regression which, if you remember, is assumed to be a normal distribution. This restores the variability in the missing values (that we lost in regression imputation), which those values would have had if they weren't missing.

However, as far as subsequent analysis and inference on the imputed dataset goes, stochastic regression results in standard errors and confidence intervals that are smaller than they should be. Since it produces *only one* imputed dataset, it does not capture the extent to which we are uncertain about the residuals and our coefficient estimates. Nevertheless, stochastic regression forms the basis of still more sophisticated imputation methods.

There are two sophisticated, well-founded, and recommended methods of dealing with missing data. One is called the **Expectation Maximization (EM)** method, which we do not cover here. The second is called *Multiple Imputation,* and because it is widely considered one of the most effective methods, it is the one we explore in this chapter.

Multiple imputation

The big idea behind multiple imputation is that instead of generating one set of imputed data with our best estimation of the missing data, we generate multiple versions of the imputed data where the imputed values are drawn from a distribution. The uncertainty about what the imputed values should be is reflected in the variation between the multiple imputed datasets.

We perform our intended analysis separately with each of these *m* amounts of completed datasets. These analyses will then yield *m* different parameter estimates (like regression coefficients, and so on). The critical point is that these parameter estimates are different solely due to the variability in the imputed missing values, and hence, our uncertainty about what the imputed values should be. This is how multiple imputation integrates uncertainty, and outperforms more limited imputation methods that produce one imputed dataset, conferring an unwarranted sense of confidence in the filled-in data of our analysis. The following diagram illustrates this idea:

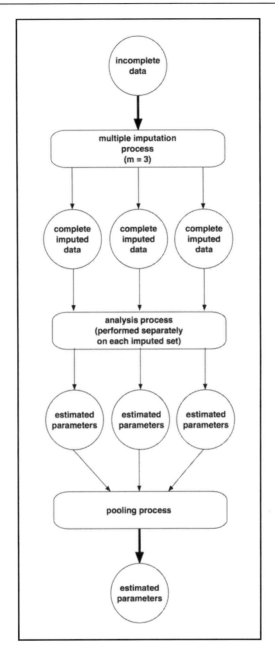

Figure 13.2: Multiple imputation in a nutshell

So how does mice come up with the imputed values?

Let's focus on the univariate case, where only one column contains missing data and we use all the other (completed) columns to impute the missing values before generalizing to a multivariate case.

mice actually has a few different imputation methods up its sleeve, each best suited for a particular use case. mice will often choose sensible defaults based on the data type (continuous, binary, non-binary categorical, and so on).

The most important method is what the package calls the norm method. This method is very much like stochastic regression. Each of the m imputations is created by adding a normal *noise* term to the output of a linear regression predicting the missing variable. What makes this slightly different than just stochastic regression repeated m times is that the norm method also integrates uncertainty about the regression coefficients used in the predictive linear model.

Recall that the regression coefficients in a linear regression are just estimates of the population coefficients from a random sample (that's why each regression coefficient has a standard error and confidence interval). Another sample from the population would have yielded slightly different coefficient estimates. If, through all our imputations, we just added a normal residual term from a linear regression equation with the *same coefficients*, we would be systematically understating our uncertainty regarding what the imputed values should be.

To combat this, in multiple imputation, each imputation of the data contains two steps. The first step performs stochastic linear regression imputation using coefficients for each predictor estimated from the data. The second step chooses slightly different estimates of these regression coefficients, and proceeds into the next imputation. The first step of the next imputation uses the slightly different coefficient estimates to perform stochastic linear regression imputation again. After that, in the second step of the second iteration, still other coefficient estimates are generated to be used in the third imputation. This cycle goes on until we have m multiply imputed datasets.

How do we choose these different coefficient estimates at the second step of each imputation? Traditionally, the approach is Bayesian in nature; these new coefficients are drawn from each of the coefficient's posterior distribution, which describes credible values of the estimate using the observed data and uninformative priors. This is the approach that norm uses. There is an alternate method that chooses these new coefficient estimates from a sampling distribution that is created by taking repeated samples of the data (with replacement) and estimating the regression coefficients of each of these samples. mice calls this method norm.boot.

The multivariate case is a little more hairy, since the imputation for one column depends on the other columns, which may contain missing data of their own.

For this reason, we make several passes over all the columns that need imputing, until the imputation of all missing data in a particular column is informed by informed estimates of the missing data in the predictor columns. These passes over all the columns are called *iterations*.

So that you really understand how this iteration works, let's say we are performing multiple imputation on a subset of miss_mtcars containing only mpg, wt, and drat. First, all the missing data in all the columns is set to a placeholder value like the mean or a randomly sampled non-missing value from its column. Then, we visit mpg where the placeholder values are turned back into missing values. These missing values are predicted using the two-part procedure described in the univariate case. Then we move on to wt; the placeholder values are turned back into missing values, whose new values are imputed with the two-step univariate procedure using mpg and drat as predictors. Then this is repeated with drat. This is one iteration. On the next iteration, it is not the placeholder values that get turned back into random values and imputed but the imputed values from the previous iteration. As this repeats, we shift away from the starting values and the imputed values begin to stabilize. This usually happens within just a few iterations. The dataset at the completion of the last iteration is the first multiply imputed dataset. Each *m* starts the iteration process all over again.

The default in mice is five iterations. Of course, you can increase this number if you have reason to believe that you need to. We'll discuss how to tell if this is necessary later in the section.

Methods of imputation

The method of imputation that we described for the univariate case, `norm`, works best for imputed values that follow an *unconstrained* normal distribution; it could lead to some nonsensical imputations otherwise. For example, since the weights in `wt` are so close to zero (because it's in units of 1,000 pounds) it is possible for the norm method to impute a negative weight. Though this will no doubt balance out over the other *m-1* multiply imputed datasets, we can combat this situation by using another method of imputation called *predictive mean matching*.

Predictive mean matching (`mice` calls this `pmm`) works a lot like `norm`. The difference is that the `norm` imputations are then used to find the *d* closest values to the imputed value among the non-missing data in the column. Then, one of these *d* values is chosen as the final imputed value; *d=3* is the default in `mice`.

This method has a few great properties. For one, the possibility of imputing a negative value for `wt` is categorically off the table; the imputed value would have to be chosen from the {1.513, 1.615, 1.835} set, since these are the three lowest weights. More generally, any natural constraint in the data (lower or upper bounds, integer count data, numbers rounded to the nearest one half, and so on) is respected with predictive mean matching, because the imputed values appear in the actual non-missing observed values. In this way, predictive mean matching is like hot-deck imputation. Predictive mean matching is the default imputation method in mice for numerical data, though it may be inferior to `norm` for small datasets and/or datasets with a lot of missing values.

Many of the other imputation methods in `mice` are especially suited for one particular data type. For example, binary categorical variables use `logreg` by default; this is like `norm` but uses logistic regression to impute a binary outcome. Similarly, non-binary categorical data uses multinomial regression; `mice` calls this method `polyreg`.

Multiple imputation in practice

There are a few steps to follow and decisions to make when using this powerful imputation technique:

- *Is the data MAR?* And be honest! If the mechanism is likely not MAR, then more complicated measures have to be taken.

- *Are there any derived terms, redundant variables, or irrelevant variables in the data set?* Any of these types of variables will interfere with the regression process. Irrelevant variables—such as unique IDs—will not have any predictive power. Derived terms or redundant variables, such as having a column for weight in pounds and grams, or a column for an area in addition to a length and width column, will similarly interfere with the regression step.
- Convert all categorical variables to factors, otherwise `mice` will not be able to tell that the variable is supposed to be categorical.
- Choose number of iterations and *m*, by default, these are both five. Using five iterations is usually okay, and we'll be able to tell if we need more. Five imputations are usually okay, too, but we can achieve more statistical power from more imputed datasets. I suggest setting *m* to 20, unless the processing power and time can't be spared.
- Choose an imputation method for each variable, you can stick with the defaults as long as you are aware of what they are and think they're the right fit.
- Choose the predictors, let mice use all the available columns as predictors as long as derived terms and redundant/irrelevant columns are removed. Not only does using more predictors result in reduced bias, but it also increases the likelihood that the data is MAR.
    - Perform the imputations.
    - Audit the imputations.
    - Perform analysis with the imputations.
    - Pool the results of the analyses.

Before we get down to it, let's call the `mice` function on our data frame with missing data, and use its default arguments, just to see what we *shouldn't do* and why, using the following code:

```
# we are going to set the seed and printFlag to FALSE, but
# everything else will the default argument
imp <- mice(miss_mtcars, seed=3, printFlag=FALSE)
print(imp)
---------------------------------
Multiply imputed data set
Call:
mice(data = miss_mtcars, printFlag = FALSE, seed = 3)
Number of multiple imputations:  5
Missing cells per column:
 mpg  cyl disp   hp drat   wt qsec   vs   am gear carb
   5    5    0    0    7    3    4    3    0    0    0
```

```
Imputation methods:
   mpg    cyl   disp     hp  drat      wt  qsec      vs     am  gear  carb
 "pmm"  "pmm"     ""     "" "pmm"  "pmm" "pmm"  "pmm"     ""    ""    ""
VisitSequence:
  mpg  cyl drat    wt qsec    vs
    1    2    5     6    7     8
PredictorMatrix:
      mpg cyl disp hp drat wt qsec vs am gear carb
mpg     0   1    1  1    1  1    1  1  1    1    1
cyl     1   0    1  1    1  1    1  1  1    1    1
disp    0   0    0  0    0  0    0  0  0    0    0
...
Random generator seed value:   3
```

The first thing we notice (on line four of the output) is that `mice` chose to create five multiply imputed datasets, by default. As we discussed, this isn't a bad default, but more imputation can only improve our statistical power (if only marginally); when we impute this dataset in earnest, we will use *m=20*.

The second thing we notice (on lines *8–10* of the output) is that it used predictive mean matching as the imputation method for all the columns with missing data. If you recall, predictive mean matching is the default imputation method for `numeric` columns. However, `vs` and `cyl` are binary categorical and non-binary categorical variables, respectively. Because we didn't convert them to factors, `mice` thinks these are just regular `numeric` columns. We'll have to fix this.

The last thing we should notice here is the predictor matrix (starting on line *14*). Each row and column of the predictor matrix refers to a column in the dataset to impute. If a cell contains a 1, it means that the variable referred to in the column is used as a predictor for the variable in the row. The first row indicates that all available attributes are used to help predict `mpg` with the exception of `mpg` itself. All the values in the diagonal are 0, because `mice` won't use an attribute to predict itself. Note that the `disp`, `hp`, `am`, `gear`, and `carb` rows all contain 0s—this is because these variables are complete and don't need to use any predictors.

Since we thought carefully about whether there were any attributes that should have been removed before we performed the imputation, we can use `mice`'s default predictor matrix for this dataset. If there were any non-predictive attributes (such as unique identifiers, redundant variables, and so on), we would have either had to remove them (easiest option), or instruct `mice` not to use them as predictors (harder).

Let's now correct the issues that we've discussed, with the help of the following code:

```
# convert categorical variables into factors
miss_mtcars$vs <- factor(miss_mtcars$vs)
miss_mtcars$cyl <- factor(miss_mtcars$cyl)

imp <- mice(miss_mtcars, m=20, seed=3, printFlag=FALSE)
imp$method
----------------------------------------
       mpg       cyl      disp        hp      drat
     "pmm" "polyreg"        ""        ""     "pmm"
        wt      qsec        vs        am      gear
     "pmm"     "pmm"  "logreg"        ""        ""
      carb
        ""
```

Now `mice` has corrected the imputation method of `cyl` and `vs` to their correct defaults. In truth, `cyl` is a kind of discrete numeric variable called an *ordinal variable*, which means that yet another imputation method may be optimal for that attribute, but for the sake of simplicity, we'll treat it as a categorical variable.

Before we get to use the imputations in an analysis, we have to check the output. The first thing we need to check is the *convergence* of the iterations. Recall that for imputing data with missing values in multiple columns, multiple imputation requires iteration over all these columns a few times. At each iteration, `mice` produces imputations—and samples new parameter estimates from the parameters' posterior distributions—for all columns that need to be imputed. The final imputations, for each multiply imputed dataset *m*, are the imputed values from the final iteration.

In contrast to when we used MCMC in *Bayesian Methods*, the convergence in `mice` is much faster; it usually occurs in just a few iterations. However, as in *Bayesian Methods*, visually checking for convergence is highly recommended. We even check for it similarly; when we call the `plot` function on the variable that we assign the `mice` output to, it displays trace plots of the mean and standard deviation of all the variables involved in the imputations.

Each line in each plot is one of the *m* imputations:

```
plot(imp)
```

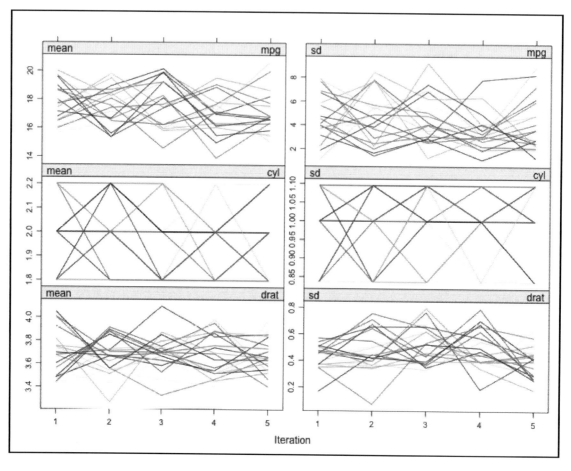

Figure 13.3: A subset of the trace plots produced by plotting an object returned by a mice imputation

As you can see from the preceding trace plot on `imp`, there are no clear trends and the variables are all overlapping from one iteration to the next. Put another way, the variance within a chain (there are *m* chains) should be about equal to the variance between the chains. This indicates that convergence was achieved.

If convergence was not achieved, you can increase the number of iterations that `mice` employs by explicitly specifying the `maxit` parameter to the `mice` function.

 To see an example of non-convergence, take a look at Figures 7 and 8 in the paper that describes this package written by the authors of the package themselves. It is available at `http://www.jstatsoft.org/article/view/v045i03`.

The next step is to make sure the imputed values are reasonable. In general, whenever we quickly review the results of something to see if they make sense, it is called a *sanity test* or sanity check. With the following line, we're going to display the imputed values for the five missing mpgs for the first six imputations:

```
imp$imp$mpg[,1:6]
```

```
                         1    2    3    4    5    6
Duster 360            19.2 16.4 17.3 15.5 15.0 19.2
Cadillac Fleetwood    15.2 13.3 15.0 13.3 10.4 17.3
Chrysler Imperial     10.4 15.0 15.0 16.4 10.4 10.4
Porsche 914-2         27.3 22.8 21.4 22.8 21.4 15.5
Ferrari Dino          19.2 21.4 19.2 15.2 18.1 19.2
```

These sure look reasonable. A better method for sanity checking is to call `densityplot` on the variable that we assign the `mice` output to:

```
densityplot(imp)
```

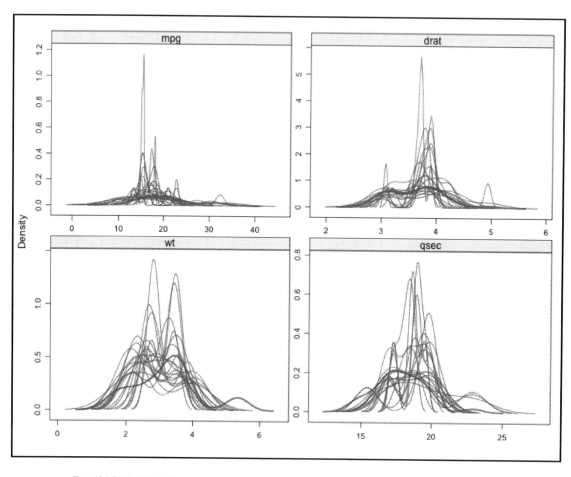

Figure 13.4: Density plots of all the imputed values for mpg, drat, wt, and qsec. Each imputation has its own density curve in each quadrant

This displays, for every attribute imputed, a density plot of the actual non-missing values (the thick line) and the imputed values (the thin lines). We are looking to see that the distributions are similar. Note that the density curve of the imputed values extend much higher than the observed values' density curve in this case. This is partly because we imputed so few variables that there weren't enough data points to properly smooth the density approximation. Height and non-smoothness notwithstanding, these density plots indicate no outlandish behavior among the imputed variables.

We are now ready for the analysis phase. We are going to perform linear regression on each imputed dataset and attempt to model `mpg` as a function of `am`, `wt`, and `qsec`. Instead of repeating the analyses on each dataset manually, we can apply an expression to all the datasets at one time with the `with` function, as follows:

```
imp_models <- with(imp, lm(mpg ~ am + wt + qsec))
```

We could take a peek at the estimated coefficients from each dataset using `lapply` on the `analyses` attribute of the returned object, as shown in the following code:

```
lapply(imp_models$analyses, coef)
-------------------------------

[[1]]
(Intercept)          am           wt         qsec
 18.1534095   2.0284014   -4.4054825    0.8637856

[[2]]
(Intercept)          am           wt         qsec
  8.375455     3.336896    -3.520882     1.219775

[[3]]
(Intercept)          am           wt         qsec
  5.254578     3.277198    -3.233096     1.337469
. . . . . . . . .
```

Finally, let's pool the results of the analyses (with the `pool` function), and call `summary` on it, as shown in the following code:

```
pooled_model <- pool(imp_models)
summary(pooled_model)
--------------------------------
                    est          se          t         df       Pr(>|t|)
(Intercept)    7.049781   9.2254581   0.764166   17.63319   0.454873254
am             3.182049   1.7445444   1.824000   21.36600   0.082171407
wt            -3.413534   0.9983207  -3.419276   14.99816   0.003804876
qsec           1.270712   0.3660131   3.471765   19.93296   0.002416595
                   lo 95       hi 95  nmis          fmi        lambda
(Intercept)  -12.3611281   26.460690    NA    0.3459197     0.2757138
am            -0.4421495    6.806247     0    0.2290359     0.1600952
wt            -5.5414268   -1.285641     3    0.4324828     0.3615349
qsec           0.5070570    2.034366     4    0.2736026     0.2042003
```

Though we could have performed the pooling ourselves using the equations that Donald Rubin outlined in his 1987 classic *Multiple Imputation for Nonresponse in Surveys*, it is less of a hassle and will be less error-prone to have the pool function do it for us. Readers who are interested in the pooling rules are encouraged to consult the aforementioned text.

As you can see, for each parameter, pool has combined the coefficient estimate and standard errors, and calculated the appropriate degrees of freedom. These allow us to t-test each coefficient against the null hypothesis that the coefficient is equal to zero, produce p-values for the t-test, and construct confidence intervals.

The standard errors and confidence intervals are wider than those that would have resulted from linear regression on a single imputed dataset, but that's because it is appropriately taking into account our uncertainty regarding what the missing values would have been.

There are, at the present time, a limited number of analyses that can be automatically pooled by mice—the most important being *lm/glm*. If you recall, though, the generalized linear model is extremely flexible, and can be used to express a wide array of different analyses. By extension, we could use multiple imputation for not only linear regression but logistic regression, Poisson regression, t-tests, ANOVA, ANCOVA, and more.

Exercises

The following are a few exercises for you to strengthen your grasp of the concepts learned in this chapter:

- Normally, when there is missing data for a question such as *"What is your income?"*, we strongly suspect an MNAR mechanism, because we live in a dystopia that equates wealth with worth. As a result, the participants with the lowest income may be embarrassed to answer that question. In the relevant section, we assumed that because the question was poorly worded and we could account for whether English was the first language of the participant, the mechanism is MAR. If we were wrong about this reason, and it was really because the lower income participants were reticent to admit their income, *what would the missing data mechanism be now?* If, however, the differences in income were fully explained by whether English was the first language of the participant, *what would the missing data mechanism be in that case?*
- Find a dataset on the web with missing data. What does it use to denote that data is missing? Think about that dataset's missing data mechanism. Is there a chance that this data is MNAR?
- When two autonomous individuals decide to voluntarily trade, the transaction can be in both parties' best interests. *Does it necessarily follow that a voluntary trade between nations benefits both states? Why or why not?*

Summary

In case you dozed off, this chapter addressed a fairly common problem in real-world data analysis—*especially* for data collected outside your control or organization: missing data.

We first learned how to visualize missing data patterns, and how to recognize different types of missing data. You saw a few unprincipled ways of tackling the problem, and learned why they were suboptimal solutions. Specifically, most of the naïve solutions produced biased estimates on *at least some* crucial statistics and, in particular, almost always underestimated the variance and would produce confidence intervals that were way too narrow.

Multiple imputation, so we learned, addresses the shortcomings of these approaches and, through its usage of several imputed datasets, correctly communicates our uncertainty surrounding the imputed values. We used `mice` to perform this procedure. We discussed the different imputation methods for different types of variables, like *predictive mean matching* for continuous variables and *polynomial regression* for categorical variables. We then got a sense of two ways we can use to verify that the MI procedure went smoothly. Finally, we got a chance to actually *use* these imputed datasets to perform linear regression on the `mtcars` dataset, which yielded correct results and confidence intervals which appropriately estimated the uncertainty in our beta coefficient estimates.

Missing data problems are often considered a subset of *messy data problems*. In the next chapter, we'll be looking into the obstacles that other brands of *messy* data present and how to overcome them.

14
Dealing with Messy Data

As mentioned in the last two chapters, analyzing data in the real world often requires some know-how outside of the typical introductory data analysis curriculum. For example, rarely do we get a neatly formatted, tidy dataset with no errors, junk, or missing values. Rather, we often get *messy*, unwieldy datasets.

What makes a dataset messy? Different people in different roles have different ideas about what constitutes *messiness*. Some regard any data that invalidates the assumptions of the parametric model as messy. Others see messiness in datasets with a grievously imbalanced number of observations in each category for a categorical variable. Some examples of things that I would consider messy are:

- Many missing values (NAs)
- Misspelled names in categorical variables
- Inconsistent data coding
- Numbers in the same column being in different units
- Mis-recorded data and data entry mistakes
- Extreme outliers

Since there are an infinite number of ways that data can be messy, there's simply no chance of enumerating every example and their respective solutions. Instead, we are going to talk chiefly about two tools that help combat the bulk of the messiness issues that I cited just now with the exception of missing data, which we addressed in the previous chapter.

Checking unsanitized data

Very often, there will be errors or mistakes in data that can severely complicate analysis—especially with public data or data outside of your organization. We will refer to this data as *unsanitized data* in this chapter. For example, say there is a stray comma or punctuation mark in a column that was supposed to be `numeric`. If we aren't careful, R will read this column as `character`, and subsequent analysis may, in the best case scenario, fail. It is also possible, however, that our analysis will silently chug along and return an unexpected result. This will happen, for example, if we try to perform linear regression using the punctuation-containing-but-otherwise-numeric column as a predictor, which will compel R to convert it into a `factor`, thinking that it is a categorical variable.

In the worst-case scenario, an analysis with *unsanitized* data may not error out or return nonsensical results, but return results that look plausible but are actually incorrect. For example, it is common (for some reason) to encode missing data with 999 instead of `NA`; performing a regression analysis with 999 in a `numeric` column can severely adulterate our linear models, but often not enough to cause clearly inappropriate results. This mistake may then go undetected indefinitely.

Some problems like these could, rather easily, be detected in small datasets by visually auditing the data. Often, however, mistakes like these are notoriously easy to miss. Further, visual inspection is an untenable solution for datasets with thousands of rows and hundreds of columns. Any sustainable solution must off-load this auditing process to R. But how do we describe aberrant behavior to R so that it can catch mistakes on its own?

The `assertr` package seeks to do this by introducing a number of data-checking verbs. Using `assertr` grammar, these *verbs* (functions) can be combined with subjects (data) in different ways to express a rich vocabulary of data validation tasks.

More prosaically, `assertr` provides a suite of functions designed to verify the assumptions about data early in the analysis process, before any time is wasted computing on bad data. The idea is to provide as much information as you can about how you expect the data to look upfront so that any deviation from this expectation can be dealt with immediately.

Given that the `assertr` grammar is designed to be able to describe a bouquet of error-checking routines, rather than list all the functions and functionalities that the package provides, it would be more helpful to visit particular use cases.

Two things before we start. First, make sure you install `assertr`. Second, bear in mind that all data verification verbs in `assertr` take a data frame to check as their first argument, and either (a) return the same data frame if the check passes, or (b) produce a fatal error (by default).

Since the verbs return a copy of the chosen data frame if the check passes, the main idiom in `assertr` involves the reassignment of the returning data frame after it passes the check:

```
a_dataset <- CHECKING_VERB(a_dataset, ....)
```

Checking for out-of-bounds data

It's common for numeric values in a column to have a natural constraint on the values that it should hold. For example, if a column represents a percent of something, we might want to check if all the values in that column are between zero and one (or 0 and 100). In `assertr`, we typically use the `within_bounds` function in conjunction with the `assert` verb to ensure that this is the case. For example, if we added a column to `mtcars` that represented the percent of the heaviest car's weight, the weight of each car is:

```
library(assertr)
mtcars.copy <- mtcars

mtcars.copy$Percent.Max.Wt <- round(mtcars.copy$wt /
                                      max(mtcars.copy$wt),
                                    2)

mtcars.copy <- assert(mtcars.copy, within_bounds(0,1),
                      Percent.Max.Wt)
```

`within_bounds` is actually a function that takes the lower and upper bounds and returns a predicate, a function that returns TRUE or FALSE. The `assert` function then applies this predicate to every element of the column specified in the third argument. If there are more than three arguments, `assert` will assume there are more columns to check.

Using `within_bounds`, we can also avoid the situation where NA values are specified as *999*, as long as the second argument in `within_bounds` is less than this value.

`within_bounds` can take other information such as whether the bounds should be inclusive or exclusive, or whether it should ignore the NA values. To see the options for this, and all the other functions in `assertr`, use the `help` function on them.

Let's see an example of what it looks like when the `assert` function fails, in the following code:

```
mtcars.copy$Percent.Max.Wt[c(10,15)] <- 2
mtcars.copy <- assert(mtcars.copy, within_bounds(0,1),
                      Percent.Max.Wt)
-------------------------------------------------------------
Column 'Percent.Max.Wt' violates assertion 'within_bounds(0, 1)' 2 times
    verb redux_fn          predicate          column index value
1 assert         NA within_bounds(0, 1) Percent.Max.Wt    10     2
2 assert         NA within_bounds(0, 1) Percent.Max.Wt    15     2

Error: assertr stopped execution
```

We get an informative error message that tells us how many times the assertion was violated, and the indices and values of the wayward data.

With `assert`, we have the option of checking a condition on multiple columns at the same time. For example, none of the measurements in `iris` can possibly be negative. Here's how we might make sure our dataset is compliant:

```
iris <- assert(iris, within_bounds(0, Inf),
               Sepal.Length, Sepal.Width,
               Petal.Length, Petal.Width)

# or simply " Species" because that
# will include all columns *except* Species
iris <- assert(iris, within_bounds(0, Inf),
               -Species)
```

On occasion, we will want to check elements for adherence to a more complicated pattern. For example, let's say we had a column that we knew was either between -10 and -20, or 10 and 20. We could check for this by using the more flexible `verify` verb, which takes a logical expression as its second argument; if any of the results in the logical expression are FALSE, `verify` will cause an error, as shown in the following code:

```
set.seed(1)
vec <- runif(10, min=10, max=20)
# randomly turn some elements negative
vec <- vec * sample(c(1, -1), 10,
                    replace=TRUE)

example <- data.frame(weird=vec)

example <- verify(example, ((weird < 20 & weird > 10) |
                           (weird < -10 & weird > -20)))
```

```
# or

example <- verify(example, abs(weird) < 20 & abs(weird) > 10)
# passes

example$weird[4] <- 0
example <- verify(example, abs(weird) < 20 & abs(weird) > 10)
# fails
------------------------------------
verification [abs(weird) < 20 & abs(weird) > 10] failed! (1 failure)

    verb redux_fn                          predicate column index value
1 verify         NA abs(weird) < 20 & abs(weird) > 10      NA     4    NA

Error: assertr stopped execution
```

Note that the way that `verify` works prevents it from showing the *values* of the offending data but it *does* tell you the index of the failure.

Checking the data type of a column

By default, most of the data import functions in R will attempt to guess the data type for each column at the import phase. This is usually nice, because it saves us from tedious work. However, it can backfire when there are, for example, stray punctuation marks in what are supposed to be numeric columns. To verify this, we can use the `assert` function with the `is.numeric` base function, as shown in the following code:

```
iris <- assert(iris, is.numeric, -Species)
```

We can use the `is.character` and `is.logical` functions with `assert`, too.

An alternative method that will disallow the import of unexpected data types is to specify the data type that each column should have at the data import phase, with the `colClasses` optional argument:

```
iris <- read.csv("PATH_TO_IRIS_DATA.csv",
                 colClasses=c("numeric", "numeric",
                              "numeric", "numeric",
                              "character"))
```

This solution comes with the added benefit of speeding up the data import process, since R doesn't have to waste time guessing each column's data type.

Checking for unexpected categories

Another data integrity impropriety that is unfortunately very common is the mislabeling of categorical variables. There are two types of mislabeling of categories that can occur: an observation's class is mis-entered/mis-recorded/mistaken for that of another class, or the observation's class is labeled in a way that is not consistent with the rest of the labels. To see an example of what we can do to combat the former case, read `assertr` vignette. The latter case covers instances where, for example, the species of iris could be misspelled (such as *versicolour* or *verginica*) or cases where the pattern established by the majority of class names is ignored (*iris setosa, i. setosa,* or *SETOSA*). Either way, these incorrect specifications prove to be the bane of data analysts for several reasons. For example, an analysis that is predicated upon a two-class categorical variable (for example, logistic regression) will now have to contend with more than two categories. Yet another way in which unexpected categories can haunt you is by producing statistics grouped by different values of a categorical variable; if the categories were extracted from the main data manually—with `subset`, for example, as opposed to with `by`, `tapply`, or `aggregate`—you'll be missing potentially crucial observations.

If you know what categories you are expecting from the start, you can use the `in_set` function, in concert with `assert`, to confirm that all the categories of a particular column are squarely contained within a predetermined set:

```
# passes
iris <- assert(iris, in_set("setosa", "versicolor",
                            "virginica"), Species)

# mess up the data
iris.copy <- iris
# We have to make the 'Species' column not
# a factor
iris.copy$Species <- as.vector(iris$Species)
iris.copy$Species[4:5] <- "SETOSA"
iris.copy$Species[135] <- "verginica"
iris.copy$Species[95] <- "i. versicolor"

# fails
iris.copy <- assert(iris.copy, in_set("setosa", "versicolor",
                                      "virginica"), Species)
-------------------------------------------
Column 'Species' violates assertion 'in_set("setosa", "versicolor",
"virginica")' 4 times
    verb redux_fn                                 predicate   column index
value
1 assert        NA in_set("setosa", "versicolor", "virginica") Species    4
```

```
          SETOSA
2 assert        NA in_set("setosa", "versicolor", "virginica") Species      5
SETOSA
3 assert        NA in_set("setosa", "versicolor", "virginica") Species     95
i. versicolor
4 assert        NA in_set("setosa", "versicolor", "virginica") Species    135
verginica

Error: assertr stopped execution
```

If you don't know the categories that you should be expecting *a priori*, the following code, which will tell you how many rows each category contains, may help you identify the categories that are either rare or misspecified:

```
by(iris.copy, iris.copy$Species, nrow)
```

Checking for outliers, entry errors, or unlikely data points

Automatic outlier detection (sometimes known as *anomaly detection*) is something that a lot of analysts scoff at and view as a pipe dream. Though the creation of a routine that automagically detects *all* erroneous data points with 100 percent specificity and precision is impossible, unmistakable mis-entered data points and flagrant outliers are not hard to detect even with very simple methods. In my experience, there are a lot of errors of this type.

One simple way to detect the presence of a major outlier is to confirm that every data point is within some *n* number of standard deviations away from the mean of the group. assertr has a function, within_n_sds, in conjunction with the insist verb, to do just this; if we wanted to check that every numeric value in iris was within five standard deviations of its respective column's mean, we could express it like this:

```
iris <- insist(iris, within_n_sds(5), -Species)
```

An issue with using standard deviations away from the mean (z-scores) for detecting outliers is that both the mean *and* standard deviation are influenced heavily by outliers; this means that the very thing we are trying to detect is obstructing our ability to find it.

There is a more robust measure for finding central tendency and dispersion than the mean and standard deviation: the median and median absolute deviation. The *median absolute deviation* is the median of the absolute value of all the elements of a vector subtracted by the vector's median.

`assertr` has a sister to `within_n_sds`, `within_n_mads`, which checks every element of a vector to make sure it is within *n* median absolute deviations away from its column's *median*, as shown in the following code:

```
iris <- insist(iris, within_n_mads(4), -Species)
iris$Petal.Length[5] <- 15
iris <- insist(iris, within_n_mads(4), -Species)
--------------------------------------------
Column 'Petal.Length' violates assertion 'within_n_mads(4)' 1 time
     verb redux_fn          predicate          column index value
1 insist          NA within_n_mads(4) Petal.Length     5    15

Error: assertr stopped execution
```

In my experience, `within_n_mads` can be an effective guard against illegitimate univariate outliers if *n* is chosen carefully.

The examples here have been focusing on outlier identification in the *univariate* case—across one dimension at a time. Often, there are times where an observation is truly anomalous but it wouldn't be evident by looking at the spread of each dimension individually. `assertr` has support for this type of multivariate outlier analysis, but a full discussion of it would require a background outside the scope of this text. Please see the `assertr` vignette for a comprehensive look at that and other topics.

Chaining assertions

The `assertr` check aims to make the checking of assumptions so effortless that the user never feels the need to hold back any implicit assumption. Therefore, it's *expected* that the user uses multiple checks on one data frame.

The usage examples that we've seen so far are really only appropriate for one or two checks. For example, a usage pattern such as the following is clearly unworkable:

```
iris <-
CHECKING_CONSTRUCT4(CHECKING_CONSTRUCT3(CHECKING_CONSTRUCT2(CHECKING_CONSTR
UCT1(this, ...), ...), ...), ...)
```

To combat this visual cacophony, `assertr` provides direct support for chaining multiple assertions by using the *piping* construct from the `magrittr` package.

The pipe operator of `magrittr`, `%>%`, works as follows: it takes the item on the left-hand side of the pipe and inserts it (by default) into the position of the first argument of the function on the right-hand side. The following are some examples of simple `magrittr` usage patterns:

```
library(magrittr)
4 %>% sqrt              # 2
iris %>% head(n=3)      # the first 3 rows of iris
iris <- iris %>% assert(within_bounds(0, Inf), -Species)
```

Since the return value of a passed `assertr` check is the validated data frame, you can use the `magrittr` pipe operator to tack on more checks in a way that lends itself to easier human understanding. Take a look at the following code, for example:

```
iris <- iris %>%
  assert(is.numeric, -Species) %>%
  assert(within_bounds(0, Inf), -Species) %>%
  assert(in_set("setosa", "versicolor", "virginica"), Species) %>%
  insist(within_n_mads(4), -Species)

# or, equivalently

CHECKS <- . %>%
  assert(is.numeric, -Species) %>%
  assert(within_bounds(0, Inf), -Species) %>%
  assert(in_set("setosa", "versicolor", "virginica"), Species) %>%
  insist(within_n_mads(4), -Species)

iris <- iris %>% CHECKS
```

When chaining assertions, I like to put the most integral and general one right at the top. I also like to put the assertions most likely to be violated right at the top so that execution is terminated before any more checks are run.

The last topic I want to touch upon regarding `assertr` is that of *comprehensive error checking*.

Sometimes, you just want to fail at the first sign of an error. Other times—especially if you *know* that the dataset is suspect—you want to get a comprehensive list of all failures. You can do this in `assertr` by putting all of your checks in between `chain_start` and `chain_end`. Take a look at the following code, for example:

```
mtcars %>%
  chain_start %>%
  assert(in_set(1, 2, 3, 4), carb) %>%
  assert_rows(rowMeans, within_bounds(0,5), gear:carb) %>%
  verify(nrow(.)==10) %>%
  verify(mpg < 32) %>%
  chain_end
----------------------------------
There are 7 errors across 4 verbs:
-
          verb redux_fn               predicate        column index value
1       assert     <NA>   in_set(1, 2, 3, 4)          carb    30   6.0
2       assert     <NA>   in_set(1, 2, 3, 4)          carb    31   8.0
3  assert_rows  rowMeans within_bounds(0, 5)  ~gear:carb     30   5.5
4  assert_rows  rowMeans within_bounds(0, 5)  ~gear:carb     31   6.5
5       verify     <NA>        nrow(.) == 10        <NA>     1    NA
6       verify     <NA>             mpg < 32        <NA>    18    NA
7       verify     <NA>             mpg < 32        <NA>    20    NA

Error: assertr stopped execution
```

The package recognized that we used four checking verbs and that there were a total of seven errors. We get a nice print-out of all the violation information that we want. Often, though, we want to save this information as a `data.frame` to inspect thoroughly, or write to a file or email. To do that, you can tell `chain_end` that you'd like to return this violation `data.frame`:

```
...
chain_end(error_fun=error_df_return)
```

This can be assigned to a variable and written to a file.

As mentioned before, there are many other capabilities built into the `assertr`, including multivariate outlier checking. For more information about these, read the package's vignette (written by yours truly), using the following code:

```
> vignette("assertr")
```

On the `magrittr` side, besides the *forward-pipe* operator, this package sports some other very helpful pipe operators. Additionally, `magrittr` allows the substitution at the right side of the pipe operator to occur at locations other than the first argument. For more information about the wonderful `magrittr` package, read its vignette.

Regular expressions

Suppose you find that there are commas separating every third digit of the numbers in a numeric column. How would you remove them? Or suppose you needed to strip a currency symbol from values in columns that hold monetary values so that you can compute with them as numbers. These, and vastly more complicated text transformations, can be performed using a most powerful tool, *regular expressions*.

What are regular expressions?

Regular expressions (or *regexes*, as it is commonly abbreviated) is a formal grammar for describing patterns in text/strings. In general purpose programming languages, it is often used for things like verifying user input, but it is most often used in the context of statistical programming to transform the textual representation of raw data. Regular expressions are—at once—the plural form of a *single* regular expression, a powerful tool, an idea, and a *language* for describing patterns in text.

You might ask yourself: *How do I work with this?* You might *first* ask yourself: *How does regex help me with data analysis?* I compute on *numbers*, not strings!

Well, first, there are often strings/character vectors in datasets specifying binary and categorical variables. In this book so far, we've only once or twice worked with data that was purely numeric. But that doesn't fully cover the answer to your question.

The answer to this question is simple: even *if* your data is purely numeric (which is rare), your data very often *starts* its life as text. Every time we import data from a file, we convert some text into data types that can be manipulated and computed on in R. It is only a matter of time until you, dear reader, run into spreadsheets that should contain only numeric data but actually include stray punctuation marks, commas, or leading and trailing whitespace (spaces, tabs, and so on).

It is *absolutely impossible* for me to overstate the utility of learning to wield regex. It is no exaggeration to say that I work with regex, in one form or another, at least once *every single workweek*. Often, the problems I solve with regex in a few minutes, or even seconds, would have taken hours otherwise—if even tractable at all.

If other analysts don't use regular expressions very often, it's because either they're given perfect data every time, or because they don't know much about them. If they learn about them, they'll undoubtedly start to see problems that they've previously regarded as unsolvable (or, at the very least, prohibitively time-consuming) as relatively simple to solve. As you become a more and more experienced regex user, you'll be able to spot regex-based solutions in your own work (with incredible frequency) as well as in the work of the people you work with. Once they catch wind of what you're capable of, still others will come out of the woodwork and ask you to transform their data. This will make you feel important and loved.

Some shy away from learning regular expressions because they look difficult and seem impossible to read. Regex apologists will counter this by saying that once regex is mastered, the previously unreadable will look simple, concise, and easy to understand. This is only partially true. I'm not gonna front, some of the regexes you'll write will still appear barely readable a few minutes after writing them. In spite of this concession, I strongly urge you to carefully walk through the examples in this section. I haven't led you wrong to date; believe me that every minute of your time learning regex will be well worth it.

Have I talked up regular expressions enough? Let's get started...

Following the language analogy proposed in the beginning of this section, pretend that regex is like Quechua (a language family from the highlands of South America). Most regular expression tutorials—and there are many excellent ones available for free on the web—take the approach of teaching *the grammar* of Quechua to provide a very solid foundation on which to build a comprehensive knowledge of the regex landscape. Another approach is the *phrasebook* style, which teaches commonly used phrases that you can use to merely *get around* in the Andes mountains. I mean, this provides a sort of *cookbook* for particular regex solutions. If you learn enough of these recipes, knowledge of the grammar is tacitly learned by contrasting known examples without conscious awareness. Here I present a hybrid approach where I present regex in the context of a true-to-life problem and try to introduce concepts along the way.

Getting started

Base R functions to wield regular expressions have been around since the project got started in the form of functions like gsub and grep. It seems, though, that a recent and popular approach is to use the stringr package (which is based on the excellent and more extensive stringi package). Both because the format/argument order of the stringr functions are more consistent than their base R counterparts and because I would like to keep you abreast of popular trends in R programming, we'll be using this package to learn regex in R. Since all of the functions that we'll be using take a string (or vector of strings) to perform regex operations on as the first argument, we'll also be using the magrittr pipe operator (introduced in the previous section to enhance readability).

The data we'll be looking at is a small, hand-crafted dataset containing bibliographic information of a small library of nine books.

Let's get started by loading our packages and data from the web, printing the table, and looking at a vector of book titles:

```
> library(magrittr)
> library(stringr)
>
download.file("https://raw.githubusercontent.com/tonyfischetti/dawr/master/
working-with-messy-data/small-library.dat", "small-library.dat")
> lib <- read.delim("./small-library.dat", stringsAsFactors=FALSE,
+                   na.strings=c("NA", ""))
> lib
                 ISBN            OCLC
1        9781447286813       930016590
2          147460725X      1005289838
3         144205374-7  (OCoLC)320194791
4        9780525433576       957617619
5         1-405-88229-8       960887987
6   8496886611fsds34Recur     1003766525
7                 <NA>  \\\\$a405610020
8          889882002x        947993663
9       978-0060000578        795634598
                                               TITLE       DD
1              Are You There, God? It's Me, Margaret  813.540
2                                   The Color Purple  813.540
3                                          Tar Beach  741.642
4                              De Amor y de sombra        NA
5                       The Picture of Dorian Grey   823.800
6                           ¿Recuerda Aquella Vez?        NA
7 Friends from the other side = Amigos del otro lado     NA
8                                   Finnegan's Wake  823.912
```

```
9                          El Ratoncito De   La   Moto         NA
>
> lib$TITLE
[1] "Are You There, God? It's Me, Margaret"
[2] "The Color Purple"
[3] "Tar Beach"
[4] "De Amor y de sombra"
[5] "The Picture of Dorian Grey"
[6] "¿Recuerda Aquella Vez?"
[7] "Friends from the other side = Amigos del otro lado"
[8] "Finnegan's Wake"
[9] "El Ratoncito De   La   Moto"
```

The first function I'll introduce is `str_detect`, which takes a string (a vector of 1) or a vector of strings and a regular expression and returns a logical vector of the same length of the input vector that is TRUE, if the corresponding input string matches the regular expression.

Our first regular expression is, very literally, going to be the definite article *The*. It will match any input that contains *The* anywhere in it:

```
> lib$TITLE %>% str_detect("The")
[1]   TRUE   TRUE FALSE FALSE   TRUE FALSE FALSE FALSE FALSE
```

To make it easier to read, the same information is presented here with the input strings beside the result:

	TITLE	result
1	Are You There, God? It's Me, Margaret	TRUE
2	The Color Purple	TRUE
3	Tar Beach	FALSE
4	De Amor y de sombra	FALSE
5	The Picture of Dorian Grey	TRUE
6	¿Recuerda Aquella Vez?	FALSE
7	Friends from the other side = Amigos del otro lado	FALSE
8	Finnegan's Wake	FALSE
9	El Ratoncito De La Moto	FALSE

The `str_subset` function takes the same kind of arguments but returns only the strings that match the regex, as shown in the following code:

```
> lib$TITLE %>% str_subset("The")
[1] "Are You There, God? It's Me, Margaret"
[2] "The Color Purple"
[3] "The Picture of Dorian Grey"
```

So *The Color Purple* and *The Picture of Dorian Grey* make sense, but it also matched *Are You There, God? It's Me, Margaret*. What gives?

Because the regex `"The"` matches those three characters *anywhere* in the test string, it is matching the `"The"` in `"Are you There..."`. To prevent this, we can use a special code in the regex that denotes a *word boundary*, `"\b"`. In order to tell the regex engine that we don't want to match a literal `"b"` character, we need to precede it with a backslash; this makes it an *escape sequence*. Because strings in R have escape sequences of their own, in order to use the `"\b"` in R, we need to "escape" the backslash in `"\b"` with another backslash, making it `"\\b"`:

```
> lib$TITLE %>% str_subset("\\bThe\\b")
[1] "The Color Purple"          "The Picture of Dorian Grey"
```

You may have noticed that there is another title that contains the definite article, namely `"Friends from the other side...."`, which wan't included. If you guessed that it was because the `"t"` is lower case, then you were right!

In order to match the definite article in both cases, we are going to use a *character class*. It looks like this:

```
> lib$TITLE %>% str_subset("\\b[Tt]he\\b")
[1] "The Color Purple"
[2] "The Picture of Dorian Grey"
[3] "Friends from the other side = Amigos del otro lado"
```

If you noticed, the new addition is the `[Tt]`. What's inside the square brackets is the character class. The regex engine will match (once) any of the characters in the class. Note that if you wanted to match a literal `[`, you'd have to escape it using `\\[`.

If we wanted to only match titles with the definite article as the first word of the title, we can use what is called an *anchor*. The `^` anchor will direct the engine to match what comes after it only if it is at the start of the string, as shown in the following code:

```
> lib$TITLE %>% str_subset("^The\\b")
[1] "The Color Purple"          "The Picture of Dorian Grey"
```

The counterpart to the `^` beginning of the string anchor is the `$` end of the string anchor.

There is only one occurrence of the word Beach in any of the titles but, just as an example, if we wanted to only match Beach if it were the *last* component of a string, we could do so:

```
> lib$TITLE %>% str_subset("\\bBeach$")
[1] "Tar Beach"
```

If you noticed, there's a few Spanish titles in our library. Unlike in English, Spanish has two different definite articles for each gender: La and El for female and male, respectively. Let's first try to match all titles with the former article, matching both lower and upper case versions:

```
> lib$TITLE %>% str_subset("[Ll]a")
[1] "¿Recuerda Aquella Vez?"
[2] "Friends from the other side = Amigos del otro lado"
[3] "El Ratoncito De  La  Moto"
```

Whoops! We can tell from the inclusion of ...Aquel**la**.. and ...otro **la**do that we forgot the word boundaries:

```
> lib$TITLE %>% str_subset("\\b[Ll]a\\b")
[1] "El Ratoncito De  La  Moto"
```

Much better!

Now how about the *masculine* definite article:

```
> lib$TITLE %>% str_subset("\\b[Ee]l\\b")
[1] "El Ratoncito De  La  Moto"
```

OK, so here's where we run into another obstacle... in Spanish of the where the definite article is feminine is *De La* as seen in *El Ratoncito De La Moto* (*The Mouse of the Motorcycle*). If the definite article is masculine, however, instead of it being *De El*, it is contracted to *Del*. So, in order to correctly match strings with the masculine article, we have to account for this.

The first step is to get a regex that will match the *del* where both *D* and *E* can be upper or lower case and do not appear as part of a larger word:

```
> lib$TITLE %>% str_subset("\\b[Dd][Ee]l\\b")
[1] "Friends from the other side = Amigos del otro lado"
```

Now, we have to let the regex engine know that the *[Dd]* is *optional*. For this we can use the *?* special character:

```
> lib$TITLE %>% str_subset("\\b[Dd]?[Ee]l\\b")
[1] "Friends from the other side = Amigos del otro lado"
[2] "El Ratoncito De  La  Moto"
```

The *?* means match the preceding character, character class, or group *zero or one times*. Both *del* and *el* fit this pattern.

Before we get to matching both Spanish definite articles, I want to more gently introduce another component of regex grammar: the *alteration*.

There are two different spellings of the main color between black and white, *grey* and *gray*. If you wanted to write a regex to match either one, you could use *gr[ae]y*. But we could also use the *alteration* construct to match this, as shown in the following code:

```
> lib$TITLE %>% str_subset("Gr(a|e)y")
[1] "The Picture of Dorian Grey"
```

In this case, the alteration construct acts like a character class expect that we have to tell it either *a* or *e* by separating the two characters with a *|*.

Because the *|* alteration operator has very low *precedence*, we couldn't have written the regex as *gra|ey* as this would have matched *gra* or *ey*. But exploiting the low precedence of this operator, we can equivalently match either *gray* or *grey*:

```
> lib$TITLE %>% str_subset("Grey|Gray")
[1] "The Picture of Dorian Grey"
```

Knowing this, let's now attempt to match both Spanish definite articles, using the following code:

```
> lib$TITLE %>% str_subset("\\b([Ll]a|[Dd]?[Ee]l)\\b")
[1] "Friends from the other side = Amigos del otro lado"
[2] "El Ratoncito De  La  Moto"
```

Rad!

Try to read the regex by translating it as you read it. This is really good practice for learning how to *think* in regular expression.

A translation might read like this: *At the start of a word, match either [Ll]a or [Dd]?[Ee]l (if it is the end of a word), where the former means match an L or l followed by an a and the latter means E or e followed by an l and possibly preceded by a D or d.*

If the paragraph above sounds scary, just remember that it doesn't introduce anything we haven't learned already! It is just combining constructs that we've already seen!

Do you want to try matching all definite articles in English *and* Spanish? Of course you do:

```
> lib$TITLE %>% str_subset("\\b([Tt]he|[Ll]a|[Dd]?[Ee]l)\\b")
[1] "The Color Purple"
[2] "The Picture of Dorian Grey"
[3] "Friends from the other side = Amigos del otro lado"
[4] "El Ratoncito De  La  Moto"
```

Regex for data normalization

The process of getting errant data into some kind of standardized format is sometimes called **data normalization**. This process is sometimes critical for a large array of common data manipulation tasks such as matching/retrieving records and aggregation.

To demonstrate the importance of data normalization, watch what happens when we try to match all titles containing an apostrophe in the following code:

```
> lib$TITLE %>% str_subset("'")
[1] "Are You There, God? It's Me, Margaret"
```

Fans of modernist Irish literature everywhere yell, *What about Finnegans Wake?* What indeed:

```
> lib$TITLE %>% str_subset("'")
[1] "Finnegan's Wake"
```

If you look closely, you might notice a slight aesthetic difference between the two apostrophes. There are two common ways of representing an apostrophe in text, and these titles use two different ones. Although this may seem like a silly example, I assure you that it is not. Even if you never run into a problem with apostrophes, I can all but guarantee that you'll run into a similar problem that requires careful data normalization.

The process of finding records that refer to the same entity across datasets or sources is called *record linkage* and it is an extremely common task in data analysts. Carrying out this process often necessitates aggressive data normalization.

Let's say we have one dataset (this one) with the book titles and bibliographic information for a bunch of books, and another dataset with book titles and the number of times the book was lent out. Deriving a dataset of ISBN codes and sales figures requires joining these two tables by the common column: book title. Here's the problem... book titles are extraordinarily notorious for being difficult to match to a particular *canonicalized* entity. For example, *Finnegans Wake* may be referred to as *Finnegans Wake, Finnegan's Wake,* or *Finnegan's Wake (Joyce)*. As another example, *Dr. Strangelove or: How I Learned to Stop Worrying and Love The Bomb* is often to just called *Dr. Strangelove*. Any complete solution to book record linkage (without using the entity disambiuation service of some sort of *knowledge database*) requires a hefty dose of domain expertise and a *whole lot* of regular expressions.

The easiest approach to linking book entities requires that we remove all extraneous symbols and subtitles that are not important for the disambiguation of book enitities. For our approach here, we are going to be stripping the titles of all *whitespace* characters (tabs, spaces, new line characters, and so on), removing all punctuation marks, converting all characters to lower case, and removing all definite articles. A complete solution would involve much more (removing any parenthesized author names in the title, removing *indefinite* articles, and so on), but this isn't a section about record linking books; bear in mind that this is just an example of the need for data normalization and how regex could help us achieve this goal.

A solid approach to the removal of all pieces of text that fit a particular pattern is to use the `str_replace` function. It takes a string, a regex pattern to match, and a string to replace any text that fits the pattern with. If you want to *remove* any text that fits the pattern, you simply replace the pattern with an empty string (`""`).

Using the special code `[:punct:]`, let's remove some punctuation from our titles:

```
> lib$TITLE %>% str_replace("[:punct:]", "")
 [1] "Are You There God? It's Me, Margaret"
 [2] "The Color Purple"
 [3] "Tar Beach"
 [4] "De Amor y de sombra"
 [5] "The Picture of Dorian Grey"
 [6] "Recuerda Aquella Vez?"
 [7] "Friends from the other side = Amigos del otro lado"
 [8] "Finnegans Wake"
 [9] "El Ratoncito De  La  Moto"
```

It might appear, at a glance, that our efforts have failed, but a closer look reveals that punctuation marks *were* removed... but only the first punctuation mark in each title. Let's try it again with the `str_replace_all` function, as shown in the following code:

```
> lib$TITLE %>% str_replace_all("[:punct:]", "")
[1] "Are You There God Its Me Margaret"
[2] "The Color Purple"
[3] "Tar Beach"
[4] "De Amor y de sombra"
[5] "The Picture of Dorian Grey"
[6] "Recuerda Aquella Vez"
[7] "Friends from the other side = Amigos del otro lado"
[8] "Finnegans Wake"
[9] "El Ratoncito De  La  Moto"
```

If you notice, *El Ratoncito De La Moto* contains some weird word spacing. If we were to try to match this with a record in another table with proper spacing, we wouldn't get a match. Now let's remove some whitespace!

The first thing you might try would be the following:

```
> lib$TITLE %>% str_replace_all(" ", "")
```

That definitely works for this example, but there are other types of whitespace than just a single *space*. We could enumerate all possible whitespace in, say, a *character class*, but luckily for us, there are some character classes that are so common that there exists *shorthand* classes that are ready to use!

The `\s` character class shorthand matches any whitespace character, so let's use that instead, as shown in the following code:

```
> lib$TITLE %>% str_replace_all("\\s", "")
[1] "AreYouThere,God?It'sMe,Margaret"
[2] "TheColorPurple"
[3] "TarBeach"
[4] "DeAmorydesombra"
[5] "ThePictureofDorianGrey"
[6] "¿RecuerdaAquellaVez?"
[7] "Friendsfromtheotherside=Amigosdelotrolado"
[8] "Finnegan'sWake"
[9] "ElRatoncitoDeLaMoto"
```

This is great, but now we have the issue of the punctuation. We could chain to calls to `str_replace_all` to do the job, but let's see if we can do better than that.

The \w is a shorthand for any *word* character. Let's see what happens when we remove all *word* characters, using the following code:

```
> # the output is formatted to make it easier to see
> lib$TITLE %>% str_replace_all("\\w", "")
                                            TITLE     result
1               Are You There, God? It's Me, Margaret    , ? ' ,
2                              The Color Purple
3                                    Tar Beach
4                        De Amor y de sombra
5                 The Picture of Dorian Grey
6                         ¿Recuerda Aquella Vez?    ¿   ?
7 Friends from the other side = Amigos del otro lado    =
8                              Finnegan's Wake         '
9                El Ratoncito De  La  Moto
```

Wow! The characters that remain are exactly the ones we want to *remove*. Luckily, for many of the special shorthands, there exists an *inverse* shorthand that means *everything except this*. It is often the character after the backslash but capitalized. In this case, *anything but a word character* is \W:

```
> lib$TITLE %>% str_replace_all("\\W", "")
[1] "AreYouThereGodItsMeMargaret"              "TheColorPurple"
[3] "TarBeach"                                 "DeAmorydesombra"
[5] "ThePictureofDorianGrey"                   "RecuerdaAquellaVez"
[7] "FriendsfromtheothersideAmigosdelotrolado" "FinnegansWake"
[9] "ElRatoncitoDeLaMoto"
```

This is great!

To get this all into lower case, all we have to do is chain a call to str_to_lower, as shown in the following code:

```
> lib$TITLE %>% str_replace_all("\\W", "") %>% str_to_lower
[1] "areyoutheregoditsmemargaret"              "thecolorpurple"
[3] "tarbeach"                                 "deamorydesombra"
[5] "thepictureofdoriangrey"                   "recuerdaaquellavez"
[7] "friendsfromtheothersideamigosdelotrolado" "finneganswake"
[9] "elratoncitodelamoto"
```

Almost there! Now all we have to do is remove the definite articles using the regex we built before, using the following code:

```
> lib$title_norm <- lib$TITLE %>%
+     str_to_lower %>%
+     str_replace_all("\\b(the|la|d?el)\\b\\s+", "") %>%
+     str_replace_all("\\W", "")
```

```
>
> lib$title_norm
[1] "areyoutheregoditsmemargaret"       "colorpurple"
[3] "tarbeach"                          "deamorydesombra"
[5] "pictureofdoriangrey"               "recuerdaaquellavez"
[7] "friendsfromothersideamigosotrolado" "finneganswake"
[9] "ratoncitodemoto"
```

Since the procedure is complete, I assigned the results to a new column in the `data.frame` called `title_norm`.

I recently had to do something similar (albeit more complicated) on a dataset of millions of book titles. Although we could have probably normalized the titles above by hand, imagine if you were tasked to do this manually on millions of titles!

More normalization

Since titles are so finicky, a more common method of linking book entities (if available) is to use bibliographic codes like ISBNs. Unfortunately for us (but, I suppose, fortunate from a pedagogical point of view), a quick look at our ISBNs reveals there's nonsense going on there, too, as you can see in the following code:

```
> lib$ISBN
[1] "9781447206813"   "147460725X"      "144205374-7 "
[4] "9780525433576"   "1-405-88229-8"   "8496886611fsds34Recur"
[7] NA                "889882002x"      "978-0060000578"
```

Some of the problems that we can spot are:

- ISBN-13s are mixed with ISBN-10s
- Some of the check digits (the last character of an ISBN) are x and some are upper case
- Some of the ISBNs are hyphenated and some are not
- One of the ISBNs have trailing whitespace
- One has complete nonsense after what appears to be a valid ISBN

Let's get cracking!

The shorthand for any digit character is \d. The inverse is \D. Let's see what happens when we remove all non-digit characters....

As with our very first example, some of the output in this subsection is formatted to make it easier for you, dear reader, to learn from:

```
> lib$ISBN %>% str_replace_all("\\D", "")
                    ISBN         result
1          9781447286813 9781447286813
2              147460725X     147460725
3             144205374-7     1442053747
4          9780525433576 9780525433576
5             1-405-88229-8     1405882298
6 8496886611fsds34Recur   849688661134
7                   <NA>          <NA>
8             889882002x     889882002
9          978-0060000578 9780060000578
```

Both fortunately and unfortunately, this worked exactly as we intended. There are two problems with this:

- The ISBN in line six, which is legitimate up to the *fsds*, contains garbage digits after it
- The check digits of *X* were removed

Let's see if we can address these issues in order.

Let's see one incomplete solution at work and we'll go over the regex afterwards:

```
> lib$ISBN %>% str_replace_all("^(\\d+)\\D*.*", "\\1")
                    ISBN         result
1          9781447286813 9781447286813
2              147460725X     147460725
3             144205374-7     144205374
4          9780525433576 9780525433576
5             1-405-88229-8             1
6 8496886611fsds34Recur    8496886611
7                   <NA>          <NA>
8             889882002x     889882002
9          978-0060000578           978
```

OK, so what's going on in the regex ^(\\d+)\\D*.*? There are three operators we've never seen before, .+, ., and *:

- The + operator is a little like the ? operator that we've already seen. Where ? meant match zero or one times, + means *match one or more times*. So, the part in the parentheses means *make sure there is at least one digit and match as many contiguous digits as you can.*

- The `*` operator means *match zero or more times*. Whereas with +, the component preceding it was *required* to appear at least once, `*` is more tolerant. `\\D*` can thus be read as *if there are any non-digits, match as many as you can.*
- Finally, the `.` is a special character that matches *any* character (except a newline character). `. +` can be read as *any characters, any amount of times*

Taken as a whole, our regex can be read as:

At the start of a string, first match any digit character, as many times as you can, ensuring that there is at least one. Then match any non-digit character, if there is one, as many times as you can. Finally, match anything that remains (as many times as you can).

You may have noticed that, for the first time, the third argument to `str_replace_all` (the string that specifies the replacement text) is not empty. In place of `""`, it now contains `\\1`. What's this?

In addition to the contents of parentheses in regular expressions signifying that the contents should be grouped (which allows you to match the *nana* in *banana* with *(na)+*), it also tells the regex engine to *capture* the contents of that part of the pattern and save it to a special variable. The contents of the first captured group are stored in `\\1`, the second in `\\2`, and so on. The use of these special variables of captured patterns is often called *back-referencing*. So, using the back-referenced group here, we extract only the part of the pattern that we want and get rid of the rest.

So the `^(\\d+)\\D*` part makes a good deal of sense but you might be wondering why we need the last `.*`. Well, let's take a look at the example at row six without it:

```
> str_replace_all("8496886611fsds34Recur", "^(\\d+)\\D*", "\\1")
[1] "849688661134Recur"
```

The `(\\d+)\\D*` only matches **8496886611fsds**34Recur. Only *this* part is removed and replaced with the back-referenced group. So, in order to ensure that the rest of the string is also replaced, we have to add the `.*` catch-all that will gobble up everything else.

Crafting regex to clean up errant data points that you *have* seen is great. But the real trick to wielding regexes with finesse is to construct your regex patterns in order to combat nonsense that you *haven't* seen. Case in point: although you can write regex to right the wrongs of this nine-book library, if you were doing this for millions of ISBNs, you couldn't possibly look at every ISBN to see in what manner it was malformed.

Taking it back to this example, some low-hanging fruit for constructing a robust regex pattern reveals itself when we look at the very first character of the regex. Is it *really* correct of us to *require* that the string start with a digit? What if there were leading spaces, or what if one were *ISBN: 123456789X*?

Can you think of a way to modify our pattern to deal with this case?

Really try, though.

A quick and dirty way to deal with it is to change the line to:

```
> str_replace_all("ISBN: 8496886611fsds34Recur", "\\D*(\\d+)\\D*", "\\1")
[1] "849688661134"
```

With this, we optionally match any amount of non-digits at the start of the string. Since we don't capture it, any text that matches will now be removed.

One more thing... since we *require* that digits be present in the string, if there are none, then no replacement of garbage characters takes place:

```
> str_replace_all("ISBN: uh, idk bruh", "\\D*(\\d+)\\D*", "\\1")
[1] "ISBN: uh, idk bruh"
```

Uh, I don't know about you, dear reader, but it seems to me that we should just replace this whole thing with an empty string by making the \\d optional, too:

```
> str_replace_all("ISBN: uh, idk bruh", "\\D*(\\d*)\\D*", "\\1")
[1] ""
```

Later, if we'd like, we can use an `ifelse` to transform all empty strings into NA.

Let's take what we've learned and bring it back to our original problem:

```
> lib$ISBN %>% str_replace_all("\\D*(\\d*)\\D*.*", "\\1")
                  ISBN        result
1       9781447286813 9781447286813
2          147460725X     147460725
3         144205374-7     144205374
4       9780525433576 9780525433576
5        1-405-88229-8             1
6 8496886611fsds34Recur    8496886611
7                <NA>          <NA>
8         889882002x     889882002
9       978-0060000578           978
```

Two failures remain: (a) our regex fails us when hyphens are present, and (b) the "X" check digits are still removed.

Let's quickly solve the first issue using chaining:

```
> lib$ISBN %>%
+    str_replace_all("-", "") %>%
+    str_replace_all("\\D*(\\d*)\\D*.*", "\\1")
                    ISBN           result
1          9781447286813 9781447286813
2             147460725X      147460725
3             144205374-7     1442053747
4          9780525433576 9780525433576
5             1-405-88229-8    1405882298
6 8496886611fsds34Recur     8496886611
7                  <NA>           <NA>
8             889882002x      889882002
9          978-0060000578 9780060000578
```

Finally we get to the issue of the X check digit...

One (not so great) solution is to replace the $(\d*)$ with a character class that will allow Xs (and upper case our input):

```
> lib$ISBN %>%
+    str_to_upper %>%
+    str_replace_all("-", "") %>%
+    str_replace_all("\\D*([X\\d]*)\\D*.*", "\\1")
                    ISBN           result
1          9781447286813 9781447286813
2             147460725X     147460725X
3             144205374-7     1442053747
4          9780525433576 9780525433576
5             1-405-88229-8    1405882298
6 8496886611fsds34Recur     8496886611
7                  <NA>           <NA>
8             889882002x     889882002X
9          978-0060000578 9780060000578
```

It appears to work great, but remember, the key to using regex effectively is to guard against all contingencies:

```
> "1234XX56789X" %>%
+    str_to_upper %>%
+    str_replace_all("-", "") %>%
+    str_replace_all("\\D*([X\\d]*)\\D*.*", "\\1")
[1] "1234XX56789X"
```

Our pattern will let in any amount of *X*s. The *X* check digit should only only occur in ISBN-10s and only once after nine preceding digits. Properly taking this into account is one of the exercises at the end of this chapter.

So that's as far as we're going to go with regular expressions! We've learned a lot together but there's still so much to know. I urge you to take out a book on the topic from your local library, or read one of the many excellent free tutorials online.

Other tools for messy data

As we've discussed before, there are countless ways that a dataset could be messy. There are many other messy situations and solutions that we can't discuss at length here. So that you, dear reader, are not left in the dark regarding other custodial solutions, here are some other tools that you may find helpful on your analytics journey.

OpenRefine

Though OpenRefine (formerly Google Refine) doesn't have anything to do with R *per se*, it is a sophisticated tool for working with and cleaning up messy data. Among its numerous, sophisticated capabilities is the ability to auto-detect misspelled or misspecified categories and fix them with the click of a button.

Fuzzy matching

In order to prepare for record linkage on book titles, we *normalized* the strings by performing a few operations on them. An alternative is to use what is referred to as *fuzzy matching*.

An exact match between two strings requires that the strings be... well... exactly the same. For example, *Finnegans Wake* and *Finnegan's Wake* are *obviously* referring to the same entity but a join operation on exact string equality will not make this connection. A *fuzzy join* operation can use a measure of string *similarity* and join records with above a certain threshold of similarity. There are many different types of string similarity metrics but most of them would rate both versions of the work by James Joyce as highly similar.

You can perform a fuzzy join in R in a lot of ways, but a really great tool for the job is the `fuzzyjoin` package. At the time of writing, this package is not available on CRAN, but installation instructions (as well as great documentation) can be found at this URL: `https:/ /github.com/dgrtwo/fuzzyjoin`.

Note that I introduced fuzzy matching as an *alternative* to data normalization. I misspoke. Often, the best and most complete record linking tasks use both normalization (often achieved via regular expressions) *and* fuzzy matching!

Exercises

- Find a freely available government dataset on the web. Read the dataset's description, and think about what assumptions you might make about the data when planning a certain analysis. Translate these into actual code so that R can check them for you. *Were there any deviations from your expectations?*
- An ISBN-10 is a unique identifier for books. It is 10 characters long. The last digit is called a check digit and is determinable from the preceding digits using modular arithmetic. When the check digit is "10", it is represented with an "X". To review, an ISBN-10 is either 10 digits or nine digits, with an "X" at the end. Write a function that uses regular expressions to check if an input string (or vector of strings) is in the format of a valid ISBN-10. As a bonus, write code to check if the check digit matches what it is supposed to be after learning about how the check digit is computed on Wikipedia! Use this predicate function in an assertr construct, like `lib %>% assert(YOUR_FUNCTION_HERE, ISBN)`.
- Does P=NP? Provide a proof.

Summary

Messy data, no matter what definition you use, presents a huge roadblock for people who work with data. This chapter focused on two of the most notorious and prolific culprits: missing data and data that has not been cleaned or audited for quality.

On *unsanitized* data, we saw that the perhaps optimal solution (visually auditing the data) was untenable for moderately sized datasets or larger. We discovered that the grammar of the package `assertr` provides a mechanism to offload this auditing process to R. You now have a few `assertr` checking *recipes* under your belt for some of the more common manifestations of the mistakes that plague data that have not been scrutinized.

15
Dealing with Large Data

In the previous chapter, we spoke of solutions to common problems that fall under the umbrella term of *messy data*. In this chapter, we are going to solve some of the problems related to working with large datasets.

Problems, in case of working with large datasets, can occur in R for a few reasons. For one, R (and most other languages, for that matter) was developed during a time when commodity computers only had one processor/core. This means that the vanilla R code can't exploit multiple processor/multiple cores, which can offer substantial speed-ups. Another salient reason why R might run into trouble analyzing large datasets is because R requires the data objects that it works with to be stored completely in RAM memory. If your dataset exceeds the capacity of your RAM, your analyses will slow down to a crawl.

When one thinks of problems related to analyzing large datasets, they may think of big data. One can scarcely be involved (or even interested) in the field of data analysis without hearing about big data. I will be staying away from that term in this chapter for two reasons:

- The problems and techniques in this chapter will still be applicable long after the buzzword begins to fade from public memory
- Problems related to truly big data are relatively uncommon, and often require specialized tools and know-how that is beyond the scope of this book.

Some have suggested that the definition of big data be *data that is too big to fit in your computer's memory at one time*. Personally, I call this large data-and not just because I have a penchant for splitting hairs! I reserve the term big data for data that is so massive that it requires many hundreds of computers and special consideration in order to be stored and processed.

Sometimes, problems related to high-dimensional data are considered large data problems, too. Unfortunately, solving these problems often requires a background and mathematics beyond the scope of this book, and we will not be discussing high-dimensional statistics. This chapter is more about optimizing the R code to squeeze higher performance out of it, so that calculations and analyses with large datasets become computationally tractable.

So, perhaps this chapter should more aptly be named **High Performance R**. Unfortunately, this title is more ostentatious, and wouldn't fit the naming pattern established by the previous chapter.

Each of the top-level sections in this chapter will discuss a specific technique for writing higher-performing R code.

Wait to optimize

Prominent computer scientist and mathematician Donald Knuth famously stated:

> *Premature optimization is the root of all evil.*

I, personally, hold that *money* is the root of all evil, but premature optimization is definitely up there!

Why is premature optimization so evil? Well, there are a few reasons. First, programmers can sometimes be pretty bad at identifying what the bottleneck of a program - the routine or routines that have the slowest throughput - is, and optimize the wrong parts of a program. Identification of bottlenecks can most accurately be performed by *profiling* your code after it's been completed in an un-optimized form.

Secondly, *clever* tricks and shortcuts for speeding up code often introduce subtle bugs and unexpected behavior. Now, the speedup of the code (if there is any!) must be taken in context with the time it took to complete the bug-finding and bug-fixing expedition; occasionally, a net *negative* amount of time has been saved when all is said and done.

Lastly, since premature optimization literally necessitates writing your code in a way that is different than you normally would, it can have deleterious effects on the readability of the code and your ability to understand it when we look back on it after some period of time. According to *Structure and Interpretation of Computer Programs*, one of the most famous textbooks in computer science, *programs must be written for people to read, and only incidentally for machines to execute*. This reflects the fact that the bulk of the time updating or expanding code that is already written is spent on a human having to read and understand the code, not the time it takes for the computer to execute it. When you prematurely optimize, you may be causing a huge reduction in readability in exchange for a marginal gain in execution time.

In summary, you should probably wait to optimize your code until you are done, and the performance is demonstrably inadequate.

Using a bigger and faster machine

Instead of rewriting critical sections of your code, consider running the code on a machine with a faster processor, more cores, more RAM memory, faster bus speeds, and/or reduced disk latency. This suggestion may seem like a glib cop-out, but it's not. Sure, using a bigger machine for your analytics sometimes means extra money, but your time, dear reader, is money too. If, over the course of your work, it takes you many hours to optimize your code adequately, buying or renting a better machine may actually prove to be the more cost-effective solution.

Going down this road needn't require that you purchase a high-powered machine outrightly; there are now *virtual* servers that you can rent online for finite periods of time at reasonable prices. Some of these virtual servers can be configured to have 2 terabytes of RAM and 40 virtual processors. If you are interested in learning more on this option, look at the offerings of Digital Ocean, Amazon Elastic Compute Cloud, or many other similar service providers.

Ask your employer or research advisor if this is a feasible option. If you are working for a non-profit with a limited budget, you may be able to work out a deal with a particularly charitable cloud computing service provider. Tell 'em that 'Tony' sent you! But don't actually do that.

Be smart about your code

In many cases, the performance of the R code can be *greatly* improved by simple restructuring of the code; this doesn't change the output of the program, just the way it is represented. Restructurings of this type are often referred to as *code refactoring*. The refactorings that really make a difference performance-wise usually have to do with either improved allocation of memory or vectorization.

Allocation of memory

Refer all the way back to Chapter 5, *Using Data to Reason About the World*. Remember when we created a mock population of women's heights in the US, and we repeatedly took 10,000 samples of 40 from it to demonstrate the sampling distribution of the sample means? In a code comment, I mentioned in passing that the snippet numeric(10000) created an empty vector of 10,000 elements, but I never explained why we did that. Why didn't we just create a vector of 1, and continually tack on each new sample mean to the end of it? This is demonstrated as follows:

```
set.seed(1)
all.us.women <- rnorm(10000, mean=65, sd=3.5)

means.of.our.samples.bad <- c(1)
# I'm increasing the number of
# samples to 30,000 to prove a point
for(i in 1:30000){
  a.sample <- sample(all.us.women, 40)
  means.of.our.samples.bad[i] <- mean(a.sample)
}
```

It turns out that R stores vectors in contiguous addresses in your computer's memory. This means that every time a new sample mean gets tacked onto the end of means.of.our.samples.bad, R has to make sure that the next memory block is free. If it is not, R has to find a contiguous section of memory than *can* fit all the elements, copy the vector over (element by element), and free the memory in the original location. In contrast, when we created an empty vector of the appropriate number of elements, R only had to find a memory location with the requisite number of free contiguous addresses once.

Let's see just what kind of difference this makes in practice. We will use the `system.time` function to time the execution time of both the approaches:

```
means.of.our.samples.bad <- c(1)
system.time(
  for(i in 1:30000){
    a.sample <- sample(all.us.women, 40)
    means.of.our.samples.bad[i] <- mean(a.sample)
  }
)

means.of.our.samples.good <- numeric(30000)
system.time(
  for(i in 1:30000){
    a.sample <- sample(all.us.women, 40)
    means.of.our.samples[i] <- mean(a.sample)
  }
)
-----------------------------------
   user  system elapsed
  2.024   0.431   2.465
   user  system elapsed
  0.678   0.004   0.684
```

Although an elapsed time saving of less than one/two seconds doesn't seem like a big deal, (a) it adds up, and (b) the difference gets more and more dramatic as the number of elements in the vector increase.

By the way, this preallocation business applies to matrices, too.

Vectorization

Were you wondering why R is so adamant about keeping the elements of vectors in adjoining memory locations? Well, if R *didn't*, then traversing a vector (like when you apply a function to each element) would require hunting around the memory space for the right elements in different locations. Having the elements all in a row gives us an enormous advantage, performance-wise.

To fully exploit this vector representation, it helps to use vectorized functions, which we were first introduced to in Chapter 1, *RefresheR*. These vectorized functions call optimized and blazingly fast C code to operate on vectors instead of on the comparatively slower R code. For example, let's say we wanted to square each height in the all.us.women vector. One way would be to use a for-loop to square each element as follows:

```
system.time(
    for(i in 1:length(all.us.women))
        all.us.women[i] ^ 2
)
------------------------
    user  system elapsed
   0.003   0.000   0.003
```

Okay, not bad at all. Now, what if we applied a lambda squaring function to each element using sapply? Let's have a look:

```
system.time(
    sapply(all.us.women, function(x) x^2)
)
-----------------------
    user  system elapsed
   0.006   0.000   0.006
```

Okay, that's worse. But we can use a function that's like sapply, and which allows us to specify the type of return value in exchange for a faster processing speed:

```
> system.time(
+     vapply(all.us.women, function(x) x^2, numeric(1))
+ )
------------------------
    user  system elapsed
   0.006   0.000   0.005
```

Still not great. Finally, what if we just square the entire vector, as shown in the following code?

```
system.time(
    all.us.women ^ 2
)
-----------------------
    user  system elapsed
       0       0       0
```

This was so fast that `system.time` didn't have the resolution to detect any processing time at all. Further, this way of writing the squaring functionality was by far the easiest to read.

 The moral of the story is to use vectorized options whenever you can. All of core R's arithmetic operators (`+`, `-`, `^`, `sqrt`, `log`, and so on) are of this type. Additionally, using the `rowSums` and `colSums` functions on matrices is faster than `apply(A_MATRIX, 1, sum)` and `apply(A_MATRIX, 2, sum)` respectively, for much the same reason.

Speaking of matrices, before we move on, you should know that certain matrix operations are blazingly fast in R, because the routines are implemented in compiled C and/or Fortran code. If you don't believe me, try writing and testing the performance of OLS regression without using matrix multiplication.

If you have the linear algebra know-how, and have the option to rewrite a computation that you need to perform using matrix operations, you should definitely try it out.

Using optimized packages

Many of the functionalities in base R have alternative implementations available in contributed packages. Quite often, these packages offer a faster or less memory-intensive substitute for the base R equivalent. For example, in addition to adding a ton of extra functionality, the `glmnet` package performs regression far faster than `glm`, in my experience.

For faster data import, you might be able to use `fread` from the `data.table` package, or the `read_*` family of functions from the `readr` package. It is not uncommon for data import tasks that used to take several hours to take only a few minutes with these read functions.

For common data manipulation tasks, such as merging (joining), conditional selection, sorting, and so on, you will find that the `data.table` and `dplyr` packages offer incredible speed improvements. Both of these packages have a ton of users who swear by them, and the community support is solid. You'd be well advised to become proficient in one of these packages when you're ready.

As it turns out, the `sqldf` package that I mentioned in passing in `Chapter 12`, *Sources of Data* - the one that can perform SQL queries on data frames - can sometimes offer performance improvements for common data manipulation tasks, too. Behind the scenes, `sqldf` (by default) loads your data frame into a temporary SQLite database, performs the query in the database's SQL execution environment, returns the results from the database in the form of a data frame, and destroys the temporary database. Since the queries run on the database, `sqldf` can (a) sometimes perform the queries faster than the equivalent native R code, and (b) somewhat relaxes the constraint that the data objects, which R uses, be held completely in memory.

The constraint that the data objects in R must be able to fit into memory can be a real obstacle for people who work with datasets that are rather large, but just shy of being big enough to necessitate special tools. Some can thwart this constraint by storing their data objects in a database, and only using selected subsets that will fit in the memory. Others can get by using random samples of the available data instead of requiring the whole dataset to be held at once. If none of these options sound appealing, there are packages in R that will allow importing data that is larger than the memory available by directly referring to the data as it's stored on your hard disk. The most popular of these seem to be `ff` and `bigmemory`; however, there is a cost to this. Not only are the operations slower than they would be if they were in memory, but since the data is processed piecemeal (in chunks), many standard R functions won't work on them. Be that as it may, the `ffbase` and the `biganalytics` packages provide methods to restore some of the functionality lost for the two packages respectively. Most notably, these packages allow `ff` and `bigmemory` objects to be used in the `biglm` package, which can build generalized linear models using data that is too big to fit in the memory.

`biglm` can also be used to build generalized linear models using data stored in a database!

Remember the CRAN *Task Views* we talked about in the last chapter? There is a whole Task View dedicated to High Performance Computing (`https://cran.r-project.org/web/views/HighPerformanceComputing.html`). If there is a particular statistical technique that you'd like to find an optimized alternative for, this is the first place I'd recommend you check.

Using another R implementation

R is both a language and an implementation of that language. So far, when we've been talking about the R environment/platform, we've been talking about the GNU Project started by R. Ihaka and R. Gentleman at the University of Auckland in 1993, and hosted at http://www.r-project.org. Since R has no standard specification, this canonical implementation serves as R's de facto specification. If a project is able to implement this specification, and rewrite the GNU-R functionality-for-functionality and bug-for-bug-any valid R code can be run on that implementation.

Some time around 2009, various other implementations of R started to crop up. Among these were:

- **Renjin** (running on the Java Virtual Machine)
- **pqR** (which stands for Pretty Quick R, and written in a mix of C, R, and Fortran), **FastR** (which is written in Java)
- **Riposte** (which is written mainly in C++)

These alternative implementations promise compelling improvements to GNU-R, such as automatic **multithreading** (parallelization), ability to handle larger data, and tighter integration with Java.

Unfortunately, none of these projects are complete as yet. Because of this, not everything you'd expect has been implemented; some of your favorite packages may stop working, and by and large, these implementations are difficult to install. For these reasons, I would only recommend this for highly advanced users and/or for the extremely desperate.

Although it doesn't qualify as another R implementation, there is another R distribution that is gaining popularity, called **Revolution R Enterprise**, put out by a commercial enterprise named Revolution Analytics. This distribution boasts automatic parallelization for certain rewritten functions, improved ability to work on and model datasets that will not fit in RAM (for certain rewritten functions), facilities for distributed computing, and tighter integration with big data databases. This is a paid distribution of R, but you can it use for free if you are a student, or for a discount if you work in the non-profit public service sector.

Revolution Analytics also puts out a free alternative distribution of R called **Revolution R Open**. The primary benefit of this distribution, from a performance perspective, is the ease with which it can be installed and used with the high performance **Intel Math Kernel Library** (**MKL**). The MKL is a drop-in substitute for the linear algebra libraries that are bundled automatically with GNU-R. While the linear algebra library that ships with GNU-R is single-threaded, the MKL can exploit multiple cores transparently. This makes computations like matrix decomposition, matrix inversion, and vectorized math (very common, whether explicitly used or not) much faster.

Before we go on, it should be noted that you don't have to use Revolution R Open to take advantage of the MKL or any other multithreaded linear algebra libraries like **OpenBLAS**, **ATLAS**, and **Accelerate** (which comes with OS X and is Mac-only) - I don't. However, linking GNU-R with these other libraries can sometimes get messy, and requires care. Interested readers can find instructions on how to do this linking on the web, mostly in the form of blog posts from R enthusiasts.

 The Macintosh version of Revolution R Open, by default, integrates with the multithreaded Accelerate framework, instead of MKL.

Using parallelization

As we saw in this chapter's introduction, one of the limitations of R (and most other programming languages) was that it was created before commodity personal computers had more than one processor or core. As a result, by default, R runs only one process and thus, makes use of one processor/core at a time.

If you have more than one core on your CPU, it means that when you leave your computer alone for a few hours during a long-running computation, your R task is running on one core while the others are idle. Clearly this is not ideal; if your R task took advantage of all the available processing power, you can get massive speed improvements.

Parallel computation (of the type we'll be using) works by starting multiple processes at the same time. The operating system then assigns each of these processes to a particular CPU. When multiple processes run at the same time, the time to completion is only as long as the longest process, as opposed to the time to complete all the processes added together:

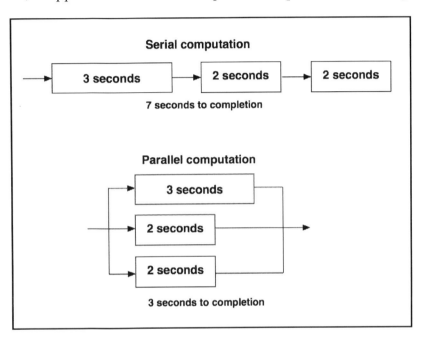

Figure 15.1: Diagram of the parallelization and the resultant reduced time to completion

For example, let's say we have four processes in a task that takes 1 second to complete. Without using parallelization, the task would take 4 seconds; but *with* parallelization on four cores, the task would take 1 second.

 A word of warning: This is the ideal scenario; but in practice, the cost of starting multiple processes constitutes an overhead that will result in the time to completion not scaling linearly with the number of cores used.

All this sounds great, but there's an important catch: each process has to be able to run independent of the output of the other processes. For example, if we wrote an R program to compute the nth number in the Fibonacci sequence, we couldn't divide that task up into smaller processes to run in parallel, because the *n* Fibonacci number depends on what we compute as the n-1th Fibonacci number (and so on, *ad infinitum*). The parallelization of the type we'll be using in this chapter only works on problems that can be split up into processes, such that the processes don't depend on each other, and there's no communication between processes. Luckily, there are many problems like this in data analysis! Almost as luckily, R makes it easy to use parallelization on problems of this type!

Problems of the nature that we just described are sometimes known as *embarrassingly parallel* problems, because the entire task can be broken down into independent components very easily. As an example, summing the numbers in a `numeric` vector of 100 elements is an embarrassingly parallel problem, because we can easily sum the first 50 elements in one process and the last 50 in another, in parallel, and just add the two numbers at the end to get the final sum. The pattern of computation we just described is sometimes referred to as *split-apply-combine*, *divide and conquer*, or *map/reduce*.

 Using parallelization to tackle the problem of summing 100 numbers is silly, since the overhead of the splitting and combining will take longer than it would to just sum up all the 100 elements serially. Also, `sum` is already really fast and vectorized.

Getting started with parallel R

Getting started with parallelization in R requires minimal setup, but that setup varies from platform to platform. More accurately, the setup is different for Windows than it is for every other operating system that R runs on (GNU/Linux, Mac OS X, Solaris, *BSD, and others).

If you don't have a Windows computer, all you have to do to start is to load the `parallel` package:

```
# You don't have to install this if your copy of R is new
library(parallel)
```

If you use Windows, you can either switch to the free operating system that over 97% of the 500 most powerful supercomputers in the world use, or you can run the following setup code:

```
library(parallel)
cl <- makeCluster(4)
```

You may replace the 4 with however many processes you want to automatically split your task into. This is usually set to the number of cores available on your computer. You can query your system for the number of available cores with the following incantation:

```
detectCores()
-----------------------
[1]  4
```

Our first silly (but demonstrative) application of parallelization is the task of sleeping (making a program become temporarily inactive) for 5 seconds, four different times. We can do this serially (not parallel) as follows:

```
for(i in 1:4){
  Sys.sleep(5)
}
```

```
Or, equivalently, using lapply:
```

```
# lapply will pass each element of the
# vector c(1, 2, 3, 4) to the function
# we write but we'll ignore it
lapply(1:4, function(i) Sys.sleep(5))
```

Let's time how long this task takes to complete by wrapping the task inside the argument to the `system.time` function:

```
system.time(
  lapply(1:4, function(i) Sys.sleep(5))
)
------------------------------------------
   user   system elapsed
  0.059    0.074  20.005
```

Unsurprisingly, it took 20 (4*5) seconds to run. Let's see what happens when we run this in parallel:

```
#######################
# NON-WINDOWS VERSION #
#######################
system.time(
  mclapply(1:4, function(i) Sys.sleep(5), mc.cores=4)
)
###################
# WINDOWS VERSION #
###################
system.time(
  parLapply(cl, 1:4, function(i) Sys.sleep(5))
)
------------------------------------------
   user   system elapsed
  0.021    0.042   5.013
```

Check that out! 5 seconds! Just what you would expect if four processes were sleeping for 5 seconds at the same time!

For the non-Windows code, we simply use the `mclapply` (the non-Windows parallel counterpart to `lapply`) instead of `lapply`, and pass in another argument named `mc.cores`, which tells `mclapply` how many processes to automatically split the independent computation into.

For the Windows code, we use `parLapply` (the Windows parallel counterpart to `lapply`). The only difference between `lapply` and `parLapply` that we've used here is that `parLapply` takes the cluster we made with the `makeCluster` setup function as its first argument. Unlike `mclapply`, there's no need to specify the number of cores to use, since the cluster is already set up to the appropriate number of cores.

Before R got the built-in parallel package, the two main packages that allowed for parallelization were multicore and snow. Multicore used a method of creating different processes called **forking** that was supported on all R-running OSs except Windows. Windows users used the more general snow package to achieve `parallelization.` `snow`, which stands for Simple Network of Workstations, not only works on non-Windows computers as well, but also on a cluster of different computers with identical R installations. Multicore did not support cluster computing across physical machines like snow does. Since R version 2.14, the functionality of both the multicore and snow packages have essentially been merged into the parallel package. The multicore package has since been removed from CRAN.

From now on, when we refer to the Windows counterpart to X, know that we really mean the snow counterpart to X, because the functions of snow will work on non-Windows OSs and clusters of machines. Similarly, by the non-Windows counterparts, we really mean the counterparts cannibalized from the multicore package.

You might ask, *Why don't we just always use the snow functions?* If you have the option to use the multicore /forking parallelism (you are running processes on just one non-Windows physical machine), the multicore parallelism tends to be lightweight. For example, sometimes the creation of a snow cluster with `makeCluster` can set off firewall alerts. It is safe to allow these connections, by the way.

An example of (some) substance

For our first *real* application of parallelization, we will be solving a problem that is loosely based on a real problem that I had to solve during the course of my work. In this formulation, we will be importing an open dataset from the web that contains the airport code, latitude coordinates, and longitude coordinates for 13,429 US airports. Our task will be to find the average (mean) distance from every airport to every other airport. For example, if LAX, ALB, OLM, and JFK were the only extant airports, we would calculate the distances between JFK to OLM, JFK to ALB, JFK to LAX, OLM to ALB, OLM to LAX, and ALB to LAX, and take the arithmetic mean of these distances.

Why are we doing this? Well, besides the fact that it was inspired by an actual, real-life problem (a problem that I covered in no fewer than three blog posts), this problem is perfect for parallelization for two reasons:

- **It is embarrassingly parallel** - This problem is very amenable to splitting-applying-and-combining (or map/reduction); each process can take a few of the airport-to-airport combinations (several hundreds, really). The results can then be summed and divided by the number of distance calculations performed.
- **It exhibits combinatorial explosion** - The term *combinatorial explosion* refers to the problems that grow very quickly in size or complexity due to the role of combinatorics in the problem's solution. For example, the number of distance calculations we have to perform exhibits polynomial growth as a function of the number of airports we use. In particular, the number of different calculations is given by the binomial coefficient, $\binom{n}{2}$, or n (n−1) /2. 100 airports require 4,950 distance calculations; all 13,429 airports require 90,162,306 distance calculations. Problems of this type usually require techniques like those discussed in this chapter in order to be computationally tractable.

The birthday problem:

Most people are unfazed by the fact that it takes a room of 367 to guarantee that two people in the room have the same birthday. Many people are surprised, however, when it is revealed that it only requires a room full of 23 people for there to be a 50% chance of two people sharing the same birthday (assuming that birthdays occur on each day with equal probability). Further, it only takes a room full of 60 for there to be over a 99% chance that a pair will share a birthday. If this surprises you too, consider that the number of pairs of people that could possibly share their birthday grows polynomially with the number of people in the room. In fact, the number of pairs that can share a birthday grows just like our airport problem - then the number of birthday pairs is exactly the number of distance calculations we would have to perform if the people were airports.

First, let's write the function to compute the distance between two latitude/longitude pairs.

Since the Earth isn't flat (strictly speaking, it's not even a perfect sphere), the distance between the longitude and latitude degrees is not constant, meaning you can't just take the Euclidean distance between the two points. We will be using the *haversine formula* for the distances between the two points. The haversine formula is given as follows:

$$a = \sin^2\left(\Delta\phi / 2\right) + \cos\phi_1 + \cos\phi_2 + \sin^2\left(\Delta\lambda\right)$$

$$c = 2.\arctan 2\left(\sqrt{a}, \sqrt{(1-a)}\right)$$

$$distance = r.x$$

Where φ and λ are the latitude and longitude respectively, *r* is the Earth's radius, and Δ is the difference between the two latitudes or longitudes:

```
haversine <- function(lat1, long1, lat2, long2, unit="km"){
    radius <- 6378      # radius of Earth in kilometers
    delta.phi <- to.radians(lat2 - lat1)
    delta.lambda <- to.radians(long2 - long1)
    phi1 <- to.radians(lat1)
    phi2 <- to.radians(lat2)
    term1 <- sin(delta.phi/2) ^ 2
    term2 <- cos(phi1) * cos(phi2) * sin(delta.lambda/2) ^ 2
    the.terms <- term1 + term2
    delta.sigma <- 2 * atan2(sqrt(the.terms), sqrt(1-the.terms))
    distance <- radius * delta.sigma
    if(unit=="km") return(distance)
    if(unit=="miles") return(0.621371*distance)
}
```

Everything must be measured in radians (not degrees), so let's make a helper function as shown in the following code for conversion to radians, too:

```
to.radians <- function(degrees){
    degrees * pi / 180
}
```

Now let's load the dataset from the web. Since it's from an outside source and it might be messy, this is an excellent chance to use our `assertr` chops to make sure the foreign data set matches our expectations: the dataset is 13,429 observations long, it has three named columns, the latitude should be 90 or below, and the longitude should be 180 or below.

We'll also just start with a subset of all the airports. Because we are going to be taking a *random* sample of all the observations, we'll set the random number generator seed so that my calculations will align with yours, dear reader. The following code illustrates this technique:

```
set.seed(1)

the.url <-
"http://opendata.socrata.com/api/views/rxrh-4cxm/rows.csv?accessType=DOWNLO
AD"
all.airport.locs <- read.csv(the.url, stringsAsFactors=FALSE)

library(magrittr)
library(assertr)
CHECKS <- . %>%
    verify(nrow(.) == 13429) %>%
```

```
    verify(names(.) %in% c("locationID", "Latitude", "Longitude")) %>%
    assert(within_bounds(0, 90), Latitude) %>%
    assert(within_bounds(0,180), Longitude)

all.airport.locs <- CHECKS(all.airport.locs)
# Let's start off with 400 airports
smp.size <- 400
# choose a random sample of airports
random.sample <- sample((1:nrow(all.airport.locs)), smp.size)
airport.locs <- all.airport.locs[random.sample, ]
row.names(airport.locs) <- NULL

head(airport.locs)
-----------------------------------
  locationID Latitude Longitude
1        LWV  38.7642   87.6056
2        LS77 30.7272   91.1486
3        2N2  43.5919   71.7514
4        VG00 37.3697   75.9469
```

Now let's write a function called `single.core`, which computes the average distance between every two pairs of airports not using any parallel computation. For each lat/long pair, we need to find the distance between it and the rest of the lat/long pairs. Since the distance between point a and b is the same as the distance between b and a, for every row, we need to only compute the distance between it and the remaining rows in the `airport.locs` data frame:

```
single.core <- function(airport.locs){
  running.sum <- 0
  for(i in 1:(nrow(airport.locs)-1)){
    for(j in (i+1):nrow(airport.locs)){
      # i is the row of the first lat/long pair
      # j is the row of the second lat/long pair
      this.dist <- haversine(airport.locs[i, 2],
                             airport.locs[i, 3],
                             airport.locs[j, 2],
                             airport.locs[j, 3])
      running.sum <- running.sum + this.dist
    }
  }
  # Now we have to divide by the number of
  # distances we took. This is given by
  return(running.sum /
        ((nrow(airport.locs)*(nrow(airport.locs)-1))/2))
}

# Now, let's time it!
```

```
system.time(ave.dist <- single.core(airport.locs))
--------------------------------
   user  system elapsed
  5.400   0.034   5.466
[1] 1667.186
```

Alright, 5-and-a-half seconds for 400 airports.

In order to use the parallel surrogates for `lapply`, let's rewrite the function to use `lapply`. Observe the output of the following incantation:

```
# We'll have to limit the output to the
# first 11 columns
combn(1:10, 2)[,1:11]
--------------------------------------
     [,1] [,2] [,3] [,4] [,5] [,6] [,7] [,8] [,9]
[1,]    1    1    1    1    1    1    1    1    1
[2,]    2    3    4    5    6    7    8    9   10
     [,10] [,11]
[1,]     2     2
[2,]     3     4
```

The preceding function used the `combn` function to create a matrix that contains all pairs of two numbers from 1 to 10, stored as columns in two rows. If we use the `combn` function with a vector of integer numbers from 1 to *n* (where *n* is the number of airports in our dataframe), each column of the resultant matrix will refer to all the different indices with which to index the airport data frame, in order to obtain all the possible pairs of airports. For example, let's go back to the world where LAX, ALB, OLM, and JFK were the only extant airports; consider the following:

```
small.world <- c("LAX", "ALB", "OLM", "JFK")
all.combs <- combn(1:length(small.world), 2)

for(i in 1:ncol(all.combs)){
  from <- small.world[all.combs[1, i]]
  to <- small.world[all.combs[2, i]]
  print(paste(from, " <-> ", to))
}
--------------------------------------
[1] "LAX  <->  ALB"
[1] "LAX  <->  OLM"
[1] "LAX  <->  JFK"
[1] "ALB  <->  OLM"     # back to olympia
[1] "ALB  <->  JFK"
[1] "OLM  <->  JFK"
```

Formulating our solution around this matrix of indices, we can use `lapply` to loop over the columns in the matrix, as shown in the following code:

```
small.world <- c("LAX", "ALB", "OLM", "JFK")
all.combs <- combn(1:length(small.world), 2)

# instead of printing each airport pair in a string,
# we'll return the string
results <- lapply(1:ncol(all.combs), function(x){
  from <- small.world[all.combs[1, x]]
  to <- small.world[all.combs[2, x]]
  return(paste(from, " <-> ", to))
})

print(results)
------------------------

[[1]]
[1] "LAX  <->  ALB"

[[2]]
[1] "LAX  <->  OLM"

[[3]]
[1] "LAX  <->  JFK"
. . . . . . . .
```

In our problem, we will be returning `numerics` from the anonymous function in `lapply`. However, because we are using `lapply`, the `results` will be a `list`. Because we can't call `sum` on a `list` of `numerics`, we will use the `unlist` function to turn the list into a vector, as shown in the following code:

```
unlist(results)
--------------------
[1] "LAX  <->  ALB" "LAX  <->  OLM" "LAX  <->  JFK"
[4] "ALB  <->  OLM" "ALB  <->  JFK" "OLM  <->  JFK"
```

We have everything we need to rewrite the `single.core` function using `lapply`. We will use the following code for the same:

```
single.core.lapply <- function(airport.locs){
  all.combs <- combn(1:nrow(airport.locs), 2)
  numcombs <- ncol(all.combs)
  results <- lapply(1:numcombs, function(x){
      lat1  <- airport.locs[all.combs[1, x], 2]
      long1 <- airport.locs[all.combs[1, x], 3]
      lat2  <- airport.locs[all.combs[2, x], 2]
      long2 <- airport.locs[all.combs[2, x], 3]
      return(haversine(lat1, long1, lat2, long2))
  })
  return(sum(unlist(results)) / numcombs)
}

system.time(ave.dist <- single.core.lapply(airport.locs))
print(ave.dist)
---------------------------------------
   user   system elapsed
  5.890    0.042   5.968
 [1] 1667.186
```

This particular solution is a little bit slower than our solution with the double `for` -loops, but it's about to pay enormous dividends; now we can use one of the parallel surrogates for `lapply` to solve the problem, as shown in the following code:

```
#######################
# NON-WINDOWS VERSION #
#######################
multi.core <- function(airport.locs){
  all.combs <- combn(1:nrow(airport.locs), 2)
  numcombs <- ncol(all.combs)
  results <- mclapply(1:numcombs, function(x){
      lat1  <- airport.locs[all.combs[1, x], 2]
      long1 <- airport.locs[all.combs[1, x], 3]
      lat2  <- airport.locs[all.combs[2, x], 2]
      long2 <- airport.locs[all.combs[2, x], 3]
      return(haversine(lat1, long1, lat2, long2))
  }, mc.cores=4)
  return(sum(unlist(results)) / numcombs)
}

###################
# WINDOWS VERSION #
###################
clusterExport(cl, c("haversine", "to.radians"))
```

```
multi.core <- function(airport.locs){
  all.combs <- combn(1:nrow(airport.locs), 2)
  numcombs <- ncol(all.combs)
  results <- parLapply(cl, 1:numcombs, function(x){
      lat1  <- airport.locs[all.combs[1, x], 2]
      long1 <- airport.locs[all.combs[1, x], 3]
      lat2  <- airport.locs[all.combs[2, x], 2]
      long2 <- airport.locs[all.combs[2, x], 3]
      return(haversine(lat1, long1, lat2, long2))
  })
  return(sum(unlist(results)) / numcombs)
}

system.time(ave.dist <- multi.core(airport.locs))
print(ave.dist)
------------------------------
   user   system elapsed
  7.363    0.240   2.743
 [1] 1667.186
```

Before we interpret the output, direct your attention to the first line of the Windows segment. When `mclapply` creates additional processes, these processes share the memory with the parent process, and have access to all the parent's environments; however, with `parLapply`, the procedure that spawns new processes is a little different, and requires that we manually export all the functions and libraries we need to load onto each new process beforehand. In this example, we need the new workers to have the `haversine` and `to.radians` functions.

Now to the output of the last code snippet. On my Macintosh machine with four cores, this brings what once was a 5.5-second affair down to a 2.7-second affair. This may not seem like a big deal, but when we expand and start to include more than just 400 airports, we start to see the multicore version really pay off.

To demonstrate just what we've gained from our hassles in parallelizing the problem, I ran this on a GNU/Linux cloud server with 16 cores, and recorded the time it took to complete the calculations for different sample sizes with 1, 2, 4, 8, and 16 cores.

The results are depicted in the following image:

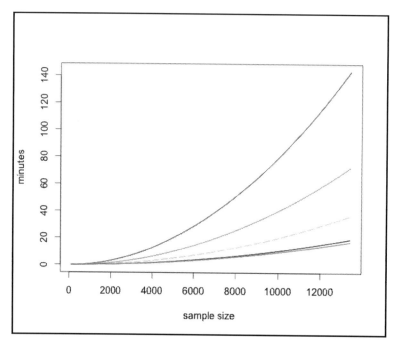

Figure 15.2: The running times for the average-distance-between-all-airports task at different sample sizes for 1, 2, 4, 8, and 16 cores. For reference, the dashed line is the 4 core performance curve, the top most curve is the single core performance curve, and the bottom most curve is the 16 core curve.

It may be hard to tell from the plot, but the estimated times to completion for the task running on 1, 2, 4, 8, and 16 cores are 2.4 hours, 1.2 hours, 36 minutes, 19 minutes, and 17 minutes respectively. Using parallelized R on a 4-core machine, which is not an uncommon setup at the time of writing, has been able to shave a full two hours off the task's running time! Note the diminishing marginal returns on the number of cores used: there is barely any difference between the performances of the 8 and 16 cores. C'est la vie.

Using Rcpp

Contrary to what I sometimes like to believe, there are other computer programming languages than just R. R, and languages like Python, Perl, and Ruby, are considered high-level languages, because they offer a greater level of abstraction from computer representations and resource management than the lower-level languages. For example, in some lower-level languages, you must specify the data type of the variables you create and manage the allocation of RAM manually - C, C++, and Fortran are of this type.

The high level of abstraction R provides allows us to do amazing things very quickly, such as import a data set, run a linear model, and plot the data and regression line in no more than four lines of code! On the other hand, nothing quite beats the performance of carefully crafted lower-level code. Even so, it would take hundreds of lines of code to run a linear model in a low-level language, so a language like that is inappropriate for agile analytics.

One solution is to use R abstractions when we can, and be able to get down to lower-level programming where it can really make a large difference. There are a few paths for connecting R and lower-level languages, but the easiest way by far is to combine R and C++ with Rcpp.

 There are differences in what is considered *high-level*. For this reason, you will sometimes see people and texts (mostly older texts) refer to C and C++ as a high-level language. The same people may consider R, Python, and so on as very high-level languages. Therefore, the *level* of a language is somewhat relative.

A word of warning before we go on: This is an advanced topic, and this section will (out of necessity) gloss over some (most) of the finer details of C++ and Rcpp. If you're wondering whether a detailed reading will pay off, it's worth taking a peek at the conclusion of this section to see how many seconds it took to complete the average-distance-between-all-airports task that would have taken over 2 hours to complete unoptimized.

If you decide to continue, you must install a C++ compiler. On GNU/Linux, this is usually done through the system's package manager. On Mac OS X, XCode must be installed; it is available free in the App Store. For Windows, you must install the **Rtools** available at http://cran.r-project.org/bin/windows/Rtools/. Finally, all users need to install the Rcpp package. For more information, consult sections *1.2* and *1.3* of the Rcpp FAQ (http://dirk.eddelbuettel.com/code/rcpp/Rcpp-FAQ.pdf).

Essentially, our integration of R and C++ is going to take the form of us rewriting certain functions in C++, and calling them in R. Rcpp makes this very easy; before we discuss how to write C++ code, let's look at an example. Put the following code into a file, and name it our_cpp_function.cpp:

```
#include <Rcpp.h>

// [[Rcpp::export]]
double square(double number){
    return(pow(number, 2));
}
```

Congratulations, you've just written a C++ program! Now, from R, we'll read the C++ file, and make the function available to R, using the following code. Then, we'll test out our new function:

```
library(Rcpp)

sourceCpp("our_cpp_functions.cpp")

square(3)
--------------------------------
[1] 9
```

The first two lines with text have nothing to do with our function, per se. The first line is necessary for C++ to integrate with R. The second line (`// [[Rcpp::export]]`) tells R that we want the function directly below it to be available for use (exported) within R. Functions that aren't exported can only be used in the C++ file, internally.

 The `//` is a comment in C++, and it works just like # in R. C++ also has another type of comment that can span multiple lines. These multiline comments start with `/*` and end with `*/`.

Throughout this section, we'll be adding functions to `our_cpp_functions.cpp`, and *re-sourcing* the file from R to use the new C++ functions.

The following modest `square` function can teach us a lot about the differences between the C++ code and R code. For example, the preceding C++ function is roughly equivalent to the following in R:

```
square <- function(number){
  return(number^2)
}
```

The two `doubles` denote that the return value and the argument respectively are both of data type `double`. `double` stands for *double-precision floating-point* number, which is roughly equivalent to R's more general `numeric` data type.

The second thing to notice is that we raise numbers to powers using the `pow` function, instead of using the `^` operator, like in R. This is a minor syntactical difference. The third thing to note is that each statement in C++ ends with a semicolon.

Believe it or not, we now have enough knowledge to rewrite the `to.radians` function in C++, as follows:

```
/* Add this (and all other snippets that
   start with "// [[Rcpp::export]]")
   to the C++ file, not the R code. */

// [[Rcpp::export]]
double to_radians_cpp(double degrees){
    return(degrees * 3.141593 / 180);
}
# with goes with our R code
sourceCpp("our_cpp_functions.cpp")
to_radians_cpp(10)
------------------------
[1] 0.174533
```

Incredibly, with the help of some `search-engine-fu` or a good C++ reference, we can rewrite the whole `haversine` function in C++, as follows:

```
// [[Rcpp::export]]
double haversine_cpp(double lat1, double long1,
                     double lat2, double long2,
                     std::string unit="km"){
    int radius = 6378;
    double delta_phi = to_radians_cpp(lat2 - lat1);
    double delta_lambda = to_radians_cpp(long2 - long1);
    double phi1 = to_radians_cpp(lat1);
    double phi2 = to_radians_cpp(lat2);
    double term1 = pow(sin(delta_phi / 2), 2);
    double term2 = cos(phi1) * cos(phi2);
    term2 = term2 * pow(sin(delta_lambda/2), 2);
    double the_terms = term1 + term2;
    double delta_sigma = 2 * atan2(sqrt(the_terms),
                                   sqrt(1-the_terms));
    double distance = radius * delta_sigma;
    /* if it is anything *but* km it is miles */
    if(unit != "km"){
        return(distance*0.621371);
    }
    return(distance);
}
```

Now, let's re-source it, and test it, as shown in the following code:

```
sourceCpp("our_cpp_functions.cpp")
haversine(51.88, 176.65, 56.94, 154.18)
haversine_cpp(51.88, 176.65, 56.94, 154.18)
----------------------------------------------
[1] 1552.079
[1] 1552.079
```

Are you surprised to see that R and the C++ are so similar?

The only things that are unfamiliar in this new function are the following:

- The `int` data type (which just holds an integer)
- The `std::string` data type (which holds a string, or a `character` vector, in R parlance)
- The `if` statement (which is identical to R's)

Other than those things, this is just building upon what we've already learned with the first function.

Our last matter of business is to rewrite the `single.core` function in C++. To build up to that, let's first write a C++ function called `sum2`, which takes a `numeric` vector and returns the sum of all the numbers, as shown in the following code:

```
// [[Rcpp::export]]
double sum2(Rcpp::NumericVector a_vector){
    double running_sum = 0;
    int length = a_vector.size();
    for( int i = 0; i < length; i++ ){
        running_sum = running_sum + a_vector(i);
    }
    return(running_sum);
}
```

There are a few new things in this function that require our attention:

- We have to specify the data type of all the variables (including function arguments) in C++, but what's the data type of the R vector that we're to pass into `sum2`? The import statement at the top of the C++ file allows us to use the `Rcpp::NumericVector` data type (which does not exist in standard C++).
- To get the length of a `NumericVector` (like we would in R with the length function), we use the `.size()` method.

- The C++ `for`-loop is a little different than its R counterpart. To wit, it takes three fields, separated by semicolons: the first field initializes a counter variable; the second field specifies the conditions under which the for-loop will continue (we'll stop iterating when our counter index is the length of the vector); and the third is how we update the counter from iteration to iteration (`i++` means add 1 to `i`). All in all, this for-loop is equivalent to a `for`-loop in R that starts with `for(i in 1:length)`.
- The way to subscript a vector in C++ is by using parentheses, not brackets. We will also be using parentheses when we start subscripting matrices.

At every iteration, we use the counter as an index into the `NumericVector` and extract the current element, we update the running sum with the current element, and when the loop ends, we return the running sum.

Please note before we go on that the first element of any vector in C++ is the 0th element, not the first. For example, the third element of a vector called `victor` is `victor[3]` in R, whereas it would be `victor(2)` in C++. This is why the second field of the for-loop is `i < length`, and not `i <= length`.

Now, we're finally ready to rewrite the `single.core` function as shown in the following code, from the last section in C++:

```
// [[Rcpp::export]]
double single_core_cpp(Rcpp::NumericMatrix mat){
    int nrows = mat.nrow();
    int numcomps = nrows*(nrows-1)/2;
    double running_sum = 0;
    for( int i = 0; i < nrows; i++ ){
        for( int j = i+1; j < nrows; j++){
            double this_dist = haversine_cpp(mat(i,0), mat(i,1),
                                             mat(j,0), mat(j,1));

            running_sum = running_sum + this_dist;
        }
    }
    return running_sum / numcomps;
}
```

Nothing here should be too new. The only two new components are that we are taking a new data type, a `Rcpp::NumericMatrix`, as an argument, and that we are using `.nrow()` to get the number of rows in a matrix.

Let's try it out! When we used the R function `single.core`, we called it with the whole airport `data.frame` as an argument. But since the C++ function takes a matrix of latitude/longitude pairs, we will simply drop the first column (holding the airport name) from the `airport.locs` data frame, and convert what's left into a `matrix`.

```
sourceCpp("our_cpp_functions.cpp")
the.matrix <- as.matrix(all.airport.locs[,-1])
system.time(ave.dist <- single_core_cpp(the.matrix))
print(ave.dist)
------------------------------------
   user  system elapsed
  0.012   0.000   0.012
[1] 1667.186
```

Okay, the task that used to take 5.5 seconds now takes less than one tenth of a second, and the outputs match, to boot! Astoundingly, we can perform the task on *all* the 13,429 airports quite easily now, as shown in the following code:

```
the.matrix <- as.matrix(all.airport.locs[,-1])
system.time(ave.dist <- single_core_cpp(the.matrix))
print(ave.dist)
----------------------------
   user  system elapsed
 12.310   0.080  12.505
[1] 1869.744
```

Using Rcpp, it takes a mere 12.5 seconds to calculate and average 90,162,306 distances-a feat that would have taken even a 16-core server 17 minutes to complete.

Being smarter about your code

In a blog post that I penned showcasing the performance of this task under various optimization methods, I took it for granted that calculating the distances on the full dataset with the unparallelized/un-Rcpp-ed code would be a multi-hour affair, but I was seriously mistaken.

Shortly after publishing the post, a clever R programmer commented on it stating that they were able to slightly rework the code so that the serial/pure-R code took less than 20 seconds to complete, with all the 13,429 observations. How? **Vectorization.** The following code illustrates the technique:

```
single.core.improved <- function(airport.locs){
  numrows <- nrow(airport.locs)
  running.sum <- 0
```

```
    for (i in 1:(numrows-1)) {
      this.dist <- sum(haversine(airport.locs[i,2],
                                 airport.locs[i, 3],
                                 airport.locs[(i+1):numrows, 2],
                                 airport.locs[(i+1):numrows, 3]))
      running.sum <- running.sum + this.dist
    }
    return(running.sum / (numrows*(numrows-1)/2))
  }

  system.time(ave.dist <- single.core.improved(all.airport.locs))
  print(ave.dist)
  ----------------------------------------------------------------
     user   system elapsed
   15.537    0.173  15.866
   [1] 1869.744
```

Not even 16 seconds. It's worth following what this code is doing.

There is only one `for`-loop that is making its rounds down the number of rows in the `airport.locs` data frame. On each iteration of the `for`-loop, it calls the `haversine` function just once. The first two arguments are the latitude and longitude of the row that the loop is on; however, the third and fourth arguments are the vectors of the latitudes and longitudes below the current row. This returns a vector of all the distances from the current airport to the airports below it in the dataset. Since the `haversine` function could just as easily take vectors instead of single numbers, there is no need for a second for-loop.

So the `haversine` function was already *vectorized*, I just didn't realize it. You'd think that this would be embarrassing for someone who professes to know enough about R to write a book about it. Perhaps it should be. But I found out that one of the best ways to learn, *especially* about code optimization, is through experimentation and making mistakes.

For example, when I started learning about writing high-performance R code for both fun and profit, I made quite a few mistakes. One of my first blunders/failed experiments was with this very task; when I first learned about Rcpp, I used it to translate the `to.radians` and `haversine` functions only. Having the loop remain in R proved to only give a slight performance edge - nothing compared to the 12.5-second business we've achieved together. Now I know that the bulk of the performance degradation was due to the millions of function calls to `haversine`, not the actual computation in the `haversine` function. You could learn that and other lessons most effectively by continuing to try and messing up on your own.

The moral of the story: *When you think you've vectorized your code enough, find someone smarter than you to tell you that you're wrong.*

Exercises

Practice the following exercises to revise the concepts learned so far:

- Is multiple imputation amenable to parallel computation? Why, or why not?
- How is the way we call `to.radians` wasteful? Is there any way to refactor our code to use `to.radians` in a more efficient way?
- When I was gathering the data from *Figure 12.2*, I didn't check every sample size from 1 to the full data set; yet, I've obtained a smooth curve. What I did was test the performance of a handful of sample sizes from 100 to only 2,000. Then I used `nls` (*non-linear least squares*) to fit an equation of the form $x.n^2$ (where n is the sample size) to the data points, and extrapolated with this equation after solving for x. What are some benefits and drawbacks of this approach? Do this on your own machine, if applicable. Do your performance curves match mine?
- There is a thought among some scholars that there is an incongruence between Adam Smith's two seminal works, *The Wealth of Nations* and *The Theory of Moral Sentiments*, namely that the preoccupation of self-interest of the former is at odds with the stress placed on the role of what Smith referred to as *sympathy* (caring for the well being of others) in guiding moral judgments in the latter. Why are these scholars wrong?

Summary

We began this chapter by explaining some of the reasons why large datasets sometimes present a problem for unoptimized R code, such as no auto-parallelization and no native support for out-of-memory data. For the rest of the chapter, we discussed specific routes to optimizing R code in order to tackle large data.

First, you learned of the dangers of optimizing code too early. Next, we saw (much to the relief of slackers everywhere) that taking the lazy way out (and buying or renting a more powerful machine) is often the more cost-effective solution.

After that, we saw that a little knowledge about the dynamics of memory allocation and vectorization in R can often go a long way in performance gains.

The next two sections focused less on changing our R code, and more on changing how we use our code. Specifically, we discovered that there are often performance gains to be had by just changing the packages we use, and/or our implementation of the R language.

In another section, you learned how parallelization works and what *embarrassing parallel problems* are. Then we restructured the code by solving a real-world problem to employ parallelization. You learned how to do this for both Windows and non-Windows systems, and saw the performance gains you might expect to see when you parallelize embarrassingly parallel problems.

After that, we solved the same example from the last section using Rcpp, and saw that:

- Connecting R and C++ doesn't have to be as scary as it sounds
- The performance often blows all other alternatives out of the water

We conclude with a parable that suggests that learning how to write performant R code is a journey and an art, rather than a topic that can be mastered at once.

16

Working with Popular R Packages

In this book thus far, we've used over 30 packages with functionalities ranging from data visualization to MCMC to connecting R to other languages. In this chapter, we will be focusing on a few *very* popular R packages that we haven't mentioned before, or that we only mentioned in passing. These packages—namely `data.table`, `dplyr`, and `tidyr`—are very widely used and revered in R circles.

These packages, which stress speed of computation and ease of use (at least after an initial learning curve) are essential components to many useRs' workflows. Note, however, that R was an extraordinarily effective and popular tool before these packages came on the scene and even if these packages were to somehow magically disappear from public memory, R would live on. Therefore, this chapter may be thought of as optional material. I strongly encourage you, however, to *at least* skim through this chapter; the problems illustrated and solutions demonstrated in this chapter are exceedingly common in day-to-day data analysis and familiarity with the material herein will give you a better idea of how to approach certain problems and, more generally, what R can do for you—even if you don't wind up using these packages!

If you're reading this chapter for the purpose of adopting one or more of the packages that we will be exploring, it is important that you actually follow along with (type and run) the code on your own computer. *Very* few will be able to effectively learn how to use these powerful packages just by reading about them. It's crucial that exploration of these packages is interactive so that the reader can make mistakes, fix them, and experiment with modifying the code for herself.

This chapter will be split into two main sections: one for `data.table`, and one for `dplyr` and `tidyr` (which are synergistic and designed based on the same principles). The same non-trivial, true-to-real-life, and (I hope) interesting example of analysis will be used in each section to better facilitate contrasting two substantially different approaches but obtaining the same results.

Even if you are going into this knowing that you are going to choose `dplyr`/`tidyr` over `data.table`—or vice versa—you *still* need to read the material from the other section. For example, the language of the second section will assume knowledge imparted, in detail, in the first section. Further, we will learn a fair bit more about R in general by contrasting these approaches.

One last thing! The preceding text and much sentiment about these packages online imply a somewhat false dilemma between `data.table` and `dplyr`/`tidyr`. The truth of the matter is that you are free to mix-and-match functionality from any of these packages in whatever way you see fit—even within the same script! In fact, in my personal research, for better or worse, I do this all the time… largely depending on my mood. That being said, it is indisputable that the packages in these two sections adhere to a different (and, in some ways, incompatible) philosophies of data manipulation. For this reason, I don't mix approaches within the same project or mix them in code that could be read or interest anyone else besides me.

Remember the website/service called `Last.fm` that we used in Chapter 12, *Sources of Data*. Well, it's back again! I've been using this service since January 2008 and collecting the track name, artist, and album info of almost every song I've listened from then until now. As a music-lover, statistician, and a hopelessly neurotic navel-gazing cataloger, this site has been a really great tool for me to practice data manipulation and new R/programming approaches. Instead of using a built-in , or using a strange online data set of (even more) limited interest, we'll be using the information that I've gathered on my listening habits to answer a few questions. This includes my listening history from January 2008 to November 2016 and we will be downloading it from GitHub.

These data sets haven't been chosen *solely* because they might be of more interest to the average reader than the old-standby data sets about flowers or old cars. These data sets (which I have made publicly available to have my music taste scrutinized by everyone with access to the internet) have also been thoughtfully chosen because they lend themselves nicely to a demonstration of a goodly array of the capabilities of the packages in both sections in a less contrived manner than is customary.

The data.table package

One of the morals that I hope came across manifest in the previous chapter is that R is capable of much better performance than many expect. And, outside of calling low-level code and using parallelization, it is very widely agreed that there is no single best approach (taking personal preference and the largely subjective concept of readability out of the equation) to high-performance R than to learn how to properly wield `data.table`.

Many would be amazed at what previously intractable problems could be solved using this package. Often, problems that the uninitiated are keen to tackle with powerful remote servers, industrial databases, and trendy tools can be handled quite easily and gracefully by data.table. And, with every update, `data.table` keeps getting faster and faster.

Before, we jump right into the code, it would behoove us to discuss what the `data.table` package gives us.

 Note that we will be using the made up variable, **DT**, to refer to a `data.table` in a generic manner in the example code. DF will refer to a vanilla `data.frame`

The name `data.table` refers to both a *package* and *data structure*. The data structure `data.table` is a kind of `data.frame`... like the ones we've been working with. In spite of its apparent similarities to the `data.frame`, though, make no mistake, the `data.table` is a far more powerful structure.

The first difference that most people notice is that printing a `data.table` (for example, by running DT in the interactive interpreter) only prints the first and the last five rows of the data, by default. Contrast this with the result of executing `iris` in the interpreter and it's easy to see why this is so useful. This property of the `data.table` often obviates the need for using the `head(DF)` idiom that we've frequently been using to control the output of certain functions, although we will still be using `head` on occasion in this chapter to save space.

Apart from this rather aesthetic improvement, the main advantage of this special structure is the what it allows us to express within the square brackets.

In a traditional `data.frame`, the contents of the square brackets (in R this is actually a function called `[`) are the familiar...

DF[i, j]

where, *i* are the indices (rows) and *j* are the columns of the data.frame.

Now, it is true that even this gives us the ability to perform some sophisticated queries. For example:

```
# select columns "Petal.Width" and "Petal.Length" for setosas and
virginicas
> iris[iris$Species %in% c("setosa", "virginica"),
                    c("Petal.Width", "Petal.Length")]
```

But to the `data.table` guru, this is quite limited. In contrast, the `data.table` actually changes the semantics of the `[` (square bracket) operator in to allow for a more powerful syntax. The syntax—whose powerful constructs we will be learning by example—can be summarized in this way:

DT [i, j, by]

where, *i* are the indices, *j* are the columns, and *by* are the variables we are grouping by. If you are familiar with SQL, the proper translation of this outline is:

```
SELECT <j> WHERE <i> GROUP BY <by>
```

However, as you'll see, we need not specify all three components of the square bracket operator where certain clauses are unnecessary.

We mentioned that data tables are a type of `data.frame`. In fact, if you run **class (DT)**, you will see that it is both a `data.table` *and* a `data.frame`. Because of this, you can usually use a `data.table` anywhere you might have normally used a `data.frame`. Though the semantics of the `[` operator are different (and, for the most part, incompatible), the package will intelligently switch to using the semantics of data frames where necessary—for example, in packages that aren't `data.table`-aware. This allows us to reap the manifold benefits of the data tables whilst preserving your ability to not have to convert your data back into a more familiar form.

Let's get started with some code, shall we? By the way, in order to make some of the output of the code in this chapter easier to read, on occasion an *image* of the output will be shown in lieu of the text returned by the R interpreter.

As you might imagine, the first step will be to use the *library* to load the data.table package and load our into memory. The function that loads the file will be the venerable fread function that we briefly mentioned in the previous chapter. We will use the following code for this technique:

```
> library(data.table)
>
download.file("https://raw.githubusercontent.com/tonyfischetti/dawr/master/
working-with-packages/data/tracks-2016-26-11.txt", "./tracks.txt")
> tracks <- fread("./data/tracks.txt")
> head(tracks, n=3)
```

```
             V1                V2      V3          V4
1: 1480053547 A Perfect Match A*Teens Greatest Hits
2: 1480024902       Mamma Mia A*Teens Greatest Hits
3: 1479933058     Upside Down A*Teens Greatest Hits
                                       V5                                  V6
1: f9a829f5-8f57-4c4a-9e4c-439e227ae82c 69d9cb53-5b8f-41b0-ac84-49eabea535b2
2: aa6f618f-2887-45de-a585-f33616ebf852 69d9cb53-5b8f-41b0-ac84-49eabea535b2
3:                                      69d9cb53-5b8f-41b0-ac84-49eabea535b2
                                    V7
1: 2fcb4813-13bf-35c2-8fe6-7a45c84b6de1
2: 2fcb4813-13bf-35c2-8fe6-7a45c84b6de1
3: 2fcb4813-13bf-35c2-8fe6-7a45c84b6de1
```

The fread function is a very incredible one, indeed. Here are *some* of the advantages of using fread:

- We automatically get back a data.table but we can choose, if we wanted to, to get back a vanilla data.frame (by using the data.table=FALSE argument)
- We don't have to specify the sep argument to tell R what the delimiter is. fread will automatically determine whether a is delimited by commas, tabs, and so on.
- fread, as mentioned in the last chapter is *blazingly* fast. Like... orders of magnitude faster than the read.table family. (PS: fread stands for "fast and friendly file reader")

- A lot of the familiar arguments to the `read.table` family are available for `fread`, including `strip.white` (which will strip whitespace, and `colClasses` for manually specifying the data types of columns. This speeds up the data import process even further (for both import methods), as R doesn't have to use expensive heuristics to determine the data types automatically. It should be noted, for the record, that `fread` is *extremely* adept at auto-recognizing column data types.

- `fread` will never convert strings into factors unless you direct it to... `stringsAsFactors=not a chance`.

- For really big files, `fread` will give us a progress bar so we can get a sense of how long an import is going to take.

- `fread` provides us with the `select` and `drop` arguments to choose which columns we want to select (or drop) from the to be imported, respectively. This is great for big data sets which contain columns that we don't need and it will save us a lot of memory.

- Like, the `read.table` family of functions, `fread` can read directly from a URL, though we chose to download the file manually in this example.

- `fread` is often able to correctly read questionably-formatted files where other import methods will choke or, much worse, silently return incorrect results.

So, in light of all these other benefits and the fact that `fread` can return a regular `data.frame` if we so choose, using the `fread` function everywhere you've previously used the `read.table` family is a reasonable tactic and we will see a powerful example of why we might want to do this in the next section!

If you notice from the output, `fread` automatically detected that there is no header to the that specifies the column names, so they are labeled `V1`, `V2`, and so on.

Let's manually add more informative names to the columns:

```
> names(tracks) <- c("thedate", "trackname", "artist", "album",
                     "trackmbid", "artistmbid", "albummbid")
> tracks
```

```
> tracks
             thedate                                    trackname      artist
      1: 1480053547                             A Perfect Match     A*Teens
      2: 1480024902                                  Mamma Mia     A*Teens
      3: 1479933058                                 Upside Down     A*Teens
      4: 1479932828                                 Upside Down     A*Teens
      5: 1479932618                                  Mamma Mia     A*Teens
    ---
 138131: 1199682596                             Young Liars TV on the Radio
 138132: 1199680339         Neighborhood #4 (7 Kettles)     Arcade Fire
 138133: 1199680084                           Big Day Coming   Yo La Tengo
 138134: 1199679962 Will You Come And Fetch Me (LP Version)   of Montreal
 138135: 1199679766                            Keep It Clean Camera Obscura
                                  album                             trackmbid
      1:                Greatest Hits f9a829f5-8f57-4c4a-9e4c-439e227ae82c
      2:                Greatest Hits aa6f618f-2887-45de-a585-f33616ebf852
      3:                Greatest Hits
      4:                Greatest Hits
      5:                Greatest Hits aa6f618f-2887-45de-a585-f33616ebf852
    ---
 138131:                Young Liars 93630f15-5659-4183-9e2a-ecc6706d87f5
 138132:                     Funeral 42c9cb8b-23f1-4ad2-903d-34a5cd6be85f
 138133:                     Painful 425f5f79-c202-4a88-8d7c-8297439d0c45
 138134:       Satanic Panic in the Attic
 138135: Underachievers Please Try Harder e238d0f6-82bc-4b47-b458-eacab956b7ed
                                  artistmbid
      1: 69d9cb53-5b8f-41b0-ac84-49eabea535b2
      2: 69d9cb53-5b8f-41b0-ac84-49eabea535b2
      3: 69d9cb53-5b8f-41b0-ac84-49eabea535b2
      4: 69d9cb53-5b8f-41b0-ac84-49eabea535b2
      5: 69d9cb53-5b8f-41b0-ac84-49eabea535b2
    ---
 138131: eb872766-98f6-453d-883f-2ae908a18315
 138132: 52074ba6-e495-4ef3-9bb4-0703888a9f68
 138133: 3f542031-b054-454d-b57b-812fa2a81b11
 138134: 8475297d-fb78-4630-8d74-9b87b6bb7cc8
 138135: ef43cee7-13f5-4d10-844e-879aba3d8b19
                                  albummbid
      1: 2fcb4813-13bf-35c2-8fe6-7a45c84b6de1
      2: 2fcb4813-13bf-35c2-8fe6-7a45c84b6de1
      3: 2fcb4813-13bf-35c2-8fe6-7a45c84b6de1
      4: 2fcb4813-13bf-35c2-8fe6-7a45c84b6de1
      5: 2fcb4813-13bf-35c2-8fe6-7a45c84b6de1
    ---
 138131: c15e9bc3-825f-41fe-9cd6-29d5e609450f
 138132: 26cdc327-38f2-4200-b5dc-f2fa0e13fcfe
 138133: a6e8c16e-ebfb-47a0-abe7-582e606cb353
 138134: b73b15da-8d85-4f6e-9a0e-89752c37772b
 138135: 132e4ef7-8abb-4e41-8019-6d9057f0a440
```

Now that we've seen the complete output of that command, we will be truncating output judiciously from now on (another reason to follow along with this code on your own!).

The i in DT [i, j, by]

In this subsection, we focus on the first third of `data.table` square bracket syntax. Specifically, this is the third responsible for selecting and filtering *rows*: the WHERE clause, using SQL parlance.

Take the four simplest examples in the following code. These select (a) the first row, (b) the first, second, and third rows, (c) the first row (again), and second row, and (d) the last row. This is illustrated in the following code:

```
> tracks[1, ]
> tracks[1:3, ]
> tracks[c(1,1,2)]
> tracks[.N, ]
```

There are two main things to note here. We can see the first by taking a closer look at the third statement. Note that, unlike the others, we don't use a comma at the end. If this were a `data.frame`, the result would be a selection of the first, first, and second *column*. In a `data.table`, however, the result of a clause in the square brackets missing a single comma are to select *rows*. That being said, I believe it is good practice and enhances readability to include the comma, so we will be doing so from here on out.

The second thing that you probably noticed is the heretofore unseen `.N` variable. `.N` is a special variable provided by this package that holds the number of observations (or, more accurately, as we'll see, the number of observations in each *group*). The consequence of using `.N` to index `tracks` is that it extracts the last row. Similarly, `tracks[.N-1, ]` will extract the second to last row:

```
> tracks[artist=="Belle and Sebastian", ]
        thedate                  trackname             artist
1: 1433898050     A Century Of Elvis Belle and Sebastian
2: 1433898049     A Century Of Elvis Belle and Sebastian
3: 1433897713         Dog On Wheels Belle and Sebastian
4: 1433897712         Dog On Wheels Belle and Sebastian
5: 1433887855   The Power Of Three Belle and Sebastian
```

Note that using `data.table` executing something like `tracks[**tracks$**artist=="Belle and Sebastian", ]` like we would with a `data.frame` is unnecessary. Just using the bare `artist` in square brackets is enough in a `data.table`

```
> tracks[artist=="Belle and Sebastian" | artist=="The Smiths", ]
> # Semantically equivalent to expression above
> tracks[artist %in% c("Belle and Sebastian", "The Smiths"), ]
> tracks[artist=="Belle and Sebastian" & trackname=="The Model", ]
```

Finally, we can, quite easily use *i* to reorder/sort any column. One method is to use the `order` function in base R, as shown in the following code:

```
> tracks[order(artist),]
          thedate         trackname              artist
    1: 1351629570   Canadian Idiot  "Weird Al" Yankovic
    2: 1254940363    ESENA MONO (Remix)  Keti Garbi
    3: 1257488339   Baby Come On                  +44
```

There is another faster, more efficient way to sort our data table:

```
> backup <- copy(tracks)
> tmp <- copy(tracks)
> setorder(tmp, artist)
> # tmp is now sorted
```

In order to justify why we used this bizarre `copy` function, we need to have a chat about something called *by reference* semantics.

What in the world are by reference semantics?

In order to properly extol the virtues of `setorder` and understand the price we pay for it, we need to discuss what it means to modify a structure *by reference* as opposed to *by value*. This is a somewhat advanced topic but I feel that it is essential for (a) learning how `data.table` is so powerful and fast, and (b) preventing you, dear reader, from corrupting your data accidentally. In addition, the material in this discussion introduces concepts and terms in computer science that will serve you well to know for programming in other languages.

Most R programs use expressions that use *by value* semantics.

Here's an example code.

Let's make a two copies of `mtcars`, called `mtcopy` and `mtcopy2`, using the following code:

```
> mtcopy <- mtcars
> mtcopy2 <- mtcopy
```

Suppose we want to sort the mtcars built-in on its `mpg` column (with base R). We've seen how to do this several times within this book, using the following code:

```
> mtcopy[order(mtcopy$mpg), ]
```

This expression immediately returns the `data.frame` we want and prints it to the interactive console. In order to capture the new sorted `data.frame`, we could either assign the return value to another variable, or—if we'd like to overwrite the original `mtcopy`, we can do so like this:

```
> mtcopy <- mtcopy[order(mtcopy$mpg), ]
```

So far so good. Convince yourself that the data frame `mtcopy2` is exactly how we left it by printing it to the console.

The operation we just performed used *by value* semantics. The result of the expression `mtcopy[order(mtcopy$mpg), ]` was a *value* that we then reassigned back to the original variable. `mtcopy` and `mtcopy2`—which were previously pointing to the same memory location—have now been separated because `mtcopy` has changed. R made a copy of the *values* of `mtcopy` before changing it so that the row ordering of `mtcopy2` was preserved in a separate place in the computer's memory.

For an example of *by reference* semantics, we'll be using the `setorder` function in `data.table`; this is other (faster) approach to sorting rows in `data.table` that we spoke of earlier.

Let's turn `mtcars` into a `data.table` called `mtDT` and assign `mtDT` to another `data.table` called `mtDT2`, using the following code:

```
> mtDT <- data.table(mtcars)
> mtDT2 <- mtDT
```

Now let's use `setorder` to order by the `mpg` column. The arguments to `setorder` are the `data.table` to sort (by reference) and the column (or columns) to sort by. We will use the following code for this process:

```
> setorder(mtDT, mpg)
```

If you print `myDT` to the console, you'll see that the data table has now been sorted. Note that we didn't have to reassign the value returned by `setorder` to a variable of the same name to make that change permanent. It changed the data in `myDT` *in place*.

Now, just for kicks, print `myDT2` to the console. The astute reader (you!) will realize that `myDT2` has *also* been changed. What gives?

Remember that, in an effort to save precious memory space, when R created `mtcopy2` from `mtcopy`, `mtcopy2` pointed to the same memory location as `mtcopy` in RAM. If `mtcopy` stayed the way it always was, we would save the space that the duplicate data frame would have taken up. If `mtcopy` were a 3 GB `data.frame` stored in RAM, we would save 3 GB of space.

When, however, we assigned the result of our *by value* sorting back into the variable `mtcopy`, R (quite intelligently) knew to copy the entire contents of `mtcopy` into a safe place, as we've previously pointed out. It is critical to note that these contents were only copied because `mtcopy` was *modified*. This resource-saving technique (that would have saved us 3 GB of memory if `mtcopy` were, hypothetically, a non-modified 3 GB data frame) is called *copy-on-modify*, or (and, for some reason, more commonly known as) *copy-on-write*.

E contrario, `setorder` bypassed this whole *copy-on-write* business because it made it's changes to the actual *physical* memory addresses that held the contents of `mtDT`. As a result, `mtDT2` was *not* copied.

By reference semantics are, in general, faster and use less memory than their *by value* counterparts—sometimes to a *very significant extent*. The *by reference* antics of `data.table` are particularly fast because this wonderful package is very finely designed to do these operations as efficiently as possible. The cost, as you might be able to see, is that *by reference* modifications to data tables can modify other copies of that data table that you didn't mean to change if you are not careful. For example, if you pass a data table into a function and the function modifies that table *by reference*, the data table is now modified even after the function returns. When using *pass by value* semantics, this would never occur. This is the price of `data.table`'s efficiency. However, for certain situations—especially when dealing with data sets that are several GBs in size, the price is well worth it... so long as you are careful.

Before we conclude this rather heady, computer-science-y tangent, there are two important things to note.

The first is that we can use `data.table`'s *by reference* tools in a safer manner by creating "deep copies" of the data tables we are planning on modifying using the `copy` function:

```
> DT <- data.table(mtcars)
> DT2 <- copy(DT)
> setorder(DT, mpg)
> DT[1:2,   ]
     mpg cyl disp  hp drat    wt  qsec vs am gear carb
1: 10.4   8   472 205 2.93 5.250 17.98  0  0    3    4
2: 10.4   8   460 215 3.00 5.424 17.82  0  0    3    4
> DT2[1:2,  ]
     mpg cyl disp  hp drat    wt  qsec vs am gear carb
1: 21.0   6   160 110 3.90 2.620 16.46  0  1    4    4
2: 21.0   6   160 110 3.90 2.875 17.02  0  1    4    4
```

The second important thing to keep in mind is that no one is forcing you to use the *by reference* tools of `data.table`. For example, we can also sort `mtDT` in a more familiar manner, like this:

```
> DT <- data.table(mtcars)
> DT2 <- DT
> DT <- DT[order(mpg), ]
> DT[1:2, ]
     mpg cyl disp  hp drat    wt  qsec vs am gear carb
1: 10.4   8   472 205 2.93 5.250 17.98  0  0    3    4
2: 10.4   8   460 215 3.00 5.424 17.82  0  0    3    4
> DT2[1:2, ]
     mpg cyl disp  hp drat    wt  qsec vs am gear carb
1: 21.0   6   160 110 3.90 2.620 16.46  0  1    4    4
2: 21.0   6   160 110 3.90 2.875 17.02  0  1    4    4
```

`data.table` will *not* use copy-on-write with the `<-` or `=`, only the `set*` functions and using the `:=` operator.

There was a period in my life, in the recent past, where I did a lot of international travel. Though I've been hitting the gym regularly—and, thus, more confident in my ability to fend off ne'er-do-wells—I had to account for the possibility of robbery.

To lessen the negative impact in the case of theft or lost luggage, I decided to take a $150 netbook instead of my regular laptop. This netbook, with a 1 GHz processor and 2 GB of RAM, was the laptop that I used for work—including analyzing data sets that were a little over a GB large—the whole time. It's fair to say that without data.table, I wouldn't have been able to finish all of my work while traveling.

All of this is to say, even if you don't work with large data sets, you might find yourself in a situation where you are working on a machine with very limited resources like a remote server, a $150 netbook, a decade old desktop computer, and so on. In these situations—which occur more commonly than you might think—"big data" tools won't help you. But this heavily-optimized, memory-efficient R package just might.

Anyway… back to business…

The *j* in DT[i, j, by]

In this subsection, we focus on the second third of data.table's square bracket syntax; this is the third responsible for selecting and filtering *columns* like the SELECT clause in SQL.

Much like we didn't have to use the name of the data table and the $ operator when selecting and filtering rows, we can just use the bare names of columns in the *j* section.

Check out the following four lines of code:

```
> tracks[, trackname]
[1] "A Perfect Match" "Mamma Mia"      "Upside Down"     "Upside Down"
"Mamma Mia"
> tracks[, .(trackname)]
                                    trackname
     1:                       A Perfect Match
     2:                             Mamma Mia
     3:                           Upside Down
# ....
> tracks[, .(trackname, artist)]
```

```
                                    trackname        artist
      1:                      A Perfect Match        A*Teens
      2:                            Mamma Mia        A*Teens
      3:                          Upside Down        A*Teens
> # semantically equivalent to above
> tracks[, c("trackname", "artist"), with=TRUE]
```

In the first line, we put `trackname` in the *j* position and the return value was a vector of the values in the trackname column, as if we had run `tracks$trackname` on a regular data frame.

The second line, in contrast, wraps the column name in `.()`. We use this to both extract multiple columns at the same time, and serve notice to data.table that we want to return a `data.table`—even when we are only extracting a single column.

In the third line, we use the our new friend `.()` to extract two columns: `trackname` and `artist`.

Finally, in the fourth line, we get the same return value as with the third line, but the inclusion of the `with=TRUE` argument allows us to specify the columns we want as strings (as opposed to bare *symbols*). Even if you don't use this much in interactive exploration, you will need to be abreast of this capability if you, for example, have to dynamically select rows that we don't know in advance (like based on user input). Hint: you will also need to know this to do one of the exercise questions!

Note that we could, as with the *i* section, use numbered indices to extract columns from the data table but this is not terribly common.

Quite conveniently, we can use a colon to specify a range of columns that we'd like to extract:

```
> # extract all columns in the data.table from thedate to album
> tracks[, thedate:album]
> # we can also use the ! to select a range of columns we'd like to
*exclude*
> tracks[, !(trackmbid:albummbid)]
```

If we wanted to get back a data table without all the unsightly "mbid" fields (these, by the way, are unique identifiers that link to information on the open music database "Music Brainz"), we can do one of the following:

- Extract the columns `thedate` to `album` (as shown in the preceding code) and assign the returned data table back into the `tracks` variable

- Remove the columns `trackmbid` to `albummbid`
- Remove the offending columns *by reference*.

Since we have no need for the columns `trackmbid` and `albummbid`, let's remove them *by reference* using the following incantation:

```
> tracks[, c("trackmbid", "albummbid") := NULL]
```

Print `tracks` to the interactive console for yourself to verify that the unnecessary columns have been removed.

Since, `artistmbid` is the only Music Brainz ID that we have left, let's rename it to just `mbid` by running the following code:

```
> tracks[, .(mbid=artistmbid)]
```

This will return a data table with the column that we want renamed, but only that column. We can include more columns within the `.()`, if we want, as shown in the following code:

```
> tracks[, .(artist, mbid=artistmbid)]
                    artist                                 mbid
     1:            A*Teens 69d9cb53-5b8f-41b0-ac84-49eabea535b2
     2:            A*Teens 69d9cb53-5b8f-41b0-ac84-49eabea535b2
     3:            A*Teens 69d9cb53-5b8f-41b0-ac84-49eabea535b2
     4:            A*Teens 69d9cb53-5b8f-41b0-ac84-49eabea535b2
     5:            A*Teens 69d9cb53-5b8f-41b0-ac84-49eabea535b2
     ---
138131: TV on the Radio eb872766-98f6-453d-883f-2ae908a18315
138132:      Arcade Fire 52074ba6-e495-4ef3-9bb4-0703888a9f68
138133:      Yo La Tengo 3f542031-b054-454d-b57b-812fa2a81b11
138134:      of Montreal 8475297d-fb78-4630-8d74-9b87b6bb7cc8
138135:   Camera Obscura ef43cee7-13f5-4d10-844e-879aba3d8b19
```

But if we wanted to keep all the columns and rename *just* `artistmbid`, typing all those other column names is a drag.

The better (not to mention *more efficient*) option is to use the `setnames` function to rename the column we want to abbreviate, as shown in the following code:

```
> setnames(tracks, "artistmbid", "mbid")
```

Say we wanted to change all the values in column x to the result of applying the values to some function. The *j* field gives us enormous flexibility when it comes to performing arbitrary computations on columns.

In this example, we are going to want to change the values in the thedate column (which are expressed as UNIX timestamps [the number of seconds since 12:00am January 1, 1970]) into the more familiar date/time objects used in R by using the anytime function from the package of the same name, as shown in the following code:

```
> library(anytime)
> tracks[, .(thedate=anytime(thedate))]
```

Note that this command returned only the updated thedate column. As before, you can certainly tack on as many other columns as you'd like within the .(), but, again (as before), you can achieve the same end by modifying the thedate column *by reference*:

```
> tracks[, thedate:=anytime(thedate)]
```

Just remember that since this is done *by reference*, if you make a mistake on the right-hand side of the := in-place update operator, you will permanently muck up your tracks data table. It is advisable to (a) use caution when modifying by reference, and (b) make a backup copy of the original data.table (using the copy function), if your computer memory space allows.

Using both *i* and *j*

Let's combine what we've learned about the first two-thirds of the allowable square bracket expressions by using both *i* and *j* in the same statements, as shown in the following code:

```
> tracks[artist=="Belle and Sebastian", trackname]
[1] "A Century Of Elvis" "A Century Of Elvis" "Dog On Wheels"...
> tracks[artist=="Belle and Sebastian", .(artist, trackname)]
                        artist                            trackname
   1: Belle and Sebastian                  A Century Of Elvis
   2: Belle and Sebastian                  A Century Of Elvis
   3: Belle and Sebastian                      Dog On Wheels
   4: Belle and Sebastian                      Dog On Wheels
   5: Belle and Sebastian                  The Power Of Three
   ---
5553: Belle and Sebastian                             Fiction
5554: Belle and Sebastian                  Your Cover's Blown
5555: Belle and Sebastian         I Don't Want To Play Football
5556: Belle and Sebastian                      Dog On Wheels
5557: Belle and Sebastian Take Your Carriage Clock And Shove It
> tracks[artist=="Belle and Sebastian" & trackname=="The Model", .N]
[1] 53
```

For many readers, the first and second incantations are moderately easy to follow, even if we haven't seen an example of both the *i* and *j* clauses being used at the same time. The third statement, though, is pretty special. We use the aforementioned special variable .N to get a count of the number of times I played *The Model* by Belle and Sebastian (as opposed to *The Model* by Kraftwerk).

For kicks, let's use the .N variable to get a count of all the songs I listened to in January of 2016! Well… at least the ones I remembered to have sent to last.fm, using the following code:

```
> jan1 <- anytime("2016-1-01 00:00:01")
> jan31 <- anytime("2016-1-31 23:59:59")
> tracks[thedate > jan1 & thedate < jan31, .N]
[1] 895
```

Super!

In order to demonstrate more advanced usage of *j*, let's first use the month function (from the lubridate package) to add a column *by reference* that stores the month that the date takes place in. We will use the label=TRUE argument in month to get a more friendly output (for example, *Jan* instead of 1), as shown in the following code:

```
> library(lubridate)
> tracks[, themonth:=month(thedate, label=TRUE)]
```

We can use a whole lot of arbitrary functions in the *j* field. In this example, we use the table function to get a count of rows (or, the number of songs I've listened to) by month:

```
> tracks[, table(themonth)]
themonth
  Jan   Feb   Mar   Apr   May   Jun   Jul   Aug   Sep   Oct   Nov   Dec
11875 10468 11400  9025 12743 13609  9439  9861 13509 13264 12175 10767
```

Let's get a count of the number of unique artists that I have listened to since 2008. We'll also get a count of the number of unique artist Music Brainz IDs. Since each artist is uniquely identifiable by their mbid, the numbers should be identical, as shown in the following code:

```
> tracks[, .(uniqueartists = sum(!duplicated(artist)))]
   uniqueartists
1:          2202
> tracks[, .(uniquembids=sum(!duplicated(mbid)))]
   uniquembids
1:        1960
```

OK.... why the discrepancy?

Let's investigate! We can take a closer look at what's going on by filtering rows by wherever `mbid` is duplicated but `artist` is not! To control the volume of output and restrict our focus on the task at hand, let's also extract just those two columns, as shown in the following code:

```
> tracks[duplicated(mbid) & !duplicated(artist), .(artist, mbid)]
                       artist                            mbid
  1:       Reservoir Ticklers
  2:           Chucky Danger
  3:  Bonnie 'Prince' Billy
  4:             Oro Solido
  5:           Kinito Mendez
 ---
238:             Yesan Damen
239:  Iron & Wine & Calexico  c3f28da8-662d-4f09-bdc7-3084bf685930
240:           Feist/Gonzales
241:         Feist/Jane Birkin
242:             Halfpastfour
```

From this investigation, we might gather that the main cause for the discrepancy between the number of unique artists and artist mbids is because there are a lot of artists for whom Last.fm was unable to match with a Music Brainz ID. Additionally, in the case of line 239, the same mbid that maps to *Iron & Wine* also maps to *Iron & Wine & Calexico*.

We'll deal with this complication later in the section.

Before we move on to the last third of the square bracket syntax, let's see how we can easily combine multiple `data.table` data manipulations by *chaining*.

For example, let's look at an excerpt of the data for the times I've listened to *The Model* by Belle and Sebastian, as shown in the following code:

```
> tracks[artist=="Belle and Sebastian" & trackname=="The Model", .(artist,
trackname, album)]
                  artist trackname
album
 1: Belle and Sebastian The Model Fold Your Hands Child, You Walk Like a
Peasant
 2: Belle and Sebastian The Model Fold Your Hands Child, You Walk Like a
Peasant
 3: Belle and Sebastian The Model Fold Your Hands Child, You Walk Like a
Peasant
```

Cool. From the first three rows, it would appear that the only times I've listened to this song, it's been off of the album called *Fold Your Hands Child, You Walk Like a Peasant*.

Let's confirm or disconfirm this by tacking on another set of square brackets and filtering by unique values in the album column, as shown in the following code:

```
> tracks[artist=="Belle and Sebastian" & trackname=="The Model", .(artist,
trackname, album)][!duplicated(album),]
              artist trackname
album
1: Belle and Sebastian The Model Fold Your Hands Child, You Walk Like a
Peasant
2: Belle and Sebastian The Model                      Hollywood Bowl
Live
3: Belle and Sebastian The Model              (2006.07.06) Hollywood
Bowl
4: Belle and Sebastian The Model
> # now just return a vector of the unique album names
> tracks[artist=="Belle and Sebastian" & trackname=="The Model", .(artist,
trackname, album)][!duplicated(album), album]
[1] "Fold Your Hands Child, You Walk Like a Peasant" "Hollywood Bowl Live"
[3] "(2006.07.06) Hollywood Bowl"                    ""
```

As it turns out, I've listened to four distinct versions of this song by this artist... including a version on an unnamed album, as seen in the fourth position of the vector returned in the last statement.

The reader who is on top of her game might object that we could have easily placed the unique-ness condition in the *i* field of the first square bracket. This is true, but chaining is a really powerful construct and can often greatly aid readability and ease of interactive exploration.

We'll be using chaining quite often for the remainder of this section.

Using the by argument for grouping

Finally we get to the last third of the square bracket syntax structure, by. This controls which variable (or variables) to group on. Learning to use this argument will allow us to answer some more interesting questions about my listening habits.

Since each record in our data set is one track listened to, if we group by the artist, and get a count of the number of records in each group, we should get a count of songs listened to by artist. Can you guess how we might do this using data.table?

::author pauses and looks at the reader painfully long::

That's right! We use the .N special variable while grouping on artist. Let's do this and chain a call to order the N variable in descending order using order(-N) in the second *i* field, and only return the first 10 results, as shown in the following code:

```
> tracks[, .N, artist][order(-N)[1:10]]
                 artist     N
 1: Belle and Sebastian 5557
 2:          The Smiths 4881
 3: The Magnetic Fields 4622
 4:              P:ano 3888
 5:            The Cure 3792
 6:               Stars 3554
 7:        Bad Religion 2977
 8:      Elvis Costello 2908
 9:         The Beatles 2461
10:           Radiohead 2198
```

Now we're on to something!

How about we get a count of the number of tracks listened to by month, just like we did with tracks[, table(themonth)] but now using *by* and returning a data.table instead of a regular table (as is returned by the table function), as shown in the following code:

```
> tracks[, .N, themonth]
     themonth     N
 1:       Nov 12175
 2:       Oct 13264
 3:       Sep 13509
 4:       Aug  9861
```

One really neat feature of the *by* is that we can perform arbitrary calculations in the field. For example, had we not added a column called themonth previously, we can group by the month, on the fly, *directly in* the *by* field:

```
tracks[, .N, month(thedate, label=TRUE)]
```

To demonstrate the ability to group by more than one variable, let's get a count of the number of plays by artist and album to get a list of my most listened to albums. Again, we'll order (in a descending fashion) by the N variable:

```
> tracks[, .N, .(artist, album)][order(-N), ]
                    artist                           album    N
   1:               P:ano     When It's Dark And It's Summer 2355
   2: The Magnetic Fields           69 Love Songs, Vol. 1 1336
   3:       Elvis Costello                    Armed Forces 1037
```

That sounds about right.

It was important to group by both the artist *and* the album title because, had we not, we would have had a lot of inflated numbers for albums titled "Greatest Hits", and so on.

Here's a tough one, but really try to think this one through. How might I get a data.table of the number of albums I've listened to by artist?

This requires us to chain two group by operations: one to group by artist and album, and to finally group by artist, using the following code:

```
> tracks[, .N, .(artist, album)][, .N, artist][order(-N)]
          artist  N
   1:   The Beatles 43
   2: Elvis Costello 36
   3:   The Smiths 32
   4:    Radiohead 32
   5:        Stars 28
```

It looks like the artist for whom I've listened to the highest number of records is The Beatles with 43 distinct albums.

Please study this incantation carefully. Understanding it will greatly expand the vocabulary of questions you can answer using data.table.

In order to demonstrate that we don't *have* to only use .N in the *j* field when performing grouping, let's try to solve a (rather contrived, I admit) problem: how can we get the mean number of tracks I listened to per month by year?

Let's start slow. The first thing we have to do is group by the year and month, using the following code:

```
> tracks[, .N, .(year(thedate), themonth)]
       year themonth     N
  1: 2016       Nov   124
  2: 2016       Oct   258
  3: 2016       Sep   225
  4: 2016       Aug   215
  5: 2016       Jul   411
  ---
103: 2008       May   952
104: 2008       Apr  1101
105: 2008       Mar  1486
106: 2008       Feb   984
107: 2008       Jan   877
```

Now let's assign that to a variable `tmp`. In the final step, we group by the year and take the mean of the `N` column, as shown in the following code:

```
> tmp <- tracks[, .N, .(year(thedate), themonth)]
> tmp[, mean(N), year]
year            V1
1: 2016   361.0000
2: 2015   948.0833
3: 2014 1464.4167
. . .
```

We could, as an alternative, have decided to chain these two operations, give the V1 column a more informative name, and split the chained expression over multiple lines, as shown in the following code:

```
> tracks[, .N, .(year(thedate), themonth)][
+         , .(mean_number_of_plays_per_month=round(mean(N))), year][
+      order(year), ]
   year mean_number_of_plays_per_month
1: 2008                            1082
2: 2009                             750
3: 2010                            1551
. . .
```

Joining data tables

No discussion of data manipulation/wrangling is complete without discussing joins. We first saw joins in `Chapter 12`, *Sources of Data*, when we were merging an SQL table of artwork information to a table of artist information. We'll begin this subsection with a closer look on what a join is.

Very often in data analysis, information we need is spread across two or more data sets. In the example in `Chapter 12`, *Sources of Data*, we wanted to get the mean age of the artists at the time of the completions of the artwork for all artworks in a table. The critical piece that was missing from that table, though, was the date of birth for that artist. For this we had to *join* (or, sometimes, called a *merge*) the two tables. In order to do the job, we had to specify the common columns that we would match on. In joining parlance, we often say that we are matching *on* a particular column (or columns) or refer to these columns as a *key*.

There are many different variants of the general join operation but the four most common are the *left join*, *right join*, *inner join*, and *full join*. The difference between these four types is how we handle situations where variables in the column that is to be joined are missing from one of the tables.

The following is a crude illustration (I tried my best!) of how these operations differ along with the code for how to join them in data.table syntax:

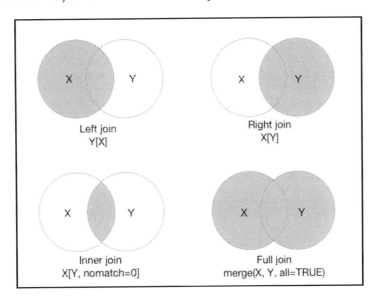

In a left join, all keys that exist in the left (we are calling this "X") are included in the joined data set, even if there is no corresponding key in the right table ("Y"). In an *inner* join, as another example, only records that have a key in both "X" and "Y" are included.

It is, perhaps, helpful to look at a toy example in code to get a better sense of the differences between the different join operations.

In the following code , we are creating two data tables (left and right). The former will be a five record set of the names and ages of budding expert statisticians (the ages are generated randomly from a normal distribution centered at 30 years-old). The data table named right contains the names of some of those statisticians, other statisticians, and their favorite color:

```
> left <- data.table(age=round(rnorm(5, 30, 5)),
+                     name=c("Isabella", "Marisol", "Aniyah",
+                            "DeAndre", "Taylor"))
> right <- data.table(fav_color=c("red", "black", "green",
+                                  "yellow", "purple", "orange"),
+                      name=c("Marisol", "Taylor", "Ethan",
+                             "DeAndre", "Isabella", "Nathan"))
> left
    age       name
1:   27  Isabella
2:   31   Marisol
3:   26    Aniyah
4:   38   DeAndre
5:   32    Taylor
> right
   fav_color       name
1:        red   Marisol
2:      black    Taylor
3:      green     Ethan
4:     yellow   DeAndre
5:     purple  Isabella
6:     orange    Nathan
```

Note that "Aniyah" is not present in right and "Ethan" and "Nathan" are not present in left.

In an inner join, only the statisticians common to *both* tables are included in the final merged data table, as shown in the following code:

```
> # inner join
> left[right, on="name", nomatch=0]
   age    name fav_color
1:  31  Marisol       red
2:  32   Taylor     black
3:  38  DeAndre    yellow
4:  27 Isabella    purple
```

In contrast, a left join, will include all statisticians in `left` even if there is no matching record in `right`, as shown in the following code:

```
> # note the, perhaps, counter-intuitive
> # placement of the tables
> right[left, on="name"]
   fav_color     name age
1:    purple Isabella  27
2:       red  Marisol  31
3:        NA   Aniyah  26
4:    yellow  DeAndre  38
5:     black   Taylor  32
```

Since we are missing information for Aniyah's favorite color, the field is filled with an NA.

Note that the `right` table now appears on the outside of the square brackets. In a right join, the command is the same except that `left` is now on the *outside* of the square brackets.

Finally, in a full join, all statisticians from both tables are thrown into the mix, as shown in the following code:

```
> merge(left, right, all=TRUE)
      name age fav_color
1:   Aniyah  26        NA
2:  DeAndre  38    yellow
3:    Ethan  NA     green
4: Isabella  27    purple
5:  Marisol  31       red
6:   Nathan  NA    orange
7:   Taylor  32     black
```

All the fields for with we are missing information are populated with NAs.

Now that we have a clear understanding of what joins are and how to perform them using data.table, let's turn our attention back to the analysis of my last.fm listening history.

Curious about how many bands I listen to from each country, I used the Music Brainz API to get the country name for each of the artists I've listened to by using the artist mbid as an identifier. Let's load it and take a look:

```
>
download.file("https://raw.githubusercontent.com/tonyfischetti/dawr/master/
working-with-packages/data/artist-info.txt", "./artist-info.txt")
> artistinfo <- fread ("./artist-info.txt", encoding="UTF-8")
> artistinfo
```

```
                               mbid          artistmb countrycode
   1: 69d9cb53-5b8f-41b0-ac84-49eabea535b2       A★Teens          SE
   2: 9552398b-27e6-43b6-9da0-a7e582b7aa08          Vår          DK
   3: a4ea3572-0b7b-4586-bad4-02508b10f5dd The Foreign Resort     DK
   4: 7de3b7b4-8288-4baf-929b-98af9224c0cb Lebanon Hanover        DE
   5: 9efaf639-6332-44b8-94ae-c25896320ca7      Protomartyr       US
  ---
1560: 96774518-0e32-4a69-8aa3-8df0527fb6af    Lewis Black         US
1561: c0a05ed0-9dde-43c1-91fa-3c1b02756c8f  Demetri Martin        US
1562: 420ca290-76c5-41af-999e-564d7c71f1a7         Queen          JP
1563: 9d98662f-48d3-4243-9bf8-36b697458ffc    Save Ferris         US
1564: 2aab61bc-67f4-4722-8c6e-e1821b2e32a6  Violent Femmes        US
            country
   1:       Sweden
   2:      Denmark
   3:      Denmark
   4:      Germany
   5: United States
  ---
1560: United States
1561: United States
1562:         Japan
1563: United States
1564: United States
```

We had to manually specify the `encoding` argument in `fread` for reasons that aren't terribly important for our purposes. You can ignore it.

For fun, let's get a count number of bands I listen to by country; I know you got this one :)

```
> artistinfo[, .N, country][order(-N)]
           country   N
1:    United States 652
2:   United Kingdom 374
3:           Canada  78
4:           Sweden  63
5:           France  63
```

That's pretty interesting but comports with my intuition. What would also be interesting is to get the counts of *the number of tracks played* by country of artist. Even *more* interesting would be to compare the results of both, side by side, right?... Right?!

You may have guessed it... in order to do this we have to join the `tracks` and the `artistinfo` data tables... but which join operation should be use? Let's explore our different options, using the following code:

```
> nrow(tracks[artistinfo, on="mbid"])   # right join
[1] 122242
> nrow(artistinfo[tracks, on="mbid"])   # left join
[1] 138135
```

Choosing to join the tables such that all artists in `tracks` are in the output, even if I'm missing country information for them, yields a joined table that has 138,135 rows. In contrast, including every artist from `artistinfo` yields a joined table of 122,242 rows.

Since, we only want to include artists for whom I have plays for and artist/country information for only the artists that I've actually listened to, an *inner join* is a sensible choice, as shown in the following code:

```
> tmp <- tracks[artistinfo, nomatch=0, on="mbid"]
> nrow(tmp)
[1] 122241
```

The merged data table `tmp` has one fewer record than the right join gave us. This is because I snuck the artist/country info for an artist I've never listened to in the `artistinfo` frame.

As mentioned before, joining is a very common operation in data analysis (which is why I wanted to give the topic a thorough treatment). Unfortunately, even with the power of `data.table`, it is an expensive operation from a computational and memory-usage standpoint. The joins we performed, it is true, are more efficient and faster than their base R counterparts but `data.table`, always out-doing itself, provides a way to do even faster and more efficient joins. The solution: setting a *key* on the variables that we're joining on:

```
> setkey(tracks, "mbid")
> setkey(artistinfo, "mbid")
> # do an inner join and extract only some columns
> withcountry <- tracks[artistinfo, nomatch=0][, .(artist, trackname,
album, country)]
> withcountry
```

```
          artist                                        trackname
  1:       Hayden                                  In Field & Town
  2: Cocteau Twins                                              Ivo
  3: Cocteau Twins                               Carolyn's Fingers
  4: Cocteau Twins                                           Donimo
  5: Cocteau Twins                                           Amelia
 ---
122237: Cobra Starship Damn You Look Good And I'm Drunk (Scandalous)
122238: Cobra Starship                                   Kiss My Sass
122239: Israel Vibration                               Friday Evening
122240: Israel Vibration                                     Survive
122241: Israel Vibration                               Friday Evening
                album          country
  1:    In Field & Town          Canada
  2:           Treasure United Kingdom
  3:   Blue Bell Knoll United Kingdom
  4:           Treasure United Kingdom
  5:           Treasure United Kingdom
 ---
122237:      ¡Viva La Cobra!  United States
122238:      ¡Viva La Cobra!  United States
122239: Unconquered People         Jamaica
122240: Unconquered People         Jamaica
122241: Unconquered People         Jamaica
```

The `setkey` function (which takes a `data.table` and a column, or columns to make keys out of) is a *by reference* transformation on the `data.table` supplied in the first argument. The main thing you'll notice by using `setkey` is that it sorts the `data.table` on the key.

Why do we want to do this again?

Setting the key will result in much faster filtering, grouping, sorting, and joining operations on the keyed column. Note that another benefit is that we no longer have to use the `on=mbid` argument to perform the join, although you still may want to for readability.

Now that we have the joined `data.table` we want, let's waste no more time finding out the countries that I've listened to the most tracks from:

```
> withcountry[, .N, country][order(-N),]
           country     N
 1:  United Kingdom 51366
 2:   United States 41260
 3:          Canada 10799
 4:          France  4222
 5:         Germany  3125
```

Super interesting! In order to really see and interpret the difference between these two aggregations by country, let's join both, as shown in the following code:

```
> playspercountry <- withcountry[, .(playspercountry=.N), country]
> playspercountry[artistspercountry, on="country"][order(-
playspercountry)[1:10]]
           country playspercountry artistspercountry
 1:  United Kingdom           51366               374
 2:   United States           41260               652
 3:          Canada           10799                78
 4:          France            4222                63
 5:         Germany            3125                52
 6:       Australia            2555                31
 7:           Italy            1931                39
 8:          Sweden            1473                63
 9:         Jamaica            1378                22
10:          Russia             679                 6
```

Let's see what insights we can glean from these results.

The first thing that stuck out to me was that tracks from bands from the UK got more plays than tracks by bands from the US, even though I listen to almost twice as many bands from the US than from the UK. Amusingly, I've only listened to six musical artists from Russia (primarily ДДТ) but the country is in the top 10 for when taking into account total tracks played (again, it's ДДТ).

Reshaping, melting, and pivoting data

In this final subsection, we will show how to perform another very common operation quickly and efficiently in `data.table`. This operation has many names—*pivot-table-ing, reshaping, melting/casting, spreading/gathering, converting from long to wide (or vice-versa)*. But while the nomenclature, I admit, can get pretty complicated, understanding the concept doesn't have to be! The best first step to explaining this is by the following example:

Here is an example of data that we will, heretofore, refer to as in *long format:*

```
        year themonth   N
  1: 2016       Sep 225
  2: 2016       Aug 215
  3: 2016       Jul 411
  4: 2016       Jun 169
  5: 2016       May 478
 ---
103: 2008       Feb 984
104: 2008       Jan 877
105: 2016       Mar 360
106: 2016       Oct 258
107: 2016       Nov 124
```

In contrast, here is the same data in a *wide format:*

```
     year  Jan  Feb  Mar  Apr  May  Jun  Jul  Aug  Sep  Oct  Nov  Dec
1: 2008   877  984 1486 1101  952  508  355  924 1244 1690 1873  984
2: 2009  1145 1475  654  728  321  590   46  972  861  690  870  642
3: 2010    88   22  308 1016 2629 2518  885  356 3330 2671 1898 2889
4: 2011  2372 2272 1340  642 1777 1788 1138 1253 2111 2427 1829 1695
5: 2012  2118 1720 2597 1584 3112 1718 2444 2093 1847 2704 2025 1279
6: 2013  1305 1034 1050  764 1215 2848 1701 1943 1974 1077 1659 2177
7: 2014  1767 1838 1521 1449 1149 2024 1499 1674 1264 1153 1395  840
8: 2015  1308  842 2084 1186 1110 1446  960  431  653  594  502  261
9: 2016   895  281  360  555  478  169  411  215  225  258  124   NA
```

Another *wide* representation of this same data may look like this:

```
    themonth 2008 2009 2010 2011 2012 2013 2014 2015 2016
1:      Jan  877 1145   88 2372 2118 1305 1767 1308  895
2:      Feb  984 1475   22 2272 1720 1034 1838  842  281
3:      Mar 1486  654  308 1340 2597 1050 1521 2084  360
4:      Apr 1101  728 1016  642 1584  764 1449 1186  555
5:      May  952  321 2629 1777 3112 1215 1149 1110  478
6:      Jun  508  590 2518 1788 1718 2848 2024 1446  169
7:      Jul  355   46  885 1138 2444 1701 1499  960  411
8:      Aug  924  972  356 1253 2093 1943 1674  431  215
```

```
   9:      Sep 1244   861 3330 2111 1847 1974 1264  653  225
  10:      Oct 1690   690 2671 2427 2704 1077 1153  594  258
  11:      Nov 1873   870 1898 1829 2025 1659 1395  502  124
  12:      Dec  984   642 2889 1695 1279 2177  840  261   NA
```

In the *long* format, each observation (a year, a month, and a count) is on it's own separate row in our table. In the first *wide* example, the very same data was "stretched" or *widened* so that each month has its own separate column. Looking up a count for a specific year/month pair, using this representation, requires identifying the row (year) we want and following the row to the column of the month we are looking for. The last example is similar but now it is the *year* that lives in it's own separate columns.

Given that all of these representations of data are semantically equivalent, a question may be raised: *Why spend time learning about long/wide representations and how to convert between formats at all?* As it turns out, there are a quite a few reasons:

- For some operations—especially linear algebra operations such as matrix multiplication and factorization—wide data not only visually looks more like the matrices we are operating on, but many functions/operators *require* it
- Some packages—such as ggplot2 and many functions/packages in the *tidyverse* (see the next section) prefer—or even require—data in long format.
- In some cases, we receive data from arbitrary sources in a particular format but to communicate better what we'd like to show, we need to express it by using a different representation
- Finally, it doesn't have to be the case that long and wide formats have to show the very same data. Very often (and we'll be seeing an example of this) converting from long to wide requires the use of an *aggregation function*. A result of this data transformation is that the long format holds more information but the wide representation contains summary information that we are interested in. Users familiar with Microsoft Excel can think of a transformation like this as a *pivot table*

Without further ado, let's see how these operations are performed using `data.table`...

First, let's create a table in *long* format using the `last.fm` data. This table will be a count of the number of tracks listened to by month and year, as shown in the following code:

```
> long <- tracks[, .N, .(year(thedate), themonth)]
> long
    year themonth   N
 1: 2016      Sep 225
 2: 2016      Aug 215
 3: 2016      Jul 411
```

```
  4: 2016        Jun 169
  5: 2016        May 478
  .
  .
  .
103: 2008        Feb 984
104: 2008        Jan 877
105: 2016        Mar 360
106: 2016        Oct 258
107: 2016        Nov 124
```

This is the data from the long representation example.

To convert this table into a *wide* format, we use the `dcast` function. The non-optional arguments that this function takes are as follows:

- A `data.table` to convert to wide format
- A formula specifying which columns will stay in their own columns and which ones will be spread across rows
- The column whose values will be the ones that occupy each new cell of the wide table

Here's an example of how to convert the long format to the *first* example of the wide format representation (the one where the months are spread across columns):

```
> dcast(long, year ~ themonth, value.var="N")
   year  Jan  Feb  Mar  Apr  May  Jun  Jul  Aug  Sep  Oct  Nov  Dec
1: 2008  877  984 1486 1101  952  508  355  924 1244 1690 1873  984
2: 2009 1145 1475  654  728  321  590   46  972  861  690  870  642
3: 2010   88   22  308 1016 2629 2518  885  356 3330 2671 1898 2889
...
```

Note that the variable that is to be spread is on the right-hand side of the ~ in the formula. Also note that the value column was specified by using the `value.var` argument by name and putting the column name in quotation marks?

Can you think of how we can modify the preceding expression in order to convert from the long format to the last example of the wide format where the years are on separate columns?

That's right! We only have to slightly modify the formula and switch the places of the left-hand and right-hand side:

```
> dcast(long, themonth ~ year, value.var="N")
   themonth 2008 2009 2010 2011 2012 2013 2014 2015 2016
 1:      Jan  877 1145   88 2372 2118 1305 1767 1308  895
 2:      Feb  984 1475   22 2272 1720 1034 1838  842  281
...
```

In order to demonstrate how to use dcast and an *aggregation function* to get a wide format summary table, we'll be making a two column data table that provides a crosswalk between months and Northern Hemisphere seasons and joining it to our long data table, as shown in the following code snippet:

```
> seasonsDT <- data.table(season=c(rep("spring", 3),
+                                  rep("summer", 3),
+                                  rep("fall", 3),
+                                  rep("winter", 3)),
+                          themonth=c("Mar", "Apr", "May", "Jun",
+                                     "Jul", "Aug", "Sep", "Oct",
+                                     "Nov", "Dec", "Jan", "Feb"))
> seasonsDT
     season themonth
 1: spring      Mar
 2: spring      Apr
 3: spring      May
...
10: winter      Dec
11: winter      Jan
12: winter      Feb
>
> # join the tables
> longwithseason <- long[seasonsDT, on="themonth"]
> longwithseason    year themonth    N season
 1: 2015       Mar 2084 spring
...
> setcolorder(longwithseason, c("year", "season", "themonth", "N"))
> longwithseason
     year season themonth    N
 1: 2015 spring     Mar 2084
 2: 2014 spring     Mar 1521
 3: 2013 spring     Mar 1050
 4: 2012 spring     Mar 2597
 5: 2011 spring     Mar 1340
 ---
103: 2012 winter     Feb 1720
104: 2011 winter     Feb 2272
```

```
105:  2010  winter      Feb    22
106:  2009  winter      Feb  1475
107:  2008  winter      Feb   984
```

Note that we used the `setcolorder` function to change the order of the columns, *by reference*, to a more sensible scheme.

Suppose we want to get a count of the number of tracks I listened to for each season in each year.

Note that in all of our other `dcast` incantations, the combinations specified by the formula uniquely identified a cell value. Concretely, in our last statement using `dcast`, there was only *one* observation for each month/year pair.

In contrast, directly above we have a table with multiple values for N for each year/season pair. How to we distill all of those (three) numbers into one to fit in the proper cell?

Well, since we want to get a grand total of the tracks for each year/season pair, using `sum` as the aggregation function should yield the value we are looking for. Pay close attention to the syntax of the incantation:

```
> pivoted <- dcast(longwithseason, year ~ season, value.var="N",
fun.aggr=sum)
> pivoted
   year fall spring summer winter
1: 2008 4807   3539   1787   2845
2: 2009 2421   1703   1608   3262
3: 2010 7899   3953   3759   2999
4: 2011 6367   3759   4179   6339
5: 2012 6576   7293   6255   5117
6: 2013 4710   3029   6492   4516
7: 2014 3812   4119   5197   4445
8: 2015 1749   4380   2837   2411
9: 2016  607   1393    795   1176
```

It's as simple as that.

Note that we can use any other function that consumes a vector and outputs a single value as our aggregation function—using `fun.aggr=max` would give us the maximum value of the tracks played for the months in the season, and using `fun.aggr=mean` would give us the mean number of tracks played per month in that season.

`dcast` is the function we use to turn long tables into wide ones; `melt` is the function to do the reverse.

To reverse the widening we performed to create the data table named `pivoted`, we call the `melt` function with two arguments: (a) the name of the `data.table` we want to *melt* (lengthen), and (b) a vector of column names that we want to boil down and have in one column. In this example, the columns we want to have put into one are the season columns, as shown in the following code:

```
> melt(pivoted, measure.vars=c("fall", "spring", "summer", "winter"))
    year variable value
 1: 2008     fall  4807
 2: 2009     fall  2421
 3: 2010     fall  7899
 4: 2011     fall  6367
...
    year variable value
# same thing
> melt(pivoted, measure.vars=2:5)
...
```

The last expression in the preceding code shows how to identify the columns to boil down by index using ranges. This is particularly useful for *very* wide tables and absolves us of the need to type all of those column names by hand.

The new columns created by the *melting* procedure are named *variable* and *value* by default. You can override them and get prettier names, if you so wish, with the following code:

```
> melt(pivoted, measure.vars=c("fall", "spring", "summer", "winter"),
+        variable.name="season", value.name="N")
    year season    N
 1: 2008   fall 4807
 2: 2009   fall 2421
...
    year season    N
```

So that's it... that's `data.table`!

The package is chock full of other goodies that we didn't get to cover but we covered a very large proportion of its most useful and popular features.

Now it's time to turn our attention to `dplyr` and `tidyr`.

Using dplyr and tidyr to manipulate data

It's perhaps a little unfair to say that `data.table` is *opinionated*. If it were, though, its main point of view is that the potential pitfalls of *call by reference* are sometimes a more than fair price to pay for unparalleled speed and memory-efficiency. It could probably also be said that `data.table` also prefers conciseness and prefers to (sometimes drastically) modify the semantics of a function by the use of arguments, instead of creating other functions.

There is, however, a new approach to *non-base-R data manipulation* on the scene. This package also puts efficiency at a premium, but not at the expense of code safety, readability, consistency, and interpretability. (This, by the way, is not to say, that `data.table` is unreadable, uninterpretable, or inconsistent; it's just that this other package very *explicitly* states that these things are its top priorities. Judgements of readability are largely a function of habit and subjective tastes.) As you might have guessed, this package is `dplyr`.

As it turns out, dplyr is just one package (albeit, probably the flagship) in a suite of packages collectively referred to as the *tidyverse*—which is a portmanteau of *tidy* and *universe*. All of these packages, at least to a large degree, follow the same conventions and philosophy of data manipulation, which we will get into shortly. The *tidyverse* has become a huge topic of interest in the R community as of late; it is scarcely possible to be plugged into the community and not hear about the *tidyverse* all of the time.

 By the tidyverse website's (`https://www.tidyverse.org/`) own admission, the packages that form the suite are pretty opinionated. The opinions/points of view that unite these packages are outlined in the Tidy Tools Manifesto (`https://cran.r-project.org/web/packages/tidyverse/vignettes/manifesto.html`).

Functional programming as a main tidyverse principle

It would serve us well to point out some of these principles before we get to using dplyr--this will help us contrast these tidy tools with `data.table`'s approach and add context to the types of manipulations that we'll be seeing shortly. There is one main principle, in particular, that I believe underlies a lot of the other doctrines of the manifesto: the call to embrace *functional programming*.

Functional programming is a hot topic in computer science research. There's a whole lot to know about this programming paradigm, and any attempt to distill it down to a paragraph explanation (which we are about to do) will be an oversimplification. But, mainly, this paradigm strongly advocates for the use of functions as routines that (a) do not modify their arguments, (b) do not modify *anything*, and (c) whose behavior is always the same given the same inputs. The functional approach, as a consequence of its ideals, lends itself to the creation and use of simple functions that do one thing and one thing well. Computation, here, is better expressed as the *composition* of many of these simple functions, by feeding the return value of one function as an input to another.

For example, using the := operator in `data.table` to modify columns by reference is *not* taking a functional approach: this is used in *statements* that do not return values but rather modify their arguments *in place*. This approach is often referred to as *imperative programming*. In contrast, the types of expressions we saw in data.table not using the := operator or the `set*` family of functions were (without particularly meaning to) compliant with the functional approach since they returned data tables as *values* and allowed for seamless *chaining* of expressions. It did, however, stray from the functional tradition insofar as an almost astounding amount of arbitrary computation could take place in the arguments (`[` and `]`) of these expressions; within the square brackets we could filter rows, modify columns, perform aggregation and even create plots. This is a violation of the functional programming ethic of chaining simple functions with very clear purposes.

Virtually all functions in `dplyr`, in particular, take a `data.frame` (or a `data.frame`-like object) as its first argument and return a (possibly modified) `data.frame` type. Data manipulation is performed by passing this object through a series of other `dplyr` functions until the intended result is achieved. Although it is not strictly necessary, the `magrittr` pipe operator (`%>%`) that we saw in the `Chapter 14`, *Dealing with Messy Data*, is used to connect these `dplyr` functions to enhance readability and to allow the reader of the code to better understand the chain of operations, in the order in which they are executed.

Recall that the pipe operator, by default, takes the value on the left side (sometimes the return value of a function call) and inserts it into the position of the first argument of the function on the right side. Since, as we've discussed, `dplyr` functions almost always take a `data.frame`type as its first argument and return a `data.frame` type, the chaining is seamless. Though `dplyr` is a particularly great example of this paradigm in action, heavy use of chain-able constructs and consistent argument/return-types positions is something that is common (to varying degrees) in all of the packages in the *tidyverse*.

It is important to note, since we'll be using the pipe operator(s) heavily, when we speak of, for example, the second argument of a `dplyr` function, we are usually talking about the argument that appears right after the open parenthesis after the function name. Concretely, the following two function calls are equivalent:

```
> arg_one %>% dplyr_function(arg_two, arg_three)
> dplyr_function(arg_one, arg_two, arg_three)
```

But, please remember, when you look up the documentation for a `dplyr` function, the first argument is usually called `data` but, if you use the pipe operator, this will *not* be in the position of the first argument, visually.

We've learned all we can about the philosophy of `dplyr` without actually diving into a concrete example. In the next section, we'll be repeating the same analysis that we performed in the `data.table` section.

Loading data for use in dplyr

Loading the data can be performed using whichever data import function you prefer. Personally, I almost always use `fread` but the `read.*`-family of functions will work just fine. But it seems the most popular for most *tidyverse*-ers is to use the `read_*`-family of functions from the `readr` package.

It can be looked at like this: `fread` is to `data.table` as the `readr` import functions are `dplyr`/tidyverse. This analogy holds for two main reasons: (a) each method, by default, returns a special type of data.frame that is optimized in various ways to the functionality of the respective packages, and (b) the use of the import alternative is not strictly necessary but often helpful for speed.

On the former point, the object of type `data.table` returned by `fread` is actually necessary for the proper functioning of its respective package. In the case of the `readr` import functions, the object of type `tibble` (a special type of `data.frame`) is not strictly necessary to work with `dplyr` but has a few advantageous properties. Here we'll be using `tibbles` instead of `data.frames` and demonstrating these advantages as we go on.

Let's get started with the following code:

```
> library(readr)
> library(magrittr)
> library(dplyr)
>
>
```

```
download.file("https://raw.githubusercontent.com/tonyfischetti/dawr/master/
working-with-packages/data/tracks-2016-26-11.txt", "./tracks.txt")
> tracks <- read_delim("./tracks.txt", delim="\t", col_names=FALSE)
Parsed with column specification:
cols(
  X1 = col_integer(),
  X2 = col_character(),
  X3 = col_character(),
  X4 = col_character(),
  X5 = col_character(),
  X6 = col_character(),
  X7 = col_character()
)
Warning: 142 parsing failures.
>
> tracks %>% class
[1] "tbl_df"      "tbl"            "data.frame"
```

A few things to note... First, the arguments to `read_delim` (equivalent to `read.delim` from base R) are different than their semantic equivalents from the base version. To wit, here we are telling `readr` via `delim` that the is tab-delimited (instead of using `sep`) and telling `readr` that the does not contain a row of column names as its header row via `col_names=FALSE` (instead of `header=FALSE`). This stands in stark contrast to `fread` that tries hard to use the familiar argument names of the base R's `read.*` family. Both of these import methods, by the way, do not read strings as factors by default. This is almost always a good thing.

The second thing to note is that the class of the returned object is `tbl_df`. This tells us that `tracks` is a `tibble`, though, as you can see, the `tbl_df` is a special case of the `data.frame` as `tracks` is also of class `data.frame`.

Finally, note that there were parsing failures in the import process; if this happens to you, **please pay attention to it**. In this case, `read_delim` failed to read 22,000 of the rows in our data set:

```
> tracks %>% nrow
[1] 116276
```

Investigation reveals that the culprit is the row containing the song *Tempation (7" version).* Because `readr` wanted to read this as a string, the import process skipped all rows between this song and the next song that contained quotation marks. Let's fix this by specifying the `quote` argument of `read_delim`, as follows:

```
> tracks <- read_delim("./tracks.txt", delim="\t", col_names=FALSE,
+                       quote="")
> tracks %>% nrow
[1] 138135
```

Again, please pay attention to parsing errors as it may indicate that a large number of rows have not been imported properly. Unfortunately, the `read.delim` function in base R does *not* alert you of parsing errors and, had the user not checked if the number of rows matches what is expected, any analysis done would have incorrect results. Remember that you can check if the number of rows matches expectations using (`tracks %>% verify(nrow(.) == 138135`) from `assertr`.

In this case, `fread` correctly intuits our intent; this is why we like `fread` here.

As before, let's set the names of the columns and take a look at the `tracks` object:

```
> names(tracks) <- c("thedate", "trackname", "artist", "album",
"trackmbid", "artistmbid", "albummbid")
> tracks
```

```
# A tibble: 138,135 x 7
       thedate trackname        artist     album   trackmbid    artistmbid      albummbid
         <int> <chr>            <chr>      <chr>   <chr>        <chr>           <chr>
1   1480053547 A Perfect Ma...  A*Teens    Great...  f9a829f5-8... 69d9cb53-5b...  2fcb4813-1...
2   1480024902 Mamma Mia        A*Teens    Great...  aa6f618f-2... 69d9cb53-5b...  2fcb4813-1...
3   1479933058 Upside Down      A*Teens    Great...  " "           69d9cb53-5b...  2fcb4813-1...
4   1479932828 Upside Down      A*Teens    Great...  " "           69d9cb53-5b...  2fcb4813-1...
5   1479932618 Mamma Mia        A*Teens    Great...  aa6f618f-2... 69d9cb53-5b...  2fcb4813-1...
6   1479932414 Can't Help F...  A*Teens    Great...  8c5e7209-e... 69d9cb53-5b...  2fcb4813-1...
7   1479932232 A Perfect Ma...  A*Teens    Great...  f9a829f5-8... 69d9cb53-5b...  2fcb4813-1...
8   1479932026 Dancing Queen    A*Teens    Great...  13006b38-4... 69d9cb53-5b...  2fcb4813-1...
9   1479931794 Gimme Gimme ...  A*Teens    Great...  340e219b-9... 69d9cb53-5b...  2fcb4813-1...
10  1479931578 Upside Down      A*Teens    Great...  " "           69d9cb53-5b...  2fcb4813-1...
# ... with 138,125 more rows
```

Like the type `data.frame`, the `tibble` has a special way of displaying/printing its contents to the console. By default, it only prints the first 10 rows, tells us how many rows it excluded, fits the contents to the width of the console window (by abbreviating the values), and displays the data type of each column. This is super helpful for spotting column-type errors.

Let's look at some of the ways that we can index our `tibble` by rows:

```
> tracks[1, ]
> tracks[1:3, ]
> tracks[c(1, 1, 2), ]
> tracks %>% tail(n=1)
> tracks %>% slice(n())
```

```
> tracks[1, ]
# A tibble: 1 x 7
    thedate trackname           artist   album  trackmbid    artistmbid   albummbid
      <int> <chr>               <chr>    <chr>  <chr>        <chr>        <chr>
1 1480053547 A Perfect Match    A*Teens  Great… f9a829f5-8…  69d9cb53-5b… 2fcb4813-…
> tracks[1:3, ]
# A tibble: 3 x 7
    thedate trackname           artist   album  trackmbid    artistmbid   albummbid
      <int> <chr>               <chr>    <chr>  <chr>        <chr>        <chr>
1 1480053547 A Perfect Match    A*Teens  Great… f9a829f5-8…  69d9cb53-5b… 2fcb4813-…
2 1480024902 Mamma Mia          A*Teens  Great… aa6f618f-2…  69d9cb53-5b… 2fcb4813-…
3 1479933058 Upside Down        A*Teens  Great… ""           69d9cb53-5b… 2fcb4813-…
> tracks[c(1,1,2),]
# A tibble: 3 x 7
    thedate trackname           artist   album  trackmbid    artistmbid   albummbid
      <int> <chr>               <chr>    <chr>  <chr>        <chr>        <chr>
1 1480053547 A Perfect Match    A*Teens  Great… f9a829f5-8…  69d9cb53-5b… 2fcb4813-…
2 1480053547 A Perfect Match    A*Teens  Great… f9a829f5-8…  69d9cb53-5b… 2fcb4813-…
3 1480024902 Mamma Mia          A*Teens  Great… aa6f618f-2…  69d9cb53-5b… 2fcb4813-…
> tracks %>% tail(n=1)
# A tibble: 1 x 7
    thedate trackname       artist            album   trackmbid artistmbid albummbid
      <int> <chr>           <chr>             <chr>   <chr>     <chr>      <chr>
1 1199679766 Keep It Clean  Camera Obscura    Under… e238d0f6… ef43cee7-… 132e4ef7…
> tracks %>% slice(n())
# A tibble: 1 x 7
    thedate trackname       artist            album   trackmbid artistmbid albummbid
      <int> <chr>           <chr>             <chr>   <chr>     <chr>      <chr>
1 1199679766 Keep It Clean  Camera Obscura    Under… e238d0f6… ef43cee7-… 132e4ef7…
>
```

There are a few things I want to point out here:

- We can extract certain rows just as before by putting the row number in the position before the comma
- If we want to extract the last row, we can either use base R's `tail` function with 1 as the n argument (for one row), or we can use `dplyr`'s `slice` operator with the `n()` argument. `n()` in `dplyr` is a little like `.N` from `data.table`
- If we use an index and don't explicitly specify whether it is a column or row (by using a comma in the square brackets), both a `tibble` and a `data.frame` will return a *column*, whereas a `data.table` will return the corresponding *row*.

Manipulating rows

As we did in the last section, let's start in earnest by learning how to subset our data by condition. For this, we use `dplyr`'s `filter` function which takes an expression that returns a logical vector:

```
> tracks %>% filter(artist=="Belle and Sebastian")
> tracks %>% filter(artist=="Belle and Sebastian" | artist=="The Smiths")
> tracks %>% filter(artist %in% c("Belle and Sebastian", "The Smiths"))
> tracks %>% filter(artist=="Belle and Sebastian" & trackname=="The Model")
```

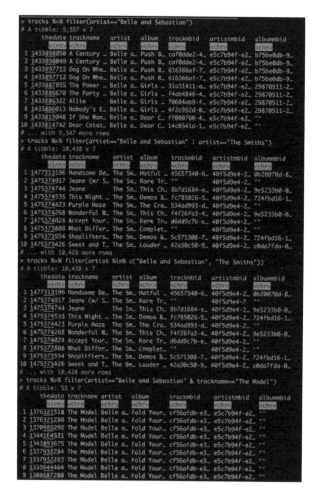

Really simple stuff so far!

Where we previously used the `order` function in the `i` field to sort by a column, the `dplyr` way is to use the `arrange` function:

```
> tracks %>% arrange(artist)
```

```
> tracks %>% arrange(artist)
# A tibble: 138,135 x 7
       thedate trackname        artist  album   trackmbid   artistmbid    albummbid
         <int> <chr>            <chr>   <chr>   <chr>       <chr>         <chr>
1  1411137793  Soylent Green   :Wumps… Music F… 66e8af50-a… e4e79264-c1…  ""
2  1431356009  Breaking Sta…   ¡Forwa… Indie/R… 29e8b7e3-6… 939af253-eb…  ""
3  1312423094  Alice Makes …   ¡Hot B… LIve at… ""          ""            ""
4  1312422897  Alice Makes …   ¡Hot B… LIve at… ""          ""            ""
5  1312422766  Alice Makes …   ¡Hot B… LIve at… ""          ""            ""
6  1312422556  The Day Yoma…   ¡Hot B… LIve at… ""          ""            ""
7  1312422394  Heartbroke      ¡Hot B… LIve at… ""          ""            ""
8  1271655652  Heartbroke      ¡Hot B… LIve at… ""          ""            ""
9  1244655431  Heartbroke      ¡Hot B… LIve at… ""          ""            ""
10 1244655310  Heartbroke      ¡Hot B… LIve at… ""          ""            ""
# ... with 138,125 more rows
> []
```

Note that there is no *by reference* equivalent to this as there is in `data.table`, as the tidyverse strongly eschews *by reference* semantics.

Selecting and renaming columns

The primary way to select columns in `dplyr` is by using the `select` function. At its simplest, `select` just takes the `tibble` (or `data.table` or `data.frame`, and so on) to operate on and an arbitrary number of columns. But, as we'll see, `select` has a few tricks up its sleeve and is far more powerful than it seems, as shown in the following code:

```
> # select trackname and artist
> tracks %>% select(trackname, artist)
# A tibble: 138,135 x 2
  trackname                          artist
  <chr>                              <chr>
 1 A Perfect Match                   A*Teens
 2 Mamma Mia                         A*Teens
 3 Upside Down                       A*Teens
...
# ... with 138,125 more rows
>
> # same thing using the standard-evaluation version
> tracks %>% select_("trackname", "artist")
```

```
# A tibble: 138,135 x 2
   trackname                          artist
   <chr>                              <chr>
 1 A Perfect Match                    A*Teens
 2 Mamma Mia                          A*Teens
 3 Upside Down                        A*Teens
...
# ... with 138,125 more rows
>
> tracks %>% select(trackname)
# A tibble: 138,135 x 1
   trackname
   <chr>
 1 A Perfect Match
 2 Mamma Mia
 3 Upside Down
...
# ... with 138,125 more rows
> tracks %>% pull(trackname)
[1] "A Perfect Match" "Mamma Mia"      "Upside Down"  ...
```

There are a few things I'd like to call attention to here:

- The first two incantations are semantically equivalent but the latter (note the underscore at the end of the function name) allows you to select columns using strings instead of unquoted symbols. Most `dplyr` functions have *underscored* equivalents that allow for this so-called *standard evaluation*. By the way, `assertr` has these, too.

- In contrast to `data.table` when we select only one column, we don't get back a `vector` but a data frame with one column. In order to extract a `vector`, you need to use the `pull` function. The example using `pull` is, thus, equivalent to `tracks$trackname`.

Now let's turn our attention to the *tricks* that we mentioned that `select` has up its sleeve. For example, we can select a range of columns using the `:` operator. Let's say that we wanted to select all rows from `thedate` to `album`. We will use the following code for this:

```
> tracks %>% select(thedate:album)
# A tibble: 138,135 x 4
     thedate trackname                 artist  album
       <int> <chr>                     <chr>   <chr>
 1 1480053547 A Perfect Match          A*Teens Greatest
Hits
 2 1480024902 Mamma Mia                A*Teens Greatest
Hits
 3 1479933058 Upside Down              A*Teens Greatest
```

```
Hits
...
# ... with 138,125 more rows
```

We could also use the – operator to explicitly *de-select* the complementary columns, as shown in the following code:

```
> # equivalent
> tracks %>% select(-(trackmbid:albummbid))
```

Another really helpful trick is to use `select helpers`, which are functions that can help select columns by condition. For example, if we wanted to remove all columns that end with "mbid", we can combine the – operator and the `ends_with` function, as shown in the following code:

```
> tracks %>% select(-ends_with("mbid"))
# A tibble: 138,135 x 4
      thedate trackname                 artist    album
        <int> <chr>                     <chr>     <chr>
 1 1480053547 A Perfect Match           A*Teens   Greatest Hits
 2 1480024902 Mamma Mia                 A*Teens   Greatest Hits
 3 1479933058 Upside Down               A*Teens   Greatest Hits
```

Run `?select_helpers` at the console to view the list and documentation of all of these *select helpers* provided by `dplyr` for use in `select`.

As before, we want to remove the `trackmbid` and `albummbid` columns, which we do not use. Whereas in `data.table` we removed these columns *by reference*, we have to use `select` and *reassign* the return value to the original variable:

```
> # this is commented out
> # tracks <- tracks %>% select(-c(trackmbid, albummbid))
```

Another option—and the one we will be using most here—is to use the `%<>%` operator from the `magrittr` package. Like, the `%>%`, this "pipes" the left-hand side into the first argument position of the function on the right side. In addition, though, it then reassigns the value returned on the right side to the variable name of the left. Thus, the following incantation is equivalent to the one immediately previous one:

```
> tracks %<>% select(-c(trackmbid, albummbid))
```

Let's now rename the `trackmbid` column to, simply, `mbid` (using `dplyr`'s rename function). Note the use of the `%<>%` operator:

```
> tracks %<>% rename(mbid=artistmbid)
> tracks
# A tibble: 138,135 x 5
        thedate trackname                                      artist   album
mbid
          <int> <chr>                                          <chr>    <chr>
<chr>
 1 1480053547 A Perfect Match                                  A*Teens Greatest
Hits 69d9cb53-5b8f-41b0-ac84-49eabe~
 2 1480024902 Mamma Mia                                        A*Teens Greatest
Hits 69d9cb53-5b8f-41b0-ac84-49eabe~
 3 1479933058 Upside Down                                      A*Teens Greatest
Hits 69d9cb53-5b8f-41b0-ac84-49eabe~
...
# ... with 138,125 more rows
```

Before moving on, let's see a demonstration of *chaining* in `dplyr` a little earlier than we had in the `data.table` section. Let's, for example, combine both `filter` and `select` to get a list of the track names (and name of artist) I've listened to by Belle and Sebastian, as shown in the following code:

```
> tracks %>%
+   filter(artist--"Belle and Sebastian") %>%
+   select(artist, trackname)
# A tibble: 5,557 x 2
   artist               trackname
   <chr>                <chr>
 1 Belle and Sebastian A Century Of Elvis
 2 Belle and Sebastian A Century Of Elvis
 3 Belle and Sebastian Dog On Wheels
 4 Belle and Sebastian Dog On Wheels
...
# ... with 5,547 more rows
```

Remember that the + is the line-continuation indicator of the R console and not something that you should type in when running this code yourself.

Computing on columns

Following the procedures in the previous section, let's convert the `thedate` column from UNIX time to regular-people time using the `anytime` package. For this we use the `mutate` function, as shown in the following code:

```
> library(anytime)
> tracks %<>% mutate(thedate=anytime(thedate))
> tracks
# A tibble: 138,135 x 5
    thedate            trackname                    artist
album          mbid
    <dttm>                   <chr>                  <chr>
<chr>          <chr>
 1 2016-11-25 00:59:07 A Perfect Match              A*Teens
Greatest Hits 69d9cb53-5b8f-41b0-ac~
 2 2016-11-24 17:01:42 Mamma Mia                    A*Teens
Greatest Hits 69d9cb53-5b8f-41b0-ac~
 3 2016-11-23 15:30:58 Upside Down                  A*Teens
Greatest Hits 69d9cb53-5b8f-41b0-ac~
...
# ... with 138,125 more rows
```

Now we can just that count of tracks I listened to in January of 2016, using the following code:

```
> jan1 <- anytime("2016-1-01 00:00:01")
> jan31 <- anytime("2016-1-31 23:59:59")
>
> tracks %>%
+    filter(thedate > jan1 & thedate < jan31) %>%
+    nrow
[1] 895
```

Super!

Let's now use `mutate` to *add* a column which is the name of the month that is specified in the `thedate` column. We'll also be making a contingency table of the counts of tracks listened to for every month by `pull`-ing the vector of months and feeding it into the `table` function, using the following code:

```
> library(lubridate)
> tracks %<>% mutate(themonth=month(thedate, label=TRUE))
>
> tracks %>% pull(themonth) %>% table
.
   Jan   Feb   Mar   Apr   May   Jun   Jul   Aug   Sep   Oct   Nov   Dec
 11875 10468 11400  9025 12743 13609  9439  9861 13509 13264 12175 10767
```

Same results as before!

We know now, from the other section, that the number of unique artist MusicBrainz IDs is not equal to the number of unique artists, but let's see how this could have been determined using `dplyr`, using its `n_distinct` function, which returns the number of distinct items, using the following code:

```
> tracks %>% pull(artist) %>% n_distinct
[1] 2202
> tracks %>% pull(mbid) %>% n_distinct
[1] 1960
>
> # these incantations are another way to do this
> tracks %>% filter(!duplicated(artist)) %>% nrow
[1] 2202
> tracks %>% filter(!duplicated(mbid)) %>% nrow
[1] 1960
```

Before moving on to the next section, for the sake of equivalency, let's get a list of all the albums from which I've listened to *The Model* by Belle and Sebastian, as we did before, using the following code:

```
> tracks %>%
+    filter(artist=="Belle and Sebastian" & trackname=="The Model") %>%
+    select(artist, trackname, album) %>%
+    distinct(album)
# A tibble: 4 x 1
  album
  <chr>
1 Fold Your Hands Child, You Walk Like a Peasant
2 Hollywood Bowl Live
3 (2006.07.06) Hollywood Bowl
4 NA
```

Try to see how easily you can follow this code.

One of the really cool things about dplyr (especially in conjunction with the pipe operator) is how you can follow the manipulation steps easily, even without necessarily knowing the details of how to use the dplyr *verbs*.

Grouping in dplyr

If you recall, the way we performed grouping in data.table was by using the by argument and performing our aggregation in the *j* section. In dplyr, we perform grouping and aggregation using the group_by and summarise functions, respectively.

As our first example, let's get sorted count of tracks I've listened to by artist. We'll use the slice function to only return the top 10, as shown in the following code:

```
> tracks %>%
+    group_by(artist) %>%
+    summarise(N=n()) %>%
+    arrange(desc(N)) %>%
+    slice(1:10)
# A tibble: 10 x 2
    artist                    N
    <chr>                 <int>
 1 Belle and Sebastian    5557
 2 The Smiths             4881
 3 The Magnetic Fields    4622
 4 P:ano                  3888
 5 The Cure               3792
 6 Stars                  3554
 7 Bad Religion           2977
 8 Elvis Costello         2908
 9 The Beatles            2461
10 Radiohead              2198
```

Here, the second argument to group_by (remember that the first one is technically the data) is the column we want to group by. As for summarise, we use the aforementioned n() and assign it to a new column named N. Note that summarize is an alias for summarise, so you can use that too, if you prefer.

To group by multiple columns, we just add another argument to `group_by`. Let's, again, get the count of the number of plays by artist *and* album, as shown in the following code:

```
> tracks %>%
+    group_by(artist, album) %>%
+    summarise(N=n()) %>%
+    arrange(desc(N))
# A tibble: 5,273 x 3
# Groups: artist [2,202]
     artist              album                               N
     <chr>               <chr>                           <int>
  1 P:ano                When It's Dark And It's Summer    2355
  2 The Magnetic Fields  69 Love Songs, Vol. 1             1336
  3 Elvis Costello       Armed Forces                      1037
  4 Bad Religion         Stranger Than Fiction              955
  5 Wild Nothing         Gemini                             873
  6 Belle and Sebastian  Push Barman to Open Old Wounds     840
...
# ... with 5,263 more rows
```

We can get the answer to the question *How many unique albums have I listened to by each artist?* by using two `group_by`/`summarise` constructs:

```
> tracks %>%
+    group_by(artist, album) %>%
+    summarise(N=n()) %>%
+    group_by(artist) %>%
+    summarise(N=n()) %>%
+    arrange(desc(N))
# A tibble: 2,202 x 2
     artist              N
     <chr>           <int>
  1 The Beatles        43
  2 Elvis Costello     36
  3 Radiohead          32
  4 The Smiths         32
  5 Guided by Voices   28
  6 R.E.M.             28
  7 Stars              28
...
# ... with 2,192 more rows
```

Finally, to demonstrate that we can summarize by more than just the count in each group, let's get the mean number of tracks I've listened to per month by year, using the following code:

```
> tracks %>%
+    mutate(year=year(thedate)) %>%
+    group_by(year, themonth) %>%
+    summarise(N=n()) %>%
+    group_by(year) %>%
+    summarise(mean_number_of_plays_per_month=mean(N))
# A tibble: 9 x 2
    year mean_number_of_plays_per_month <dbl>                    <dbl>
1   2008                           1082
2   2009                            750
3   2010                           1551
...
```

Joining data

Luckily, we have already spoke at length of the basics of joining/merging s in the last section so we can jump right into how to actually perform them here.

Joining data sets in `dplyr` could scarcely be simpler! Just as in the last section, let's inner join the tracks `tibble` and the with the artist info (including country of origin), using the following code:

```
> # download the artist info
>
download.file("https://raw.githubusercontent.com/tonyfischetti/dawr/master/
working-with-packages/data/artist-info.txt", "./artist-info.txt"
> artistinfo <- read_delim("./artist-info.txt", delim="\t")
>
> tmp <- tracks %>% inner_join(artistinfo)
Joining, by = "mbid"
> tmp %>% nrow
[1] 122241
```

How simple is that!?

There are two things I'd like to point out.

First, note that we didn't have to specify the column that we wanted to join by; by default, the joining functions of dplyr will join on the column that is common to both data sets. If there are multiple common columns, the joining will join on all of them. If this is not what you want, make sure you prevent this behavior by using the by argument of the joining functions.

Remember that in data.table, we used an argument in the square bracket to denote that we wanted an inner join. As we've mentioned, dplyr generally prefers to keep things that drastically change the semantics of routines in separate functions. For example, inner_join is its own function in dplyr. If we wanted to perform a left, outer, right, or full join, we would use the left_join, right_join, and full_join functions, respectively. (Run ?dplyr::join to see all the joining options/functions available).

Reshaping data with tidyr

Finally, we get to turn our attention to the other staple of the *tidyverse*, tidyr.

Though this package offers more functionality, the main purpose of this package is to reshape data (convert from *long* to *wide* format) in a *tidy* manner.

Let's recreate long, a *long* format that contains the play counts for each year/month, using the following code:

```
> long <- tracks %>%
+   group_by(theyear=year(thedate), themonth) %>%
+   summarise(N=n())
> long
# A tibble: 107 x 3
# Groups: theyear [?]
    theyear themonth       N
      <dbl> <ord>      <int>
  1    2008 Jan          877
  2    2008 Feb          984
  3    2008 Mar         1486
  4    2008 Apr         1101
...
# ... with 97 more rows
```

Now let's get this into *wide* format with the different month in its own columns.

The tidyr equivalent of the `dcast` function is `spread`. As its arguments, it takes the data to transform, the column that contains the categories to be spread across different columns, and the value.

This is equivalent to the `value.var` argument in `dcast`:

```
> long %>% spread(themonth, N)
# A tibble: 9 x 13
# Groups: theyear [9]
   theyear   Jan   Feb   Mar   Apr   May   Jun   Jul   Aug   Sep   Oct ...
     <dbl> <int> <int> <int> <int> <int> <int> <int> <int> <int> <int>
*
1     2008   877   984  1486  1101   952   508   355   924  1244  1690
2     2009  1145  1475   654   728   321   590    46   972   861   690
3     2010    88    22   308  1016  2629  2518   885   356  3330  2671
...
```

Done!

As you might imagine, the incantation to perform the widening procedure that makes the years columns is `long %>% spread(theyear, N)`.

Using `dcast` and `melt` in tidyverse, you might think that the `dcast` and `melt` functions we saw in the data.table section are unique to that package. The truth, though, is a little more nuanced.

Before `tidyr`, a very common method for converting between long and wide formats was using the `reshape2` package. It was actually *this* package that popularized the `dcast` and `melt` semantics. data.table then re-implemented dcast and melt to be optimized with data.table-specific enhancements.

So, if you'd prefer the syntax of `dcast`/`melt` to the `spread`/`melt` of tidyr, you can just load the `reshape2` package and use those familiar functions to reshape your data!

In keeping with the *rosetta stone* tradition—where we perform the same exact manipulations in data.table and the *tidyverse*—the next thing we should be doing is showing how to use aggregation functions in tidyr to mimic the functionality of a "pivot table". To do this in data.table, if you recall, we joined our long data table to a table we made of the crosswalk between months and North American seasons, and then used the `fun.aggr=sum` argument to denote that we wanted to get a of the sum of all the tracks I listened to per month by year.

For better or worse, `tidyr` does not have the ability to specify an aggregation function. In other words, the spreading operation has to identify *at most* one value for each season/year pair. Luckily, we needn't use an aggregation function for this; we can perform this operation in two steps using `group_by`/`summarise` and *then* spreading on the summarized value.

First, let's recreate the crosswalk using a `tibble`, and full-join it to the `long` , as shown in the the following code:

```
> seasonstbl <- tibble(season=c(rep("spring", 3), rep("summer", 3),
+                           rep("fall", 3), rep("winter", 3)),
+                 themonth=c("Mar", "Apr", "May", "Jun", "Jul",
+                           "Aug","Sep", "Oct", "Nov", "Dec",
+                           "Jan", "Feb"))
> longwithseason <- long %>%
+    full_join(seasonstbl) %>%
+    select(theyear, season, themonth, N)
Joining, by = "themonth"
>
> longwithseason
# A tibble: 107 x 4
# Groups: theyear [9]
    theyear season themonth      N     <dbl> <chr>  <chr>       <int>
  1    2008 winter Jan        8772     2008 winter Feb           984
  3    2008 spring Mar        1486
...
# ... with 97 more rows
```

Now we will use the following code to recreate the pivot table from the last section:

```
> pivoted <- longwithseason %>%
+    group_by(theyear, season) %>%
+    summarise(thesum=sum(N)) %>%
+    spread(season, thesum)
> pivoted
# A tibble: 9 x 5
# Groups: theyear [9]
    theyear   fall spring summer winter
  *   <dbl>  <int>  <int>  <int>  <int>
  1    2008   4807   3539   1787   2845
  2    2009   2421   1703   1608   3262
  3    2010   7899   3953   3759   2999
  4    2011   6367   3759   4179   6339
  5    2012   6576   7293   6255   5117
```

```
6    2013  4710  3029  6492  4516
7    2014  3812  4119  5197  4445
8    2015  1749  4380  2837  2411
9    2016   607  1393   795  1176
```

As you can see, we don't lose much by using `spread` over `dcast`. We just have to perform the aggregation from `dplyr` using `group_by/summarise`, first.

For our last trick, we'll be converting back from *wide* format to *long* format. In `data.table/reshape2`, this was by using `melt`... in `tidyr`, `gather`.

`gather` takes the data as its first argument. It's next two arguments are the column names to use as the key/value columns. Finally, `gather` takes an arbitrary amount of other column names to boil down. The column name will by in the *key* column, and the value in the cell will be the in the *value* column.

In this example, we'd like the key value to be called *season* (again) and the value column to be called *N* (again). The columns to boil down (*gather*, if you will) are *fall, spring, winter,* and *summer*. The following code illustrates this technique:

```
> pivoted %>%
+   gather(season, N, fall, spring, summer, winter)
   theyear season    N
1     2008    fall 4807
2     2009    fall 2421
3     2010    fall 7899
. . .
10    2008 spring 3539
11    2009 spring 1703
12    2010 spring 3953
. . .
19    2008 summer 1787
20    2009 summer 1608
27    2016 summer  795
. . .
28    2008 winter 2845
29    2009 winter 3262
30    2010 winter 2999
```

It is very common to *gather* tens or even hundreds of columns. As strenuous as typing out each and every season was, specifying all of these hypothetical hundreds of columns would be even more harrowing—not to mention error-prone. Luckily, we can, instead, simply specify the column that we *don't* want to gather (which, in this case, is *year)* and use the – operator. `spread` will then know to gather every column other column and leave the one specified untouched. The following code illustrates this technique:

```
> pivoted %>%
+    gather(season, N, -theyear)
# A tibble: 36 x 3
# Groups: theyear [9]
   theyear season      N
     <dbl> <chr>   <int>
  1    2008 fall    4807
  2    2009 fall    2421
...
  9    2016 fall     607
 10    2008 spring  3539
# ... with 26 more rows
```

Pretty cool, right!?

Exercises

- Write a function called `dt_table` similar to the `table` function in base R. The arguments will be a `data.table`, and a *string* specifying a column name. Do the same thing for `tibbles` and call it `dp_table`.
- Read some of the documentation for `data.table` and `dplyr/tidyr`. Of the former, learn about `.SD` and `.SDcols`. Of the later, learn about the `separate_` functions. These are life-savers.
- Learn about some of the other popular packages of the tidyverse. What do all of these have in common, again?
- Describe the four major voting bloc "cleavages" defined by Lipset and Rokkan in *Party systems and voter alignments*. Since its publication in 1967, have any other potential cleavage points emerged in your nation or state? How do these cleavages manifest themselves in political party differences?

Summary

For both `data.table` *and* `dplyr/tidyr` we went on a very substantial walk-through of the functions and abilities they offer, but not of all of them. Feel free to read the documentation on all of these packages to learn about some of the niceties that we didn't have the space to mention here.

I hope that you, dear reader, got a lot out of this chapter. Even if you don't eventually end up using `data.table` or the *tidyverse*, I hope you've gained a better sense of how flexible R is, learned that R is just as powerful at manipulating data as it is analyzing it, and that we don't have to settle for base R computation speeds if we don't want to. Most of the functions we've seen in this chapter—in both sections—are a full order of magnitude faster than their base R equivalents. This can be (and often is for very large data sets) the difference between your data wrangling taking a few hours and it taking a few minutes or seconds.

17
Reproducibility and Best Practices

At the close of some programming texts, the user, now knowing the intricacies of the subject of the text, is nevertheless bewildered on how to actually get started with some serious programming. Very often, discussion of the tooling, environment, and the like - the things that inveterate programmers of language x take for granted - are left for the reader to figure out on their own.

Take R, for example: when you click on the R icon on your system, a rather Spartan window with a text-based interface appears, imploring you to enter commands interactively. Are you to program R in this manner? By typing commands one at a time into this window? This was more or less permissible up until this point in the book, but it just won't cut it when you're out there on your own. For any kind of serious work, for example, requiring the rerunning of analyses with modifications, and so on, you need knowledge of the tools and typical workflows that professional R programmers use.

To not leave you in this unenviable position of not knowing how to get started, dear reader, we will be going through a whole chapter's worth of information on typical workflows and common and best practices.

You may have also noticed (via the enormous text at the top of this page) that the subject discussed in the previous paragraphs is sharing the spotlight with **reproducibility**. What's this, then?

Reproducibility is the ability for you, or an independent party, to repeat a study, experiment, or line of inquiry. This implies the possession of all the relevant and necessary materials and information. It is one of the tenets of scientific inquiry. If a study is not replicable, it is simply not science.

If you are a scientist, you are likely already aware of the virtues of reproducibility (if not, shame on you!). If you're a non-scientist data analyst, there is great merit in your taking reproducibility seriously, too. For one, starting an analysis with reproducibility in mind requires a level of organization that makes your job a whole lot easier, in the medium and long run. Secondly, the person who is likely going to be reproducing your analyses the most is *you*; do yourself a favor, and take reproducibility seriously so that when you need to make changes to an analysis, alter your priors, update your data source, adjust your plots and figures, or rollback to an established checkpoint, you make things easier on yourself. Lastly, and true to the intended spirit of reproducibility, it makes for more reliable and trustworthy dissemination of information.

By the way, all these benefits still hold even if you are working for a private or otherwise confidential enterprise, where the analyses are not to be repeated or known about outside of the institution. The ability of your coworkers to follow the narrative of your analysis is invaluable, and can give your firm a competitive edge. Additionally, the ability for supervisors to track and audit your progress is helpful, if you're honest. Finally, keeping your analyses reproducible will make your coworkers' lives much easier when you finally drop everything to go live on the high seas.

Anyway, we are talking about best practices and reproducibility in the same chapter, because of the intimate relationship between the two goals. More explicitly, it is best practice for your code to be as reproducible as possible.

Both reproducibility and best practices are wide and diverse topics, but the information in this chapter should give you a great starting point.

R scripting

The absolute first thing you should know about standard R workflows is that programs are not generally written directly at the interactive R interpreter. Instead, R programs are usually written in a text file (with an `.r` or `.R` file extension). These are usually referred to as **R scripts**. When these scripts are completed, the commands in this text file are usually executed all at once - we'll get to see *how*, soon. During development of the script, however, the programmer usually executes portions of the script interactively to get feedback and confirm proper behavior. This interactive component to R scripting allows for building each command or function *iteratively*.

I've known some serious R programmers who copy and paste from their favorite text editor into an interactive R session to achieve this effect. To most people, particularly beginners, the better solution is to use an editor that can send R code from the script that is actively being written to an interactive R console, line-by-line (or block-by-block). This provides a convenient mechanism to run code, get feedback, and tweak code (if need be) without having to constantly switch windows.

If you're a user of the venerable Vim editor, you may find that the Vim-R-plugin achieves this nicely. If you use the equally revered Emacs editor, you may find that **Emacs Speaks Statistics** (**ESS**) accomplishes this goal. If you don't have any compelling reason not to, though, I strongly suggest you use RStudio to fill this need. RStudio is a powerful, free **Integrated Development Environment** (**IDE**) for R. Not only does RStudio give you the ability to send blocks of code to be evaluated by the R interpreter as you write your scripts, but it also provides all the affordances you'd expect from the most advanced of IDEs, such as syntax highlighting, an interactive debugger, code completion, integrated help and documentation, and project management. It also provides some very helpful R-specific functionality, such as a mechanism for visualizing a data frame in memory as a spreadsheet, and an integrated plot window. Lastly, it is very widely used within the R community, so there is an enormous amount of help and support available.

Given that RStudio is so helpful, some of the remainder of the chapter will assume you are using it.

RStudio

First things first: go to `http://www.rstudio.com`, and navigate to the Downloads page, `https://www.rstudio.com/products/rstudio/download/page`. Download and install the Open Source Edition of the RStudio Desktop application.

When you first open RStudio, you may only see three panes (as opposed to the four paned windows in *Figure 13.1*). If this is the case, click the button labeled **e** in *Figure 13.1*, and click **R Script** from the dropdown. Now the RStudio window should look a lot like the one from *Figure 13.1*.

The first thing you should know about the interface is that all of the panes serve more than one function. The pane labeled *a* is the source code editor. This will be the pane wherein you edit your R scripts. This will also serve as the editor panel for **LaTeX**, **C++**, or **RMarkdown**, if you are writing these kinds of files. You can work on multiple files at the same time, using tabs to switch from document to document. **Panel *a*** will also serve as a data viewer that will allow you to view datasets loaded in memory in a spreadsheet-like manner.

Panel *b* is the interactive R console, which is functionally equivalent to the interactive R console that shipped with R from CRAN. This pane will also display other helpful information, or the output of various goings-on in secondary or tertiary tabs.

Panel *c* allows you to see the objects that you have defined in your global environment. For example, if you load a dataset from a disk or the web, the name of the dataset will appear in this panel; if you click on it, RStudio will open the dataset in the data viewer in panel *a*. This panel also has a tab labeled **History**, which you can use to view R statements we've executed in the past.

Panel *d* is the most versatile one; depending on which of its tabs are open, it can be a file explorer, a plot-displayer, an R package manager, and a help browser. The following image illustrates the Rstudio interface in Mac OS:

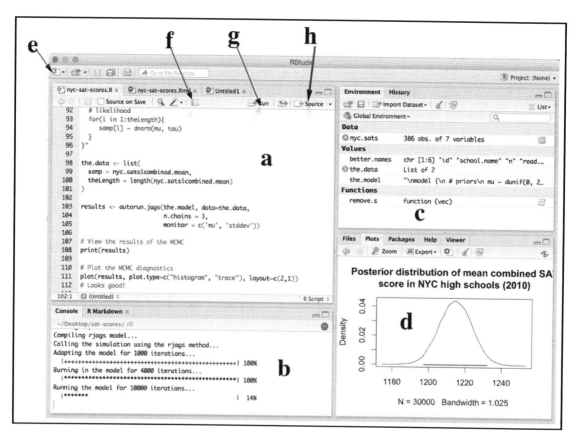

Figure 17.1: RStudio's four-panel interface in Mac OS X (version 0.99.486)

The typical R script development workflow is as follows: R statements, expressions, and functions are typed into the editor in panel *a*; statements from the editor are executed in the console in panel *b* by putting the cursor on a chosen line and clicking the **Run** button (component *g* from the figure), or by selecting multiple lines and then clicking the **Run** button. If the outputs of any of these statements are plots, panel *d* will automatically display these. The script is named and saved when the script is complete (or, preferably, many times while you are writing it).

To learn your way around the RStudio interface, write an R script called `nothing.R` with the following content:

```
library(ggplot2)
nothing <- data.frame(a=rbinom(1000, 20, .5),
                      b=c("red", "white"),
                      c=rnorm(1000, mean=100, sd=10))
qplot(c, data=nothing, geom="histogram")
write.csv(nothing, "nothing.csv")
```

Execute the statements one by one. Notice that the histogram is automatically displayed in panel *d*. After you are done, type and execute `?rbinom` in the interactive console. Notice how panel *d* displays the help page for this function?. Finally, click on the object labeled nothing panel *c* and inspect the data set in the data viewer.

Running R scripts

There are a few ways to run saved R scripts, like `nothing.R`. First - and this is RStudio-specific - is to click the button labeled **Source** (component *h*). This is roughly equivalent to highlighting the entire document and clicking **Run**.

Of course, we would like to run R scripts without being dependent on RStudio. One way to do this is to use the `source` function in the interactive R console: either RStudio's console, the console that ships with R from CRAN, or your operating system's command prompt running R. The `source` function takes a filename as it's first and only required argument. The filename specified will be executed, and when it's done, it will return you to the prompt with all the objects from the R script now in your workspace. Try this with `nothing.R`; executing the `ls()` command after the `source` function ends should indicate that the `nothing` data frame is now in your workspace. Calling the `source()` function is what happens under the hood when you press the **Source** button in RStudio. If you have trouble making this work, make sure that either (a) you specify the full path to the file `nothing.R` in the `source()` function call, or (b) you use `setwd()` to make the directory containing `nothing.R` your current working directory, before you execute `source("nothing.R")`.

A third, less popular method is to use the `R CMD BATCH` command on your operating system's command/terminal prompt. This should work on all systems, out of the box, except Windows, which may require you to add the R binary folder (usually, something like: `C:\Program Files\R\R-3.2.1\bin`) to your `PATH` variable. There are instructions on how to accomplish this on the web.

 Your system's command prompt (or *terminal emulator*) will depend on which operating system you use. Window users' command prompt is called `cmd.exe` (which you can run by pressing *Windows-key+R*, typing `cmd`, and striking *enter*). Macintosh users' terminal emulator is known as `Terminal.app`, and is under `/Applications/Utilities`. If you use GNU/Linux or BSD, you know where the terminal is.

Use the following incantation:

```
R CMD BATCH nothing.R
```

This will execute the code in the file, and automatically direct its output into a file named `nothing.Rout`, which can be read with any text editor.

R may have asked you, anytime you tried to quit R, whether you wanted to *save your workplace image*. Saving your workplace image means that R will create a special file in your current working directory (usually named `.RData`) containing all the objects in your current workspace that will be automatically loaded again if you start R in that directory. This is super useful if you are working with R interactively and you want to exit R, but be able to pick up and write where you left off some other time. However, this can cause issues with reproducibility, since another user won't have the same `.RData` file on their computer (and you won't have it when you rerun the same script on another computer). For this reason, we use `R CMD BATCH` with the `--vanilla` option, as shown in the following code:

```
R --vanilla CMD BATCH nothing.R
```

Which means, *don't restore previously saved objects from .RData, don't save the workplace image when the R script is done running, and don't read any of the files that can store custom R code that will automatically load in each R session, by default*. Basically, this amounts to: don't do anything that would be able to be replicated using another computer and R installation.

The final method, which is my preference, is to use the `Rscript` program that comes with recent versions of R. On GNU/Linux, Macintosh, or any other Unix-like system that supports R, this will automatically be available to use from the command/terminal prompt. On Windows, the aforementioned R binary folder must be added to your PATH variable.

Using `Rscript` is as easy as typing the following code:

```
Rscript nothing.R
```

Or, if you care about reproducibility (and you do!), go for the following code:

```
Rscript --vanilla nothing.R
```

This is the way I suggest you to run R scripts when you're not using RStudio.

If you are using a Unix or Unix-like operating system (like Mac OS X or GNU/Linux), you may want to put a line like `#!/usr/bin/Rscript --vanilla` as the first line in your R scripts. This is called a *shebang line*, and will allow you to run your R scripts as a program without specifying Rscript at the prompt. For more information, read the article *Shebang (Unix)* on Wikipedia.

An example script

Here's an example R script that we will be referring to for the rest of the chapter:

```
#!/usr/bin/Rscript --vanilla
############################################################
##                                                        ##
##    nyc-sat-scores.R                                    ##
##                                                        ##
##                Author: Tony Fischetti                  ##
##                        tony.fischetti@gmail.com        ##
##                                                        ##
############################################################

##
## Aim: to use Bayesian analysis to compare NYC's 2010
##      combined SAT scores against the average of the
##      rest of the country, which, according to
##      FairTest.com, is 1509
##

# workspace cleanup
rm(list=ls())

# options
options(echo=TRUE)
options(stringsAsFactors=FALSE)

# libraries
```

```
library(assertr)    # for data checking
library(runjags)    # for MCMC

# make sure everything is all set with JAGS
testjags()
# yep!


## read data file
# data was retrieved from NYC Open Data portal
# direct link:
https://data.cityofnewyork.us/api/views/zt9s-n5aj/rows.csv?accessType=DOWNL
OAD
nyc.sats <- read.csv("./data/SAT_Scores_NYC_2010.csv")

# let's give the columns easier names
better.names <- c("id", "school.name", "n", "read.mean",
                  "math.mean", "write.mean")
names(nyc.sats) <- better.names


# there are 460 rows but almost 700 NYC schools
# we will *assume*, then, that this is a random
# sample of NYC schools

# let's first check the veracity of this data...
#nyc.sats <- assert(nyc.sats, is.numeric,
#                   n, read.mean, math.mean, write.mean)

# It looks like check failed because there are "s"s for some
# rows. (??) A look at the data set descriptions indicates
# that the "s" is for schools # with 5 or fewer students.
# For our purposes, let's just exclude them.


# This is a function that takes a vector, replaces all "s"s
# with NAs and make coverts all non-"s"s into numerics
remove.s <- function(vec){
  ifelse(vec=="s", NA, vec)
}

nyc.sats$n          <- as.numeric(remove.s(nyc.sats$n))
nyc.sats$read.mean  <- as.numeric(remove.s(nyc.sats$read.mean))
nyc.sats$math.mean  <- as.numeric(remove.s(nyc.sats$math.mean))
nyc.sats$write.mean <- as.numeric(remove.s(nyc.sats$write.mean))

# Remove schools with fewer than 5 test takers
nyc.sats <- nyc.sats[complete.cases(nyc.sats), ]
```

```
# Calculate a total combined SAT score
nyc.sats$combined.mean <- (nyc.sats$read.mean +
                           nyc.sats$math.mean +
                           nyc.sats$write.mean)

# Let's build a posterior distribution of the true mean
# of NYC high schools' combined SAT scores.

# We're not going to look at the summary statistics, because
# we don't want to bias our priors

# Specify a standard gaussian model
the.model <- "
model {
  # priors
  mu ~ dunif(0, 2400)
  stddev ~ dunif(0, 500)
  tau <- pow(stddev, -2)

  # likelihood
  for(i in 1:theLength){
     samp[i] ~ dnorm(mu, tau)
  }
}"

the.data <- list(
  samp = nyc.sats$combined.mean,
  theLength = length(nyc.sats$combined.mean)
)

results <- autorun.jags(the.model, data=the.data,
                        n.chains = 3,
                        monitor = c('mu', 'stddev'))

# View the results of the MCMC
print(results)

# Plot the MCMC diagnostics
plot(results, plot.type=c("histogram", "trace"), layout=c(2,1))
# Looks good!

# Let's extract the MCMC samples of the mean and get the
# bounds of the middle 95%
results.matrix <- as.matrix(results$mcmc)
mu.samples <- results.matrix[, 'mu']
bounds <- quantile(mu.samples, c(.025, .975))

# We are 95% sure that the true mean is between 1197 and 1232
```

```
# Now let's plot the marginal posterior distribution for the mean
# of the NYC high schools' combined SAT grades and draw the 95%
# percent credible interval.
plot(density(mu.samples),
     main=paste("Posterior distribution of mean combined SAT",
              "score in NYC high schools (2010)", sep="\n"))
lines(c(bounds[1], bounds[2]), c(0, 0), lwd=3, col="red")


# Given the results, the SAT scores for NYC high schools in 2010
# are *incontrovertibly* not at par with the average SAT scores of
# the nation.
```

There're a few things I'd like you to note about this R script, and its adherence to best practices.

First, the filename is `nyc-sat-scores.R`, not `foo.R`, `do it.R`, or any of that nonsense; when you are looking through your files in 6 months, there will be no question about what the file was supposed to do.

The second is that comments are sprinkled liberally throughout the entire script. These commands serve to state the intentions and purpose of the analysis, separate sections of code, and remind ourselves (or anyone who is reading) where the data file came from. Additionally, comments are used to block out sections of code that we'd like to keep in the script, but which we don't want to execute. In this example, we commented out the statement that calls `assert`, since the assertion fails. With these comments, anybody, even an R beginner, can follow along with the code.

There are a few other manifestations of good practice on display in this script: indention that aids in following the code flow, spaces, and new lines that enhance readability, lines that are restricted to under 80 characters, and variables with informative names (no `foo`, `bar`, or `baz`).

Lastly, take note of the `remove.s` function we employ instead of copying and pasting `ifelse(vec=="s", NA, ...)` four times. An angel loses its wings every time you copy and paste code, since it is a notorious vector for mistakes.

Scripting and reproducibility

Put any code that is not *one-off*, and is meant to be run again, in a script. Even for one-off code, you are better off putting it in a script, because (a) you may be wrong (and often are) about not needing to run it again, (b) it provides a record of what you've done (including, perhaps, unnoticed bugs), and (c) you may want to use similar code at another time.

Scripting enhances reproducibility, because now, the *only* things we need to reproduce in this line of inquiry on another computer are the script and the data file. If we didn't place all this code in a script, we would have had to copy and paste our interactive R console history, which is ugly and messy to say the absolute least.

It's time to come clean about a fib I told in the preceding paragraph. *In most cases*, all you need to reproduce the results are the data file(s) and the R script(s); however, in some cases, some code you've written that works in your version of R may not work on another person's version of R. Somewhat more common is that the code you write, which uses a functionality provided by a package, may not work on another version of that package.

For this reason, it's good practice to record the version of R and the packages you're using. You can do this by executing `sessionInfo()`, and copying the output and pasting it into your R script at the bottom. Make sure to comment all of these lines out, or R will attempt to execute them the next time the script is run. For a prettier/better alternative to `sessionInfo()`, use the `session_info()` function from the `devtools` package. The output of `devtools::session_info()` for our example script looks like this:

```
> devtools::session_info()
Session info -------------------------------------
 setting  value
 version  R version 3.2.1 (2015-06-18)
 system   x86_64, darwin13.4.0
 ui       RStudio (0.99.486)
 language (EN)
 collate  en_US.UTF-8
 tz       America/New_York
 date     1969-07-20

Packages -----------------------------------------
 package  * version date       source
 assertr  * 1.0.0   2015-06-26 CRAN (R 3.2.1)
 coda       0.17-1  2015-03-03 CRAN (R 3.2.0)
 devtools   1.9.1   2015-09-11 CRAN (R 3.2.0)
 digest     0.6.8   2014-12-31 CRAN (R 3.2.0)
 lattice    0.20-33 2015-07-14 CRAN (R 3.2.0)
 memoise    0.2.1   2014-04-22 CRAN (R 3.2.0)
 modeest    2.1     2012-10-15 CRAN (R 3.2.0)
```

```
rjags        3-15     2015-04-15 CRAN (R 3.2.0)
runjags    * 2.0.2-8 2015-09-14 CRAN (R 3.2.0)
```

The packages that we explicitly loaded are marked with an asterisk; all the other packages listed are packages that are used by the packages we loaded. It is important to note the version of these packages, too, as they can potentially cause cross-version irreproducibility.

R projects

Although rare, there are some cases where a single R script contains the totality of your research/analyses. This may happen if you are doing simulation studies, for example. For most cases, an analysis will consist of a script (or scripts), and at least one data set. I refer to any R analysis that uses at least two files as an R project.

In R projects, special attention must be paid to how the files are stored relative to each other. For example, if we stored the file SAT_Scores_NYC_2010.csv on our desktop, the data import line would have read:

```
read.csv("/Users/bensisko/Desktop/SAT_Scores_NYC_2010.csv")
```

If you want to send this analysis to a contributor to be replicated, we would send them the script and the data file. Even if we instructed them to place the file on their desktop, the script would *still* not be reproducible. Our collaborators on Windows and Unix would have to manually change the argument of read.csv to C:/Users/jameskirk/Desktop/SAT_Scores_NYC_2010.csv, or /home/katjaneway/Desktop/SAT_Scores_NYC_2010.csv, respectively.

A far better way to handle this situation is to organize all your files in a neat hierarchy that will allow you to specify *relative* paths for your data imports. In this case, it means making a folder called sat-scores (or something like that), which contains the script nyc-sat-scores.R, and a folder called data that contains the file SAT_Scores_NYC_2010.csv:

Figure 17.2: A sample file/folder hierarchy for an R analysis project

The function call `read.csv("./data/SAT_Scores_NYC_2010.csv")` instructs R to load the dataset inside the `data` folder in the *current working directory*. Now, if we wanted to send our analysis to a collaborator, we would just send them the folder (which we can compress, if we want), and it will work no matter what our collaborator's username and operating system is. Additionally, everything is nice and neat, and in one place. Note that we put a file called `README.txt` into the root directory of our project. This file would contain information about the analysis, instructions for running it, and so on. This is a common convention.

Anyway, never use absolute paths!

In projects that use more than one R script, some choose a slightly different project layout. For example, let's say we divided our preceding script into `load-and-clean-sat-data.R` and `analyze-sat-data.R`; we might choose a folder hierarchy that looks like this:

Figure 17.3: A sample file/folder hierarchy for a multiscript R analysis project

Under this organizational paradigm, the two scripts are now placed in a folder called `code`, and a new script `master.R` is placed in the project's root directory. `master.R` is called a *driver* script, and it will call our two non-driver scripts in the right order. For example, `master.R` may look like this:

```
#!/usr/bin/Rscript --vanilla
source("./code/load-and-clean-sat-data.R")
source("./code/analyze-sat-data.R")
```

Now, our collaborator just has to execute `master.R`, which will, in turn, execute our analysis scripts.

There are a few alternatives to using an R script as a driver. One common alternative is to use a *shell script* as a driver. These scripts contain code that is run by the operating system's command-line interpreter. A downside of this approach is that shell scripts are, in general, not portable across the Windows versus all-other-operating-systems divide. A common, but somewhat more advanced alternative, is to replace master.R with a dependency-tracking build utility like make, shake, sake, or drake. This offers a host of benefits, including extensibility and identification of redundant computations.

Version control

A very compelling benefit to our neat hierarchical organization scheme is that it lends itself to easy integration with version control systems. Version control systems, at a basic level, allow one to track changes/revisions to a set of files, and easily roll back to previous states of the set of files.

A simple (and inadequate) approach is to compress your analysis project at regular intervals, and post-fix the filename of each compressed copy with a timestamp. This way, if you make a mistake, and would like to revert to a previous version, all you have to do is delete your current project and un-compress the project from the time you want to roll back to.

A far more sane solution is to use a remote file synchronization service that features revision tracking. The most popular of these services at the time of writing is Dropbox, though there are others such as **TeamDrive** and **Box**. These services allow you to upload your project *into the cloud*. When you make changes to your local copy, these services will track your changes, resynchronize the remotely stored copy, and version your project for you. Now you can revert to a previous version of just one file, instead of having to revert the entire project hierarchy.

Beware! Some of these services have a limit on the number of revisions they track. Make sure you look into this for the service that you choose to use.

A great benefit of using one of these services is that any number of collaborators can be invited to work on the project simultaneously. You can even set permissions for the files each collaborator can read/write to. The service you choose should be able to track the changes made by the collaborators, too.

Perhaps, the sanest solution is to use an *actual* version control system such as **Git**, **Mercurial**, **Subversion**, or **CVS**. These are traditionally used for software projects that contain hundreds of files and many, many contributors, but it's proving to be a crackerjack solution to data analysts with just a few files and little to no other contributors. These alternatives offer the most flexibility in terms of rollback, revision tracking, conflict (incompatible changes) resolution, compression, and merging. The combination of Git and **GitHub** (a remote Git repository hosting service) is proving to be a particularly effective and common solution to statistical programmers.

Version control enhances reproducibility. Since all the changes to the entire project (scripts/data/folder-structure layouts) are documented, all the changes are *repeatable*.

If your data files are small to medium-sized, keeping them in your project will play nicely with your version control solution; it will even offer great benefits, including the assurance that no one can tamper with your data. If your data is too large, though, you might look into other data storage solutions such as remote database storage.

Package version management

Some R analysts who rely heavily on the use of add-on CRAN packages may choose to use a tool to manage these packages and their versions. The two most popular tools to do this are the packages **packrat** and **checkpoint**.

The **packrat**, which is the more popular of the two, maintains a library of the packages an analysis uses inside the project's root directory. This allows the analysis and the packages it depends on to be version controlled.

The checkpoint allows you to use the versions of CRAN packages, as they were on a particular date. An analyst would store the date of the CRAN snapshot used at the top of a script, and the proper versions of these packages would automatically download on a collaborator's machine.

Communicating results

Unless an analysis is performed *solely* for the personal edification of the analyst, the results are going to be communicated, either to teammates, your company, your lab, or the general public. Some very advanced technologies are in place for R programmers to communicate their results accurately and attractively.

Following the pattern of some of the other sections in this chapter, we will talk about a range of approaches, starting with a bad alternative, and giving an explanation for why it's inadequate.

The terrible solution to the creating of a statistical report is to copy R output into a Word document (or PowerPoint presentation) mixed with prose. *"Why is this terrible?"* you ask. Because if one little thing about your analysis changes, you will have to re-copy the new R output into the document, manually. If you do this enough times, it's not a matter of *if*, but a matter of *when* you will mess up and copy the wrong thing, or forget to copy the new output, and so on. This method just opens up too many vectors for mistakes. Additionally, any time you have to make a slight change to a plot, update a data source, alter priors, or even change the number of multiple imputation iterations to use, it requires a Herculean effort on your part to keep the document up to date.

All better solutions involve having R directly output the document that you will use to communicate your results. RStudio (along with the `knitr` and `rmarkdown` packages) makes it very easy for you to have your analysis spit out a paper rendered with **LaTeX**, a slideshow presentation, or a self-contained HTML webpage. It's even possible to have R directly output a Word document, whose contents are dynamically created using R objects.

The least attractive, but easiest of the alternatives, is to use the `Compile Notebook` function from the RStudio interface (the button labeled *f* in *Figure 13.1*). A pop-up should appear, asking you if you want the output in HTML, PDF, or a Word document. Choose one, and look at the output. It would look like the following image:

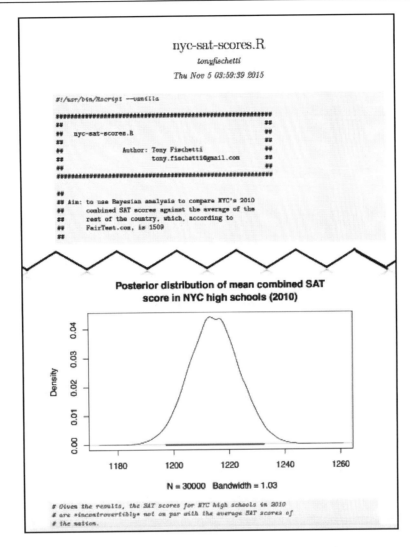

Figure 17.4: An excerpt from the output of Compile Notebook on our example script

Sure, this may not be the prettiest document in the world, but at least it combines our code (including our informative comments) and results (plots) in a single document. Further, any change to our R script followed by recompiling the notebook will result in a completely updated document for sharing. It's a little bit weird to have our narrative told completely via comments, though, right?

Literate programming is a novel programming paradigm put forth by genius computer scientist Donald Knuth (whom we mentioned in the previous chapter). This approach involves interspersing computer code and prose in the same document. Whereas the *Compile Notebook* feature doesn't allow for prose (except in code comments), the RStudio/knitr/rmarkdown stack allows for an approach to report generation where the prose/narrative plays a more integral part. This is how it can be done:

1. To begin, click the **New Document** button (component *e*), and choose **R Markdown...** from the dropdown.
2. Choose a title like **example1** in the pop-up window, leave the default output format, and press **OK**. You should see a document with some unfamiliar symbols in the editor.
3. Finally, click the button labeled **Knit HTML** (it's the button with the cute image of a ball of yarn), and inspect the output.
4. Go back to the editor and re-read the code that produced the HTML output. This is **R Markdown**: a lightweight markup language with easy-to-remember formatting syntax elements, and support for the embedded R code.

Besides the auto-generated header, the document consists of a series of two components. The first of the components is stretches of prose written in Markdown. With Markdown, a range of formatting options can be written in plain text that can be rendered in many different output formats, like HTML and PDF. These formatting options are simple: *This* produces italic text; **this** produces bold text. For a handy cheat sheet of Markdown formatting options, click the question mark icon (which appears when you are editing R Markdown [.Rmd] documents), and choose **Markdown Quick Reference** from the dropdown.

The second component is snippets of R code called *chunks*. These chunks are put between two sets of backticks (```). The set of three backticks that open a chunk look like ```{r}. Between the curly braces, you can optionally name the chunk, and you can specify any number of *chunk options*. Note that in example1.Rmd, the second chunk uses the option echo=FALSE; this means that the code snippet plot(cars) will not appear in the final rendered document, even though its output (namely, the plot) will.

There's an element of R Markdown that I want to call out explicitly: *inline R code*. During stretches of prose, any text between `` `r `` and `` ` `` is evaluated by the R interpreter, and substituted with its result in the final rendered document. Without this mechanism, any specific numbers/information related to the data objects (like the number of observations in a dataset) have to be *hardcoded* into the prose. When the code changes, the onus of visiting each of these hardcoded values to make sure they are up to date was on the report author. Using inline R to offload this updating onto R eliminates an entire class of common mistakes in report generation.

What follows is a re-working of our SAT script in R Markdown. This will give us a chance to look at this technology in more detail, and gain an appreciation for how it can help us achieve our goals of easy-to-manage, reproducible, literate research. We will use the following code for the same:

```
---
title: "NYC SAT Scores Analysis"
author: "Tony Fischetti"
date: "November 1, 2015"
output: html_document
---


#### Aim:
To use Bayesian analysis to compare NYC's 2010
combined SAT scores against the average of the
rest of the country, which, according to
FairTest.com, is 1509


```{r, echo=FALSE}
# options
options(echo=TRUE)
options(stringsAsFactors=FALSE)
```


We are going to use the `assertr` and `runjags`
packages for data checking and MCMC, respectively.
```{r}
# libraries
library(assertr)    # for data checking
library(runjags)    # for MCMC
```


Let's make sure everything is all set with JAGS!
```{r}
testjags()
```
```

```
Great!
```

```
This data was found in the NYC Open Data Portal:
https://nycopendata.socrata.com
```{r}
link.to.data <-
"http://data.cityofnewyork.us/api/views/zt9s-n5aj/rows.csv?accessType=DOWNL
OAD"
download.file(link.to.data, "./data/SAT_Scores_NYC_2010.csv")

nyc.sats <- read.csv("./data/SAT_Scores_NYC_2010.csv")
```
```

```
Let's give the columns easier names
```{r}
better.names <- c("id", "school.name", "n", "read.mean",
                  "math.mean", "write.mean")
names(nyc.sats) <- better.names
```
```

```
There are `r nrow(nyc.sats)` rows but almost 700 NYC schools. We will,
therefore, *assume* that this is a random sample of NYC schools.
```

```
Let's first check the veracity of this data...
```{r, error=TRUE}
nyc.sats <- assert(nyc.sats, is.numeric,
                   n, read.mean, math.mean, write.mean)
```
```

```
It looks like check failed because there are "s"s for some rows. (??)
A look at the data set descriptions indicates that the "s" is for schools
with 5 or fewer students. For our purposes, let's just exclude them.
```

```
This is a function that takes a vector, replaces all "s"s
with NAs and make coverts all non-"s"s into numerics
```{r}
remove.s <- function(vec){
  ifelse(vec=="s", NA, vec)
}

nyc.sats$n          <- as.numeric(remove.s(nyc.sats$n))
nyc.sats$read.mean  <- as.numeric(remove.s(nyc.sats$read.mean))
nyc.sats$math.mean  <- as.numeric(remove.s(nyc.sats$math.mean))
nyc.sats$write.mean <- as.numeric(remove.s(nyc.sats$write.mean))
```
```

Now we are going to remove schools with fewer than 5 test takers
and calculate a combined SAT score
```{r}
nyc.sats <- nyc.sats[complete.cases(nyc.sats), ]

# Calculate a total combined SAT score
nyc.sats$combined.mean <- (nyc.sats$read.mean +
                           nyc.sats$math.mean +
                           nyc.sats$write.mean)
```

Let's now build a posterior distribution of the true mean of NYC high
schools' combined SAT scores. We're not going to look at the summary
statistics, because we don't want to bias our priors.
We will use a standard gaussian model.

```{r, cache=TRUE, results="hide", warning=FALSE, message=FALSE}
the.model <- "
model {
  # priors
  mu ~ dunif(0, 2400)
  stddev ~ dunif(0, 500)
  tau <- pow(stddev, -2)

  # likelihood
  for(i in 1:theLength){
    samp[i] ~ dnorm(mu, tau)
  }
}"

the.data <- list(
  samp = nyc.sats$combined.mean,
  theLength = length(nyc.sats$combined.mean)
)

results <- autorun.jags(the.model, data=the.data,
                        n.chains = 3,
                        monitor = c('mu'))
```

Let's view the results of the MCMC.
```{r}
print(results)
```

Now let's plot the MCMC diagnostics
```{r, message=FALSE}
plot(results, plot.type=c("histogram", "trace"), layout=c(2,1))
```

```
Looks good!


Let's extract the MCMC samples of the mean, and get the
bounds of the middle 95%
```{r}
results.matrix <- as.matrix(results$mcmc)
mu.samples <- results.matrix[,'mu']
bounds <- quantile(mu.samples, c(.025, .975))
```


We are 95% sure that the true mean is between
`r round(bounds[1], 2)` and `r round(bounds[2], 2)`.

Now let's plot the marginal posterior distribution for the mean
of the NYC high schools' combined SAT grades, and draw the 95%
percent credible interval.
```{r}
plot(density(mu.samples),
     main=paste("Posterior distribution of mean combined SAT",
                "score in NYC high schools (2010)", sep="\n"))
lines(c(bounds[1], bounds[2]), c(0, 0), lwd=3, col="red")
```


Given the results, the SAT scores for NYC high schools in 2010
are **incontrovertibly** not at par with the average SAT scores of
the nation.

This is some session information for reproducibility:
```{r}
devtools::session_info()
```
```

This R Markdown, when rendered by *knitting* the HTML, looks like this:

NYC SAT Scores Analysis

Tony Fischetti

November 1, 2015

Aim:

To use Bayesian analysis to compare NYC's 2010 combined SAT scores against the average of the rest of the country, which, according to FairTest.com, is 1509

We are going to use the `assertr` and `runjags` packages for data checking and MCMC, respectively.

```
# libraries
library(assertr)    # for data checking
library(runjags)    # for MCMC
```

Let's make sure everything is all set with JAGS!

```
testjags()
```

```
## You are using R version 3.2.1 (2015-06-18) on a unix machine, with
## the X11 GUI
## The rjags package is installed
## JAGS version 3.4.0 found successfully using the command
## '/usr/local/bin/jags'
```

Great!

This data was found in the NYC Open Data Portal: https://nycopendata.socrata.com

Posterior distribution of mean combined SAT score in NYC high schools (2010)

N = 30000   Bandwidth = 1.019

Given the results, the SAT scores for NYC high schools in 2010 are **incontrovertibly** not on par with the average SAT scores of the nation.

This is some session information for reproducibility:

```
devtools::session_info()
```

Figure 17.5: An excerpt from the output of Knit HTML on our example R Markdown document.

Now, that's a handsome document!

A few things to note:

- First, our contextual narrative is no longer told through code comments; the narrative, code, code output, and plots are all separate and easily distinguished.
- Second, note that both the number of observations in the data set and the bounds of our credible interval are dynamically woven into the final document. If we change our priors, or use a different likelihood function (and we should - see Exercise #3), the bounds as they appear in our final report will be automatically updated.
- Finally, take a look at the chunk options we've used. We hid the code in our first chunk so that we didn't clutter the final document with option setting. In the sixth chunk, we used the option `error=TRUE` to let the renderer know that we expected the contained code to fail. The printed error message nicely illustrates why we had to spend the subsequent chunk on data cleaning. In the ninth chunk (the one where we run the MCMC chains), we use quite a few options. `cache=TRUE` caches the result of the chunk so that if the chunk's code doesn't change, we don't have to wait for MCMC chains to converge everything we render the document. We use `results="hide"` to hide the verbose output of `autorun.jags`. We use `warning=FALSE` to suppress the warning emited by `autorun.jags` informing us that we didn't choose starting values for the chains. Lastly, we use `message=FALSE` to quiet the message produced by a `autorun.jags` that the `rjags` namespace is automatically being loaded. `autorun.jags` sure is chatty!

We may opt to use different chunk options, depending on our intended audience. For example, we could hide more of the code, and focus more on the output and interpretation, if we were communicating the results to a party of non-statistical programmers. On the other hand, we would hide less of the code if we were using the rendered HTML as a pedagogical document to teach budding R programmers how to use R Markdown.

The HTML that is produced can now be uploaded as a standalone document to a web server, so that the results can be sent to others as a hyperlink. Bear in mind, too, that we are not limited to knitting HTML; we could have just as easily knitted a PDF or Word document. We could have also used R Markdown to produce a slideshow presentation; I use this technology all the time at work.

You don't have to necessarily use RStudio to produce these handsome, dynamically-generated reports; they can be rendered using only the `knitr` and `rmarkdown` packages and a format conversion utility called `pandoc`. But RStudio makes writing them so easy, you would need a really compelling reason to use any other editor.

`knitr` is a beefy package indeed, and we only touched on the tip of the iceberg in regard to what it is capable of; we didn't cover, for example, customizing the reports with HTML, embedding math equations into the reports, and using LaTeX (instead of R Markdown) for increased flexibility. If you see that power in `knitr`, and dynamically-generated literate documents in general, I urge you to learn more about it.

Exercises

Practice the following exercises to revise the concept of reproducibility learned in this chapter:

- **Review**: When we created the data frame from nothing, we combined a vector of 1,000 binomially distributed random variables, 1,000 normally distributed random variables, and a vector of two colors, red and white. Since all the columns in a data frame have to be the same length, how did R allow this? What is the property of vectors that allows this?
- Seek out, read, and attempt to understand the source code of some of your favorite R packages. What version control system is the author of the package using?
- Carefully review the analysis that was used as an example in this chapter. In what manner can this analysis be improved upon? Look at the distribution of the combined SAT scores in NYC schools. Why was modeling the SAT scores with a Gaussian likelihood function a very bad choice? What could we have done instead?
- If both a poor and a rich person are willing to buy a pair of sneakers for no more than $40, who values the sneakers the most, and who should get the sneakers in order for that resource to be allocated most efficiently? Couch your answer in terms of the diminishing marginal utility of money. What would the law of diminishing marginal utility say about the most equitable income tax schema, with respect to different income levels?

Summary

This last chapter, which was uncharacteristically light on theory, may be one of the most important chapters in the whole book. In order to be a productive data analyst using R, you simply must be acquainted with the tools and workflows of professional R programmers.

The first topic we touched on was the link between best practices and reproducibility, and why reproducibility is an integral part of a productive and sane analyst's workflow. Next, we discussed the basics of R scripting, and how to run completed scripts all at once. We saw how RStudio - R's best IDE - can help us while we write these scripts by providing a mechanism to execute code, line-by-line, as we write it. To really cement your understanding of R scripting, we saw an example R script that illustrated clean design and adherence to best practices (informative variable names, readable layout, myriad informative comments, and so on).

Then, you learned of a few ways that you can organize multi-file analysis projects. You saw how the correct organizational structure of analysis projects naturally lend themselves to integration with version control, a powerful tool in the organized analyst's utility belt. You learned how the benefits conferred by a sophisticated version control system (ability to revert to previous versions, track all revisions, and merge incompatible revisions) could potentially save an analyst from hours of heartache.

Finally, you saw how to use the `RStudio/knitr/rmarkdown` stack to help us achieve our goals of producing a reproducible report of your analyses. You learned the dangers of ad-hoc/copy and paste manual report generation, and discovered that a better solution is to charge R with creating the report itself. The simplest solution, compiling a notebook, was, at least, better than manual alternatives, but produced reports that were somewhat lacking in the flexibility and aesthetics departments. Instead, you saw that we can use R Markdown to create fancy-pants, attractive, dynamically-generated reports that cut down on errors, complement reproducibility, and aid in the effective dissemination of information.

Other Books You May Enjoy

If you enjoyed this book, you may be interested in these other books by Packt:

R Data Analysis Cookbook - Second Edition
Kuntal Ganguly

ISBN: 9781787124479

- Acquire, format and visualize your data using R
- Using R to perform an Exploratory data analysis
- Introduction to machine learning algorithms such as classification and regression
- Get started with social network analysis
- Generate dynamic reporting with Shiny
- Get started with geospatial analysis
- Handling large data with R using Spark and MongoDB
- Build Recommendation system- Collaborative Filtering, Content based and Hybrid
- Learn real world dataset examples- Fraud Detection and Image Recognition

R Data Analysis Projects
Gopi Subramanian

ISBN: 9781788621878

- Build end-to-end predictive analytics systems in R
- Build an experimental design to gather your own data and conduct analysis
- Build a recommender system from scratch using different approaches
- Use and leverage RShiny to build reactive programming applications
- Build systems for varied domains including market research, network analysis, social media analysis, and more
- Explore various R Packages such as RShiny, ggplot, recommenderlab, dplyr, and find out how to use them effectively
- Communicate modeling results using Shiny Dashboards
- Perform multi-variate time-series analysis prediction, supplemented with sensitivity analysis and risk modeling

Leave a review - let other readers know what you think

Please share your thoughts on this book with others by leaving a review on the site that you bought it from. If you purchased the book from Amazon, please leave us an honest review on this book's Amazon page. This is vital so that other potential readers can see and use your unbiased opinion to make purchasing decisions, we can understand what our customers think about our products, and our authors can see your feedback on the title that they have worked with Packt to create. It will only take a few minutes of your time, but is valuable to other potential customers, our authors, and Packt. Thank you!

Index

columns
  computing 507, 508
  renaming 503, 504, 506
  selecting 503, 504, 506
comments 8
communicating results 534, 535, 537, 540, 542, 543
complete case analysis 378
Comprehensive R Archive Network (CRAN) 29
confidence intervals 206, 207
confusion matrices 272, 273
continuous variables
  relationship 75
copy-on-modify 471
copy-on-write 471
correlation coefficients 78, 79, 82, 84
covariance 77
CRAN Task Views
  reference 367
cross-tabulation 73
cross-validation 245
CVS 533

D

data formats 366
data manipulation
  with dplyr 496
  with tidyr 496
data normalization 414
data points
  checking 403
data type of column
  checking 401
data.table package
  about 463, 464, 466
  by argument, used for grouping 479, 481, 482
  by reference semantics 469, 470, 472
  data tables, joining 483, 484, 486, 488
  data, melting 490, 491, 492, 495
  data, pivoting 490, 491, 492, 495
  data, reshaping 490, 491, 492, 494
  i and j arguments, using 476, 477, 479
  i argument, in DT [i, j, by] 468, 469
  j argument, in DT[i, j, by] 473, 474, 476
data

fuzzy matching 424
loading, into R 26
messy situations 423
OpenRefine 423
decision trees 279, 280, 281, 283, 284
degrees of freedom 48
directional hypothesis 137
discrete numeric variable 34
DOM (Document Object Model) 360
double exponential smoothing 328
dplyr
  data, joining 511
  data, loading 498, 499, 501
  grouping 509, 511
  used, for data manipulation 496

E

Emacs Speaks Statistics (ESS) 521
ensemble learning 285
entry errors
  checking 403
Error, Trend, and Seasonal (ETS)
  space model 337
errors, NHST 138, 139
estimate 48
Expectation Maximization (EM) method 382

F

FastR 435
flow of control construct 12
forecasting
  about 298
  difficulties 300
  uncertainity 299
forking 441
frequency distributions 34, 35, 37
functional programming
  about 496
  columns, computing 507, 508
  columns, renaming 503, 504, 506
  columns, selecting 503, 504, 506
  data, joining in dplyr 511
  data, loading in dplyr 498, 499, 501
  grouping, in dplyr 509, 511
  rows, manipulating 502, 503

functions 21
fuzzy matching 423

G

Gaussian distribution 42
Gaussian white noise 311
Generalized Additive Models (GAMs) 258
Generalized Linear Model (GLM) 276
Git 533

H

H0 (null hypothesis) 134
H1 (alternative hypothesis) 134
Holm-Bonferroni correction 156
hot deck imputation 380
hyperplane 237

I

imperative programming 497
independence of proportions
  testing 157, 158
independent samples t-test
  assumptions 153
indexing 15
Integrated Development Environment (IDE) 521
Intel Math Kernel Library (MKL) 436
interaction terms 258, 259
interpretations 103
interval estimation
  about 122, 124
  qnorm function, using 124, 125
Iteratively Re-Weighted Least Squares (IWLS) 234

J

Jaccard index 356, 357
JavaScript Object Notation (JSON) 351, 353, 354, 355
joint distribution 181
Just Another Gibbs Sampler (JAGS)
  using 183, 185, 187

K

k-fold cross validation 247
k-Nearest neighbors

about 264, 265, 266
limitations 273
using, in R 268, 269, 270
kernel density estimation 55
kitchen sink regression 241, 243

L

lambda functions 22
LaTeX 534
left-tailed distribution 42
linear models 220, 221, 222
linear regression diagnostics
  about 251, 252
  fourth Anscombe relationship 255, 256
  second Anscombe relationship 252, 253
  third Anscombe relationship 254
list-wise deletion 378
logistic regression
  about 274, 275
  using, in R 277, 278

M

Mann-Whitney U test 161
Markov chain Monte Carlo (MCMC) 180, 182
mathematical operators
  arithmetic 8
  assignments 8
  characters 11
  logical 10
matrices 23, 25
Maximum Likelihood Estimate (MLE) 167, 276
mean height
  estimating 115, 116, 117, 118
mean of one sample
  testing 141, 142, 144, 145, 146
Mean Squared Error (MSE) 225
mean substitution 380
Mercurial 533
methods, for missing data
  complete case analysis 378
  hot deck imputation 380
  mean substitution 380
  multiple imputation 382
  pairwise deletion 380
  regression imputation 381